Transport and Economy:

The Turnpike Roads of Eighteenth Century Britain

Transport and Economy:

The Turnpike Roads of Eighteenth Century Britain

ERIC PAWSON

*Department of Geography,
University of Canterbury,
Christchurch, New Zealand*

1977

ACADEMIC PRESS
London · New York · San Francisco

A Subsidiary of Harcourt Brace Jovanovich, Publishers

ACADEMIC PRESS LTD.
24/28 Oval Road
London NW1

U.S. Edition published by
ACADEMIC PRESS INC.
111 Fifth Avenue
New York, New York 10003
Copyright © 1977 By ACADEMIC PRESS LTD.

Library of Congress Catalog Card Number: 76–48386
ISBN: 0–12–546950–0

Printed in Great Britain by
Willmer Brothers Limited, Birkenhead

For my parents

Preface

One of the hardest parts of a book to write must be its preface, being in most cases the last part that is written but the first part that is read. Scanning the contents of other people's prefaces is not much help. Some are just summaries of the contents of the book, others are detailed explanations of them. Some are long, even interminable, lists of acknowledgements, others are near autobiographies. But one worthwhile type that has been gaining ground is the methodological preface—and this does seem an ideal place for a public airing of one's thoughts on the broader issues of one's trade, provided of course that it does not develop into an extended exercise in self justification. I make no apology therefore for writing a 'methodological' preface.

One of the more entertaining critiques of British historical geography to have appeared in the last few years described its practitioners as being unduly concerned with sources rather than with problems.† It seems that the major and often sufficient research problem, in fact, has been the discovery of an historical source, its reorganization, and detailed analysis. The aim is to allow the source to speak for itself, to see 'what the source tells us'. The drawback of this research method is simply that more pressing problems, defined in terms of particular historical questions, have tended to be lost in the minutiae. On occasions this approach has certainly produced valuable results, but all too often it has produced no publishable results at all.

This 'source domination' has not been the only notable characteristic of work in British historical geography. One might also mention the preoccupation with agriculture, but far more important, and probably most damaging, has been the almost total lack of concern with research at anything other than the local scale. Justified under that mysterious title of 'historical scholarship' this last policy has bred some very good local studies, but far more that lie dusting on the shelves, at best of interest to

† M. J. Bowden, *Economic Geography*, **48**, 214–6 (1972).

the worthies of Draynflete, at worst to no one. Where instead are the historical geographers' answers to the major problems, or questions, of history: for example, their thoughts on the growth of cities or the unfolding of the Industrial Revolution?

Recently, however, historical geography has been changing, just as the main discipline in which most of us are trained, has changed. Geography itself has become more scientific and analytical, addressing itself to general themes and pertinent problems, rather than to local syntheses and regional descriptions. Historical geography has begun to follow, albeit with a suitable—maybe scholarly?—time lag. A similar process has been occuring in economic history, with the injection of ideas and manpower from main stream economics, promoting the so-called 'New Economic History'. This book is written very much in sympathy with this more recent stance. I hope that it will appeal, then, not only to historical geographers, but to some geographers and economic historians as well.

The central problem with which I have been concerned is the role of transport in economic change, or the interrelationship between transport and economy. The book explores this problem by discussing the origins, development and impact of one particular transport innovation, and the system that it produced: the turnpike trust of the eighteenth century. The perspective is essentially general, encompassing the whole of Britain, but with particular emphasis on England and Wales. The discussion has been set within a theoretical deductive framework, building on simple concepts derived from economics and geographical diffusion theory.

All theoretical work, however, must be carefully wedded to empirical sources. The sources I have used, mainly Parliamentary records and Acts, and local trust archives, will be familiar to many. But despite this familiarity, and their accessibility, they have not been previously used in a study at the general scale. Where appropriate systematic sampling procedures have been adopted, and although such methods used in an historical context may dismay some, they do offer the only means of tackling large scale problems effectively, as social scientists long ago discovered.

I hope that the end result of this project may contribute beneficially to the new, and as yet relatively unexplored path of macro-level problem-orientated work in British historical geography. It is surely only by opening up this path that historical geographers will find something worth saying both to the rest of the historical fraternity as well as to their fellow geographers.

I am grateful to many people who have helped at various stages during the preparation of the book. I owe much to John Patten, who not only suggested, quite rightly, that the problem would prove interesting in the first place, but who subsequently gave many hours to it as the Supervisor of the doctoral thesis on which the book is based. I shall long remember lunches in the Kings Arms and tea in Hertford at four. I am also very fortunate to have held a two year Studentship at Nuffield College, Oxford, and being able to call whilst there on the advice of Max Hartwell and the late Denys Munby. The final form of the book, whatever its remaining faults, is much the better for all their ideas and criticisms.

I would also like to thank David Vaisey, for introducing me, as a geographer, to some of the fundamentals of historical research; Miss Betty Kemp, for guiding me initially through the maze of Parliamentary records; and Professor Peter Mathias, Dr Kenneth Warren and Dr Patrick O'Brien for their helpful suggestions. The staffs of local record offices all round the country have always been cooperative and frequently very interested. I am most grateful to Mr C.S.A. Dobson, the Librarian of the House of Lords, for his assistance.

Finally I must thank many friends and helpers, in College, in the School of Geography and outside Oxford, in particular: Mark Teversham; Penny Timms, who drew the maps I couldn't draw; Clive Payne and Samir Shah who showed me how to win with a computer; and many typists who laboured long, especially, Hazel Dempsey, Miss Iris Trask and Mrs Janet Day. The most important acknowledgement, however, is in the dedication.

Nuffield College,
Oxford.
January, 1976

ERIC PAWSON

Acknowledgements

The author and publisher are grateful to the following for permission to reproduce copyright material:

J. M. Dent and Sons Ltd for permission to quote from *A Tour through the Whole Island of Great Britain* by Daniel Defoe, Everyman's Library; to Cambridge University Press for permission to use an extract from *The Stages of Economic Growth* by W. W. Rostow; to Heinemann Educational Books Ltd for permission to use an extract from *Economic Growth and Structure* by Simon Kuznets; to Edinburgh University Press for permission to use an extract from *Men of Iron* by M. W. Flinn; to Manchester University Press for permission to use an extract from *An Eighteenth Century Shopkeeper: Abraham Dent of Kirkby Stephen* by T. S. Willan, and to use Figure 2 from *River Navigation in England* by T. S. Willan (reproduced here as Fig. 4); to Essex County Record Office for permission to use a table from *Essex at Work 1700–1835* by A. F. J. Brown (reproduced here as Table LI); and to Earl Fitzwilliam and his Trustees and the Director of Sheffield City Libraries for permission to quote from documents in the *Fitzwilliam Papers*.

Contents

Part One: Transport and Economy

Part Two (A): Innovation and Diffusion

Part Two (B): Implementation

Part Three: Impact

List of Illustrations

xv

List of Tables

Note on References and Abbreviations

The Harvard system is used to refer to printed works cited in the text. The date of publication, and the page number of the reference follow the name of the author: e.g. Brown 1969 : 100. All works used are listed in the Bibliography at the end of the book.

Printed Parliamentary material is referred to in the text by the use of standardized shorthand schemes. The normal method is adopted for Parliamentary Papers: e.g. BPP 1840 (289) XLV 159: 16. The abbreviation JHC is used for the Journals of the House of Commons, and the exact reference given by volume and then page number: e.g. JHC 15 : 402.

Turnpike trust documents which have been used in the text are cited in the footnotes by the date of the reference in the original document, and Record Office in which the document is deposited. The footnotes are located at the end of each chapter, and all documents used are listed by order of Record Office, in the first part of the Bibliography. E.g. Wells Minutes, 27 March 1754 (Somerset RO) refers to the Minute Book of the Wells Trust (1753–67) in the Somerset Record Office.

The abbreviations used in the references and footnotes are:

AO   Archives Office.
BPP   British Parliamentary Papers.
CRO   County Record Office.
JHC   Journals of the House of Commons.
JOJ   *Jackson's Oxford Journal.*
RO   Record Office.
WR   West Riding, Registry of Deeds.

The normal county name abbreviations are used.

Note on Acts of Parliament

In order to avoid excessive quotation of Act references, a shorthand method has been used:

Local turnpike acts are referenced in the text according to an individual index number. The key to these is given in Appendix 1. Act No. 152, for example, established the Crickley Hill to Oxford Trust in 1751, 24 Geo. II, c. 28.

General highway and turnpike Acts are referred to simply by date alone. Their full notations are given below:

1555	Statute for Mending of Highways	2 & 3 Philip & Mary, c. 8
1562	General Highway Act	5 Eliz., c. 13
1586	General Highway Act	29 Eliz., c. 5
1662	Act for enlarging and repairing common highways	14 Car. II, c. 6
1670	General Highway Act	22 Car. II, c. 12
1691	General Highway Act	3 Wm and Mary, c. 12
1697	General Highway Act	8 & 9 Wm III, c. 16
1741	Weighing Engines Act	14 Geo. II, c. 42
1751	Weighing Engines Amendment Act	24 Geo. II, c. 43
1753	Broad Wheels Act	26 Geo. II, c. 30
1755	Broad Wheels Amendment Act	28 Geo. II, c. 17
1757	General Highways Act	30 Geo. II, c. 28
1767	General Turnpike Act	7 Geo. III, c. 40
	General Highways Act	7 Geo. III, c. 42
1773	General Highways Act	13 Geo. III, c. 78
	General Turnpike Act	13 Geo. III, c. 84
1822	Turnpike Act	3 Geo. IV, c. 126
1835	General Highways Act	5 & 6 Wm IV, c. 50

Transport and Economy

1

Introduction

Britain, in the eighteenth and nineteenth centuries, experienced a fundamental discontinuity in her history, a discontinuity which although the first of its kind, has since been repeated in regions and in countries across the globe. The relative stability of pre-industrial life gave way in a process of accelerating change and development. The organization of economy and society was radically altered: population exploded, industry boomed, science and technology flourished, trading links expanded, towns and cities grew rapidly and customs, habits and standards altered for better or for worse. The Industrial Revolution brought to a close that period of four or five thousand years of agricultural dependence and dominance that had begun in Neolithic times.

The processes of change and development underlying this discontinuity were, however, extremely complex. Few economists or historians would dispute such an assertion and the wealth of ideas about the chief causes, prerequisites, necessary and sufficient conditions and leading sectors of the Industrial Revolution underlines this very forcibly. Support can be found in the literature for agricultural expansion, population growth, the boom in foreign trade or the rise in the rate of productive investment as prime movers. Laissez faire, transport improvements, commercial and educational development and fortunate factor endowments have all been singled out as prerequisites. Even the exact identity of the Industrial Revolution is in some dispute; it has been seen as 'the Rise of Modern Industry', the transfer to inanimate sources of power and inorganic supplies of raw material, the Demographic Transition, Immiseration and most recently—and reasonably—as economic transformation and growth. Indeed, one can agree that 'the lesson of history is that any single theory of, or policy for, growth is absurd. The study of history shows that growth is a highly complicated process.' (Hartwell, 1971:8.)

The role of transport in this process is of great interest. Transport is basic to the operation of economy and society: in a space-bound system it is vitally necessary in overcoming the friction of distance. Consequently, an inefficient transport sector will adversely affect the progress of development, whilst improvements in transport may have far reaching effects. Thus it is a sector that is partially responsible for change, and one that is itself in constant change. As economies grow, so does the provision of transport facilities: this provision is positively correlated with the level of economic development (Kindleberger 1965: 145–55, Haggett 1965: 76–8).

Transport and Economic Development

The contribution of transport to economic development has long occupied the minds of those who have constructed models of economic growth. For Adam Smith, transport improvements performed the basic function of widening the market. This encouraged the division of labour, and hence its growing productive power. This he identified as the mainspring of the growth in the Wealth of Nations:

> 'As it is the power of exchanging that gives occasion to the division of labour, so the extent of this division must always be limited by the extent of the market . . .
> Good roads, canals and navigable rivers, by diminishing the cost of carriage, put the remote parts of the country more nearly upon a level with those in the neighbourhood of the town. They are upon that account the greatest of all improvements . . . though they introduce some rival commodities into the old market, they open up many new markets to its produce.' (Smith 1904: 19, 148)

The neoclassical economists built upon this basic idea of the extension of the market with the concept of internal and external economies of scale, introduced by Marshall and developed by Young (1928). As the market grows, firms cannot only practice the division of labour, but they can also make other internal economies, by the use of better machinery, the substitution of factor inputs, management delegations and the improvement of marketing methods. At the same time, external economies, available to whole numbers of firms in industrializing areas become important. New firms and industries emerge to service the existing ones. A pool of skilled labour is attracted, and infrastructure facilities can be improved. Hence there is progressive division of labour between and within firms, and eventually between regions, dependent upon the widening market) The classic process of circular and cumulative causation is encouraged.

The focus of neoclassical analysis was not, however, the long run of development. 'Rather it centred upon the functioning of the market system and its major objective was to clarify the choices open to producers and consumers in a market situation.' (Barber 1967: 215.) The role of transport was implicit, but again central. Without it a reasonably competitive market system could not operate. Good communications are needed to maintain flows of information to suppliers and consumers: information about factor and product price changes, shifts in interest rates and the emergence of new lines. The response, of changes in factor and product flows, has to be effected by transportation. A perfect market system will not, of course, be achieved, but a market system, no matter how imperfect, will only emerge with adequate transport and communications. Its emergence is one of the essential characteristics of development (Hicks 1969).

The role of transport in development can now be seen more clearly It is responsible for creating increasing returns to firms and regions in a market economy, by widening the physical and material extent of the market. It is also responsible, in large measure, for allowing the market system to emerge and operate effectively. These points are basic and cannot be disputed. However, some writers have gone rather further than this, to offer stimulating but often controversial interpretations of the timing of transport improvements, and the degree and character of their impact.)

One of the best known theories of development is that of Schumpeter, expounded in his *Theory of Economic Development* (1934), and illustrated in *Business Cycles* (1939). It is a cyclical theory of expansion, with boom periods being based on the application of credit-financed innovations. It lays special emphasis on the role of the entrepreneur as innovator and in the place of the 'great innovations' in the last two hundred years: the steam engine, the railway, electric power and the car. He underlined the importance of canals and railways in British economic development in changing the location of industry and stimulating the growth of output, and of shipping, in providing cheap sources of food and raw materials (Schumpeter 1939: 341–6, 368–9).

This theory has been responsible for encouraging a widely expressed belief in the importance of great transport innovations. These innovations rather than merely permitting growth, are elevated to the status of special cases, or 'prime-movers', actually responsible for engineering growth. It is a belief that has received strong backing and illustration in one of the most popular of development theories, Rostow's *Stages of Economic Growth* (1971). He has depicted the growth process as one of rapid transformation in the 'take-off' period, as the slowly changing traditional society gives way to the industrialized state. Take-offs, characterized by a rapid rise in the level of productive investment, are led by certain 'leading sectors' and 'the introduction of the railroad has been historically the most powerful single initiator of take-offs', although admittedly not in Britain, where the first take-off was based on cotton textiles (Rostow 1971: 53–5).

Rostow's thesis, however, is of further interest as he specifies the ways in which railroads encouraged growth, far more clearly in fact than does Schumpeter:

'The railroad has had three major kinds of impact on economic growth during the take-off period. First, it has lowered internal transport costs, brought new areas and products into commercial markets and, in general, performed the Smithian function of widening the market. Second, it has been a prerequisite in many cases, to the development of a major new and rapidly enlarging export sector which, in turn, has served to generate capital for internal development, as, for example, the American railroads before 1914. Third, and perhaps most important for the take-off itself, the development of railways has led on to the development of modern coal, iron and engineering industries. In many countries the growth of modern basic industrial sectors can be traced in the most direct way to the requirements for building and, especially, for maintaining substantial railway systems.' (Rostow 1971: 55)

The key role of transport, as outlined by Rostow and Schumpeter, has received strong backing from other writers. Flinn, in his analysis of the origins of the British Industrial Revolution, is quite categoric:

'A . . . major field of change essential as a prerequisite to the Industrial Revolution was transport . . .' (Flinn 1966: 96)

Kuznets, in discussing the requirements for industrialization in a more general context, implies the same:

'The other sector [other than agriculture] in the economy whose efficiency is crucial to the development of modern industry is transport and communication . . . transportation and public utility facilities are capital-intensive . . . and they are needed early in the economic development of a country.' (Kuznets 1966: 199)

And Youngson, in his study of overhead capital in development is sure that:

> 'Most people would agree that improved transport plays a key role in economic development. This, indeed, is one of the few general truths which it is possible to derive from a study of economic history.' (Youngson 1967: 73)

There are two distinct and separate stands in these arguments. The first is that transport improvements lead, initiate or are prerequisites to growth, in chronological terms; the second is that they make an outstanding directive contribution to the general process of growth. Both these assertions have been questioned by recent empirical work in economic history.

The prerequisite role of transport development is widely accepted in the underdeveloped world today. The theory of social overhead capital assumes this role: transport facilities are part of the economic infrastructure, the development of which is said to permit the growth of direct production (Hirschman 1958: 84). Such investment is lumpy, requires a long gestation period and is therefore best provided by governments as a stimulus to growth. But although this may be a justifiable approach to modern development problems, it is not a reflection of the historical process. In Britain, the railways did not lead economic growth, but tended to lag behind booms in the trade cycle, in response to them (Mitchell 1964: 320–1). The same is true of the pattern of American railroad development (Cootner 1963: 27–8, Fishlow 1965: 306–11). A recent analysis of English canal finance has shown that the progress of inland navigation schemes was closely correlated with the growth of traffic—'when trade flourished . . . then navigation projects were numerous' (Ward 1974: 168–9). And Hunter, after a review of the literature and a study of Chinese and Soviet development concluded that 'the transport sector as a whole is a handmaiden, and not a prime-mover in the process of development' (1965: 71–84).

Secondly, the scale of the impact of the great transport innovations has been subject to re-evaluation in the last few years, by a group of quantitative economic historians. The most notable studies are those of

Fogel (1964), Fishlow (1965) and Hawke (1970). Using the concept of 'social savings', introduced by Fogel, they have attempted to show that the impact of the railroads on the economy was rather less than Rostow implied. Social savings are defined as the difference between the actual national income at a given date and the national income that would have been produced without the railroads. They are represented by the difference between the cost of shipping the goods and passengers that actually travelled by railroad and the cost of shipping them by the next best alternative. This cost difference is measured by multiplying the unit price differential between the two by the quantity of goods and passengers transported by rail.

Hawke's estimate of the social saving produced by the railways in England and Wales amounts to between 7 and 11 per cent of the national income in 1869. About 4 per cent of this is accounted for by savings on freight movements. Fogel and Fishlow, calculating social savings for freight alone, produced similar results—Fogel of 5 per cent of the United States national income in 1890 and Fishlow of 4 per cent in 1859. Fogel thereby concludes that American economic development would not have been seriously hindered without the growth of its railroad system, as improved canal and road networks could have taken its place. Gunderson then used the same techniques to test the impact of another 'great' transport innovation, the steamship, and discovered that the social savings to the American economy were still lower (1970: 218).

In a clear analysis of these results (for railroads and steamships), Gunderson decided that they undermine the importance of the 'great innovations', and instead direct attention towards 'the small, but continuous and ubiquitous increases in efficiency which amalgamate into major increases in output'. Indeed, Cootner has already proposed that to view the railroad as a 'great innovation' at all is inappropriate, as it was really a gradual evolution, the culmination of steps forward in making rails, steam engines and boilers (1963: 490). The temporal sequence of network development lends further support to this view. National systems of railroads, canals and improved roads did not emerge immediately as systems, but evolved from small-scale undertakings and only gradually developed into coherent infrastructure developments.

The impact of transport innovations through derived demands (Rostow's third category of effects), has also been challenged by these studies. In both America and Britain, the basic industrial sectors were already in existence before the advent of the railroad. Although they were stimulated by railroad construction and maintenance, only a relatively small proportion of their output was directed towards this. The use of wood and scrap cut down the level of demand for the iron industry's products to about 20 per cent of its whole output at the peak (Fishlow 1965: 141–3, Mitchell 1964: 325, Vamplew 1971: 53), even though it was of great importance in developing some regional iron-producing concentrations, such as South Wales. Nor, it seems, were the railways responsible for technical advances of lasting significance in the iron industry (Hawke 1970: 245).

Some doubt has therefore been thrown on the 'special role' of transport in economic development. But it is significant that all the studies that have been discussed have been carried out at a very general scale, being concerned either with overall theories of development, or with aggregate assessments of transport innovation impact. Rather less research has been carried out to identify the actual mechanisms by which transport improvements have effected changes, or the nature of those changes— whether economic, social or geographic. This is not to say that transport history itself has been overlooked—in fact, the opposite is true. Although Hartwell's observation is perhaps less valid than it was, it is still a telling point:

> 'the historians have not neglected the growth of services (including transport) . . . but have failed to place them in the context of essential structural change, and to relate them operationally to the process of economic change.' (1971: 208)

Thus in the British context, most transport studies have been undertaken for their own sake, rather than to consider the broader themes of 'roles and relations'. Much romantic detail has emerged, but often little of consequence, as both Hawke (1970: 1) and Dyos (1956: 186) have pointed out in respect of railway and canal histories. Most of the more general transport texts are descriptive summaries of the course of change through time (e.g. Sherrington 1934, Savage 1959, Dyos and Aldcroft 1969, Bagwell 1974). Jackman's great work (1916) is, for the most part, a description of the statutes.

Important problems, such as the effect of transport cost savings on industry—in terms of production, marketing and organizational changes, on competition and change in regional economies, or the relocation of economic activity, and the reorganization of settlement patterns have not been tackled. 'There has been surprisingly little examination of the place of the railways in the history of the UK', as

Hawke says (1970: 1). Nevertheless, their place has been more clearly identified[1] than that of the canals or turnpike roads. And in many sections of the transport sector, the omission goes one stage further, as a failure to even identify properly the course of change within transport itself. As yet, the spread of turnpiking, of horse-drawn railroads or tramways is little understood. Little has been done to improve on Willan's pioneering, but necessarily sketchy, studies of the coasting trade and river navigation in the seventeenth and eighteenth centuries. The pattern and organization of internal trade at that time remains largely a mystery.

The problem of transport and economic development in history is thus characterized by a great paradox. On the one hand, transport is obviously an important component in the development process. But on the other:

'. . . the exact relationship between transport and the growth of the economy is one of the least understood aspects of the British Industrial Revolution.' (Thompson 1973: 39)

A Dynamic Model

It is appropriate, at this point, to return to basic principles and develop a simple model to interrelate transport development and economic growth. The basic step is illustrated in Fig. 1. Three elements of a transport system are identified—transport networks, the economic structure connected by

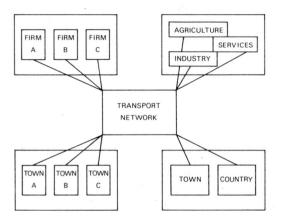

Fig. 1. Transport and the economic structure.

those networks, and the flows of traffic generated by the economic structure and channelled over the networks. The networks exist to accommodate flows from origins to destinations, the flows being made up of movements of people, goods, services and information, generated by firms, settlements or regions within the economic structure. Some networks are the products of the flows which move over them, and become articulated as these flows grow stronger: early road systems, sea-lanes and air corridors are examples. Other networks, such as railways and motorways, are created specifically to channel existing or potential flows.

This description, however, lacks a third dimension. In order to accommodate change over time, a dynamic element must be built into the model. The close relationship of transport network and the economic structure inevitably means that changes in the state of one affect, or even alter, the state of the other. An intensification of economic activity, for example, will generate greater traffic flows which may require improvements in the transport network. Similarly, improvements in the transport network will induce improvements in the performance of the economic structure by facilitating the transfer of flows.

This dynamic element is explored more systematically in the main model (Fig. 2). It consists of three parts, labelled A, B, and C. It accommodates growth in the economic structure and consequent increased traffic flows (A); the impact of this on the transport network and resulting improvements (B); and the effect of these improvements in the performance of the economic structure (C).

The model suggests that increasing traffic flows may have several effects on a transport network. Firstly, if the network has sufficient spare capacity, the transfer of these increasing flows will not be impeded, and the operation of the economy is not affected (route 1). Secondly, however, they may result in localized or generalized pressure as the capacity of the network is reached, both increasing the cost of network maintenance, and the cost of transport itself as the competition for carrying capacity intensifies (route 2). Independent factors, such as faulty construction (as was the case with some English canals) may also induce the emergence of pressure points. Unless a successful search for improvement to the network follows, a negative loop is initiated, as inland trade, and hence development, is hindered (route 3). But a successful search, which may—but need not—incorporate a technological advance, will then initiate a positive loop. This can be done by one of three routes. The capacity of the original network may be

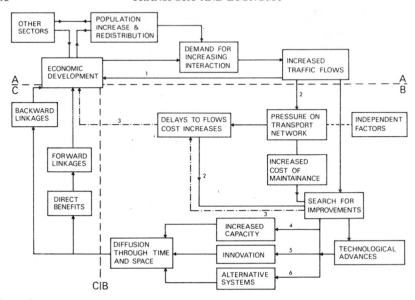

FIG. 2. Transport and economic development: a dynamic model.

improved (e.g. by double tracking of railway lines—route 4); an innovation may be adopted within the transport network (e.g. the pound lock on rivers, or the turnpike trust on roads—route 5), or traffic may be transferred to an alternative route (route 6).

These improvements or innovations themselves diffuse through time and space, as the pressure on the original network becomes more generalized, and as their superiority is demonstrated. They will produce positive stimulants to development, identified in the third part of the model (C). The direct benefits of savings on the cost of transport (such as lower rates, faster transit times, increased frequency, regularity and integration of services) are the most immediate. These savings can be used by producers to extend the market area, or to increase investment. They can be used by consumers to increase travel or consumption. These effects of direct benefits are called the *forward linkages*. In addition, the construction and maintenance of the improvement or innovation generates *backward linkages*, or derived demands, for constructional materials and employment. These forward and backward linkages in turn contribute to, and in part themselves constitute, economic development.

Several broad implications emerge from the discussion of this model. Firstly, it attempts to overcome the lack of a functional, dynamic approach to transport studies by demonstrating the intricate relationship between transport and economic development, and directing attention to the component parts of the whole process. Secondly, it does not assume a prerequisite role for transport improvements in the development process, nor does it assume that transport is the only sector contributing to change. Thirdly, it illustrates positive and negative relationships, which may be operative at the same time, but in different areas. Lastly, it implies a successive series of innovations and improvements in the transport sector.

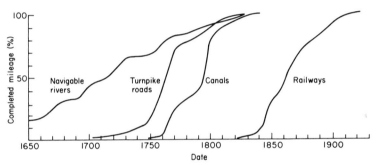

FIG. 3. The diffusion of transport innovations in Britain, 1650–1930: mileage constructed. *Sources*: canals and navigable rivers: mileage constructed in Britain (Priestley 1831); turnpike roads: mileage open in England (see Chapter 5), railways: mileage open in Britain (Mitchell 1962).

This last point is worth emphasizing. It is obviously true in the British context. Dyos has written that 'the most persistent tendency in the history of transport is creeping obsolescence.' (Dyos and Aldcroft 1969: 51.) This is a curiously negative view of a very positive process. British economic history has been characterized by successive waves of transport innovation and diffusion, some competing and some complementary: from river navigations and parish highway, to canal and turnpike road, railway and tramway, and then airline and motorway. These waves are illustrated in Fig. 3, which is a simple demonstration of the British historical dimension of this model of transport and economic development.

Turnpike road development

This book is concerned with one of these innovations and its diffusion—the turnpike trust and the emergence of the turnpike road system in eighteenth century Britain. Despite the wealth of Parliamentary and local records which the trusts have left behind, surprisingly little effort has been made to identify and understand the turnpike road system, since the early work of Jackman (1916) and the Webbs (1920). One notable exception is Albert's book on the subject (1972), which has made a brief but valuable survey. Nevertheless, the development of the system still remains to be clearly identified and analysed, and an assessment of its 'roles and relations' has not been available.[2] It is in these spheres that this book seeks to make a contribution, although it also ranges outside them to apply systematic analytical methods to the administration and financial background of turnpike trusts, still much misunderstood topics.

The book is organized into three broad parts, corresponding with the three parts of the model (Fig. 2). Part One (Chapters 1 and 2) establishes the context, and discusses the importance and growth of land traffic flows in the eighteenth century economy. Part Two (Chapters 3 to 9) discusses the emergence of the innovation, its characteristics, diffusion and operation, whilst Part Three (Chapters 10 to 12) explores the impact of the innovation, both on the road network, and more generally, on the economy.

1. Notes

1. Their relationship with the state (Cleveland-Stevens 1915, Parris 1965) and with the capital market (Reed 1975) has received attention, as has their impact on cities (Kellett 1969) and, briefly, on suburbs and resorts (Perkin 1970).
2. This is an omission for which Albert's book was quickly criticized (Hawke 1973).

2

Internal Trade and Traffic in the Eighteenth Century

The eighteenth century in Britain is in many respects a divide. It is a century of increasing change, both of growth and decline. The pre-industrial economy and society of 1700 was, by 1800, giving way in the reverberations of the Industrial Revolution. Population had begun to grow rapidly, towns were expanding, agricultural output was rising, industry and foreign trade were of increasing importance, and new regional economies were emerging. And yet this century, witnessing the beginnings of the First Industrial Nation, remains shrouded in mystery. The broad outline of developments may be clear, but because statistical sources are so limited, it is difficult to make precise identification of the changes. In some respects, as for population and migration, the sources are less useful than those of the seventeenth century. Only price data, foreign trade series, constructed estimates of population, and a few industrial output figures are available.

This obscurity extends into the sphere of internal trade. Apart from the evidence of the Port Books on the volume of the coastal traffic, little material survives, or ever existed, to indicate the detailed pattern, or size of internal trade flows. The result has been, that apart from one or two notable contributions (Willan 1938, Andrews 1954), this aspect of the eighteenth century economy has not been explored. Indeed 'while transport has been written about at length, trade, and especially internal trade, has been all but ignored by the historians.' (Hartwell 1971: 214).

It is, therefore, the purpose of this chapter to draw together the existing threads of evidence about internal trade, and to provide some new material to illustrate the nature, volume and organization of trade flows, particularly those carried overland. The general picture can, in fact, be established without difficulty, using the surrogates of general economic

expansion, and regional and local differentiation. A brief examination of
these will provide the basis for understanding the general patterns of
trade flow, and their increasing importance, in the eighteenth century:
these will then be illustrated by reference to the surviving qualitative and
quantitative evidence.

General Patterns of Internal Trade

The theoretical basis for interregional trade is the concept of comparative
advantage. A region possesses a comparative advantage in the
production of those goods which it can produce at a lower cost than other
regions. The concept, although based originally on the classical
economists' doctrine of comparative labour costs, has subsequently been
developed to incorporate variations in resource endowments, factor
supply, and factor intensities. If regions produce those goods in which
they have comparative cost advantages, trade will result with other
regions, providing the cost advantage exceeds the transport cost and if
there are no legal, institutional or technological barriers to the transfer of
goods.

There is sufficient qualitative evidence to show, in general terms, the
applicability of this principle in seventeenth and eighteenth century
Britain. The pre-industrial economy was far from being a self-sufficient
peasant economy. With wide regional variations in resource
endowments, and with a significant urban population, removed from
land, it could not have been. Coal and mineral production was restricted
to certain areas, notably the north-east and Midlands. The iron industry
was located close to raw material supplies, in Sussex and the Forest of
Dean, and later, on the West Midland plateau and in South Wales. Wool
textile production, although widespread, was focused around Exeter and
Norwich, and in the West Riding, Wiltshire and Gloucestershire.

Even within agriculture, there were significant regional variations.
'The subsistence sector did not dominate agriculture and few farms were
completely divorced from the market.' (Clarkson 1971: 45.) Defoe, in his
celebrated Tour, published between 1724 and 1726, noted the
widespread specialization of production. High value, perishable
products, such as milk and vegetables, were produced close to towns,
whilst distant upland areas were committed to rearing cattle and sheep,
which were subsequently fattened for the urban markets in East Anglia
and the Midlands. The south-eastern counties, and Bedfordshire,

Hertfordshire and Herefordshire were notable granaries. Leicestershire and the downland country were sheep producers, and Norfolk and Suffolk were famous for their turkeys and geese.

Internal trade was based on the flows of exchange between the specialized economies of these areas: exchange between agricultural regions, between regions sufficient and deficient in natural resources, between industrial and non-industrial, and between country and town. But, in the seventeenth and eighteenth centuries, internal trade was not static—it was increasing in importance, as economic and regional specialization developed, and as the economy expanded. Real output more than doubled between 1700 and 1800, and whilst agricultural production probably rose by about 50 per cent, industrial and commercial production roughly quadrupled. Coal production rose from barely 5 million tons in 1760, to 11 million tons in 1800, whilst pig iron output, at only 17,500 tons in 1720, and 30,000 tons in 1760, had reached 250,000 tons in 1800. The production of West Riding broad and narrow cloths rose steadily by about 8 per cent per decade from 1701 to 1741, then more dramatically by 13 or 14 per cent up to 1772, after which it was overshadowed by the growth of cotton textiles: the import of cotton raw material doubled between 1750 and 1775, and increased eightfold in the last 20 years of the century.

This growth in itself required increasing exchange of raw materials and finished goods, between producer and consumer areas, and ports. It was also accompanied by other important changes which intensified the expansion of internal trade. Agriculture declined in relative importance in the economy, and its share of employment fell dramatically from Gregory King's estimate of three quarters of the workforce in 1688, to about a third in 1800. Hence, a large proportion of the sustained increase in population between these two dates, from $6\frac{1}{2}$ to $10\frac{1}{2}$ million, was in the industrializing areas and urban centres. By the end of the eighteenth century, the pre-industrial concentration of population in the southern, agricultural counties had shifted to the emerging coalfield areas. The urban population had grown significantly: in 1700, about 13 per cent of the population of England and Wales lived in towns of over 5,000. In 1751, this figure had reached 16 per cent, and by 1801, 25 per cent. London had grown from an estimated 200,000 in 1600, to 575,000 in 1700, and 900,000 in 1801, symbolizing the expansion of towns elsewhere. Towns were becoming increasingly important as markets for agricultural produce, and for the distribution of processed and manufactured goods and the information services.

Defoe was one of the first observers to describe the centrality of London in this national system of internal trade. Indeed, it was one of his key themes in the Tour:

> '. . . this whole kingdom, as well as the people, as the land, and even the sea, in every part of it, are employ'd to furnish something, and I may add, the best of everything, to supply the city of London with provisions; I mean by provisions, corn, flesh, fish, butter, cheese, salt, fewel, timber, & 'c. and cloths also; with every-thing necessary for building, and furniture for their own use, or for trades. . . .' (Defoe 1962 Vol. 1:12)

London's needs had been growing rapidly for some time: its coastwise imports of corn rose from 17,380 quarters in 1579/80 to 95,714 quarters in 1638. In the following 100 years, its demand for food expanded by 75 per cent. And it was not an indiscriminate demand—'it drew on each district, not so much for food in general, but for those victuals in particular which the district was best fitted to produce.' (Fisher 1935: 47.) The London market was a powerful engine encouraging the regional specialization within agriculture. Corn came from East Anglia, the Humber and the Borders by sea, and overland by river and road, from the Thames Basin, Hertfordshire, Buckinghamshire and Bedfordshire. Essex supplied oats, Sussex—wheat, and Norfolk—malt, whilst Kent sent all three in quantity. Butter came from Yorkshire, Suffolk and the Fens, and cattle from the hill country of the north and west, via fattening pastures in the South Midlands, Essex and on the Kent marshes.

The volume of trade involved in supplying London was considerable. In the 1750s, it was estimated that Scotland was sending 80,000 black cattle and 150,000 sheep to England every year. In 1700, about half a million sheep and 75,000 cattle were sold at Smithfield market. In 1800, these figures had reached 750,000 and 100,000 respectively, with each animal travelling overland. In 1730, 115,000 firkins of butter were dispatched to London from the Yorkshire ports, 56,000 firkins from the Suffolk ports, and 16,000 from Newcastle. A further 105,000 firkins came by river and road. Hence, a total of 12,000 tons of butter was reaching the capital by this date. Twenty years later, in 1751, the London cheesemongers were being supplied with 2,000 tons of cheese from Gloucestershire, Wiltshire and Berkshire, and 500 tons from the Midland counties.

It was not only agricultural products which were involved in the London trade. In 1750, the port received 650,000 tons of coal from

Tyneside, a twofold increase in 100 years. This represented about one sixth of total national production. The great rise in population, and the increased use of coal for domestic burning, and making bricks (rather than using wood for building), were the underlying reasons for this. Building materials came coastwise from Dorset (paving and Portland stone), Cornwall (roofing stone) and North Wales (slate). The cloth trade was also important. In the seventeenth century, Hull shipped large quantities of dozens, kerseys and bays to London. Exeter sent pieces of serge in great numbers—83,000 in the year to Midsummer 1701.

London was not, however, only a centre of consumption in this system of trade flows. It was also an important centre of redistribution, both of home and imported goods. The coastwise cloth trade was almost entirely for export, for example, with London playing an entrepôt role. To a certain extent, it was balanced by return flows of imported cloth— Exeter, Yarmouth and Kings Lynn all received foreign linen from the capital for local redistribution. In 1683, London distributed nearly 1,000 tons of iron, most of it foreign, chiefly to the east coast ports. There was an important exchange trade in coal, to East Anglia and the south-eastern counties. Imported luxuries and London manufactures similarly featured as exchange products: in 1683, 99 shipments were sent to Newcastle and 84 to Hull, including such items as iron, flax, haberdashery, wine and spirits, groceries, tobacco and stationery.[1]

Two central points can be made about this growing London trade. Firstly, the importance of the coastal trade is very apparent. It is however, only a facet of the whole which has received detailed attention from historians, and this should not be allowed to promote its relative position. It is probable, in fact, that overland traffic, by river and road, accounted for six times the volume of trade brought by coaster (McGrath 1948: 119). The river basins, the road network, and the coastal routes were all important in the system of flows to and from London. Secondly, and most significantly, London's centrality was a symbol of the general pattern of inland trade. 'It would be a mistake to regard London as the only focus of inland trade in pre-industrial England, although it was certainly the most important . . . Every expanding market town in the country stood at the centre of an ever enlarging circle of commerce.' (Clarkson 1971: 122–3.) In 1750, there were 130 towns in England with populations exceeding 2,500. Many of these were small—the largest, Bristol (50,000) and Norwich (36,000) were less than one tenth the size of the capital. But many were also growing very rapidly. By 1801 the new industrial centres of Manchester (84,000) Liverpool (78,000) and

Birmingham (74,000) had moved to the top of the urban hierarchy.

All these large towns were foci of trade in their own regions, both as centres of consumption in their own right, and as important links in the London or foreign trade. On the west coast, Bristol played a similar role to that of the capital, attracting a wide range of foodstuffs from the Severn Vale and the south-western counties, and corn and wool from South Wales and Ireland. It acted as an entrepôt for Welsh coal and Cornish tin, exported large quantities of Dean timber to London, and distributed imported goods, such as sugar and tobacco, widely (Minchinton 1954). As with the London trade, much of this Bristol traffic was brought by coaster or river barge. The River Severn in particular was an important artery. Much of the agricultural produce of the Midland counties moved down it making Gloucester a major corn port. It was the export route for manufactured goods from the Birmingham plateau, and carried an exchange trade in coal and pig iron from South Wales (Willan 1937, Johnson 1951). The other river basins played similar roles in their regions—the Tyne, the Ouse, the Aire and Calder, the Trent and the Great Ouse. In fact, many of the largest eighteenth century towns were both sea ports and river towns. Kings Lynn, for example, was a substantial east coast corn port. Defoe described its trade:

'. . . there is the greatest extent of inland navigation here, of any port in England, London excepted . . . By these navigable rivers the merchants of Lynn supply about six counties wholly, and three counties in part, with their goods, especially wine and coals . . . besides the several counties, into which these goods are carryed by land carriage, from the places where the navigation of those rivers ends; which has given rise to this observation on the town of Lynn, that they bring in more coals than any sea-port between London and Newcastle; and import more wines than any port in England, except London and Bristol.' (Defoe 1962 Vol. 1: 73)

Most of the corn from the Great Ouse was sent to London (62,410 quarters out of a total of 82,795 quarters shipped in 1734/5), but a significant amount (10,012 quarters) did go to Newcastle in exchange for coal (Willan 1938: 80).

The importance of the river basins as trade routes can be seen in the history of the Thames basin. The Thames itself was one of the earliest rivers to be improved, with a series of measures from the fourteenth century onwards. The Lea was made navigable between 1571 and 1581, the Wey between 1651 and 1653, the Medway and the Mole in the 1660s, and the Kennet from 1715. The Lea was an important artery supplying London with malt and corn: as early as Elizabeth's reign a ring of towns from Enfield to Cheshunt was processing corn brought in by wagon from Bedfordshire, Buckinghamshire and Northampton. In the west, Abingdon and Reading fulfilled a similar function. Again, it was not a one-way trade, as was evident from Defoe's description of Reading:

> 'Their chief trade is by this water—navigation to and from London, though they have necessarily a great trade into the country, for the consumption of the goods which they bring by their barges from London, and particularly coal, salt, grocery wares, tobacco, oyls and all heavy goods.' (1962 Vol. 1: 291)

Farnham, the greatest corn market in the south, supplied London via the Wey Navigation. In Defoe's time, Guildford was the main port on this river, for the dispatch of both corn and timber, but after the extension of the navigation to Godalming in the 1760s, that town usurped Guildford's role. In 1766, it was estimated that 1,100 loads of timber were sent downstream from Godalming wharf in a year, 700 of which came up the Petworth road alone.[2] Further east, in Kent, the Medway carried large quantities of timber, hops, corn, fruit and building materials to London. The main port was Maidstone, described by Defoe as 'a considerable town, very populous, and the inhabitants generally wealthy; 'tis the county town, and the river Medway is navigable to it by large hoys of fifty to sixty tons burthen.' (Vol. 1: 133–4.)

The river basins therefore played an important part in the extensive system of internal trade in the seventeenth and eighteenth centuries. Many of the big towns were river ports and sea ports, thus emphasizing the role of the river barge and coaster in conveying traffic. Although evidently much internal trade was taken overland, by road, the description has slipped into an implicit, and traditional exposition of the importance of water carriage. The reasons for this are worth exploring further.

Land and Water Carriage

'The chief highway of the English during the turnpike era was not the road at all but navigable water' wrote Dyos and Aldcroft (1969: 81). Their assertion reflects a bias both common and traditional in descriptions of inland trade and transport in this period. This bias is the result of two factors—one empirical, the other theoretical. The water transport system has been both easier to study, because of the survival of evidence in the Port Books, and has been studied more intensively. There is no equivalent work to that of Professor Willan on both sea and river transport (1936, 1938). There is also important theoretical backing for the notion of the superiority of water over land transport, a notion which can be traced back to Adam Smith. It is a short step from demonstrating apparent superiority of a transport mode, to assuming its virtual dominance.

Adam Smith's discussion of the role of water transport in promoting the division of labour is well known:

'As by means of water-carriage a more extensive market is opened to every sort of industry than what land-carriage alone can afford it, so it is upon the sea-coast, and along the banks of navigable rivers, that industry of every kind naturally begins to subdivide and improve itself, and it is not frequently till a long time after that these improvements extend themselves to the inland parts of the country. A broad-wheeled waggon, attended by two men, and drawn by eight horses, in about six weeks time carries and brings back between London and Edinburgh near four ton weight of goods. In about the same time a ship navigated by six or eight men, and sailing between the port of London and Leith, frequently carries and brings back two hundred weight of goods. Six or eight men, therefore, by the help of water carriage, can carry and bring back in the same time the same quantity of goods between London and Edinburgh, as fifty broad-wheeled waggons, attended by a hundred men, and drawn by four hundred horses.' (Smith 1904 Vol. 1: 20)

This was sound economic analysis. A pack-horse could carry between 2 and 3 cwt, a wagon, needing several horses, was limited after 1662 to a load of 30 cwt in summer by law: this was raised in 1741 to 3 tons, and in 1765 to 6 tons. On water, however, a horse could tow up to 30 tons along a river, and as much as 50 tons using a well constructed canal towpath. River carriage was certainly more efficient, and because of this, it was— in general terms—considerably cheaper than land carriage. In the early eighteenth century, over long distances and away from some small rivers controlled by monopoly interests charging high tolls (such as the Wey, Idle and Chelmer), 'the rate of carriage by water was usually as low as 1d per ton per mile.' (Willan 1936: 121.) Dyos and Aldcroft considered that 'the average was probably nearer 2½d, but by road the figure was around a shilling. Even allowing for the more direct routes usually taken by roads, the relative cost of water transport was certainly no more than half that for land carriage.' (1969: 40–1.) Sea transport was even cheaper. The only detailed study of regional trade patterns in this period, for the Wealden counties south of London between 1650 and 1750, revealed that there was a well developed land and sea carriage trade from Wealden towns to London. However, the available information on rates shows that land transport was eight times as costly per mile as sea transport (Andrews 1954: 144–5).

This cost advantage was always emphasized by promoters of river improvement bills in Parliament. The information to be gained from the recordings of the procedure on these bills represents a valuable source for the study of inland trade. In 1720, the promoters of the River Weaver bill claimed that the Cheshire salt trade had lost most of its overseas markets to France and Spain because of the high cost of land carriage to the head of navigation. But, they said:

'. . . if the River Weaver . . . was made navigable from Winsford Bridge to Frodsham Bridge, the salt would be delivered at Frodsham Bridge for about three shillings per Tun, which now costs Eight or Nine Shillings, and sometimes Ten Shillings, per Tun; . . . such Navigation will likewise very much encourage and improve the Cheese Trade, which is the great Produce of the Country, and most of it brought to London, by lessening the land-carriage thereof to Frodsham Bridge near Three Shillings per Tun, which is now Ten, Fifteen and sometimes Eighteen Shillings, per Tun. . . .' (JHC 19: 227)

Although this bill was not successful, an Act was secured in the following year, and the improvements put in hand. Similar arguments were used by the promoters of many other river bills at this time.

Nevertheless, despite the apparently overwhelming economic advantage of trade by water, a well used land transport system existed. This land transport system can be classified into two parts: a *complementary* system, which was interdependent with water transport, and performed a feeder and distribution role for it, and a *competitive, independent* system, which did not rely on water transport linkages.

The complementary land transport system was a necessary adjunct of the flows of trade within the river basins. Goods had to be carried overland to and from points of navigation and the important river and sea ports. The Cheshire cheese and salt trades and the economy of the Great Ouse Basin depended on these linkages, as the illustrations above have shown. Travellers in this period often noted the heavy road traffic around such ports. Celia Fiennes, for example, in her journey round England in the 1690s made many such observations. In the north-east:

'As I drew nearer and nearer to Newcastle I met with and saw abundance of little carriages with a yoke of oxen and a pair of horses together, which is to convey the Coales from the pitts to the barges on the river . . . upon a high hill 2 mile from Newcastle I could see all about the country which was full of coale pitts.'

And at Taunton in Somerset:

'. . . this river comes from Bridgewater 7 mile, the tyde comes up beyond Bridgewater even within 3 mile of Taunton . . . and here at this little place where the boats unlade the coale the packhorses comes, and takes it in sacks and so carryes it to the places all about; this is the sea coale brought from Bristole, the horses carry 2 bushell at a tyme which at the place cost 18d. and when its brought to Taunton cost 2 shillings; the roads were full of these carryers going and returning.' (Morris 1947: 209, 243)

Sometimes, the flow of traffic to and from ports came long distances overland. Defoe was told that 'eleven hundred teams of horse, all drawing waggons, or carts, loaden with Wheat' had been seen at the great market at Farnham. These came from a wide area of the surrounding countryside. Near Chichester, 'the farmers generally speaking, carry'd all their wheat to Farnham, to market, which is very near forty miles by land-carriage, and from some parts of the country more than forty miles.' (Vol. 1: 135.) This corn was ground by millers on the River Wey, and dispatched to London, but also 'by this navigation a very great quantity of timber is brought down to London, not from the neighbourhood of (Guildford) only, but even from the woody parts of Sussex and Hampshire above thirty miles from it, the country carriages bringing it hither in the summer by land.' (Vol. 1: 145.)

In the north, there was an important trans-Pennine trade from Lancashire to Yorkshire, involving exchange of manufactures and agricultural produce, and import and export of goods through Hull:

'. . . the Towns of Manchester and Stockport are very large, and considerable Trading Towns, and send weekly great Quantities of Goods, Merchandizes, and Manufactures to Doncaster, in the County of York; which are carried from thence by Water to Hull, in order to be shipped to London, and foreign Parts; and bring back considerable Quantities of Flax, Yarn and other Commodities, which are manufactured in the said Towns of Manchester and Stockport. . . .' (JHC 23: 575)

This trade was all carried over the Pennines by pack-horses, and later, by wagon.

Quite apart from this complementary system, however, there was an important independent land transport system. This involved the transfer of people and information, as well as goods, over long distances without any recourse to water transport. Three factors underlay the existence of this independent system: the disadvantages of water transport, and its absence in many areas (the negative), and the better service often available by land transport (the positive). It is these factors which underline the danger of assuming the dominance of water transport on generalized grounds of apparent cost advantages alone. Each deserves some illustration.

Water transport, by river and sea, had obvious disadvantages. It was unsuitable for certain types of goods, notably wool, which was easily damaged. At sea, trade was subject to delays by the weather, and the additional hazards of war and piracy. Shipments were often delayed for days or weeks, whilst awaiting convoys. Although this does not seem to have diverted the trade in bulk goods, such as coal, overland (Willan 1938: 21–23), more valuable products were usually sent by road instead. William Stout, the grocer of Lancaster, for example, was forced to depart from his normal habit of coastal shipment to London several times in the 1690s and 1700s (Marshall 1967: 98, 138).

River transport was unattractive in some areas because of poor navigations, or the high monopoly charges levied by owners. In Yorkshire, in the early 1740s, this situation existed:

'the road from Leeds to Halifax is about 18 measured Miles, through which several thousand Loads of Lime are carried to manure Land; and in Summer, when the River is low, and in great Frosts, and Floods, all sorts of Goods are sent by Land Carriage . . .

That the Lock Dues, upon the Rivers Aire and Calder, being very high, the Manufactures of the Western Parts, as also Wool, Corn & c from Lincolnshire, and other Places, can be conveyed by Land Carriage . . . when (the roads) are passable, at an easier Expense than they are now carried by Water.' (JHC 23: 641)

The upper Thames, above Oxford, suffered from similar difficulties. It carried a substantial trade in the seventeenth century in building stone, cheese, butter, bacon and cider from the wharves at Radcot Bridge, near Burford, and Lechlade. But there were long delays at the weirs, and in 1695 (6 & 7 Wm & Mary, c. 16) and again in 1730 (3 Geo. II, c. 11), it was necessary to legislate to control the millers' charges. In the 1740s, there were complaints of barges getting stuck in shoals, and it became common to use 'lightening boats' into which to transfer the cargo when this happened. Later, in 1767, fourteen boats were still operating on the upper river, but river traffic was declining because high carriage rates and long delays were making merchants and producers send their goods by land (Neale 1972: 28). Two years after this, a direct road west from Oxford was opened upon the completion of Swinford Bridge, and so much trade was diverted off the river onto the road that river traffic almost ceased, and Oxford boatmen resorted to letting their craft for pleasure purposes.[3]

Many parts of the country, however, did not have the opportunity of using water transport. In 1700, large areas were more than 15 miles from a navigable river (Fig. 4). In the upland regions, there was no alternative to using the roads. Trains of pack-horses were therefore a common sight. In the north Pennines, for example, it was estimated in 1766 that two thousand horses laden with lead used the road from Nenthead to Penrith each week in summer.[4] A large part of the Midlands, before the construction of canals in the latter part of the eighteenth century, was remote from water transport. Coal and iron, as well as corn, were distributed over several counties here by road. In 1726, it was claimed in Parliament that:

> '. . . the ancient Road between Birmingham and Warwick, and from thence to Banbury, in the great Road towards London, being at least 28 miles, is become very ruinous, and almost impassable, not only by the great Number of Carriages, of late Years, employed in the Malt and Barley Trade, from the County of Oxon and Parts adjacent, but also by the return of Coals and Iron from Birmingham to London, Oxon, Berks and other Counties. . . .' (JHC 20: 584)

In the following year, it was said that the Wolverhampton to Birmingham road:

> '. . . is much used in the carrying of Iron-Wares, Coals and Lime to Birmingham, and so into the Counties of Warwick, Northampton, Oxford and other counties.' (JHC 20: 746)

In the Staffordshire potteries, producers had to relay on pack-horses to supply coal, flints and panniers of clay, and to distribute the crates of pottery to market (Thomas 1934). The Trent and Mersey Canal through the area, which was backed by many of the potters, including Wedgwood, was not begun until the late 1760s. Two hundred wagon loads of corn were brought to the weekly market in Warminster, in Wiltshire—a large rural market town—in the 1720s. It was dispatched by road as well: 'nearly half the Malt that is made in Warminster, is carried out into the Bristoll road.' (JHC 20: 803.)

Sometimes it was cheaper to use land carriers even when a competing

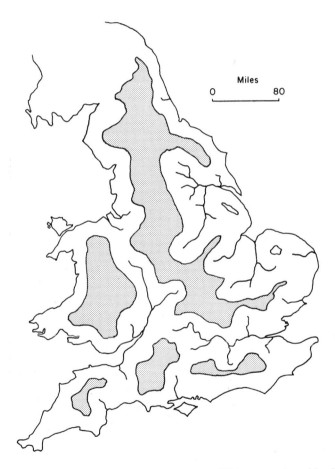

Fig. 4. The extent of the land area of England and Wales more than 15 miles from a navigable river in 1700. *Source*: Willan 1936: 32.

service was available, because of the distances involved in trading by water. In the Weald the use of coastal transport by inland towns involved a long haul to the coast, and then around the Kent peninsula to reach London. Centres such as Tonbridge, Sevenoaks, East Grinstead and Midhurst thus had a higher provision of land transport services than the coastal towns, and there was a heavy traffic on the London-bound roads in bulk goods, such as fish, wool and hops, as well as high value products (Andrews 1954: 144–6). The canals of the later eighteenth century were not always cheaper than the roads for the same reason. Not until 1805, when the Grand Junction Canal was opened, was there a direct water route between Manchester and London. Pickfords, one of the main canal carriers on this route, shipped its goods down the Trent and Mersey Canal, and then, rather than make the circuitous journey down the Oxford Canal and the Thames, transhipped goods on to wagons and carried them the rest of the way by road (Turnbull 1973: 8–9).

The land transport system therefore offered the best service on many routes, because water transport was poor, indirect or simply not available. In addition, land transport could often offer a superior service even when these disadvantages did not occur. In many respects, this superiority was little affected by the new canals.

Some types of traffic were obviously unsuited to transport by water. The great overland droves of animals came in this category. Cattle and sheep could be conveyed by boat, but it was cheaper and more convenient to allow them to walk themselves to market. This way they also arrived in a better condition, being able to rest and graze on the way. The half million sheep and 75,000 cattle that were sold at Smithfield in 1700 all came overland. In East Anglia, Defoe marvelled at the droves of turkeys walking to the capital, often, he was told, between 300 and 1,000 at a time. In Norfolk, he found that 40,000 Scots cattle were driven to St Faith's fair each year, and fattened on the marshes between Norwich and the sea. From Peterborough, fowl were sent to London 'twice a week in wagon loads at a time', and the turkey droves were beginning to be replaced by a 'new-fashion'd voiture', of four storeys (Vol. 1: 59–60, 65).

Other types of traffic required a speedier and more reliable journey to market than was available by water. This was so in the fish trade. London was supplied with fresh fish, delivered within a few hours of being caught, by packhorse from Rye and Hastings. In 1710, about 300 fish-carrier horses passed through Tunbridge Wells every day. Defoe said of the inhabitants:

'. . . they are supply'd with excellent fish, and that of almost all sorts, from Rye, and other towns on the sea-coast . . . In the season of mackarel, they have them here from Hastings, within three hours of their being taken out of the sea.' (Vol. 1: 127)

In fact, the Folkestone and Hastings roads could supply London within 12 or 15 hours, whereas the sea voyage took at leat 48 hours (McGrath 1948: 181). Fish-trains were coming to the city from Wallington, with fresh salmon, and from Newcastle and Lyme Regis. Speed and reliability were also important with manufactured goods and some raw materials, such as wool. Also, as these items had a high value to weight ratio, the cost advantage of water transport was not so pronounced. The manufactured goods of the West Midlands were distributed to their markets by road:

'The manufactures of the Towns of Wolverhampton and Walsall consist of Iron Wares, Flax, Hemp and other Goods, are carried by Land to London, Chester, Shrewsbury, Litchfield and Bridgenorth, and other Parts of this Kingdom for Sale and Exportation. . . .' (JHC 25: 506)

This was also the case with the trade of Sheffield and the surrounding country:

'. . . on Account of the large Trade and Manufacture carried on within the Limits of that Corporation, great Quantities of Goods are weekly sent away in Carriages, and on Horseback, from Sheffield, to London and other Places. . . .' (JHC 23: 302)

Wool could be carried long distances overland without a marked increase in price—the journey from Bristol to East Anglia in the early eighteenth century added less than 15 per cent to its cost, for example. Large quantities were taken by road from Romney Marsh and East Sussex to the markets at Sevenoaks and Tonbridge, and from there to London (Andrews 1954: 206). The Godmanchester to Newmarket route was heavily used by wagons taking wool from the Midlands to Norwich, (JHC 23: 593, 24: 733), as well as woollen goods to the great annual fair at Sturbridge, near Cambridge. Defoe, when he went to this fair, found that:

'Here are clothiers from Hallifax, Leeds, Wakefield, and Huthersfield in Yorkshire, and from Rochdale, Bury &c. in Lancashire, with vast quantities of Yorkshire cloths, kerseyes, pennistons, cottons, &c with all sorts of Manchester ware, fustians, and things made of cotton wool; of which the quantity is so great, that they told me there were near a

thousand horse-packs of such goods from that side of the country. . . .'
(Vol. 1: 82)

At the time Defoe wrote, however, these great fairs were in decline, and
goods were sold increasingly in the urban markets, through
warehousemen, or factors, or direct to the public. Much of the Lancashire
trade was in the hands of the Manchester men, who were wholesale
dealers, selling their wares to shopkeepers all over the country, using
trains of pack-horses and wagons to do so.[5] The manufacturers also used
'riders out', who travelled the country with sample patterns, and had
their orders dispatched by carrier. The export trade was handled by
carriers—in the 1750s, 150 pack-horses and two broad-wheeled wagons
went from Manchester to Bristol every week, in addition to the trade
through Liverpool, and across the Pennines (Wadsworth and Mann
1931: 232–40).

The use of the carrier was one great advantage that the land transport
system offered. He provided a direct link between producers, middlemen
and consumers. But he also performed more than a straightforward
carrying function. This is clearly seen from business papers and personal
correspondence of the period. The Wiltshire cloth firms used the carrying
network extensively to dispatch cloth, and to place orders for raw
materials, whilst their customers used it to place their orders, and to make
payments (Mann 1964). Samuel Oldknow, the Lancashire cotton
manufacturer, used carriers to keep in touch with his London
warehousemen in the same way (Unwin 1924). Abraham Dent, the
shopkeeper of Kirkby Stephen, a relatively remote town in Westmorland,
received year round deliveries of groceries, cloth, stationery and exotic
goods from nearly 200 suppliers all over the North and Midlands between
1750 and 1777. These deliveries were made by carriers, and Dent
forwarded payment with them, either in kind or by bill and banknote
(Willan 1970). It was not only the commercial world which relied on
these land carriers. They also provided the direct link between consumers
and markets, particularly outside the towns. The Purefoys, a mid-
eighteenth century Buckinghamshire gentry family, relied on local
carriers to keep them in touch with their London agents, and supply
goods from the capital (Davis 1966: 224–35).

The land transport system thus offered a distinctive service which
water transport could not hope to emulate. In part, this was because it
was a direct service, but the key was 'communication'—the conveyance

of information. The carrying trade, the stage-coach passenger services, the letter post, and the provincial newspaper network were the principal instruments in this, and they were essentially facets of the land transport system. The economy could not function merely by exchange of goods and raw materials: this exchange presupposed the existence of adequate information links. In the developing economy of the eighteenth century, the easier communication of information was just as important as the easier transportation of goods.

The Land Transport System

A formally organized land transport system was available from an early date. In 1637, John Taylor's *Carriers Cosmographie* had shown the existence of over two hundred carriers' services to London 'from any parts, townes, shires, and countries, of the Kingdomes of England, Principality of Wales, as also from the Kingdomes of Scotland and Ireland.' Most of these were pack-horse services, and wheeled transport was unusual, particularly in the upland areas and counties remote from London, until well into the eighteenth century. Taylor did mention, however, fifteen wagon services, mostly to towns within thirty miles of London, and Stow had referred to 'long wagons' serving the capital from Canterbury, Norwich, Ipswich and Gloucester about 1564.

The *Cosmographie* also contained details of four regular coach services, to St Albans, Cambridge, Hertford and Hatfield. Stage-coach routes were later in development than carriers' services, but provincial links were emerging in the middle of the seventeenth century. By 1660, there were regular services to the south-west, Lancashire, Newcastle and Edinburgh, as well as towns closer to London (Jackman 1916: 119). These coaches carried not only passengers, but also small parcels of goods, and, away from the official Post Office routes, both letters and money. The Post Office System itself was initially restricted to five main roads, and carried only Royal dispatches. It is difficult to say when the privilege of using this system was first extended to private letters, and private posting, but the King's proclamation of 1635, and the Post Office Act of 1660 (12 Car. II, c. 35) confirmed its operation as a public service, and increased the number of routes in the network (Fig. 5). Common carriers were, in fact, forbidden after this to carry any letters, except those referring to goods in their charge, but this was not enforceable, particularly for cross-posts. Only the Universities of Oxford and

Cambridge were exempt, and by this time they operated their own letter carrying systems.

This land transport system developed rapidly from the mid-seventeenth century, and services proliferated. A comparison of Taylor's list of 1637 with the account in Delaune's *Present State of London*, of 1680, shows a considerable increase in traffic. The four towns served by stage-coach had increased to 88. In 1705, the *Travellers' and Chapmans' Instructor* listed 180 such towns, and in 1715, the *Merchant's and Trader's Necessary*

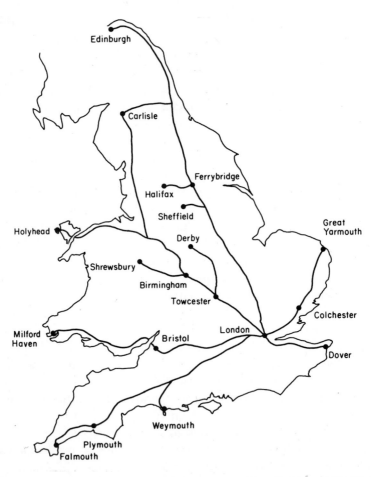

FIG. 5. The main Post Office routes, *c.* 1670. *Source:* derived from Robinson 1953: 16, 25–7.

Companion had increased this to 216. In the 1690s Celia Fiennes made note of the range of services available to one town near London, Tunbridge Wells:

> 'the Post comes every day and returns every day all the while the season of drinking the waters is, from London and to it . . . you likewise have the conveniency of Coaches every day from London for 8 shillings apiece dureing the whole season and Carriers twice a week.' (Morris 1947: 134)

In the eighteenth century, both intra- and interurban traffic services expanded. Carrying and coaching networks became better integrated in time and space. From 1720, Ralph Allen set about the serious development of the bye-and cross-post services. Provincial newspapers, which became a vital source of news and trade information, were available in 28 towns from Newcastle to Exeter by 1758 (Wiles 1965: 27). They carried the current prices of goods at market, and advertisements for industrial and imported products, and were thus instrumental in the workings of the market system, the creation of new markets, and in changing tastes and preferences. They were very widely available from agents, and their distribution networks gave an indication of the efficacy of the service offered by the post, carriers and coachmen (Fig. 6).

By 1823, London had 735 carriers' services operating from inns all over the city. In 1836, John Bates listed 342 coach services in his *Directory*. Of these, 275 were provided by the three largest proprietors, 106 by William Chaplin alone. He owned five inns in central London, and employed over 2,000 people and 1,800 horses in his business (Bagwell 1974: 50). In the same year 28 mail coaches—introduced by John Palmer in 1784—were leaving the city at 8 p.m. every night. The pattern was replicated in provincial centres, on a smaller scale. In Birmingham, for example, there were 74 individual carriers and firms operating in 1818. An entry in the local Directory for one of these gives an indication of the integration of land transport services achieved by this date:

> 'RUDGE, William and Co., from the Red Lion, Digbeth to Bath, every Tuesday, Thursday and Saturday evenings. This is the only waggon direct . . . to Bath, where it meets LYE's waggons, by whom goods are forwarded to Frome, Trowbridge . . . Salisbury and Southampton—To Bristol every Tuesday, Thursday and Saturday evenings . . . where they meet EARL's waggons, by whom goods are forwarded to Taunton, Exeter, Plymouth and all parts of the West of

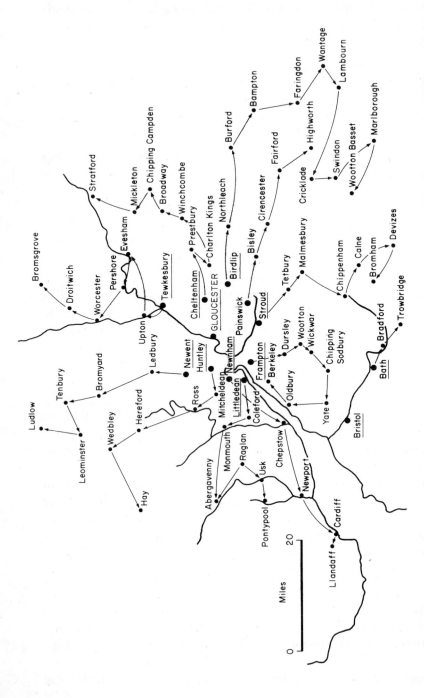

Fig. 6. The distribution network of the *Gloucester Journal*, 1725. The network was divided between 13 'distributors', each with his own 'division'. These were centred on the towns underlined on the map, and the paths of distribution followed the arrowed routes. *Source:* based on information in issue no. 160, dated 24 April 1724 (Gloucester Reference Library).

England. To Stratford-on-Avon, every Tuesday, Thursday and Saturday evenings, and conveys goods to . . . Evesham, Wootton under Edge &c.' (Wrightson, 1818: 191)

However, surprisingly little is known about these carriers, their businesses, or the carrying networks between towns. Very little research has been carried out since Jackman's pioneering efforts (1916).[6] As Professor Willan said, in discussing Abraham Dent's network of contacts:

'The presence of so many suppliers in different parts of the country suggests a developed transport system. The main man in that system was the carrier—a strangely neglected figure.' (1970: 41)

Carrying Networks

It is not possible to date precisely the emergence of the carrier. Packman and pedlars were certainly common on the roads of Tudor England, and in some areas, long before this. Oxford had services to and from its University from the mid-fifteenth century. By 1670, it had country wide connexions, with the regularity of the service declining with increasing distance (Table I). Kendal, the economic centre of Cumbria, had extensive regular carrying links all over the north, and to London, by the end of the seventeenth century. These are recorded in an unusual and detailed list (Table II, Fig. 7).[7] However, it was not only the large towns which had such services: many smaller centres and villages had their own carrier, as the example of Bedfordshire shows. Places situated on main roads were particularly well served (Fig. 8).

Some towns actually appointed their own carriers, regulating the number operating with other centres. This was the case in Ipswich, for example, where in 1613 the Corporation set the maximum rates that carriers could charge, and ordered that the two weekly London services be cut to one.[8] Evidence of this sort of regulation operating widely is not available, however. In the seventeenth century, the status of 'common carrier' gradually emerged in law, and this may have diminished the need for direct regulation. The common carrier, unlike the private carrier, was one who 'makes carrying his business, who holds himself out to the world as prepared for hire to transport from place to place the goods of any person wishing to employ him.' A common carrier was 'an insurer of the safe carriage of the goods he undertakes to carry'. He could not choose his customers, and had to charge a reasonable price—an

Table I

Oxford Carriers in the 1670s

Lincolne	Mr. Bennet lyes at the Maydenhead once in 3 weekes
Glocester	Mr. Basdell at the Crowne every weeke
Salop	Mr. Finch at the Sarazenshead every moneth
Lancashere	Mr. Richardson ⎫
	Mr. Ibing ⎬ at the Crowne every moneth
	Mr. Seddon ⎭
Cheshire	Mr. Drone ⎱ at the Roe Buck once in 6 weekes
	Mr. Lalham ⎰
Cambredge	Mr. Repuelder at the Grehound once in 3 weekes
Dorsetshire	Mr. Pope at the Fleur de Luce ⎫
	Mr. West at the Crowne ⎬ every weeke
	Mr. Reynolds at the Bull ⎭
Wiltes	Mr. Symonds at the Blewe bore every weeke
Northampton	Mr. Hickman at the Maydenhead every weeke
Warwick	Mr. Hickes at the Star ⎱ once a weeke
	Mr. Hiches at Katherin-wheele ⎰
Worcester	Mr. Newman at the Georg' once a weeke
Banbury	Mr. Fawkner at the Starr twice a weeke
Reading	Mr. Surdwer at the Checquer once a weeke
v.	
Winchester	Mr. Oades at the Blew bore once a week
Somersetshire	Mr. Besset at the Miter
Brestoll	Mr. Wharton at the Ship
Devenshere	Mr. Bartlot at the Crowne every moneth
Hereford	at the Blewbore
Manchester	Pycraft at the 3 Cuppes every 5 weekes
Derbyshire	Curle at the Miter every moneth
Cornish	Speare at the Beare once a quarter
Yorkeshire	Lydwell ⎱ at the Roe-Buck once in 5 weekes
	Steed ⎰
Coventry	at the Ship
Litchfield	

Source: This is a manuscript list from the University Archives. It is undated, but evidence from the University carriers' licences (see text) would suggest it belongs to the 1670s (Bodleian MSS Rawlinson D.317B fo. 177).

unreasonable price being tantamount to a refusal to carry (**Kahn-Freund** 1939: 2–6).

Within towns, however, efforts were certainly made in the seventeenth and eighteenth centuries to control traffic plying for hire. The hackney coach trade of London was regulated by a Board of Commissioners, and coaches were limited in number and licensed to operate for a set amount

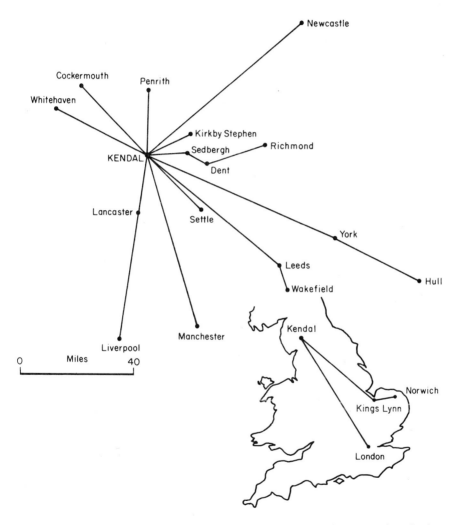

FIG. 7. Kendal carriers' network, *c.* 1699. This map illustrates the routes given in the manuscript list reproduced as Table II.

Table II

Kendal Carriers, *c.* 1699

From Kendall Carriers Names	To London	Price of Carriage thither	Days going out from Kendall	Price of Carriage back	Days Setting out home again	Lodgings	Days coming into Kendall	Number of Horses Imploy'd
Wm. Bateman Arthur Dixon Ja. Dixon Jno. Meel		ye pack 21s to 26s	Moundays	26s to 28s	Fridays	Castle Inn in Wood Street	Wednesdays	60
Ralph Whoely Jno. Wakefield	by way of Lancaster to London	20s to 25s	Thursdays Satturdays	24s to 20s	Fridays	Ditto & Swan with 2 Necks Lad Lane	Thursdays Satturdays	24
Jno. Winder	to Newcastle	7s to 8s	Satturdays sometimes Moundays	8s to 10s	Satturdays sometimes Moundays		Fridays	
Ralph Whoely Jno. Wakefield	to Liverpoole	8s	Thursdays & Satturdays	8s			Thursdays & Satturdays	
Jno. Wakefield	to Manchestr.	7s to 8s	Satturdays	8s			Thursdays & Satturdays	
Wm. Wadd	to Leeds and	8s				Talbot at Wakfield	Tuesdays	10

Jno. Holme Rond. Tatum	York & Hull	10s 14s	Satturdays & Wednesdays	10s 14s	Satturdays & Wednesdays	24
Wm. Wadd	Norwich & Linn	26s to 28s	Moundays	32s to 34s	Fridays	12
Mich. Tyson	to Cockermo.	4s	Wednesdays & Satturdays			
Jno. Holme Rond. Tatum	to Settle	4s	Wednesdays & Satturdays			
Petr. Bilboe	Kirkby Steven	2/6	Satturdays	2s to 6s		
Guy Warwick Tho. Wilson	to Dent Richmond Sedbar	4s 6s 1/6	Satturdays			
Ja. Halhead Jno. Turner	to Penrith	2/6 to 3s	Moundays & Thursdays	2/6 to 3s	Wednesdays & Fridays	

Source: This list is taken from Sir John Lowther's Memorandum Book (D/Law/W Cumbria Record Office). It is inscribed on one whole page, measuring 14 by 9 in.

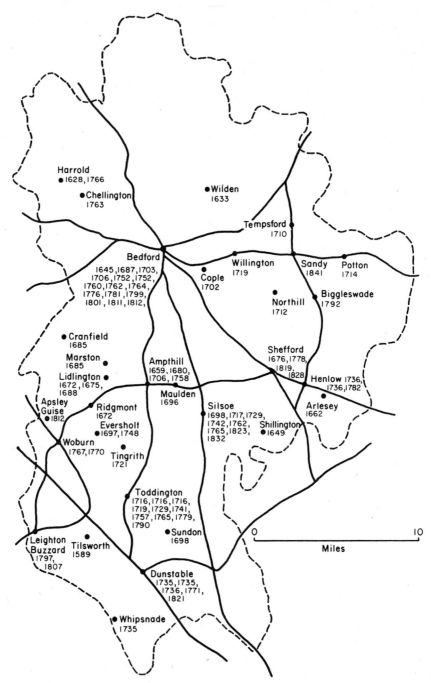

FIG. 8. Carriers in Bedfordshire. *Source*: Occupations index (Beds. CRO). The dates are those for which there is documentary evidence of a carrier working from the places indicated.

of time. Cromwell licensed 200 coachmen by Ordinance in 1654, to keep not more than 300 coaches. These figures were raised by Parliament in later Acts, so that there were 700 hackneys in 1694, and 1,000 in 1768 and 1,200 by 1832. An Act of 1694 fixed the rates to be charged (5 & 6 Wm & Mary, c. 22). Earlier, in 1606 and 1672, the London carters had found themselves subject to similar controls. The Justices of the Peace fixed and printed complete schedules for different commodities and distances. In 1677, licences were issued and the number of carts limited to 420 (Jackman 1916: 125–8).

A similar situation existed in Bristol, but here the carrying trade was controlled by the halliers, who were incorporated as a City Company in 1669. The Halliers Company required that all halliers be registered, and it set certain rules as well as fixing maximum rates. No charge of over one shilling per ton was to be made for merchants' goods conveyed from the quay to any place within the city, whilst 1s 6d per ton was the limit for lead brought in from Redcliffe Hill. After 1718, each hallier was recorded in the Register of Halliers, Brewers and Glassmakers. In 1721, for example, 22 halliers were entered in the Register. They had a total of 67 sledges, with several running four or five, and employed 56 journeymen and apprentices between them.[9]

Two other places where the carrying trade was strictly regulated were the Universities of Oxford and Cambridge. Both used licensing systems to control the trade between the Universities and other towns: these were inter- rather than intra urban carrying services. In Oxford, carriers and coachmen were controlled, but in Cambridge, with a few exceptions, only letter-carriers were involved. These licensing systems are of interest, because they give a detailed picture of the development of carrying networks.

In Oxford the regulation of the carrying trade can be traced back to the fifteenth century.[10] The earliest recorded University carrier was John Bayley, who was licensed to ply between the University and 'ye North Parts' in 1493. From then onwards, the University regularly appointed carriers, many for long distance routes into Wales, Yorkshire and the West Country, and others to closer centres such as London, Bristol and Salisbury.[11] The system in 1670 has already been revealed (Table I). From this date, a series of bonds and licences for carriers were kept in the University Archives.[12] These give a clear indication of the nature and extent of the University's carrying system up until 1825. The bonds outline the conditions under which the necessary surety money would not be forfeit, including the route to be followed, and an obligation to obey the regulations laid down by the University. Periodically, the Vice-Chancellor set the rates to be charged (Fig. 9). In return for entering into this agreement, the carrier received a monopoly of the University's trade on his particular route, and was elected to the status of 'privileged person' of the University. Privileged persons were able to engage in trade in Oxford itself without admission by the Town Corporation. The University carriers could, therefore, convey town trade as well.

'Whereas the Carriers between the University of Oxford and the City of London, to the great Prejudice of the members of the said University, and Others, have for divers years last past exacted what Rates they pleased for the Carriage of Goods and Letters (and have aggravated this their Unreasonable Practice by requiring Greater Summes from Scholars, than Towns-men) contrary to the Charters, and Antient Privileges of the said University, and to the Orders last prescribed to them in the year 1666.

Rates viz
—1 cwt goods (All Saints to Lady Day —4/–
        (by water 1/– per cwt)
        (Lady Day to All Saints) — 3/6
—carriage of any person by wagon — 4/–
—Parcels under $\frac{1}{4}$ cwt — 1/–
—Single hat and case—9d.
—any Burthen ($\frac{1}{4}$–1 cwt) — 3d, any parcel 1d.
—Letters to be left in Butteries of Colleges — $\frac{1}{2}$d.
—Ordinary 2 day Stage Coaches from the University to London to leave at/before 9 a.m. from St Marys Clock.
If anything, contrary to the fore-mentioned Orders, shall be hereafter practiced by any of the said Carriers, let the Offenders expect to undergo due Punishment; and also to make satisfaction to the Party injury, according to Right and Justice.'

                                        R. A. BATHURST V.C.
                                        4th December 1674

FIG. 9. Oxford University carriers rates in 1674.
Source: Bodleian MSS Wood 276A/318.

An analysis of the routes that were licensed shows the extent of the University's external relations (Table III, Fig. 10). Although there were several long routes in the system, these declined as a proportion of the whole in the eighteenth century. As the national system of interurban carrying links developed, becoming more integrated, so the need for long linkages from the University declined. Towns close to Oxford, situated on other main traffic routes, provided connexions to those farther away. Banbury gradually became the transit centre for Oxford's traffic to

Table III

Length of Licensed Oxford University Carriers Routes, 1670–1825

	Over 60 miles	20–60 miles	Less than 20 miles
1670–1720	12 (36 per cent)	19 (58 per cent)	2 (6 per cent)
1721–1770	5 (20)	15 (60)	5 (20)
1771–1825	4 (15)	16 (62)	6 (23)

Yorkshire, Lancashire and North Wales. Bristol and Hereford became the links to South Wales and the south-west. Significantly, the network had never been so extensive to the east of Oxford, because of the early prominence of London as the carriers' major route centre.

The carriers licensed by Oxford University carried both goods and passengers. In the eighteenth century, the proportion of coachmen awarded licenses increased, suggesting that the coach was growing in popularity over travel by horse. Carriers of goods *per se* also declined, with a steady rise in the proportion of carriers of goods and passengers, reflecting the rise in the use of wagons, rather than pack-horses. The term 'wagon' does not appear in the bonds until 1737, but after that date an increasing number of carriers are referred to as 'wagoners' (Table IV). In Cambridge, with the exception of five coach licences for the 1670s and 1680s, only letter-carriers were controlled. Licences survive for the period from 1663 to 1791.[13] Initially, they were issued for the London route alone, but from the 1680s, other important centres were gradually brought in to the system. Expansion continued until the 1740s, after which the need for a University post on many routes declined as the

Table IV

Types of Licences issued by Oxford University, 1670–1825

	Coachmen	Carriers of goods	Carriers of goods and passengers
1670–1720	10	66	0
1721–1770	10	25	12
1771–1825	45	2	24

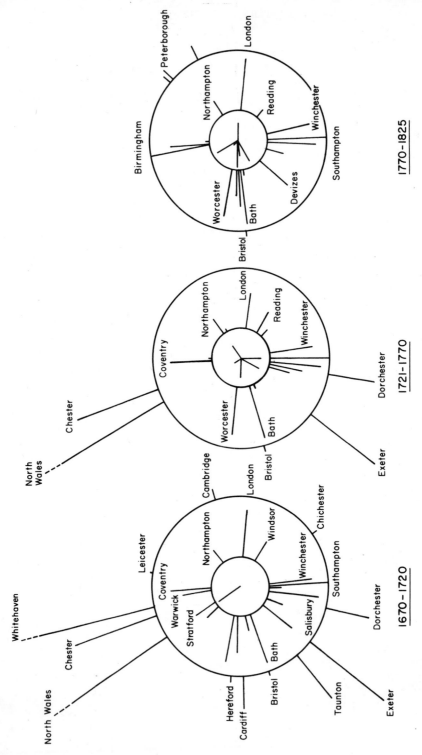

Fig. 10. The Oxford University carrying network, 1670–1825. *Source*: see text. The three maps are centred on Oxford, and plot those routes licensed by the University for which licenses survive. The circles are of 20 and 60 mile radii.

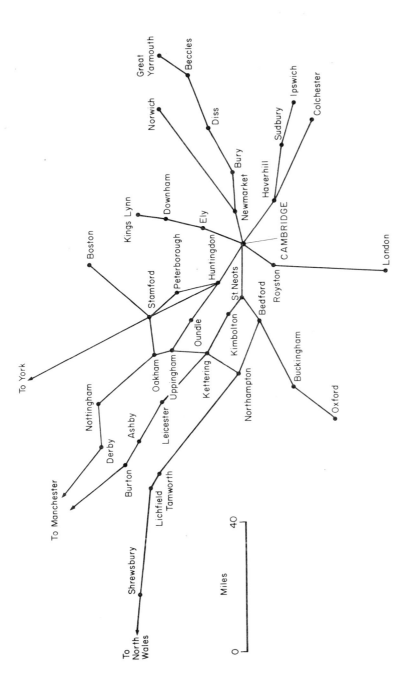

Fig. 11. The Cambridge University letter-carriers network, 1660–1800. This map shows all the routes for which licences granted between 1660 and 1800 are extant. *Source:* see text.

C

official posts improved. No London licences were issued after 1758. The maximum extent of the system is shown in Fig. 11.

From about the middle of the eighteenth century, an increasing amount of information is available about carrying networks. Lists in local directories and advertisements in local newspapers can be used to build up a picture of the evolving land transport system. The long-distance connexions of four of England's important towns in the latter half of the century are illustrated in Fig. 12. Bristol, Norwich, Newcastle and Liverpool were, respectively, the second, third, fourth and sixth largest towns in England in 1750. At the same time, Kendal, a much smaller centre of only 5,000 people, had maintained extensive packtrain connexions all over the north. Writing about the town as it was in 1753, Nicolson and Burn, (1777 Vol. 1: 66) the historians of Cumbria, said that 'the largeness of (its) trade may be estimated from the quantity of goods brought in and carried out . . . weekly, by the pack-horse carrier, before the turnpike roads were made, when wagons came into use':

One gang of pack-horses to and from London every week of about	20 horses
One gang from Wigan, weekly about	18 horses
One gang from Whitehaven, about	20 horses
From Cockermouth	15 horses
Two gangs from Barnard Castle	26 horses
Two gangs from Penrith twice a week, about 15 each gang	60 horses
One gang, about 15, from Settle, twice a week	30 horses
From York, weekly, about	10 horses
From Ulverston	5 horses
From Hawkshead, about 6, twice a week	12 horses
From Appleby, about 6 twice a week	12 horses
From Cartmel	6 horses
Two wagons from Lancaster twice a week, computed at 60 horse load	60 horses
Carriages, 3 or 4 times a week to and from Milnthorpe, computed at 40 horse load	40 horses
From Sedbergh, Kirkby, Lonsdale, Orton, Dent, and other neighbouring villages, about	20 horses
TOTAL	354 horses

Besides 24 every six weeks from Glasgow.

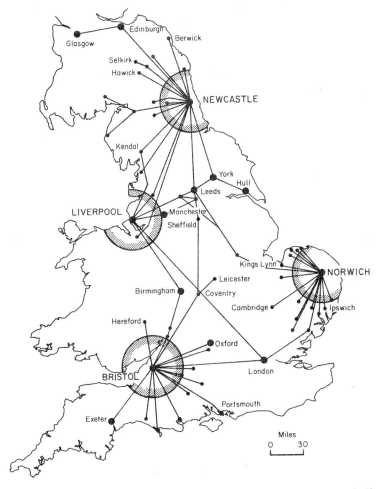

FIG. 12. Long-distance carrying links of important English towns in the latter half of the eighteenth century. This map shows all carrying links of over 30 miles for 4 large towns. *Sources*: Bath and Bristol Guide 1753, Liverpool Directory 1769, Norwich Directory 1783, Newcastle Directory 1778.

By 1790, the *Universal British Directory* showed that not only had the range of services widened, but that a qualitative change in their nature, from packtrain to wagon had taken place. Twenty-eight carriers or partnerships were operating, some to the same places:

London, twice a week	Dent, once a week
London, once a week	Sedbergh, twice
Manchester, twice	Settle, twice
Sheffield, once	Appleby, twice
York, once	Ambleside, once
Newcastle, twice	Milnethorp, six times
Newcastle, twice	Ulverstone, via Cartmel, once
Hawick, once a fortnight	Ulverstone, via Cartmel, once
Carlisle, twice	Ulverstone, via Barrow, twice
Whitehaven, twice	Ulverstone, via Barrow, once
Penrith, twice	Hawkshead, twice
Lancaster, six times	Orton, once
Lancaster, twice	Broughton, once
Bowes, once	
Hawes, once	

The town also had daily mail coaches to the north and south, and a post coach to London on every day of the week, except Sunday. These changes were part of a general trend in eighteenth century carrying systems towards increasing capacity to accommodate increasing trade. They were reflected in the London and Oxford systems, as has been seen, and gradually in the carrying networks of all other towns. Chester provides a final example—by 1781, its English hinterland was served by coach and wagon, but its Welsh hinterland was still reached by pack-horse (Fig. 13).

Carrying and Coaching Businesses

Carriers normally operated from inns, although some used their own houses, or warehouses, in their home towns. The inn was a convenient collection centre, and meeting point with other carriers. The advertised route of the Oxford to Southampton carrier, displayed in *Jackson's Oxford Journal* in 1761, demonstrates this (Fig. 14). James Croton was licensed that year by the University for this route. In fact, over one-third of the Oxford University licencees used innkeepers as bondsmen, although Croton himself did not. Carriers' entries in town directories always stated the inn or house from which their service operated. The Chester wagons to English towns, for example, nearly all went from Blossom's Inn, whereas the Welsh carriers went from the White Bear, from Messrs Wright and Sidebottom's warehouse, or from various

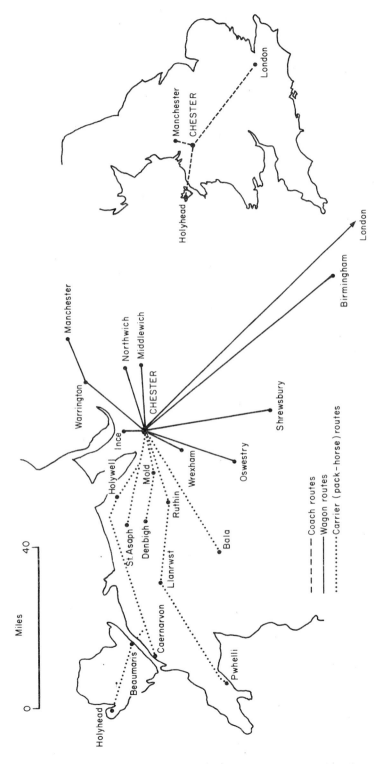

FIG. 13. Chester coach and carrier network, 1781. *Source*: Chester Guide, 1781.

JAMES CROTON

OXFORD, ABINGDON, NEWBURY, WINCHESTER, and SOTON CARRIER

Sets out from his House in the High Street, OXFORD, every Monday
Morning, by Five O'Clock; calls at the New Inn in Abingdon, at the
Pack Horse on Milton Hill, the Swan at Ilsey, the Crown in Cheveley
Lane, puts up at the Globe in Newbury; sets out from thence Tuesday
Mornings, calls at the Chequer at Whitway, the Rose & Chequer at
Whitchurch, the Old Swan at Sutton, puts up at the Three Tuns in
Winchester. He carries Goods, Passengers, &c for Romsey, Ringwood,
Lymington, or any Part of the New Forest; for Cowes, Newport, or any
Part of the I.o.W; for the Islands of Guernsey & Jersey, for Bishops-
Waltham, Wickham, Fareham, Gosport, Portsmouth, Chichester,
Alresford, Alton, Farnham, and Guildford'c. Sets out Thurs. Mornings
early for the Three Tuns in Winchester, gets to the Globe At Newbury
the same Night; from thence on Friday Mornings, and to his House in
Oxford the same Night. He brings Goods, Passengers &c. for Wantage,
Hungerford, Wallingford, and for all Parts of Oxfordshire, Warks,
Worcs, Northants, Shrops, Ches & c. Goods are desired to be delivered
at Oxford by Ten o'clock at farthest on Monday mornings . . . All
Gentlemen, &c. who will be so kind as to favour me with the Carriage or
Orders, may depend on the utmost Care and Diligence in the Delivery
of them.

Performed (if God permit) by

Their obedient and most humble Servant,

JAMES CROTON

NB It is the Waggon late Mr. James Dudley's that put up at the White
Hart Inn, in High Street, Winchester.

LSL The Master of the said Waggon will not be answerable for any
Money, Jewels, Plate, Watches, Bank-Notes or Writings, unless
delivered as such, and paid for accordingly.

FIG. 14. Advertisement of an Oxford carrier, 1761.

Source: Jackson's Oxford Journal
24 Oct. 1761

grocers in the town. In Oxford itself, the Flower de Luce Inn was popular.
It advertised itself in *Jackson's Oxford Journal* in the following terms:

'The Reading Machine, Abingdon, Coventry, Salisbury, Wallingford,
Burford Waggon and Carriers Inn at this House, where Goods are
taken in every Day in the Week, and conveyed to any Part of England.'

These services conveyed a wide variety of goods: large and small, bulky and valuable. The Account Book of a Leeds to London carrier, Robert Dawson, shows that he made a journey to London once every three or four weeks throughout the year. He spent Christmas 1750 on business in London and set out from Leeds for London on Christmas Day, 1751. His business followed a regular pattern—he carried 'packs of cloth' and 'bailes of wool' to London along with a few items (between 10 and 20) of general luggage. The return journey was nearly always a full load of small items—between 30 and 40 'parcels, barrels, chests, bags and trunks.' On 19 November 1750, he carried a barrel of oysters for Mr Dawson, another for H. Davis, with three Acts of Parliament, and a third for Sir Walter Blacket. On a return journey on 13 February of the next year, he took three hams, two turkeys, a packet of beef and an oven to London. Very occasionally, he took passengers too.[14] A similar variety of traffic is shown in the Account Book of an unnamed carrier who worked between London and King's Lynn in 1792.[15] This carrier served a number of places *en route*—entries in the book often refer to Wisbech, Upwell, March, Downham and Cambridge. He must have passed through some of these places, but others would be served by connecting carriers. Robert Dawson's Account Book refers to 'Road Goods', which were to be left at towns such as Nottingham and Northampton *en route* to London but the final destinations of items travelling the whole way are rarely given. An exception is the entry for the journey of 3 August 1758:

S. Richards	truss	5s	0d
W. Powell	1 pkt Norwich	2	0
N. Ganning	truss Norwich	3	9
Sarah Burnham	pkt Colchester	1	2
Dorothy Wilson	a box Gosport	2	10
John Nolbarrow	——Kelvedon	2	2
Ralph Thrasher	——Kelvedon	2	0
J. Seal	truss Yarmouth	7	5
J. Dixon Esq.	pkt Hampstead	0	8
John Chipendal	2 trunks	6	0
		7	6
Tho. Addington	box	3	2
		4	9
Tho. Kirkbright	box	1	6
Mrs Childer	'passage and a child' £1	7	6

These goods were then forwarded from London to their destinations by other carriers. When a fair amount of traffic passed between carriers in this way, formal agreements were sometimes made. Thomas Lidgard, who carried from Lincoln to Sheffield, and Richard Gardiner, who operated between Sheffield and Manchester had one such agreement. Lidgard promised to deliver all Manchester bound goods carried by him to Gardiner, whilst Gardiner undertook to accept goods at his warehouse in Manchester that were bound for places on Lidgard's route.[16]

These carrying businesses varied in size, but many were small—both on the long and short distance routes. The fact that all the Oxford University licences were issued to single holders does not indicate that they were one-man businesses, but it does suggest that partnerships were unusual. Family co-operation was more common—with sons, and sometimes widows, succeeding to the business. The Barkerdale family, for example, held four licences on the Oxford to Gloucester route between 1670 and 1717, the Bartlett family held four on the London route between 1698 and 1722, and the Robbins family held four on the Salisbury route between 1680 and 1732. There is no evidence that Robert Dawson employed another carrier, and the timing of his journeys, with long gaps between them, would suggest that he did not. However, he must have used or employed agents in Leeds and London, to accept and collect goods. Similarly, Thomas Lidgard and Richard Gardiner had employees to manage their warehouses. Most of the carriers operating from Kendal in 1699 (Table II) worked on a small scale. Some were apparently in partnership with one another, but only on the London route, where 60 horses were used, were there as many as four men working together. Carriers' sales notices, inserted in local newspapers, confirm that most businesses were of limited size. Those appearing in the Oxford paper, *Jackson's Oxford Journal*, over a 12-year period, are shown in Table V.

There were, however, some much larger businesses. John Hick, thought to have been a former valet to Lord Fitzwilliam, ran a coach and wagon business from the Old Kings Arms in Leeds. He wrote to Fitzwilliam in 1793 to ask for a loan of £400, and enclosed a list of his assets (Table VI). He owned two farms, and the lease of his inn, as well as 82 horses, shares in two London wagons, and a number of passenger conveyances for local use. Another North Country carrier, Richard Milnes, ran a water and road service across the Pennines. He began carrying in 1788 between Manchester and the Yorkshire navigation heads at Huddersfield and Sowerby Bridge. In April 1796, he advertised a daily boat from Huddersfield to Wakefield, and in December 1797, a daily boat from Sowerby Bridge to Hull, and three or more each week from Sowerby Bridge to Wakefield. However, he went bankrupt in the

Table V

Size of Carriers Businesses: Evidence from Sales Notices in *Jackson's Oxford Journal*

Carrier	Route	Assets	Date of advertisement
William Pope	Witney–London	Broad-wheeled wagon 7 horses farm implements	4 July 1761
James Parsons	Oxford–London	B-w wagon horses farm wagons implements	25 Dec. 1762
Samuel Cooke	Oxford–Birmingham	2 B-w wagons 8 horses	3 Nov. 1764
William Hunt	High Wycombe–London	1 B-w wagon 8 horses 1 hackney 2 tenements 2 gardens	13 June 1767
Edward Lock	Bicester–London	2 B-w wagons	24 Nov. 1770
Thomas Dorsett	Thame–London	1 Wagon and horses	5 Jan. 1771
Charles Tinson	London–Oxford	1 Wagon 16 horses farm implements	14 Sept. 1771
Washington Miles	Birmingham–London	1 Wagon 5 horses	30 Nov. 1771
John Barrett	Banbury–London	1 Wagon and horse	26 Dec. 1772
Henry Hill	Shillingford–London	1 Wagon 1 cart 4 horses	29 May 1773
—	Watlington–London	1 B-w wagon 1 narrow-wheeled wagon cart 7 horses	31 Aug. 1773
John Hearn	Chesham–London	2 B-w wagons 1 N-w wagon 1 cart 10 horses	23 Oct. 1773

Table VI

John Hick's Assets, 1793

Item	Estimated value £ s d		
82 Horses	856		
7 Chaises	140		
1 Coach, new	30		
Harnesses for 20 pairs of horses, posting only	60		
Harnesses for 36 pairs, carriages	72		
8 Setts for funerals	40		
8 Horses in the London wagon	30		
6 Horses in the London wagon	24		
6 Horses–farm only	10		
2 Farming wagons	30		
4 Carts, broad wheels, 1 water	46	6	0
2 Cows, 9 pigs	13	13	0
3½ Large haystacks	350		
8 Acres of oats to thrash	67	4	0
1 Stack of wheat/oat straw	32		
2 Acres of ground well cropped for market	30		
Farming utensils	58		
Furniture	1280		
Drink	1074		

credit of £5264 12s 8d
Estimated balance of £3121 4s 0d
(He owned two farms: Headingly Farm of 127 acres, and Squire
Pastures Farm of 82 acres, as well as the lease of the Old Kings
Arms in Leeds)

Source: Wentworth Woodhouse Muniments F106–99 (Sheffield City Libraries).

following year, apparently due to the opening of the Rochdale and Huddersfield Canals across the Pennines. Then his assets were listed as including land, collieries, a corn and malt trade and an impressively large carrying business (Table VII). But the most famous example of a large-scale carriers' firm is that of Pickfords, whose trade between Manchester and London has already been mentioned (page 28). It started business as one of six firms on this route in 1766. By the early 1780s it had six wagons, and in 1803, at least 50. In 1795, it also had ten canal boats, increased to 83 operating on the Trent and Mersey and Grand Junction Canals by 1822 (Barker and Savage 1974: 46).

Rather more is known about the organization of the coaching

business.[17] Many coach masters were innkeepers, and coaching businesses were often large-scale affairs. Quite often one partnership controlled many of the routes out of a town, as in London (above, page 33). In Gloucester, the Turner brothers operated exclusively on most of the routes in the 1760s and 1770s. William Costar occupied a similar position in Oxford—between 1777 and 1798, the University awarded him seven licences to run coaches to London, Banbury, Salisbury, Southampton, Bristol, Gloucester and Worcester.

It was common for coachmen to join in partnerships to operate particular routes. Several innkeepers along the route would combine, each providing horses for his own section, and contributing to the overall

Table VII

Richard Milnes' Assets, 1797

1. Healey Colliery, near Batley and two pits near Dewsbury.
2. Interests in the corn and malt trades. He was described as a maltster and corn factor at bankruptcy hearings.
3. The carrying trade.
4. 420 acres of land, either owned or leased.
5. A £320 annuity from a colliery, recently sold, and two mortgages for the Wakefield to Austerlands turnpike trust.

The Carrying Trade:

Wharves, warehouses, cattle and servants. These included a warehouse and stables at Portland Place, Manchester, and a wharf and stables for 20 horses at Sowerby Bridge, Yorkshire. The latter was established in 1796. In 1797, an estate at Sculcoates, with warehouse, and the Golden Lion Inn and wharf on the River Aire at Ferrybridge had to be sold.

16 sloops and other vessels.

52 horses:	12 at Manchester, 26 at Sowerby Bridge wharf, 9 at Blake Hall, Mirfield, 4 at Wakefield and one at Hull.
9 wagons:	4 at Manchester, 4 at Sowerby Bridge and one at Huddersfield.
8 carts:	4 at Manchester and 4 at Sowerby Bridge.

Estates:

97 acres owned near Dewsbury.
90 acres at Thornhill, on a 14-year lease.
200 acres three miles outside Manchester, also leased.
Small plots near Huddersfield, Wakefield and Whitely Wood.
Crows Nest near Dewbury, his residence until 1797, and the Rectory Manor of Dewsbury.

Source: Typescript notes concerning the MSS of Richard Milnes (1750–1832), by J. F. Goodchild (Archivist, Wakefield M.D.C.). I am grateful to Mr Goodchild for permission to use this material.

expenses, and sharing in the overall profit. The Oxford to London Machine in 1765 was run by S. White of the Bear Inn, Oxford, J. Shrubb of the White Hart, Benson, E. Prascey of the Red Lion, Henley, J. March of the Orkney Arms, Maidenhead Bridge, and R. Fuller of the Rose and Crown, Hounslow, and W. Dinnock, of London. The Oxford Post Coaches, which left Mrs James, the Fishmonger's in High Street Oxford, went by the same route. Sam Borton, of the Dolphin Inn, Oxford, ran post-chaises to London, in partnership with Francis Webling, of the Red Lion, Nettlebed, Mr Green of the Sun, Maidenhead, the landlord of the George Inn, Hounslow, and Thomas Brown, of the Plough, Princes Street. The High Wycombe road was also used—John Taylor's New Oxford—London Diligence was shared with Thomas Hanks of London, John Smith of Uxbridge, and R. Hutchinson of High Wycombe.[18]

John Hick, the Leeds coachmaster, again wrote to Lord Fitzwilliam in 1802.[19] He announced that he was selling his coaching and carrying business, and would therefore be able to repay his debt. He had shares in four coach routes, calculated on a mileage basis, and in the London wagon:

	£ Value
London wagon, 9 horses employed, my share (1 of 11)	700
London coach 'True Briton', 16 horses, share of 22 miles (1 of 10)	300
Manchester coach, 'The Peacemaker', share: 18 horses, 32 miles (1 of 5)	400
Newcastle coach, 'The Telegraph', 9 horses, 17 miles (1 of 7)	350
York coach, 8 horses, 15 miles	100
	£1,850

The mileage share determined the proportion of the overall profit each partner received. Each one made the necessary expenditure on coach duty, turnpike tolls, wages, lamps, greasing, printing and damage, and the receipts were then distributed to make up each partner's share of the profits. The Bedford to London coach, for which accounts survive between 1803 and 1808, was divided into three equal shares, the 'London share', the 'Hitchin' and the 'Bedford'. In January 1803, each share was worth £37 5s 8½d, after a month's duty of £9 16s 2d, a month's wages and tolls of £9 8s 0d and £1 4s 0d for book-keeping and greasing had been paid. The Kettering to London Coach, whose accounts are in the same bundle, was split between 5 partners, however, in shares of 13, 12, 10, 16 and 25 miles.[20]

Private Carrying

By the end of the eighteenth century, a sophisticated network of carriers and coaches operated between towns and villages. Even quite small centres had their own carrier, either to the nearest town, or to London itself. The carriers were common carriers, offering and advertising their services for public hire. However, outside this official network, and before the network developed extensively, private carrying was a common bye-employment. Even in the eighteenth century, much of the provincial carrying trade was carried by farmers, under private arrangement. The extent of private carrying may well explain why so few references to carriers are found in seventeenth century occupational surveys.[21] Nevertheless, many people were involved in carrying, an indication of its importance in local employment being given by the nature of much opposition to river improvement bills. A typical case was that of the Derwent Improvement Bill. In 1703, the Mayor and Burgesses petitioned against it because:

> 'it will impoverish the Petitioners' families, by Diverting their Trades, lessening their Tolls, lowering the Rents of the Lands thereabouts and will be the Utter Ruin of many families, whose only support is to bring Lead, Salt and other Commodities, from several parts of Nottingham, and carry back Malt and other Goods by Land Carriage.' (JHC 14: 60)

Two of the other four counterpetitions were in the same vein, but the bill still passed into law. In 1712, the 'Gentlemen and Freeholders of Wiltshire' protested against the Avon improvement bill, claiming:

> 'it will be a Prejudice to the Petitioners, and other Inhabitants of that County, and a publick Detriment, by hindering the Poor's Employment by Land Carriage; by lowing the Profits of their Cattle's Labour therein. . . .' (JHC 17: 134)

They were supported in this claim by three other counterpetitions, as were many other river bills. Many farmers not only carried their own produce to market, but carried for other farmers, and primary producers. Manufacturers and households also made use of their services when a regular carrier's link was not available.

Road Traffic Flows

The development of carrying networks, the use of the roads by common and private carriers and coachmen, the droves of animals, pack-horse trains, wagons, coaches, and horses all contributed to heavy traffic flows, particularly between and near large towns. In the country areas, traffic was much lighter, but on fair and market days could still be heavy. Unfortunately, statistical evidence is very limited, as few traffic censuses survive, and turnpike toll returns, where they exist, are rarely sufficiently detailed.

There is no known census for any of the roads in or near London,[22] but an indication of conditions there can be gained from the Smithfield statistics (above, p. 18), and from a Bristol census. This was taken during the week ending 2 June 1765, at Lawford's gate, a few miles north of the city on the Gloucester road. The volume of traffic is impressive: there were 259 coaches, 11,759 horses, 491 wagons, 675 asses, 722 carts and 206 drays (*Felix Farley's Bristol Journal*, 7 December 1765). Conditions further away from a big city, but on an important main road, are indicated in the three-monthly traffic totals compiled by the Gloucester–Birdlip Hill Turnpike Trust at its gate on the London to South Wales road (Table VIII). Droves of cattle and sheep, coming from the Welsh hills, were prominent on this route. This was the only easy route up the Cotswold scarp, whereas the absence of animals on the Bristol road may indicate that they were able to keep off the main turnpike, and thus avoid toll payment. Wheeled traffic was still heavy on the Gloucester road, although it is impossible to estimate the number of coaches and wagons accurately due to the nature of the return. In 1761/2, it was probably not more than 10,000.

These high totals can be compared with two other sets of turnpike gate returns, for main roads in rural areas. The traffic on the London–Hastings road, passing through the Ticehurst Town gate was surprisingly light, with wheeled traffic in particular being very limited (Table IX). A final traffic census is available for a northern route—the Sheffield to Wakefield road, at Old Mill bar, north of Barnsley (Table X). The importance of pack-horses, rather than wagons, can clearly be seen. The figures are in monthly totals, and to give an approximate comparison with the Hastings figures, the four separate months have been added together. Interesting daily variations emerge. Peak traffic flows during the week were on Wednesdays, which was a local market day, whereas the highest flow recorded was Friday 10 October 1760, a Fair Day, when 622 horses and 436 animals passed the gate.

Table VIII

Gloucester–Birdlip Hill Trust Tollgate Returns, 1761–2, 1767–8

	Beasts in draught at 4d	Single horses at 1d	Cattle at 10d score	Sheep/hogs at 5d score
6 July 1761 to 27 Sept. 1761	5173	5978	4926	1120
27 Sept. 1761 to 27 Dec. 1761	9985	6409	6807	4146
27 Dec. 1761 to 28 March 1762	9024	5400	516	2962
28 March 1762 to 20 June 1762	7120	5912	2627	2672
	31842	23699	14876	10900
21 June 1767 to 27 Sept. 1767	5380	5668	4803	1432
27 Sept. 1767 to 20 Dec. 1767	5921	5137	6683	8406
20 Dec. 1767 to 20 March 1768	6430	4870	402	3768
20 March 1768 to 19 June 1768	6652	5118	1950	2320
	23583	20793	13838	15926

Source: Minute Book, 1761–73 (Glos. RO.) These returns were printed from 1761 to 1767 in the 'State of Affairs': an annual account of the progress of the Trust.

Table IX

Hastings Road Traffic, 1769/70

May–Aug. 1769		Dec. 1769–March 1770
196	Four-wheeled carriages/wagons	50
90	Two-wheeled carriages/wagons	27
1200	single horses	933
10	mules	10
741	cattle	41
211	sheep	200

Source: Dunn MSS 52/19 (East Sussex RO).

The amount of traffic on the roads in the mid-eighteenth century was, therefore, considerable in some areas. On main roads, particularly near cities, wheeled traffic was heavy—elsewhere, it was droves of animals and pack-horse trains which constituted the larger proportion of the total. Wheeled traffic was, however, gradually increasing in importance, as peripheral areas, participating more readily in the growing economy, changed from pack-horse to wagon, as carrying networks themselves extended, and as regular coach services began to displace the horse as a means of passenger transport.[23]

Table X

Barnsley Road Traffic, 1760/61

	Oct. 1760	Jan. 1761	April 1761	July 1761	Total
Horses	1396	637	657	869	3559
Horses (2)	624	465	379	—	1468
Animals	699	179	295	167	1330
Coaches	3	—	3	6	12
Chaises	38	21	16	74	149
Wagons	62	45	76	65	248

Source: Old Mill Bar Tollgate Returns. TC 363/45 (Sheffield City Libraries).

The overall volume of traffic was increasing everywhere. The growth of the economy in the seventeenth and eighteenth centuries found its expression in increased internal trade, with the development of industry and towns, and the emergence of regional specialities. This internal trade was carried by land and water—by common and private road carrier, by river barge, and by sea coaster. Undoubtedly, much went by water, but it is pointless to debate just how much in the absence of any general statistics for river or road traffic flows. Nevertheless, it is also clear that road traffic was an important component of the total—not only in quantitative terms, in the movement of raw materials, and finished goods, but in qualitative terms, for the passage of information flows, money and people.

The road network, over which these traffic flows moved, was, however, strangely medieval in concept and construction. It was a network unsuited to the strains of eighteenth century economic expansion, for reasons, and with results, which will now be explored more fully.

2. Notes

1. The statistics in these paragraphs are drawn from Fisher 1935: 47; Fussell and Goodman 1936, 1936; Willan 1938: 93–4, 204–5; Wrigley 1967: 55–8.
2. 'The Proposal for removing the Godalming Turnpike considered.' Pamphlet, 1769 (Loseley MSS, Guildford Muniment Room).
3. I am grateful to Mrs M. Prior for this last point. See below, p. 275.
4. Letter from John Hopper to Sir James Lowther, 6 Nov. 1766 (D/Lons/L/Survey List 2, Cumbria RO).
5. The Manchester men are discussed in greater detail in Chapter 12. See below, p. 308.
6. There have been a few recent studies of nineteenth century carrying systems, notably Everitt 1973, Kennett 1974, Freeman 1975.
7. I am most grateful to Mr Andrew Butcher for bringing this list to my attention.
8. Document quoted in Thirsk and Cooper 1972: 333–4.
9. Register of Halliers, Brewers and Glassmakers 1718–56, and Ordinances for City Companies. (Bristol AO.)
10. The University's Charter of 1356 exempted 'ye scholars servants' from taxation by the town. Disputes as to which groups of tradesmen were covered eventually led to an Agreement between the University and the Corporation in 1449, in which common carriers were included as 'scholars servants'.
11. Carriers were recorded in the University Registers, and printed in Clark (1887: 315–17) for the period 1553–1642. The Twyne–Langbein MSS contains a list for 1493–1550. (Vol. 4, Bodleian Library, Oxford.)
12. Archives University Oxon Hyp. fo. 2. (Bodleian Library, Oxford.) Information has also been drawn from the Wood Papers, reprinted in Cordeaux and Merry (1968), and Clark (1887).
13. The records of the Cambridge University carriers are contained in:
    TIV 1 Bonds 1663–1711
        2 Bonds 1699–1791
        3 Miscellaneous
        4 Licences 1665–1791
    and the Vice-Chancellor's Court Records:

Acta Curiae (Neat Book)	1718–28	Vc Ct I 16
	1728–35	Vc Ct I 17
(Loose Paper)	1717–35	Vc Ct I 90–100
	1735–1800	Vc Ct I 101–109

    (Cambridge University Library).
14. Account Book of Robert Dawson, Carrier (no reference, Cumbria RO). He later transferred to the Kendal–London route, and the book contains entries for this in 1758 and 1759. The book itself then passed to another carrier, John Jackson, and for part of 1760, it records his business between Kendal and Leeds.
15. Account Book (no reference, Cambs. RO).
16. Articles of Agreement, 23 March 1772 (PC 1088, Sheffield City Libraries).

17. See, for example, Bagwell 1974.
18. *Jackson's Oxford Journal*. This information is from regular advertisements carried in the 1760s and 1770s.
19. Wentworth Woodhouse MSS, F 106–106/7 (Sheffield City Libraries).
20. Accounts of the Bedford Coach (X37–4), and Kettering Coach (X37–8, Beds. CRO).
21. Only 1·6 per cent of the working population of Gloucestershire in 1608 was engaged in transport and building (Tawney 1934). A survey of the occupational structure of towns in East Anglia in the seventeenth and eighteenth centuries found no carriers at all (Patten 1972). A sample of mid-seventeenth century probate inventories from Lichfield records 57 occupations, but no carriers (Vaisey 1969).
22. There is, in fact, an early seventeenth century reference to a census taken on the Great North Road. Unfortunately it has not survived (see below, p. 77).
23. The role of improved road surfaces in stimulating the change to wheeled traffic is explored in Chapter 11.

Innovation and Diffusion

3

The Emergence of the Innovation

The Highway: A Communal Property Right

Before the eighteenth century, the highway was not so much an actual body of land reserved and maintained for the convenience of traffic, as a 'right of passage' for every subject of the Crown over another's land. This right extended solely to passing and repassing, and in no way conferred ownership of the soil on the Crown or the community. The right of property in the soil, over which this right of passage existed, might belong to the King or to a private person. In fact, in the absence of evidence to the contrary, it was assumed that the owner of the soil was the owner of the land on either side of the highway. This situation was significantly different to that which prevails today, whereby the land in public highways is vested in the relevant local authorities, under the Local Government Acts of the late nineteenth century.

Furthermore, the actual extent of this right, in relation to the land over which it was held to pass, was not rigidly defined. It was generally assumed by the end of the seventeenth century that it was permissible to deviate either side of the usual way if this was 'founderous'. This was not an ancient right, having been established by two court cases in the mid-seventeenth century, but it was accepted by the leading legal authorities of the eighteenth century. Again, it constitutes a major difference between eighteenth century and modern practice.

A highway was established by the express or presumed dedication of the owner of the land; or through creation by statute, as was the case with the alterations brought about by turnpike trusts, estate expansion and the enclosure movement from the early eighteenth century. Most major highways came in the first category, however: the dedication usually being by presumption and continued public use, as the origins of many roads extend back beyond the limits of legal memory.

The act of dedication itself, or local custom, could restrict the use to which a particular highway could be put. By the seventeenth century, the law recognized three different categories—footpaths, bridleways and cart or wagon roads. A footpath could not be used for pack-horses or cattle and a bridleway could not be used for wheeled traffic, except by rededication or statutory alteration. But although highway rights might be restricted, it was recognized that they must benefit all people. Similarly, they could not be granted for only a limited period of time.[1]

The right of passage was thus a communal property right— 'communal' because it was intended for the benefit of, and could be exercised by, all men. Communal ownership means that 'the community denies to the State or to individual citizens the right to interfere with any person's exercise of [these] rights' (Demsetz 1967: 354). So, although the owner of the land dedicated to the public as a highway did not relinquish his right of property in the soil, he could not use that soil in any way that would interfere with its function as a highway. In addition, no one could block or divert a highway without proper authority. The consent of the King or Parliament had to be obtained, or after 1773, under the power of the General Highway Act, from the Justices of the Peace. Before this, however, a private Act was often sought. The Earl of Aylesford did this in 1760, when he wanted to 'discontinue the use' of a road in Great Packington in Warwickshire and create a new one at his own expense (1 Geo. III, c. 36). The Earl of Donegall did the same in 1766 when he wished to enclose Fisherwick Park in Stafford, and provide alternative roads around it (6 Geo. III, c. 60).

The roads of the seventeenth and eighteenth centuries suffered, however, from disadvantages similar to those of other forms of communal property, such as common grazing or hunting land. This form of ownership fails to concentrate the cost associated with any person's exercise of his communal right on that person. Thus, anyone seeking to maximize the value of his right will not contain his actions in line with the more restrictive policy which would accompany state-owned and enforced, or private property rights. In the absence of agreed rules, common land will suffer from overgrazing and overhunting, and—to take another instance—the urban atmosphere will suffer from uncontrolled pollution, because the cost of these excesses is borne largely by others. It is irrational for one or several owners to limit their actions without overall agreement amongst all owners. Those who do not comply benefit, whilst those who do lose the maximum value of their rights.

The externalities which arise from the exercise of communal property rights can, therefore, be costs or benefits. Before the advent of the turnpike road system, with no cost attached directly to the road user, there was no incentive for him to regulate his use in accordance with the maintenance of a passable road surface. Abuse of the highways was common—for example, carrying heavy loads on wagons needing many horses for haulage, using narrow wheels with spikes which broke open the surface, and dragging sledges and timber directly along the road. If the road user himself sought a remedy for the situation, either by limiting his own use or by effecting road repairs, many others benefited from his cost, thereby denying an effective return to himself.

A suitable solution to the problem involved some kind of alteration in the property right through well defined and enforced rules which internalized the cost and benefits, that is, concentrated them on those reponsible for their creation. With communal land ownership in open fields, the division into enclosures was the answer. With the highways, however, a different sort of remedy was needed.

The solution sought with the Tudor parish repair system was internalization within the framework of each parish. In economic terms, this was only reasonable if the benefits and costs associated with road use and repair could be contained within each parish. This assumption implied negligible through traffic, a situation more generally applicable in the sixteenth century when statute labour was introduced than in the eighteenth century. Within each parish, the right of passage ceased to be a free right, and hence the costs associated with road repair might have been expected to encourage responsible road use. Similarly, the containment of benefits to be gained should have encouraged a reasonable standard of road maintenance.

The Parish Repair System

The parish repair system was established on a temporary basis in 1555. The powers of this Act were renewed in 1562, and made perpetual in 1586, but were eventually abolished under the reforming General Highway Act of 1835.[2] Under the 1555 Act, each parish was required to meet annually and elect, at a Vestry meeting organized by the constable and churchwardens, two unpaid Surveyors of Highways. The function of these Surveyors was to supervise and direct the required statute labour.

This requirement was graded roughly according to wealth. Every person occupying a ploughland, or holding, worth £50 per annum, and all those keeping a draught of horses or plough in the parish, were to supply one team—i.e. a cart with horses or oxen, and two men. Everyone else was obliged to supply one man or come themselves. All these teams and labourers had to appear on the roads each year at the time fixed by the Surveyors, to work under their direction for eight hours on four, and afterwards (in 1562) on six, consecutive days. The Surveyors were to present all defaulters to a Justice of the Peace, and fines were to be levied at the rate of ten shillings per team, and one shilling per man, per day.

The responsibility of the parish for maintaining its roads did not begin however in 1555. According to common law obligations, the parish could be indicted at Quarter Sessions for failing to repair its highways long before this date. Nevertheless, the 1555 Act is important because it provided a means by which regular maintenance could be carried out, appointing special officers to oversee the process, and enabling simple enforcement through the existing legal apparatus. 'The ancient common law obligation . . . was, for the first time, definitely allocated among the several parties, and the procedure to be followed was peremptorily laid down' (Webb 1920: 14). But even the formalization of the obligation was not entirely new. Paving Acts—passed for many towns from the fourteenth century—required householders to maintain the roadway outside their house, to the middle of the street. Such Acts were passed for Chester in 1391 and 1405, Northampton in 1422, Southampton in 1477, for parts of the City of London in 1532 and 1533 and extended to the whole of the capital in 1540 (Jackman 1916: 12–13, 37). The parish system was, therefore, an attempt to enforce an ancient obligation by formal means, and an extension to all parishes of a formalization previously only extant in certain towns.

However, it was to be expected that a general system of such simplicity would not completely internalize costs and benefits, even if each parish were an almost sealed unit. Many of those who performed the six days statute labour did not use the roads themselves, except for pedestrian movement, and so had little incentive to create benefits for others. Many of the heavier users, such as tradesmen or carriers, were barely charged for the use they derived from the roads. The economic motivation for restraint in use, and a good standard of maintenance, was thereby lessened.

There were other reasons why the system could not have been expected to work well. Many parishioners liable under the law could ill afford to meet their obligations. For the labourer, or farmer with only one cart, the prospect of losing several days earnings did not encourage good attendance (Mather 1696: 44, Dowdell 1932: 98). For those who were obliged through tenure of certain landholdings to repair sections of road, the law involved an unpalatable measure of double-counting. The Surveyors, whose duty to enforce the law put them in an uneasy position within the community, were often reluctant to resort to the Justices, who were themselves often unwilling to enforce penalties (Shapleigh 1749: 45, Webb 1920: 27–42). Furthermore, the Surveyors were untrained, could not be expected to know much about road construction and repair, and were often unable or unwilling to co-ordinate effort in those places which most needed it. Their appointments were annual, and hence there was little continuity of repair or leadership.

These general circumstances were compounded by particular conditions which affected some parishes more badly than others. Each parish varied in size, mileage of road, and population density. In some, the statute labour requirement was sufficient to maintain a reasonable standard of road repair, whilst in others a particularly heavy local traffic, in timber or grain for instance, rendered it entirely insufficient. These difficulties were compounded by the uneven distribution of topographical features, such as steep hills, clay vales and rivers.

These general and particular circumstances contributing to the ineffectiveness of parish repair have, therefore, to be added to the incomplete internalization brought about by the system. Such a system was self-defeating, laying itself open to abuse simply because it did not function as well as intended. If the roads were not well repaired, there was little incentive to restrain unreasonable use. Similarly, the realization of this could not encourage effective road repair. Hence, even with a minimal amount of through traffic, the parish repair system could not have been expected to meet the needs required of it.

The apparent assumption of minimal through traffic was anyway becoming less valid during the seventeenth and eighteenth centuries, as internal trade flows increased. The type of traffic involved was often very damaging to the poorly maintained road surfaces of the day: the new wheeled coaches and carriers' wagons of the towns, and the heavy sledges, wagons and loads of timber of the producer regions. These new loads were 'free-riders' in the parishes through which they passed, contributing nothing to the cost of road repairs they made necessary. In 1804, William Marshall summarized the situation well:

'When roads are worn by the public at large tenfold more, in some instances, than by the inhabitants of the parishes they happen to pass through, it is become unreasonable, if not unjust, to impose the task of repairing them on the individuals who happen to be possessed of a plough-team, a cart, a wheelbarrow, a shovel, or a basket (what a principle of taxation in these days!), though they may never use the road they are doomed to repair.' (Marshall 1804: 293)

Parishes situated on main roads, or close to large towns, faced a difficult task as the evidence of presentments at Quarter Sessions for bad highways shows. This ancient procedure had been strengthened in 1563 by allowing any Justice of the Peace to present a highway not properly repaired. In Hertfordshire, for instance, between 1619 and 1661, 66 presentments were recorded. Thirty-nine of these were against parishes on the New Great North Road, five against those on the Old Great North Road, with many of the remainder against parishes with roads leading into one of these (Albert 1972: 18). But road maintenance was not the only problem. The growth of traffic on major routes obviously made alterations and improvements necessary as well, i.e. widening, straightening, and the provision of new bridges. However, before the end of the seventeenth century, the legal liability of the parish for its highways did not extend to altering them in any way to meet new needs.[3]

It is evident from this brief analysis that the parish repair system, in its simplest form, was neither a good means of maintaining existing highways, or of improving them, or of creating new ones. Even with the enforcement machinery of the law, it is generally accepted that the system never functioned adequately.[4] In order to meet the needs of the road user in the late seventeenth and eighteenth centuries, other measures were therefore required. They could be either inspired and imposed by Parliament, or sponsored by private individuals. They could either treat the symptoms of failure by strengthening the existing system, or they could introduce a new one.

Alternative Solutions

The simplest solution lay in strengthening the existing parish repair system, and using its enforcement procedure more effectively. Although the Justices may have been reluctant to fine statute labour defaulters, they were more willing to use the procedure of presentment and indictment when necessary (Webb 1920: 52). Upon presentment at Quarter Sessions, a parish would be ordered to repair the highway in question, under threat of indictment. If this occurred, the parish was penalized by the imposition of extra days statute labour or a money fine.

The Justices could thus raise funds outside the restriction of a fixed highway rate. In the towns, in fact, this means was commonly used throughout the eighteenth century, often to the total exclusion of statute labour (Webb 1920: 60). The funds gained could be used to pay hired labour, which need not have been under the direction of the amateur parish surveyor. They were swelled by the practice of commutation, which had become so common by the mid-eighteenth century that it was regulated by the General Highway Acts of 1766 and 1773, and standard rates laid down. In return for a fixed sum, often based on the defaulter's fine, the parishioner was relieved of his obligation to perform statute duty itself.

These sources of cash from within the existing system of road repair were supplemented by the highway rate from the mid-seventeenth century onwards. The earliest example of such a rate was provided for in the Commonwealth Ordinance of 1654. It was to be levied by parishes themselves, and was not to exceed one shilling in the pound. The power was renewed in 1662, but as a supplementary measure rather than one to replace statute work altogether, as had been the intention of the earlier measure. The Surveyors could make a levy, with the consent of the Justices, but the Act was to remain in force for only three years. It was repeated in 1670, for a further term of three years, but with the rate to be levied by the Justices themselves. Finally, in 1691, highway rates were made a permanent measure, under the control of the Justices, whose power was additionally strengthened by transferring the responsibility of appointing the Surveyor himself to Quarter Sessions, and increasing the penalties for default. Under none of these Acts, however, was the legal assessment to exceed sixpence in the pound.

The idea of a general rate, although novel for highways, was not entirely new. The 'Statute of Bridges', passed in 1531 (22 Henry VIII, c. 5) had made the county responsible for those bridges outside corporate towns, when no other liability could be proved. The Justices were empowered to appoint two County Surveyors to ensure that all bridges were adequately maintained, and they were given authority to levy a rate for this purpose; but the County Fund created by this means was sometimes used to help parishes with road repairs. Highway rates themselves were levied fairly commonly after 1691, but it seems that a relatively low proportion of parishes were assessed in this way. In St Marylebone on the outskirts of London, 13 such rates were raised between 1705 and 1723, until the parish followed the obvious course and obtained a turnpike Act for the busy Tyburn and Edgware roads (42) (Sheppard 1958: 54). Highway rates became steadily less frequent about this time, for this very reason.

When rates were levied they could be used for three purposes. They could provide money firstly to supplement statute labour repairs and secondly, to buy repair materials when these were not available locally. These were both maintenance rates, given in the 1691 Act. But in 1697, magistrates were allowed for the first time to levy a rate for improvement purposes, to enable parishes to buy land to widen a highway. Although the power to widen had been given originally in 1662, no means of providing the necessary resources had previously been available.[5]

A second solution to the problem of meeting the needs of road repair and improvement was by private initiative. It was common at this time for local landowners to subscribe money for highway repairs, or for general subscriptions to be raised. The Earl of Dumfries was active mending roads in Ayrshire (Goodwin 1790: 50). Lord Bulkeley, in North Wales, contributed towards and organized the construction of a new route over Penmaenmawr on the Anglesey post road, a scheme which was supported by the Irish Parliament and people of Dublin (Arch.Camb. 1852: 30–1). In the 1750s, the owner of Hawarden Castle in Flintshire built a new causeway over the Saltney marshes to Chester (Dodd 1925: 129). Arthur Young often noted such cases of private initiative, praising, for example, the efforts of Charles Turner and Christopher Crowe, Esquires, on the roads of Cleveland in his Northern Tour (Young 1771: 421).

Sometimes the proceedings on turnpike bills reveal instances of private road repair before resort was made to Parliament. In 1717, during the passage of the Surrey–Sussex Trust bill, it was revealed that Lambeth had spent £1,425 over and above statute work since 1712, that Streatham and Croydon had worked an extra four days and levied subscriptions, and Newington had spent £60 in a year—more than the proceeds of the 6d rate (JHC 18: 663). In 1753, the Reverend Mr Robinson, in evidence to the Committee examining the petition for turnpiking the Oundle to Alconbury road in Northamptonshire, said:

'That it is impossible to repair the Road by the Statute Work, That the Witness collected about £150 by voluntary Contribution for the repairing thereof, and the neighbouring farmers gave the Carriage of

Materials, which he apprehends would have amounted to as much more. . . .' (JHC 26: 620)

In 1759, £1,500 was raised by subscription to repair the road between Whitby and Saltersgate, five years before it was turnpiked (MacMahon 1964: 34). Private subscriptions were used in Essex to repair the Nayland–Great Horkesley road in 1778, and the Dunmow–Ongar road in 1800 (Brown 1969: 80).[6]

Many private improvements were, of course, carried out purely in self interest. New roads were built to promote the exploitation of mineral wealth within estates, and to enable landowners to divert existing highways outside areas of parkland. Sometimes an economic interest led to improvements in the surrounding area, benefiting everyone. Lord Penrhyn, on taking over his estates in 1782, built new roads to replace horse-paths and link his slate quarries with Bangor and Capel Curig (Dodd 1925: 129). However, when there was little direct return for those involved in private schemes, their efforts were primarily for the social good. It was illegal for a toll to be charged on a public highway without the consent of Parliament so it was not possible to charge those who benefited from such good works except by voluntary means.[7]

Landowners were at liberty, however, to charge travellers for the use of a private road—one which had not been dedicated to the public as a highway. They could also charge travellers for the privilege of being allowed to pass through private grounds. A well documented case of the former sort was that of the private road over two estates between Preston and Kirkham in the Lancashire Fylde. The road was two miles long, and ran over marshland, providing a convenient short cut from the winding and ill-repaired public highway. The tolls were actually leased in 1676, and were so probably in existence rather earlier. The two owners agreed to construct a new road in 1781, but it remained private and the toll continued until 1902 (Sharpe–France 1945).

Several cases of travellers being charged for passing through private grounds are revealed in the proceedings on turnpike road bills in Parliament. For example, four witnesses before the Committee examining the petition for a turnpike trust to be set up on the road between Stevenage and Biggleswade in 1720 (39) told MPs that:

'. . . Coaches have been many times overturned therein; and are obliged to pay Four Shillings and Sixpence per Coach for passing through private Grounds, to avoid the Badness of the Highways: the

Proprietors of those Lands pay nothing towards the Repair of those Roads . . .'. (JHC 19: 218)

Nevertheless, neither the solution of increasing parish liability, nor that of private improvements, tackled the fundamental disadvantage that resulted from the exercise of the communal right of passage—that of externalities. The only system which could encourage responsible use of roads, and provide an adequate fund for maintenance and improvement was, in the absence of direct and general government action, to concentrate the cost of exercising the right on the road user. However, because of the difficulty of reaching and enforcing agreements locally, Parliamentary procedure had to be used. The consent of Parliament, as representative of the community, had to be gained anyway if the right of passage was to be altered.

Parliamentary action could take two courses. It could seek to abolish, contain or minimize the harmful effects which it considered to be the cause of poor roads, or it could inflict charges on road users to compensate for this harm. In practice, the approach adopted was one of compromise, or complementarity.

With the economy expanding and trade flows increasing, it would not have been possible to eliminate the harmful effects completely, although once a definition of 'unreasonable' usage had been agreed upon, enforcement by statute of certain restrictions was possible. A long series of such measures was passed, beginning with the Proclamation of James I, issued in 1621, and reissued in 1629, that no four-wheeled wagon or carriage was to carry more than a ton load. Cromwell's Ordinance of 1654 was the first to seek to limit the number of horses used—to five. In 1741, turnpike Trustees were empowered to erect weighing engines, and charge 20s per cwt for all carriages and wagons with loads exceeding three tons. In 1753, with the first Broad Wheels Act, Parliament began to regulate the widths of wheels.

These regulations were continually altered and enlarged in successive road Acts, culminating in the General Highway and Turnpike Acts of 1773. These laid down complex schedules of maximum loads, and through turnpike toll reductions and surcharges, encouraged broad wheels and rollers, and flat tyres without protruding nails. The muddle of restrictions and exemptions prompted John Scott to produce his *Digest of the Highway Laws* in 1778, in an attempt to sort out the confusion.

Despite the complexity of these restrictive regulations, they were enforced, particularly on those turnpike roads where trusts had provided weighing engines.[8] However, although some restriction of the more harmful effects was obviously necessary, comprehensive regulation was not desirable because of the need for large-scale transfer of goods and passengers by road. It became less important, too, as road surfaces improved and could bear larger loads. The opinion that roads should be constructed in the first place to bear the traffic load, rather than a compromise situation whereby construction was aimed to accommodate artificially restricted loads, became increasingly common. It found an able voice in J. L. MacAdam, who propounded such a view before successive Parliamentary Committees from 1810 (BPP 1810–11 (240) III 855: 27–32). All these restrictions, however, were not finally abolished until the reforming General Highway Act of 1835 was passed.

The more important side of Parliamentary activity is, therefore, that concerned with directly charging road users. The easiest system to operate would have been to levy a uniform charge on all users, irrespective of the extent of the harmful effects they caused, but this would not have been effective in internalizing costs. A more equitable method was to identify the main cause of the harm, and then charge for road use on a selective basis. This had the added advantage of affecting the right of passage in only a limited number of cases. It was adopted by the late sixteenth century Wealden Road Acts, which charged ironmasters for road use in direct proportion to the number of loads they dispatched.[9] However, the difficulties of identification, and the inflexibility of a scheme which could not cope with the emergence of new harmful effects, did not encourage its adoption on a wider basis.

The fairest system that could be devised was to charge all road users according to a fixed scale, determined by the amount of harm each was considered to cause. This could be assessed on two grounds: the frequency with which the right of passage was used, and the wear and tear caused on each occasion. Such a system of charges did not have to be general as it need be applied only where relevant. Direct charges obviously had to be inflicted at source, and the simplest method of doing this was through the levy of a toll.

The collection of the toll, and the administration of the funds that it provided, had to be enforced. An administrative structure had to be organized, either centrally or locally. It is of interest that in 1657 the Commonwealth Parliament discussed a bill which would have created a centralized structure, had it passed into law. Cromwell had already appointed a Surveyor General of Highways, with authority throughout the land, and the bill would have entitled him to large funds for repair purposes. However, it was lost when Parliament was dissolved that year (JHC 7: 461–592).

Adam Smith voiced the contemporary opinion when he wrote in favour of local administration for local works, believing that they would be undertaken more effectively and with less abuse by this means (1904 Vol. 2: 218). Local *ad hoc* bodies were easily established, and were the usual means by which emerging problems were resolved in the eighteenth century. The Webbs identified four groups of such bodies: the Improvement Commissions, Courts of Sewers, Incorporated Guardians, and Turnpike Trusts (Webb 1922: 1). The last named were created to deal with the problem of road repair.

The establishment of turnpike trusts, and the consequent curtailment of the free right of passage, offered several advantages. Firstly, if the toll charges were fairly structured, and could be effectively collected, they were a suitable way of internalizing the costs of road use, and thereby providing a source of money to finance road repair. Secondly, the trusts themselves provided a system through which the general highway restrictions could be enforced. Thirdly, they overcame one of the most serious disadvantages of communal property, as they were a means by which road maintenance not only in the present, but also in the future, might be undertaken. Lastly, turnpike trusts could be given powers by Parliament not only to maintain but also to improve the highway.

The First Turnpike Act

A regular succession of Acts establishing turnpike trusts was passed from 1696. From the late 1740s, the numbers increased dramatically each year (Fig. 3). However, the first turnpike trust was set up much earlier, in 1663. The events surrounding its creation are of some interest, in the light of the preceding discussion, and will therefore be explored in some detail.

In 1609, a bill for repairing the 'Biggleswade Highways' was read in Parliament, but failed to pass into law. In 1621–2, a second bill was presented, for repair of the Great North Road between Biggleswade and Baldock. Although no details of the earlier bill are recorded, it is known that the second proposed that a toll should be taken, and the funds used for repairing the road under the direction of Surveyors appointed by the

Lord High Chancellor and the Lord High Treasurer. This second bill was defeated 'because it was a Tax upon all Passengers, thereby savouring of a Monopoly' (Emmison 1935: 108).

The nearby parish of Standon, on the New Great North Road between Wadesmill and Buntingford, was the most frequently presented in Hertfordshire. In 1631, they petitioned Quarter Sessions, and following this a census of wagons was taken on the road at Colliers End. This census was sent to the Privy Council, which ordered, as a result, that all maltsters and loaders were to carry on horseback between All Saints and May Day.[10] Despite this, the parish again had to write to Quarter Sessions in 1646, and suggested a tax on heavy loads. This was not granted, and in 1660 the parish petitioned Parliament for relief, two years after another presentment. This petition was referred to the Committee drafting the Highway Bill of 1662, but no more was heard of it. It seems probable that the Committee felt that the highway rate established in this bill would provide the necessary solution (JHC 8: 292). In the same year, a bill for repairing Watling Street was given a first reading in Parliament. No record of a petition has been found, or any details of what was proposed in the bill. It is thus not known which part of Watling Street was affected. A second reading was ordered, but the bill then disappeared (JHC 8: 439). In 1663, however, a further petition from Standon, joined by two others from parishes in Cambridgeshire and Huntingdon, was successful in bringing forward a bill, which passed on to the statute book. It established the first turnpike trust.

In the 1664–5 session, this Act was extended for 21 years for the Hertfordshire section of the road, to run in addition to its original 11 year term. At the same time, there were other significant moves. On 26 November 1664, another Committee was set up to examine the operation of the general highway laws and suggest improvements. On 5 December, they were ordered that 'they do in particular take into Consideration the repairing and making the Highway from London to West Chester'; on 17 January 1665, they reported that they could 'find no other Expedient reasonably to mend the Roads from London to Chester, than a toll' (JHC 8: 569, 572, 583). It was agreed by the House that this, and the Committee's other proposal—a continuation of the sixpenny rate of 1662—were both acceptable. The ensuing bill received two readings, and on 11 February 1665 was ordered to be committed:

'And the Committee are hereby impowered to lay an additional

Charge of Six-pence in the Pound, besides the Six-Pence per Pound already charged on the Inhabitants of the several Parishes, who are concerned in the repairing the Highways, and also to limit a time for the Toll to cease, when the Ways are so repaired, that they may be maintained without it'. (JHC 8: 599)

Unfortunately, no more was heard of this bill, although there is no record of it having been defeated, but in the same session, another highways bill was presented, on 1 December, for the repair of roads in 'Bedford, Buckingham, Northampton and Warwickshire'. It was defeated on its second reading two days later (JHC 8: 570, 1). It seems likely, however, that its concern was that considered by the above Committee after 5 December, as Watling Street, the road from London to Chester, was the only main road to pass through all four counties.

Therefore, in the 1660s, Parliament was prepared to consider granting tolls for the repair of public highways, by passing one Act in 1663, and renewing it two years later, and by giving due consideration to a proposed toll on Watling Street. However, no more turnpike petitions or bills appear before 1694, and in particular, there are none for Watling Street before 1707 (8, 9). Local opposition to road tolls does not seem a likely cause, especially in the parishes, where a toll could result in a considerable reduction in the cost of road repair. As no petitions were presented to Parliament for relief, it would seem that the existing repair procedure, with supplementary rates and fines, was adequate and not overburdensome.

The initiation of a series of petitions and turnpike bills in the last decade of the seventeenth century does indicate that by then, however, the parish system was beginning to break down. The general rise in internal trade, and consequent increasing dissatisfaction with the expense of repairs, meant that it was sensible to apply to Parliament for relief. In many cases, the Justices in Quarter Sessions initiated or supported the move. When a few turnpike Acts had been passed, and the device had become more widely known, the adoption of the innovation became self-sustaining. Established trusts acted as 'demonstrators' of the benefits to be gained by other hard-pressed parishes, and road users. Initially, there was a little opposition in Parliament, and three of the seven bills presented between 1694 and 1700 were defeated. This was indicative of an early suspicion of the innovations. After 1700, however, widespread opposition was not in evidence, and the spread of turnpiking was conditioned by other factors.

Turnpike Petitions

Many of the petitions presented to Parliament for relief and assistance in repairing parish highways are full of interesting evidence. These petitions are printed in their original form in the Journals of the House of Commons, followed by the proceedings on the subsequent bill, if this was deemed necessary. Until 1717, this matter was decided by the Commons upon hearing the petition, but after that date, all petitions were referred to a Committee. This Committee heard evidence on the claims of the petition, and afterwards presented a report to the House. These are also printed in detail, until the 1760s, and are a second valuable source of information.

In 1714, the 'Deputy Lieutenants, Justices, Gentlemen and others, living in or near the road from Kensington to Colnebrook and Staines' protested that:

'. . . by reason of the many and heavy Carriages frequenting the said Roads, the same are become so very ruinous, that it is dangerous to Her Majesty and all attending her, to travel that way; and that the Inhabitants thereof have been at great Expence in repairing the same, yet continue so bad, that it cannot by the Laws now in Force, be effectually mended, without Aid of Parliament; Gravel and other Materials, not being to be had, but at a great Distance.' (JHC 17: 540)

That the cost of road repair now exceeded reasonable proportions was a theme common to many petitions, such as this one, presented by the gentlemen and inhabitants of Reigate and Horley in 1697. Some of their roads were:

'. . . not passable without Danger, nor can they be repaired by any Law now in Force, for that the Charge will far exceed any legal Assessments, and praying leave to bring in a bill, for the better repairing and amending the said Lane by a Toll.' (JHC 11:650)[11]

This petition produced an Act, resulting in the establishment of one of the earliest trusts (4). The Kensington petition was not successful, however, the bill it produced disappearing after one reading, but it was reintroduced in 1717, in almost identical form, and an Act was secured, creating the Brentford Trust (32).

Some petitions give details of the cost to the parish of maintaining the existing system of road repair. Thomas Smith, Esquire, in evidence to the

Committee considering a petition presented in 1743 about the road from Shepherd's Shore to Marlborough, in Wiltshire, said:

'That although the Inhabitants of the Parishes of Avebury and Bishops Cannings, through which the Roads desired to be repaired lead, have constantly done their statute-work, and raised Nine-Pence in the Pound, and laid out the same in repairing and amending the said Roads; yet the same Parishes have been several times indicted on Account of the Badness of the Highways; and that the Parish of Avebury has been fined £100 and the Parish of Bishops Cannings £30, both which sums were laid out in the Repairs of the said Roads, and that the Parishes seldom escape a Year without being indicted; And the Witness also said, That if the Parishioners of the several Parishes were to do and raise twice as much as they are obliged to do and raise by Law, the Road could not be effectually amended.' (JHC 24: 365)[12]

Sometimes the problem of the state of the roads rebounded in a vicious circle. It was reported in 1738, in a petition for a turnpike from Shoreditch to Mile End, that:

'. . . many of the best Houses in the Parish are, and have been, several years empty through the Badness of the Roads, to the great Danger of the Parish, by raising the taxes on the remaining Inhabitants.' (JHC 23: 43)[13]

In addition to complaining about the cost of road repair, telling examples of the shortcomings of the present roads were usually given. Mr Francis Austen, questioned by the Committee examining the case for a turnpike road between Farnborough and Sevenoaks in Kent, said that:

'. . . in several Places, the Road is so narrow, as not to admit two Carriages to pass one another, nor even a Passenger on Horseback to pass by a Carriage; That the Witness himself has been frequently obliged to get over into the Fields to avoid a Carriage: That at the bottom of Marmscott Hill is a deep hollow Way, which was absolutely impassable last Year for the Space of a month, being filled up with Snow . . .'. (JHC 25: 675)[14]

Such descriptions were common to many petitions. The Committee would usually call three or four witnesses to satisfy itself of the truth of the claims—claims which were intended to back up the demand for an additional source of income for road repair and improvement. Often the highways in question were said to be impeding traffic flow and inhibiting trade. In 1706, the inhabitants of Droitwich complained that the road between there and Worcester was:

'. . . so very much destroyed by the great Carriage of Salt, Iron, Coals and other Wares, that they are almost impassable, several Carts and Waggons having been there broke, the Goods spoiled and many Horses lost, and the Inhabitants are incapable of repairing the same by the Laws now in Force, to the great Prejudice of Trade in that Part of the Country.' (JHC 15: 97)

In fact, a turnpike trust was not set up to look after this road until 1714 (25), the bill of 1706 having disappeared after one reading. In such cases, however, the weather was often an important factor in the timing of a petition. The merchants of Liverpool obtained the Act for the Prescot Turnpike (63) after the very wet winter and subsequent advance in coal prices of 1725 (Barker and Harris 1954: 14). The trusts of the West Riding, established because of pressure from the textile merchant community, were set up after the Aire and Calder Navigation froze over in 1741 (Wilson 1966: 111).[15]

Although negative reasons such as these predominate, sometimes the positive benefits which were expected to result from turnpiking would be stressed. In 1752, the 'Gentlemen, Clergy and Freeholders of the Vale of the White Horse' sent a petition to Westminster in support of another requesting that a turnpike trust take over the repair of the road from Faringdon to Wallingford. They said:

'the same is an exceeding rich and fertile Vale, of great Extent, both as to Length and Breadth, and producing annually immense Quantities of Corn, Butter and Cheese, which for the Want of good Roads and Markets, are rendered almost useless to the Publick, and that the Farms are hereby impoverished, and the Farmers very frequently ruined; but that the Petitioners apprehend, that in case a good Road be made through the Vale, and an easy Communication opened to the River of Thames, and Cities of London and Westminster, it must necessarily be productive of good Effects, not only to the Vale of Berkshire, but many other parts of the Kingdom.' (JHC 26: 316)

The Act was secured (161).[16]

It is therefore possible to identify a variety of reasons that were put forward in petitions to justify the call for a turnpike trust. It is evident that the majority of these represented 'demand-induced' motives—i.e. a desire to transfer the cost of road repair and maintenance to the road user, because that cost had become excessive with the increase in traffic. The actual determination of an 'excessive cost' was for the petitioners, who often included the gentlemen of Quarter Sessions, and for Parliament, to decide.

Far fewer petitions claimed to be directly concerned with what Ashton has called the 'high hopes' of projectors—i.e. the 'supply-led' thesis (Ashton 1955: 84–5). His talk of falls in the prices of foodstuffs, an end to famine, enhancement of the value of land, encouragement of new industries and the increased mobility of Troops featured in few petitions, although there is no doubt that such motives were present. Easier movement of coal, and the expansion of the market, was one of the reasons underlying the creation of an extensive turnpike road mileage in the north of England and Midlands in the 1740s. Cheap lime, for agricultural improvement, was important as a factor in the initiation of turnpiking in South Wales. Also, the military motive was a prime reason for the establishment of some of the turnpike roads in Scotland and the Borders.[17]

It is not possible to ascertain from these turnpike petitions to Parliament which group or individuals were the instigators of reform. Unfortunately this activity has left very little record. Although a general list of petitioners heads each petition, they are always in order of status group, or importance: e.g. 'the Deputy Lieutenants, Justices of the Peace, Gentlemen and Landholders'. Little can be learnt from these lists. In many cases, only one or two men were active promoters—for example, Sir William Blackstone, the leading eighteenth century legal authority, who organized several turnpike schemes around Oxford (de Villiers 1969).

Some general points are useful, however. The largest group of petitioners on those turnpike petitions presented to Parliament before 1750 were the landowning and agricultural classes. They appear on two-thirds of petitions (64 per cent), and actually head the listing in over half (51 per cent). In this second case, the county officials were always placed first—the Lieutenants, Grand Jury, or most commonly, the Justices of the Peace. Thus most rural parishes, when they petitioned Parliament, did so through Quarter Sessions, rather than by direct application. A petition formulated in this way would not only have greater weight at Westminster, but demonstrated that the Justices themselves were satisfied that the provisions of the existing law were clearly inadequate. Secondly, nearly one-third of petitions (28 per cent) were promoted by urban interests, either by an official body ('the Mayor, Alderman and

Burgesses'), or by 'the principal Inhabitants'. They were usually concerned with the difficulty of communication, and the effect of this on their trade, as in the Droitwich petition of 1706. In some cases, petitioners' trades were listed. Thirdly, although they did not actually head any lists, wagoners and carriers were included in a small, but significant, number of petitions (10 per cent). Thus the 1714 petition about the Kensington to Staines road was supported by 'several Graziers, Farmers, Gardeners, Stage-Coachmen, Carriers, Waggoners, Higglers and others who frequent and pass the said Highway'. Stage-coachmen, in particular, were often called to give evidence to Committees examining turnpike petitions.

It was usual for only one petition to be presented about a particular road. In some cases, however, petitions expressing opposition or support would be received, often from a very wide area. In an unusual case in 1741, for example, 'the Gentlemen, Clergy, Free-holders, Merchants, Tradesmen, Farmers, Mariners, Keelmen and others, of the several Townships of Halifax, Wakefield, Knottingley, and of many other Villages in the West Riding' submitted a petition for a turnpike trust to take over responsibility for the roads from Wakefield to Pontefract (JHC 23: 578). It received petitions of support from seven other towns—respectively 'the Gentlemen, Merchants, and Tradesmen of Gainsborough', 'the Mayor, Aldermen, Capital Burgesses of the Corporation of Beverley', 'the Tradesmen, and Inhabitants of Brigg', 'the Mayor, Sheriffs, Citizens and Commonalty of Lincoln', 'the Borough of Grantham', 'the Merchants and Woollen Manufacturers of Norwich' and 'the Gentlemen and Tradesmen of Manchester'. They were successful in obtaining an Act (109).

The original petition which eventually produced the Surrey-Sussex Turnpike Act in 1717 (33) was a more complex case. The 'Justices of the Peace, Gentlemen and others' living near the roads in question were supported by 'several Farmers, Gardeners, Stage-Coachmen, Carriers, Waggoners, Higglers and Carters'. This produced a protest from 'the Justices of the Peace of Sussex, Gentlemen, Constables and other inhabitants of Lewes', claiming that the toll would be a great hardship (JHC 18: 656). 'The Justices, Gentlemen, Farmers, Maltsters, Graziers, Owners of Hop-grounds, Shopkeepers, Stage-Coachmen, Waggoners, Carters, Carriers, Fishermen, Higglers and others in the Rapes of Pevensey and Hastings' petitioned to request that they might be allowed to pass toll-free (JHC 18: 692). Then 'the Grand Jury of the Borough of Southwark' petitioned in the bill's support (JHC 18: 698). However, before it finally passed into law there was another counterpetition, from 'the Gentlemen, Freeholders, Traders and Landholders' of Reigate (JHC 18: 726). In some cases, therefore, road improvement was of very wide interest, drawing both support and opposition from very different groups of people and areas. These two examples, however, are unusual. In the period up to 1750, only 15 per cent of bills were petitioned against, and only 15 per cent were supported in this way.[18]

Most turnpike petitions that were presented to Parliament resulted in the production of a bill, which normally passed into law. A certain number of petitions and bills were lost in the process, but the proportion is small.[19] Each Act established a turnpike trust, composed of large numbers of local gentlemen, a small number of whom were active.[20] These Trustees, or Commissioners, were unpaid, and forbidden to make personal profit from the trust. Their first responsibility was 'to Erect or cause to be Erected a Gate or Gates, Turnpike or Turnpikes' at which the toll, as laid down in Act, was to be collected. The Trustees appointed Collectors to man the tollgates, a Surveyor to supervise road repairs, as well as a Clerk and Treasurer to administer the business affairs of the trust.

The funds were to be applied only to those roads named in the Act. These roads were usually existing highways, although from the late 1740s, there are some cases of completely new road building, and most trusts were permitted and actually did undertake road improvements. If the tolls proved insufficient for repair purposes, the Trustees could borrow money, the maximum amount not usually being specified, although the Act fixed the rate of interest. Most turnpike Acts were to continue in force for not more than 21 years.

There were three basic reasons why it was necessary to obtain an Act of Parliament before establishing a turnpike trust. Firstly, the right to take a toll made passage along the public highway chargeable, and therefore fundamentally altered the communal right of passage. Such an alteration could only take place with the agreement of the community through its representatives in Parliament. Secondly, a grant of toll gave a monopoly to the trust concerned. Safeguards were necessary to ensure that this privilege was not abused. Parliament endeavoured to encourage efficiency, by ensuring that salaried officials were appointed, and minimize corruption, by appointing an adequate number of Trustees, with a specified quorum for meetings. Accounts were to be kept, and some provision was usually made to ensure that these were available for inspection, either by the Justices or the Trustees themselves.

Thirdly, adequate protection had to be ensured for all parties affected by the working of the trusts. Initially, this took the form of the right to petition against turnpike bills and to be heard by the Committee responsible for examining the original petition. Interested Members of Parliament could, of course, oppose turnpike bills. Once a trust was established, travellers were charged according to a scale of tolls fixed by the Act, and if they were frequent users, they were usually given a concessionary rate. Creditors were protected by a fixed rate of interest, and a known scale of tolls, which the Trustees could lower, but only with their consent. Lastly, landowners whose property was in any way damaged by the workings of trusts were to be compensated, with any disagreement to be settled by the Justices of the Peace.

It was the emergence and diffusion of this administrative innovation that represents the eighteenth century's most important attempt to come to terms with the need for an improved road transport infrastructure. It was essentially a very simple device based on a transfer of income from road user to parishioner that resulted from charging the former, and exempting the latter, in most cases, from the need to pay for the upkeep of main roads.

3. Notes

1. The discussion in the preceding paragraphs is based on Holdsworth 1938: 301–6 and Pratt and Mackenzie 1967: 1–61.
2. A similar system was established in Scotland in 1669, and confirmed in 1719. Six days statute labour had to be performed, but under the supervision of the Justices of the Peace (Hamilton 1963: 222–3).
3. A writ of *ad quod damnum* was required to divert a public highway or effect a change in its status. This was both difficult and expensive to obtain (Holdsworth 1938: 314–20). Only in Kent and Sussex was road diversion a relatively simple matter, powers having been given in two early Acts of 1523 and 1535 (14/15 Henry VIII, c. 6 and 26 Henry VIII, c. 7) for landowners to replace founderous stretches of road with the assent of the Justices and 'twelve other discreet men living in that hundred'. This had become necessary due to the difficulty of diversion from roads in this area of early enclosure.
4. Webb 1920: 28; Jackman 1916: 63–4. Their conclusions were based on the evidence of contemporary writers such as Shapleigh, Hawkins and Scott.

5. The 1662 Act decreed that all roads leading to market towns were to be made at least eight yards wide. The ineffectiveness of this measure was underlined by lowering the minimum to eight feet in 1691. However, an equally simple means of diverting highways, other than those controlled by turnpike trusts, was not provided until 1773 when the General Highway Act empowered Quarter Sessions to authorize necessary diversions.

6. See below, note 12.

7. One case of such a toll has been found. The Fornhill to Stony Stratford Trust became inoperative sometime in the 1730s, and before it was re-established in 1740, a voluntary toll of 6d was levied on regular wagon users of the road for three years (JHC) 23: 404). See below, p. 216.

8. See below, Table XXXIX.

9. In the original Act of 1585 (27 Eliz., c. 19) the payment was in kind, of road repair materials, but the amendment Act of 1598 (39 Eliz., c. 19) supplemented this with a direct tax.

10. Attempts to trace this census have not been successful, although it was certainly taken (Herts. County Records, Vol. 5, pp. 161–5). The order of the Privy Council is in the Calendar of State Papers, Domestic 1631–3 (PC 2/42 and p. 487).

11. Other similar examples can be found in: JHC 20: 595, 613, 741; 22: 372, 398, 544; 23: 561, 568; 25: 704.

12. Some further examples of the high cost to parishes of maintaining this system:
2s 6d rates in Sevenoaks (JHC 16: 235, Act 15);
Full rates and frequent additional assessments on Kent Street (JHC 18: 685, Act 34);
£1,600 spent by the Borough of Warwick on the Birmingham road (JHC 20: 584, Act 54);
10d rate and fines in Salford (JHC 26: 554, Act 193);
Rates of 6d and 9d on the York to Northallerton road (JHC 26: 641, Act 202); And JHC 18: 298; 22: 544; 23: 69, 424; 25: 675; 26: 590.

13. Further examples:
The difficulty of getting tenants for farms on the Barnhill road due to high fines (JHC 15: 83, Act 7);
Trade falling in Beverley (JHC 20: 711);
Innkeeping declining in Lichfield (JHC 21: 222, Act 80);
Housing unoccupied in Kensington (JHC 23: 412, 424).

14. Other examples: JHC 20: 289, 605, 782, 794, 803; 22: 398, 441; 23: 567; 26: 590.

15. Other examples: JHC 21: 75, 440; 22: 97, 767; 23: 239.

16. Other examples: JHC 23: 46, 613, 643–9; 24: 582; 25: 80; 29: 794.

17. These factors are discussed in Chapters 5 and 6.

18. See below, Table XV.

19. See below, p. 117.

20. Except the earliest trusts, which were run by Justices of the Peace. (See below, p. 88).

4

The Nature of the Innovation

An understanding of the nature, or characteristics, of an innovation is basic to the study of its role, diffusion and impact in time. Only by a detailed examination of the innovation itself can its relationship to, and genesis from, the existing order, and its own development as an effective mechanism be understood. It is a field of enquiry which, in the context of the turnpike trust, reveals much of interest and importance. Since the Webbs' pioneering studies (1920, 1922), it has received little attention and a reassessment is now needed, in the light of new evidence.

Three general points merit investigation. Firstly the relationship between the turnpike trust and existing organs of local government can reveal more, at the empirical level, about the emergence and nature of the turnpike trust as an administrative innovation. Secondly, the study of the evolution of the turnpike trust as a statutory instrument through time helps to demonstrate the dynamic nature of the innovation, and its adaptation to changing conditions. Thirdly, the intention and the reality is of importance: that is, whether or not the turnpike trust in legislation was closely mirrored by the turnpike trust in operation.

The Administrative Structure

The Webbs' four classes of '*ad hoc* bodies', or 'statutory authorities for special purposes' have already been mentioned. These bodies, set up to deal with the emergence of particular problems in certain areas, numbered about 1,800 in England alone by the end of the eighteenth century. This was eight times the number of Municipal Corporations, and thirty times the number of Courts of Quarter Sessions (Webb 1922: 2). These *ad hoc* bodies were functionally separate from the existing local government structure, although not necessarily unconnected with it. Incorporated Guardians were often formed by the amalgamation of several parishes, or as outgrowths of Vestries. The early Improvement Commissions were given to municipal authorities. Turnpike trusts, too, were not divorced from the existing order, despite the Webbs' assertion to the contrary (1922: 107). They developed from the administrative and legal structure of the county, not becoming more or less independent bodies until the middle of the eighteenth century.

There were four general stages in the evolution of the turnpike trust. The earliest ones were run by Justices of the Peace, and are most easily referred to as 'Justice trusts'. They were essentially a part of the county administration. Excepting the early Hertfordshire Trust of 1663, the first was set up in 1696 and the last in 1713. The last to cease operation did not do so until the nineteenth century. The first trusts to be run by independent bodies of Trustees, the second stage, were set up from 1706. They were subject to loose Justice control, and were so still subordinate, to a degree, to the county administration. Elements of this control began to disappear in the 1730s, and by the 1750s it had completely gone. The third stage is, therefore, that of the independent and almost unaccountable trusts. They were though, still subject to occasional Parliamentary enquiries, as in 1752, 1763, 1764 and 1765 (JHC 26: 490–3; 29: 648–64, 1005–9; 30: 429), and routine examination of their affairs when applying for renewal Acts. The fourth stage showed an intensification of Parliamentary interest and a reversion to limited local control. In the first half of the nineteenth century, there was a succession of Parliamentary enquiries, and in 1823 Justices were again empowered to act as full members of trusts operating within their area of jurisdiction (3 Geo. IV, c. 126).

The first Justice trust of 1663 was a local body, under control of Quarter Sessions. This was in contrast to the 1622 bill,[1] which would have created a trust administered centrally by the Lord High Chancellor and the Lord High Treasurer. Both these measures reflected the prevalent attitudes of their times. In the earlier period, Commissions of Sewers were controlled in a similar way (Holdsworth 1938: 202–3), and road repair policy itself consisted of general centrally imposed limitations. By the 1660s, however, the local parish system of road repair had been strengthened with the power to levy rates and widen roads, and later, in 1691, the influence of the Justices was extended when the authority to appoint parish Surveyors from lists submitted by each Vestry was given to them.

The Justice trusts were little more, in administrative terms, than a further development of this enhanced parish system. There were three basic similarities. Firstly, these trusts were under the ultimate control of the Justices. It was the responsibility of Quarter Sessions, or Highway Sessions, to appoint a 'convenient number' of Surveyors and toll Collectors. These officials were accountable to the Justices for the money they received. In addition, Quarter Sessions had power to authorize Surveyors to borrow money on the credit of the toll, and it could, if necessary, terminate the trust before its statutory expiry date. Secondly, the appointment as Surveyor to a Justice trust was not a matter of choice for those who served. In the parish, not only the Surveyor, but also the Churchwardens, Constable and Overseers of the Poor were appointed in the same way. At County level, the Sheriff and High Constables served compulsorily (Webb 1906: 304). The Justice trust Surveyors were chosen by the Justices, and informed in writing. They could be fined up to £5 for refusing to serve, unless they had a 'Lawful Excuse', such as being peers, Members of Parliament or clergymen. No provision was made for them to be salaried.

The Surveyors were to view the roads in their respective divisions within one week, consider the best means of repair, and prepare a report, with the estimated cost, for the next Quarter Sessions. It was then the responsibility of the Surveyors to hire labour and pay for it from the proceeds of the toll, but this labour, again, was not to be hired on the open market. The same degree of coercion was in evidence: statute labour was to be used, even though it was to be paid the local rate:

> 'And the said respective Surveyors are hereby impowered to appoint and require such Carts and Persons who are liable to work in the Highways by the Statute already in force from time to time to come and work in the said respective Places as they shall think needful and appoint for which the said Surveyor shall pay . . . according to the usual Rate of the County . . .' (7 & 8 Wm III, c. 9)

This again, reflected the contemporary situation. The Commissions of Sewers relied on the same methods.

The third similarity between the new Justice trusts and the parish system was that the office of Surveyor was a temporary one. They were to serve for one year, and retire at the annual Easter Quarter Sessions. Then they had to render 'a perfect Account in Writing', paying over any surplus to the next year's appointees. The Justices were also required to examine Collectors' accounts, the frequency varying from weekly to bi-

annually according to the Act. Justice control could thus be fairly tight, as
was the case with the parish system.

A summary of the structure of the Justice trusts, and their relationship
to the parish system and turnpike trusts proper, is given in Fig. 15. There
were fourteen Justice trusts altogether (Table XI). Little direct evidence
of their operation has survived: their administrative records are
incorporated with those of Quarter Sessions, but are usually brief and
uninformative. Only the Hertfordshire Session Records give sufficient
detail to allow the development of a Justice trust (1) to be examined (Le
Hardy 1930: 31). Only one set of accounts is known to survive.[2]

The picture which emerges from these slender sources suggests that
intention and reality in the operation of Justice trusts were rather
different. The Hertfordshire Sessions appointed nine 'County Surveyors'
each year to supervise the toll at Wadesmill on the Great North Road (1).
These appointments usually lasted for more than a year. The same men
served from 1694 to 1707. They were replaced in 1708, but reappointed
in 1709 to serve, with some exceptions, until 1719. A similar pattern of
reappointments continued until 1733, when the trust was made a normal
turnpike. Several of the Hertfordshire Surveyors combined their post

Table XI
Justice Trusts

No. of trust	Date of establishment		Date of expiry
1	1663	Wadesmill–Stilton	1733
2	1696	Shenfield–Harwich	1726
3	1696	Wymondham–Attleborough	*
4	1697	Reigate–Crawley	1717
5	1698	Gloucester–Birdlip Hill	1718
6	1703	Thornwood–Woodford	1769
7	1706	Whitchurch–Barnhill	1727
10	1707	Devizes	1784
11	1708	Bath	1757
12	1708	Cherhill–Studley Bridge	1744
22	1712	Northfleet–Rochester	*
24	1714	Shepherds' Shore–Horesley Upright Gate	1729
28	1714	Edinburgh	1751

* These Justice trusts were still operating in the nineteenth century. The others, upon
date of expiry, were transformed by a new Act into normal turnpike trusts.

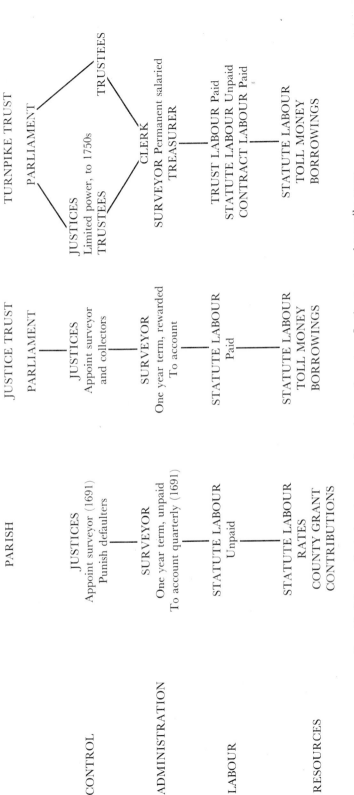

Fig. 15. Schema of relations between the parish repair system, Justice trusts and turnpike trusts.

with another County Office, such as Surveyor of Bridges, or High Constable. They were all awarded a small amount for their services—£5 a year from 1701 to 1708, and £2 10s from then until 1718. It would seem that they were appointed more by choice than by compulsion, forming an embryonic County administration outside Quarter Sessions. These Surveyors were, therefore, more closely related to the salaried turnpike Surveyor than to the impressed, unrewarded parish Surveyor.

The first turnpike trust proper was set up in 1707 (9), followed by one in each of the two succeeding years (13, 14). The transition from Justice trust to turnpike trust was not sudden, however, even taking into account the similarity in structure between them. Until 1713, new turnpike trusts and Justice trusts were being established side by side. There were also three 'hybrid' trusts, run by independent Trustees, but with power to appoint Surveyors in the same way as the Justice trusts (15, 16, 17). Two reasons may be suggested for the continued choice of Justice trusts in some areas, and the new form of organization in others. Firstly the influence of Members of Parliament who drafted bills was important. Some MPs were more conservative than others with regard to the desirable method of administration. The gentlemen of Wiltshire, who sanctioned three Justice trusts in their county after 1707 (10, 12, 24), were less willing to put the management of highway affairs under independent Trustees than those from around London. Wiltshire, in fact, was the only county to support more than one Justice trust, apart from Essex with two very early ones (2, 6), and Gloucestershire, which partly administered the Bath Trust (11),[3] in addition to the Birdlip Hill Trust (5).

Secondly, the change to independent Trustees at an early stage was probably due more to necessity than choice, as the Commission of the Peace was unable to absorb extra duties. The multiplication of Justices' functions, in addition to their basic legal role, placed severe strains on the Commission, particularly in those areas which were badly undermanned (Webb 1906: 307). In Middlesex, for example, the Justices were unable to devote much effort to the existing highway law enforcement (Dowdell 1932: 136, 190).

The new authorities were run by bodies of turnpike Trustees, sometimes known as 'Commissioners'. They were drawn from the same class of society as the gentlemen who served at Quarter Sessions. A property qualification, a common eighteenth century requirement for public service, was inserted in most turnpike Acts from the 1740s, and made general in the Act of 1767. In addition, many Justices were members of turnpike trusts, and some were very active. In Gloucestershire for instance 'a study of the surviving turnpike record shows that practically every Justice served on at least one Trust. Some, like Sir John Guise, were regular attenders at all the ones in the neighbourhood.' (Moir 1969: 125.) Thus the difference between the Justice trust and Turnpike trust Commission was technical, rather than functional.

The powers of borrowing money, and appointing Officers, were transferred from the Justices to the Trustees. The management structure which resulted from this is the main indicator of the more mature status of the turnpike trust. In most trusts, the Surveyor no longer acted as both Clerk and Treasurer. His post was salaried, and unless he was employed by a large trust with more than one division, it was not shared with others. Trust administration was divided between a salaried Clerk, and sometimes a Treasurer too, although it was common for a Trustee to fulfill the latter office. The use of the County Treasurer, as an outside holding agent for surplus money, was no longer necessary.

Justice control over these trusts was not completely relinquished. They retained the power to terminate a trust's existence if its roads were repaired and debts repaid, and they could also set up a Committee to examine trust affairs at any time. These provisions were included in most new turnpike Acts until the 1750s, but do not seem to have been implemented.[4] Justices could also check Officers' accounts upon request by the Trustees, but it was more common for the Trustees to do this themselves, and this was formally recognized in turnpike Acts from the 1730s. The control of the Justices over the administration of the new trusts appears, therefore, to have been rather weak, except when they took an interest as individual Trustees themselves. However, they continued to exercise the important legal functions of arbitration and punishment. They actively settled disputes concerning the amount of statute work due to a trust, and the level of compensation to be paid to landowners, and punished those who attempted to deceive a trust, or destroy its property.

Throughout the eighteenth century, Trustees' power increased steadily, without any commensurate increase in control over their activities. From the 1740s, turnpike Acts conferred a range of powers: to compound for statute duty and tolls, to lease and lessen the tolls, to set up side gates, to purchase land compulsorily, and to contract for road repairs. The General Turnpike Act of 1773 extended all but the last two powers to all trusts, but compulsory purchase powers, after independent valuation by a Jury if necessary, were included in most trust Acts, while contracting was not forbidden, and was extensive by the 1770s.

The Size of Trusts

The question of size is interesting in two respects: firstly, as a measure of the number of turnpike trusts compared with other institutions of local government, and secondly, as an internal measure of the range of sizes of trusts themselves. The first point is answered admirably by the Webbs, and no elaboration is necessary:

> 'Among all the Statutory Authorities the Turnpike Trusts were the most numerous. Of Courts of Sewers in England and Wales there may have been, at one time or another during the eighteenth century, a hundred or so. Of Incorporated Guardians of the Poor, we have particulars of about 125. Of separate bodies of Police or Incorporated Commissioners, large or small ... nearly three hundred may be enumerated. But of Turnpike Trusts, from the beginning of the eighteenth century, steadily increasing in number throughout a century and a quarter, there came to be, by 1835, over 1,100 simultaneously in existence; or twice as many as the other statutory authorities put together. The Turnpike Trusts were in the first quarter of the nineteenth century about five times as numerous as the Municipal Corporations, or nearly twenty times as numerous as the Courts of Quarter Sessions that governed the counties. Only the immemorially ubiquitous Parish and Manor, for which no statutory or other formal origin can be assigned, exceeded them in number.' (Webb 1922: 152)

It is more difficult to demonstrate the range of sizes of individual trusts. There are several indicators which could be adopted: the length of road mileage controlled, the number of Trustees appointed or the number active, total or toll income, or level of expenditure. The first of these is the easiest to use, and because full evidence is available it is the best means of comparison between trusts. There were often many Trustees appointed but only a small proportion were active. It is difficult to define this active proportion. Average attendance at meetings is not a good indicator. Toll income and expenditure are useful measures, but a representative sample of sizes is very hard to obtain.[5]

The mileages controlled by individual trusts may be calculated from

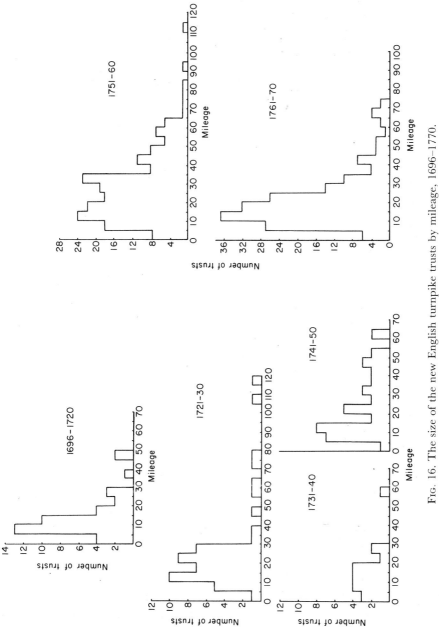

Fig. 16. The size of the new English turnpike trusts by mileage, 1696–1770.
Source: Acts of Parliament, House of Lords.

the routes given in each Act by the use of modern large-scale maps.[6] The information gathered in this way has been grouped and plotted in graph form for all new English trusts established up to 1770 (Fig. 16). The results are of interest, in the context of previous information on this subject. 'The turnpike trusts were relatively small undertakings, each concerned with only a few miles of road', wrote Ashton, which, he explained in a footnote, meant that 'between ten and twenty miles was normal' (1955: 87). The Webbs, similarly, wrote of 'this mass of local Acts, each applicable to only a few miles of road' (1920: 120).

Ashton is broadly correct, as the proportion of trusts controlling less than 30 miles of road does not fall below 60 per cent in the whole period up to 1770 (Fig. 17). Nevertheless, the number of small trusts—those controlling less than ten miles of road—only twice exceeds 20 per cent. This was in the period before 1720, when the innovation was just becoming established, and in the 1730s. The mean size of trusts was, in fact, roughly stable decade by decade, after 1720, and is appreciably higher than Ashton's figure:

Table XII

Mean Size of New English Turnpike Trusts in Miles, 1696–1770[7]

		miles
1695–1720	:	14·5
1721–30	:	27·4
1731–40	:	16·6
1741–50	:	25·7
1751–60	:	29·9
1761–70	:	28·3

The situation is rather more complex than indicated by a single summary measure. Up to 1760, there was a gradual trend towards a greater proportion of large trusts, controlling over 30 miles, decade by decade, and a lower number of small ones, controlling less than ten miles. The proportion in the former category rises from 8 per cent in the pre-1720 period, to 40 per cent in the 1750s, whilst that in the latter category falls, from 42 to 14 per cent.

Some of the large trusts were very extensive. The biggest, before 1750, were the Gloucester to Hereford Trust, with 64 miles of road (59), the Birmingham to Edgehill with 71 miles (54), the Worcester Turnpike with 76 miles (60), the Bristol Turnpike with 109 miles (69) and the Hereford Turnpike with 118 miles (85). After 1750, some even bigger trusts were

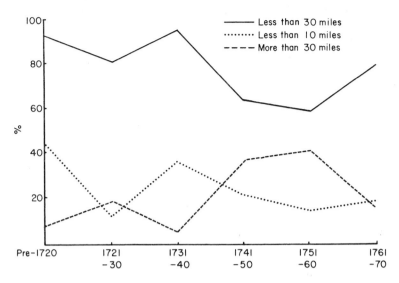

Fig. 17. Proportion of new English turnpike trusts of different sizes by mileage, 1696–1770.

established. The Exeter Trust had 112 miles of road (201), the Leeds to Blackburn had 115 miles (247), and the two county trusts for Monmouthshire and Cardigan had 196 and 164 miles respectively (288, 511). These large trusts were always divided into districts, however, often with their own separate administrations.

Domain of the Innovation

All innovations must have a defined domain, which delimits the nature and scope of their operations. This domain may be defined by existing or subsequent legislation, or it may be established by statute at the outset. This was the case with turnpike trusts.

Initially, the domain of turnpike trusts was limited to existing resources. They were entrusted with the care of established highways, which were beyond repair 'by the ordinary means'. But some early trusts were empowered to buy land to widen their roads. The Barnhill (7), Bath (11) and Northfleet (22) Justice trusts were the first, but these powers became general in turnpike Acts passed from the early 1740s. Then, from mid-century, the domain of the innovation was widened significantly, to allow it to create and supervise completely new highway resources. After 1749, several trusts were established, mostly around London, to build completely new roads, and amendment Acts were passed to allow some existing trusts to do this. The first example was the Bermondsey Trust (142), which built a new road from Southwark to Deptford through a rapidly growing part of South London.[8] In addition, from the late 1750s, most turnpike Acts gave power to trusts to buy land to divert parts of their roads, and build completely new sections.

The land in the road was not owned by the Trustees. This was both unnecessary, and undesirable. It was already effectively a public resource, even though it remained legally in the hands of those who had always owned it. Likewise, new land bought for highway improvements was deemed to be part of the 'publick and common Highway'. In this latter case the situation was more complex, as the land had to be bought from the existing owner by the Trustees, even though it did not become their property. It became part of the public resource, and was deemed to be publicly owned. The improvements brought about by trusts were thus the precursor of modern highway expansion methods. Once old sections of the road were replaced they could be sold, then ceasing to be part of the common highway. The Trustees were agents, appointed to look after the public right of passage, with power to improve it, but without any power to assume ownership.

The toll money collected was, in contrast, vested in the Trustees. The tollhouses and gates, being the means by which it was to be collected, were also owned by them. Thus trusts did have a small number of assets, in terms of money in hand, tollhouses and gates, and any tools, animals and storage facilities they might have acquired. It was partly because turnpike trusts were, in most cases, maintaining an existing resource, albeit on a more intensive scale than previously, and did not need substantial financial backing to create new assets, that they were simply trusts, and not joint-stock companies.

Two of the later important transport innovations—the canals and railways—were run by joint-stock companies. However, these innovations were not only creating completely new assets, they were also not charged with the care of an existing public right. Their aim was thus fundamentally different from turnpike trusts. The latter were non-profit-making guardians. They were not companies, they were not privately owned, and they were not intended to make a profit. These are important points, because their essential nature has been misconceived many times in the past.[9]

The activities of turnpike trusts tended to define more clearly than before the actual physical extent of the highway. It was an inevitable consequence of organized and concentrated road repair that a particular route, of certain width, would emerge as 'the road'. Attempts to maintain, and increasingly to construct, this surface of limited width, with the planting of hedges and digging of ditches alongside, hastened the acceptance of the highway as a strip of land, dedicated to a particular purpose, rather than as a right of passage which need not maintain a constant course.

The 'containment of the route' was of course a necessary prerequisite of successful trust management. Only one line along a route could be repaired. The digging of ditches was usually considered necessary to keep the road surface drained, and divergence from the route had to be eliminated if these ditches and the hedges were not to be damaged. However, it was also important to prevent the avoidance of tollgates, so that the level of toll income could be maintained in line with the level of use of the road. From about 1715, turnpike Acts gave the Justices power to levy fines on all toll evaders, and on landowners who acquiesced with, or encouraged such evasion. From the early 1740s, the Trustees themselves were given authority to erect side-gates to prevent traffic avoiding payment by entering a turnpike route above or below a gate.

The domain of the innovation was not static, and might represent an alteration from the situation prevailing before the turnpike road was established. In some cases, the status of a route was altered, so that bridleways became coach roads (12, 152, 193, 489), but when the trusts developed completely new roads, the alteration was far more radical. Their Acts actually established public rights of way over land not previously used for that purpose. It was more common for the domain to alter after the establishment of the trust. Road widening, turning and replacement schemes all affected it. Each Act provided its trust with substantial powers to back up these provisions, in the form of compulsory land purchase. If owners refused to comply with a request from a trust to sell land, or would not accept the price offered, a Jury was summoned by the High Sheriff of the county. This Jury decided the level of compensation, and the trust then bought the land it needed at that price. Great advantage was taken by trusts of their land purchase powers, and it was not uncommon for them to call on the services of a Jury.[10]

The trust's domain did, therefore, extend away from its roads to the property surrounding them. This is reflected in one more matter: their right to dig for road gravel. All turnpike Acts allowed Surveyors to seek repair materials in waste ground and commons, and failing this, to remove them from private land. Landowners were given several safeguards. Nothing was to be removed from gardens, yards, orchards, meadows, planted walks or house avenues, and the trusts had to offer compensation for any damage caused. The earliest Acts allowed trusts to obtain these materials free of charge, but from the mid-1710s, this privilege was no longer included. The 1753 general Highways Act made it necessary for gravel pits to be fenced, but the investment of trusts with compulsory purchase powers was confirmed. This was acceptable because trusts were agents, established for the social good in order to maintain and improve a public asset.

A Supplementary Measure

The obligation of parishes to repair highways derived from common law, and could not be rescinded except by statute. The 1555 Act formalizing the obligation had been made perpetual in 1568. Legislation establishing a new system of highway maintenance had, therefore, to reject statute work specifically, if the new system was to replace, and not only complement it. But turnpike Acts did not do this: rather, they made provision for its continuation on turnpike roads. For example, the Shenfield to Harwich Trust Act of 1696 stated that:

> '. . . all and every Person and Persons who by Law are chargeable toward repairing the said Highways shall still remaine so chargeable and doe their respective Works in the said Highways as before they used to do therein.' (2)

The earliest Acts did not direct the proportion of each parish's statute work that was to be performed on the turnpike road. From about 1714 it was usual for each Act to provide some means of assessing this. Either the Justices were to decide, or the Act itself fixed the number of days. This was a maximum allowance, and the Trustees, or their Surveyor, could fix the actual amount within the limit. It was also usual for Acts to allow parishes to commute their share of statute work, paying instead a mutually agreed sum to the trust. The statute labour provision was certainly used by trusts. Nearly all made some use of it, although the payment of composition money sometimes presented problems.[11]

However, because turnpike Acts did not remove the statute work obligation of the parish, neither did they cancel its responsibility for the state of the highway. It was still the parish, and not the turnpike trust, which had to be presented or indicted at Quarter Sessions if a turnpike road was not properly maintained. In 1808, in evidence to the House of Commons Committee on Highways, Sir John Hippesley said:

'As the law now stands, if any part of a turnpike road be out of repair, remedy is given by presentment or indictment of the parish, in which such road is situate, subjecting the parish, to great expense and inconvenience, although the nuisance be wholly imputable to the Trustees of the Turnpike.' (BPP 1808 (275) II 459: 136)

Very little was ever done to relieve the parish of its obligation and responsibility. A minor concession was made in the General Turnpike Act of 1766. If there was more than one turnpike road in a parish, and the statute labour requirement exceeded a total of three days, the Justices were 'to adjust the same', with regard to the relative condition and revenue of each turnpike. In 1773, the next General Turnpike Act allowed the court to apportion any fine and costs arising from presentment and indictment 'in such Manner, as to the Court, upon consideration of the case, shall seem just'. This meant at least that trusts could be charged. The same Act allowed the Justices in Special Sessions to direct that the obligation be cancelled, wholly or in part, if the roads and finances of the trust were in good order. The basic obligation, however, remained. It was stated very clearly in a legal case heard in 1832:

'It is a mistake to suppose that the object of turnpike Acts is to relieve parishes and townships from the burden of repairing the highways. Their object is to improve the road for the general benefit of the public by imposing a pecuniary tax in addition to the means already provided by law for that purpose.'[12]

Temporary Authority

The authority of turnpike trusts was of limited duration, the term being fixed by each Act. It was usual for this to be 21 years, although in the earlier Acts, it was commonly shorter.[13] Turnpike Acts were certainly not unique in this respect. The grants of toll to towns or to bridge builders in medieval times were usually limited to three or five years. The Commissions of Sewers were only temporary bodies. The original statute gave them a term of three years (23 Henry VIII, c.5), enlarged in 1549 to five years (3 & 4 Edw. VI, c. 8), and then in 1570, to ten years (13 Eliz., c.

9). And the early road Acts were of limited duration. The 1555 Statute had a term of seven years, renewed in 1562 for 20. The highway rates granted by the Acts of 1662 and 1670 were for three years only.

The implication of this is that the term allowed by turnpike Acts was considered, at the time, to be sufficient to carry out the necessary work. The Justice's power to terminate a trust's existence if the debts were repaid and the road was in good order reinforces this argument. Nonetheless in retrospect, the ongoing general increase in traffic, and the reliance on traditional methods of continuous repair maintenance, made temporary measures unrealistic.

However, the turnpike trust was certainly not a temporary institution. Renewal Acts were nearly always sought by the Trustees before the expiry of their term, and without exception, these were granted.[14] They usually extended the original term by a further 21 years, although in some cases it was shorter, with the new term taking immediate effect. Only seven of the Acts passed before 1750 were not renewed, and it seems that these were deliberately allowed to expire. All, except one, had been revived by 1760.[15] Only 14 of the Acts passed between 1751 and 1770 were not renewed.[16] In both periods, the proportion of the total is small— 4·8 per cent and 3·9 per cent respectively. With these exceptions, trusts sought not merely one, but several renewal Acts.

A letter from a London lawyer to the Treasurer of the Stevenage–Biggleswade Trust (39) concerning a draft amendment bill, illustrates the ease with which renewals were obtained[17]:

> Abingdon Street,
> 28 October, 1777
>
> Sir,
>   Inclosed I return you the Draft of your Bill, with Mr. Sprangler's Corrections and Observations.
>   As enlarging the Term of the former Act will not be attended with any additional Expence I have inserted some Words for that Purpose in Fo. 4; and if the getting a new Petition will be attended with any considerable Trouble, I believe we may get those Words inserted in the Bill, without any prolongation prayed for in the Petition, as they are almost a matter of course in every alteration of Turnpike Acts.
>   I am, Sir,
>   Your most Obedient Humble Servant,
>   Nathnl. Barwell.

Two points can be deduced from the evidence of these renewal Acts—

the first concerned with the implementation of the innovation, and the second with its permanency. It is a reasonable assumption that all trusts which sought to renew their terms had actually been established after the original Act, and were functioning. The petitions for renewal, and the Reports of the Committees which examined them, usually provide a qualitative assessment of the work carried out by the trusts, the state of the roads, their financial position, and any repairs of urgency still awaiting attention. These renewal Acts thus make the assumption that original turnpike Acts were implemented rather more sound than is the case with original canal or railway Acts. And, in addition, there is some evidence that Acts whose terms were not renewed were, in fact, implemented.[18]

Evidence of operation does not necessarily mean that road repair was put in hand immediately, or that all parts of the roads in the care of a particular trust were repaired together. Most trusts made immediate attempts to repair or reconstruct the worst parts of their roads, but a frequent claim in petitions for renewal Acts was that not all sections had yet been mended. Sometimes mileage was not repaired because it had proved superfluous, or the tolls on that section were insufficient. During the eighteenth century, there are thus 21 cases in the renewal Acts of trusts established before 1770 of sections of road actually being disturnpiked. There are a further 13 of roads being transferred to other trusts—three of these being whole trusts, and the rest just small sections.[19]

The second point concerns the permanency of the innovation. It is evident that the turnpike trust, far from being a temporary institution of local government, was in practice a most permanent one, at least until the mid-nineteenth century, when frequent disturnpiking schemes began. This does not mean that the size or domain of the innovation was everywhere permanent, but as an institution it certainly was.

There were several reasons why renewal Acts were necessary. The need for continuous road maintenance, in the face of increasing demand, is the first. It featured prominently in many petitions from trusts presented to Parliament.[20] Secondly, it was often the case that 'great improvements' had been brought about, but that parts of the road remained unfinished, or even unstarted.[21] The third reason was to safeguard the interests of creditors. Many trusts borrowed heavily, as they were permitted to do by their Acts. Although the rate of interest was always fixed by the legislation, the maximum amount that could be borrowed usually was not. Most of the early Acts, before 1720, actually stated that money was not to be borrowed for a term exceeding that of the Act, although there was nothing to indicate that these terms should coincide. There was thus an inbuilt renewal mechanism: an unpaid debt at the expiry date of the trust's life. Later Acts also abandoned the clause fixing the maximum borrowing term. A large debt often presented a conflict of interests. If a trust's income was not sufficient to maintain its roads and repay its debt, it had to disappoint either the public, or its creditors.

A typical instance was that of the Edgware Trust (19). It presented its case for a renewal Act in 1721. It had debts of £4,389, and a net income, after payment of interest, of £299. Hence:

> 'there being but Eleven Years and a Half to come of the term granted by the . . . Act, the Money arising by the said Toll during that Time will scarce repay the Money borrowed; so the Trustees, during the remainder of the said Term, will be prevented from laying out anything in amending the said Roads and the keeping them in such Repair as they now are will amount to about £300 per Annum, one Year with another, while the present Act continues in Force.' (JHC 19: 670)

There are many other examples,[22] often with an equally long gap between the application date for a renewal Act and the expiry date of the current Act (Table XIII).

The opportunity was often taken in renewal Acts to amend a trust's

Table XIII

The Gap, in Years, Between the Application Date for a Renewal Act, and the Expiry Date of the Original Act, 1721–70

(Years)	0–1	2–3	4–5	6–10	11–15	16–20	20	Total
1721–30	7	2	3	7	3	3		25
1731–40	6	2	6	10	5	1		30
1741–50	14	11	12	17	5	2		61
1751–60	6	3	5	16	15	15	5	65
1761–70	10	6	11	39	28	13		107
	43	24	37	89	56	34	5	296 (Acts)

Note: This table excludes renewal Acts passed before 1720, as there were only eight. It excludes those passed after 1770 because of the practical difficulty of knowing which trusts took advantage of the five-year extension clause allowed by the General Turnpike Act of 1773 (see text). It includes only those Acts which granted an extension of the term, and not those which amended the original Act in some other way. Hence the decadal totals differ from those in Table XIV.

powers in some other way. Likewise, renewal was sometimes the by-product of an appeal for the amendment of powers. These alterations most frequently related to a strengthening of the powers relating to statute work,[23] the number or position of tollgates,[24] and borrowing limits, where these had been imposed.[25] Most common, however, was a change in the schedule of tolls to be charged,[26] or an addition to the mileage under the control of the trust.

This last point is of importance, because it demonstrates that the domain of trusts was anything but constant. Over a third of the amendment and renewal Acts passed in the years up to 1770 added extra mileage to their respective trusts, the average amount being anything from five to fifteen miles, decade by decade (Table XIV). A considerable increment was given to some trusts in this way. An exceptional case was the Shenfield to Harwich Justice Trust, established in 1696 with 27 miles of road (2). Successive renewal Acts added eight miles in 1708, a further 70 in 1726, 33 miles in 1747, and 95 miles in 1765. The trust was by then one of the largest in the country, with 233 miles of road.

In view of the high level of trust renewals, and the ease with which Acts were obtained, it may have seemed unnecessary for Parliament to have maintained the standard 21-year term. Indeed, that it should be abandoned was one of the recommendations of the 1833 Committee investigating turnpike trusts (BPP 1833 (703) XV 409: iii). Instead, however, the Annual Turnpike Constinuance Acts were introduced. These extended the life of those trusts whose Acts were due to expire from the end of one Parliamentary session to the next, without any need for individual application.[27] They came at a time when turnpike renewal Acts were becoming increasingly expensive—in 1829, the average costs of 128 renewal Acts was estimated to be £436 3s. (ibid.: 57)—and when the pressure of other business on Parliamentary time was increasing.

The 21-year term was evidently retained until the 1830s, because it was considered a valuable means of keeping some central control over trusts' activities, and because it often gave an opportunity for any required alteration of powers. There were only two general extensions of trusts' terms in the whole of the eighteenth century: one of five years, granted by the 1755 Broad Wheels Amendment Act to protect the interests of creditors upon the reduction of tolls for broad wheeled vehicles and another of five years, offered to trusts by the 1773 General Turnpike Act, to induce them to build weighing engines.

Table XIV
Renewal and Amendment Acts

A. Numbers of Acts altering the mileage of trusts						
	A	B	C	D	E	F
1695–1720	8	2				
1721–30	16	10	2		1	
1731–40	24	10	2			1
1741–50	46	5	5		3	1
1751–60	50	17	4	2	3	3
1761–70	64	30	12	5	2	8

B. Proportion of Acts altering the mileage of trusts						
	A	B	C	D	E	F
1695–1720	80 per cent	20 per cent				
1721–30	55·2	34·5	6·9		3·4	
1731–40	64·9	27·0	5·4			2·7
1741–50	76·6	8·3	8·3		5·0	1·6
1751–60	63·3	21·5	5·1	2·5	3·8	3·8
1761–70	52·8	24·8	9·9	4·1	1·6	6·6

A = No change in mileage
B = addition of 1–10 miles
C = addition of 11–20 miles
D = addition of 21–30 miles
E = addition of over 30 miles
F = reduction of mileage

C. Mean number of miles added per Act
1695–1720 — 5·5 miles
1721–30 — 11·1 miles
1731–40 — 5·9 miles
1741–50 — 15·6 miles
1751–60 — 12·0 miles
1761–70 — 10·0 miles

Section C excludes those Acts which did not alter, or reduced, a trust's mileage.

Was it an innovation?

As a conclusion to this examination of the nature of the turnpike trust, it seems appropriate to ask whether or not it was an innovation. It did, after all, emerge from the existing local government structure, and bore similarities to it. Its domain was mainly that of existing highways, and it relied for its finance on a well tried method—the toll. In addition, it was only a supplementary measure.

The central characteristic of a turnpike road was the toll. 'The ordinary meaning of the words "turnpike road" is a road on which a turnpike is lawfully erected and the public are bound to pay tolls', and 'the distinctive mark of a turnpike road is the turning back of anyone who refuses to pay toll.'[28] But reference has already been made to the grants of toll to medieval towns for pavage, pontage and murage, and to individuals and bodies for building bridges and causeways. Some of these still existed in the eighteenth century, such as the traverse tolls at Carlisle, the murengers tolls in Chester, or the street tolls in Edinburgh.[29]

However, on turnpike roads, the toll was being used in a completely new way, in a novel situation. 'In the legislation of 1663 [and after] sanctioning tolls on roads, there was a revival of powers not, indeed, new, but never before elaborated, or, indeed, clothed in statutory form, because previous tolls had only been imposed by royal licence, or by ordinance.' (Clifford 1887: 15.) Also tolls had not been used before to repair long stretches of road. The exercise of the right of the passage had always been free, except on crossing bridges or causeways, or on entering the walls, streets, or market places of towns. Thus although the turnpike trust, as an institution, bore similarities to others, it was nevertheless an institutional innovation based on the novel use of a well known expedient.

A further question arises. Was the innovation itself innovative? Was the adoption of the innovation itself matched by an innovative approach to its task? The conventional view, propounded by the Webbs (1920) and supported by Albert (1972), is that the trusts used conventional repair methods, albeit on a far more intensive scale than previously. In the first half of the eighteenth century, this was generally true. There is little reason why an institution, taking over an existing resource, rather than creating a new one such as a railway line or canal, would have to adopt radical new methods and skills immediately. However, after 1750 there is much evidence in surviving trust records of a more professional attitude to road repair: of experimentation, detailed specifications, planning, and widespread improvements.[30]

Nevertheless, the fact that turnpike trusts were not widely innovative from the start does not in any way affect their status as innovations. Too often it has been assumed that innovations, to qualify for the title, must be technical in nature—that they must be pound-locks, steam engines, or telegraphs. But social, political, educational and administrative innovations have been just as vital, if not more so, in the history of change.

4. Notes

1. See above, p. 76–7.
2. Devizes Trust, 1707–8, 1746–83 (Wilts. RO).
3. The original Bath Trust Act of 1708 entrusted the administration of this trust to two or more Justices from Wiltshire, and two or more from both Somerset and Gloucestershire as well as one or more from Bath itself (11).
4. No cases of either measure being used have been found in any of the local turnpike records examined (Samples 2 and 3, introduced in Chapters 7 and 8.). This would seem to preclude widespread implementation of them, although individual cases may have occurred.
5. Trustee attendances did not vary greatly according to size of trust, as is seen in Chapter 7, Table XXIV. Trust income is discussed in Chapter 8.
6. For this purpose Ordnance Survey One-Inch maps were used, and supplemented when necessary by the relevant 2½-Inch sheets. Nearly all of the places named in the Acts can be found on these maps.
.7. Welsh and Scottish trusts have been excluded from this table as they were often of considerable size, representing an extreme form in the development of the innovation. See below, p. 153.
8. The whole process of new road building in London is discussed in Chapter 10, pp. 272–5.
9. Court (1938: 66) refers to trusts as 'companies', as does Iredale, in Stephens (1970: 130), but it is Vigier who commits the wildest errors: 'Invested with broad powers under various Acts of Parliament, private companies were relatively free of supervision, particularly in the choice of routes which were determined on the basis of their profit potential rather than as part of a highway system to serve the country ... Canals and turnpikes were usually initiated and financed by joint-stock companies composed of local businessmen who recognised the opportunities for profit they offered.' (1970: 24, 33).
10. See below, p. 252.
11. Composition money was in effect a rate paid in lieu of statute duty although it originated as a fine. The use of statute duty by trusts is discussed in Chapter 8, pp. 217–9.
12. Bussey v. Storey (1832) 4 B. & Ad. 98.
13. The following Acts had only 11 year terms: 30, 32, 34; 13 years: 21, 22, 23; 15 years: 2, 3, 15, 26; 20 years: 4, 5, 12.

14. There was, in fact, one exception: the renewal bill for the Hockcliffe to Woburn Trust (8), defeated in 1726. A bill for the same purpose was however accepted two years later (1 Geo. II, c. 8.).

15. The Acts passed before 1750 and allowed to expire were:

    4 in 1717, revived in 1755 as 230.

    5 in 1718, revived in 1723 as   46.

    7 in 1727, revived in 1760 as 334.

    9 in 1728, revived in 1740.

  62 in 1747, revived in 1756 as 253.

  88 in 1757, revived in 1759 as 307.

146 in 1771.

The trusts themselves may well have ceased to function before these expiry dates.

16. Acts passed between 1751 and 1770 and allowed to expire: 163, 212, 223, 229, 239, 282, 296, 300, 360, 369, 388, 473, 487, 508.

17. TP6–82 (Herts. RO).

18. Act 4 (JHC 18: 726), 5 (JHC 14: 288), 9 (JHC 23: 107–8), 223 (Young 1770 Vol. 4: 423), 369 (JHC 40: 210). See notes 15 and 16 above.

19. The disturnpiking and transfer of routes was not significant: it accounted for only 144 miles of the 14,965 miles turnpiked up to 1770. This was only 0·9 per cent of the total. Three whole trusts were terminated and their roads transferred to other trusts: the Fulham Trust (92) merged with the Kensington Trust in 1767 (65); the Droitwich Trust (239) was taken over by the Worcester to Bromsgrove Trust (25) in 1768, and in the same year the Trowbridge Trust (163) was merged with the Seend to Beckington Trust (159). Although the Fulham Trust had been in operation since 1731, the Droitwich Act was never implemented and it is doubtful if the Trowbridge one was either.

20. For example, the renewal of Act 22 (JHC 20: 360), 34 (JHC 22: 775), 57 (JHC 23: 59), 37 (JHC 23: 438), 40 (JHC 24: 115), 78 (JHC 24: 89), 80 (JHC 24: 510), 91 (JHC 24: 516), 79 (JHC 25: 691), 93 (JHC 25: 927).

21. For example, trust 2 in 1708 (JHC 15: 742), 18 in 1720 (JHC 19: 232), 15 in 1724 (JHC 20: 363), 22 in 1724 (JHC 20: 360), 20 in 1733 (JHC 22: 65), 21 in 1736 (JHC 22: 540), 77 in 1738 (JHC 23: 261), 17 in 1742 (JHC 24: 121), 54 in 1758 (JHC 28: 98), 14 in 1760 (JHC 28: 754).

22. Trust 23 in 1716 (JHC 18: 378), 34 in 1720 (JHC 19: 224), 32 in 1720 (JHC 19: 258), 11 in 1721 (JHC 19: 417), 10 in 1725 (JHC 20: 415), 27 in 1735 (JHC 22: 375), 73 in 1743 (JHC 24: 377). 84 in 1743 (JHC 24: 485), 97 in 1753 (JHC 26: 856).

23. Some examples: trust 31 in 1735 (JHC 22: 450), 23 in 1744 (JHC 24: 563), 132 in 1749 (JHC 25: 820), 115 in 1749 (JHC 25: 755–6), 276 in 1762 (JHC 29: 165), 167 in 1769.

24. Some examples: trust 9 in 1717 (JHC 18: 586), 51 in 1730 (JHC 21: 498), 57 in 1738 (JHC 23: 59), 13 in 1740 (JHC 23: 419), 78 in 1744 (JHC 24: 488), 113 in 1751 (JHC 26: 56), 148 in 1765 (JHC 30: 159), 425 in 1766 (JHC 30: 529), 465 in 1768 (JHC 31: 437), 167 in 1769 (JHC 32: 81).

25. Some examples: trust 66 in 1731 (JHC 21: 679), 201 in 1756 (JHC 27: 321), 86 in 1758 (JHC 28: 63), 59 in 1760 (JHC 28: 744), 41 in 1766 (JHC 30: 651).

26. This point is discussed in Chapter 8, pp. 203–4.

27. The first Annual Turnpike Continuance Act (1/2 Wm IV, c. 6) was in fact passed in

1831, but not until after the publication of the 1833 Committee's Report does a full series begin. Hence these Acts only become annual from 1834 (4/5 Wm IV, c. 10; 5/6 Wm IV, c. 49; 6/7 Wm IV, c. 62).

28. Parke, B., in Northern Bridge Co. v. London and Southampton Rail Co. (1842). 6 M. & W. 428 (quoted in Pratt and Mackenzie 1967: 12).

29. English Gate Tollbook (Ca/4/175), Irish Gate Toolbook (Ca/4/175) and Applebyshire Toolbook (Ca/4/161,2 Cumbria RO). Murengers Accounts (Chester Town Hall). Edinburgh tolls: Act 12 Anne stat 2, c. 10 (1713).

30. This whole area is discussed in Chapter 9.

5

The Diffusion of the Turnpike
System through Time

The task of identifying, let alone interpreting, the course of change in history is not an easy one, but the study of innovations and their diffusion is a clear way of exploring it. However, the pattern of diffusion of many innovations, particularly the agricultural and industrial improvements of the seventeenth and eighteenth centuries, cannot be established with any certainty, due to the absence of a central record.

This is fortunately not the case with the turnpike road system. Its diffusion pattern through time and space can be reconstructed in detail and with precision because of the nature of the turnpike trust innovation. Each new trust, having been established by an Act of Parliament, is well documented. The Acts are available in a continuous series in the House of Lords, in manuscript form for those passed before 1720, and in the printed volumes of the Public General Statutes after that date. It is therefore relatively simple to identify the process of turnpiking as a prologue to the analysis and interpretation of the pattern which emerges.

Identification of the Process

Theoretical and empirical study of innovations suggests that it is possible to recognize certain regularities in the process of diffusion. From a small number of initial adopters, or innovators, the successful new idea, technique or product will spread outwards through the whole population. The majority of eventual adopters will be clustered in the central time period of the process, with 'leading' adopters and 'lagging' adopters spread through the earlier and later periods. In the ideal case, the frequency distribution of adopters through time should conform to a normal curve. Adopters can then be categorized according to their position relative to the mean (Fig. 18). If, however, the information is transformed into cumulative percentage terms, the ideal curve assumes an S-shaped, or logistic form, commonly known as the diffusion curve. The steep central part of the diffusion curve, covering the majority of adopters, represents the 'bell' of the normal curve. The diffusion curve itself enables an estimate of the level of penetration of the innovation at a particular time to be made, in terms relative to its final level of penetration.

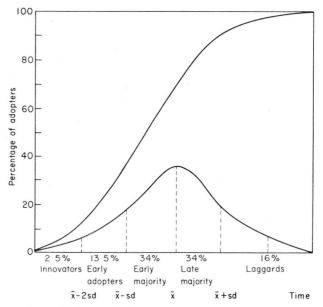

FIG. 18. Innovation and adopter distributions: frequency and diffusion curves. The bell-shaped frequencey curve and S-shaped diffusion curve, showing adopter classification on the basis of innovativeness. *Source*: based on Rogers and Shoemaker 1971: 177, 182.

The theoretical justification for the form of these two curves is quite simple. As knowledge of the innovation, and realization of the benefits to be gained from its adoption, spread through the population, the rate of adoption increases. Each new adopter acts as a 'demonstrator' to prospective future adopters. In time, though, the rate of adoption will begin to level off, and then fall, as the limits of potential adopters, or as geographical boundaries, are approached. It may be hastened by the emergence of a competing innovation.

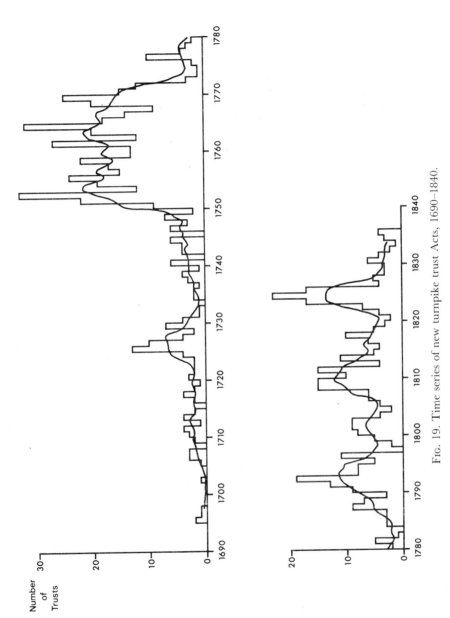

Fig. 19. Time series of new turnpike trust Acts, 1690–1840.

The time series of new turnpike Acts (i.e. those creating new turnpike trusts) is shown in Fig. 19. The years 1696 and 1836 have been taken as terminal points, as these represent the dates of the first and last new trust Acts, excluding the early Hertfordshire Trust of 1663. The similarity of form between this time series and the ideal case is readily apparent, particularly when the general trend is extracted by the use of a moving mean to smooth annual variations. This close correspondence is further emphasized when the time series is transformed into a diffusion curve (Fig. 20). The S-shape is clearly depicted, with marked turning points occurring in 1750 and 1770.

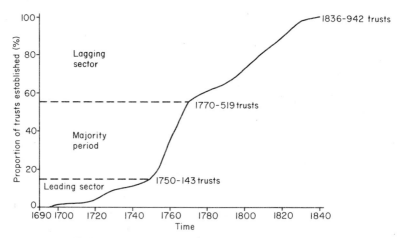

FIG. 20. Diffusion curve of new turnpike trusts, England and Wales.

Both these curves, however, are of numbers of Acts only. A more detailed measure of the pattern of turnpike trust diffusion is the actual number of miles of road affected each year. These totals, calculated from the routes detailed in each Act, have been used to construct the revised diffusion curve in Fig. 21. This revised curve emphasizes the importance of the 'majority' or 'boom' period even more. The 20 years between 1750 and 1770 saw the establishment of 40 per cent of the eventual total of new trusts, and 52 per cent of the eventual mileage. In both cases, this majority period has an important share of the total, although less than the 68 per cent of the ideal case. It is less because the majority period is short and abruptly contained, whilst the lagging sector from 1770 is longer and proportionately more important than might be expected.

The identification of the pattern of turnpike trust diffusion therefore raises several questions. Why was the majority period relatively short, and abruptly contained? Why is it located between 1750 and 1770, and not an alternative pair of dates? Why are the leading and lagging sectors so long? Why is a relatively high proportion of new trusts and mileage found in the lagging sector? There are thus three broad problems, concerned with the form and location in time of the leading, majority and lagging sectors. The analysis and interpretation of turnpike trust diffusion will be explored in this chapter within this simple framework.

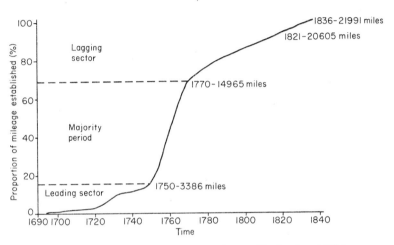

Fig. 21. Diffusion curve of turnpike road mileage, England and Wales.

Analysis of the Process

The rate of adoption of an innovation is related directly to the characteristics of that innovation, but conditioned by the general process of diffusion as already outlined. This 'contextual' factor provides an indication of the overall form of the process, but the exact timing of the phases within the process is due to independent factors. The most basic of these are the forces of demand and supply. It is therefore to the component factors affecting the demand for the innovation, and the supply of it, that the search for explanation of the diffusion process must be directed. Also important is the negative force of resistance, delaying innovation and diffusion as a result of direct opposition from interested parties. These three forces—demand for, supply of, and opposition to an innovation—can be termed in this case respectively 'a motive to adopt', 'the ability to adopt', and the attitude of local people and Parliament.

A *motive for adoption* is established by the need or desire to adopt an innovation which is believed to be better than the method or product already in use. The relative advantage of the turnpike trust was the improvement it offered as a means of road maintenance over the established parish repair system. It was the internalization of the cost of road repair, resulting in better highways for road users, and the transfer of income to parishes when they no longer had to work extra days statute duty, pay fines levied by Quarter Sessions upon indictment for poor roads, or raise highway rates.

Relative advantage is the most important factor affecting demand, but it is not the only one. There are others: the complexity of the innovation, the ease with which it can be adopted, and its observability are all significant. A simple innovation, with readily apparent advantages, and not employing radical or alien techniques, is more likely to be quickly accepted. This is particularly so if it can be observed in operation before adoption, and can then be adopted without resort to involved procedures. In these terms, the turnpike trust was relatively simple, it was easily observed in operation, but it was more difficult to adopt than most innovations because the consent of Parliament had to be obtained.

A motive for adoption, as a result of these various demand factors cannot be met, however, unless there is a favourable supply situation, i.e. *the ability to adopt*. The turnpike trust could not be costed in conventional terms, because it was not an innovation that could be sold in the open market. Nevertheless, there was a financial cost attached to its adoption. The ability to adopt depended upon the availability of capital to cover the expense of promoting the Act of Parliament, and of loaning money to a new trust on the credit of its toll for road repair programmes.

A period of rapid adoption of an innovation can now thus be interpreted as the result of the convergence of demand and supply forces: a strong motive for adoption, coupled with the ability to adopt. Similarly, periods of slower adoption are characterized by weaker forces on one or both sides. Diffusion may be delayed because there is insufficient capital to pay for widespread adoption, or because there is insufficient need for the innovation. It may also be delayed because of the third force: *direct resistance*. The novelty of the turnpike trust, particularly as it conflicted with the accepted means of road repair by the parish system, could have resulted in direct opposition, expressing itself locally, or through the Parliamentary process.

Diffusion: the Leading Sector

It has been suggested, initially by the Webbs (1920: 123–4) and again more recently (Albert 1972: 19) that this third reason, direct opposition, explains the length of the leading sector of trust diffusion, with its relatively low proportion of new trusts and total mileage. There was certainly scope for opposition both in Parliament, through the presentation of counterpetitions to turnpike bills and then the defeat of those bills, and outside Parliament in the form of riots and protests directed at existing trusts. However, the evidence shows that opposition was relatively limited, and certainly cannot be used as an explanatory factor.

The course of each turnpike bill through Parliament is recorded in detail in the Journals of both Houses. These Journals are procedural records of the business of Parliament, cataloguing the progress of each measure, and its eventual success or failure. Thus, when a bill was defeated, the event was recorded. The Journals reveal, however, that only five bills and petitions for bills were defeated in the entire period from 1665 to 1750. One of these was for a renewal bill, whilst three of the others were rejected in the 1690s.[1] Twice a bill for turnpiking roads in Islington was defeated, in 1694 (JHC 11: 45) and again in 1697 (JHC 11: 575), and two years later, a bill for the St John's Bridge to Faringdon road in Berkshire was voted out (JHC 12: 615). This does indicate that there was some initial opposition in Parliament to turnpike bills, even though four others did pass between 1696 and 1698, but it is certainly not enough to suggest concerted opposition beyond 1700. The proportion of bills defeated over the whole period to 1750 was very small—only 2·25 per cent of new trust measures, and 0·65 per cent of renewals.

Nevertheless, a rather larger number of bills and petitions for bills—53 in all—did fail to make the statute book. But 48 of these were not formally defeated: they disappeared at some stage in the Parliamentary process, probably because of lack of business time, or of promotion money in the first instance. Most of these were reintroduced and passed by Parliament soon after: 73 per cent within four years, and 66 per cent within only two years. Usually the new petition was identical with the first.

Hence, during the leading sector of turnpike trust diffusion, 16·5 per cent of the bills and petitions for bills initiated in Parliament failed to produce Acts. The failure rates for new and renewal measures were respectively 20·8 per cent and 10·4 per cent. In both cases this is a low proportion, but one that becomes quite insignificant in view of the fact that only five of the 53 failures were defeated. It is therefore not possible to sustain the argument that a hostile attitude in Parliament, except possibly in the 1690s, forestalled the more rapid adoption of the turnpike trust before 1750.

It is, however, possible that many potential turnpike schemes were never presented to Parliament because of local opposition. If this had been the case, then such opposition should have revealed itself when turnpike petitions and bills were actually read in Westminster. The normal way to do this was for the disaffected parties to present a counterpetition, stating their reasons for opposing the establishment of a turnpike trust. Few actually did so. The Journals reveal that before 1750, counterpetitions were presented against only 15 per cent of new trust bills and petitions, with the average number per measure affected being only 2·1. Fifty-seven counterpetitions were presented against 27 new trust bills, whilst the remaining 151 received none at all. The proportion of bills petitioned against before 1720 is marginally higher than in subsequent decades, but it is still less than a fifth (Table XV). Lack of information at the local level is an unlikely reason for such limited opposition, as the proceedings at Westminster were widely available through the Votes of Parliament. Cost was not a deterrent, as many small communities, often just several villages, petitioned in favour of, or for extensions to, proposed turnpike schemes. As many bills were supported in this way as were opposed. And if opposition existed, it could easily be voiced. The experience of river improvement bills demonstrates this. Between 1700 and 1730, a total of 156 counterpetitions were recorded in the Journals against 22 river bills—an average of 7·1 counterpetitions per bill. They came from villages and towns, individuals and groups, and are ample evidence that if such an innovation was controversial, then opposition could be mounted.

Outside Parliament, trusts were also uncontroversial. Although it has frequently been stated that turnpike riots were extensive (Webb 1920: 123, Ashton 1948: 44, Mantoux 1961: 115, Albert 1972: 26) there is little evidence of this. Riots have only been documented for parts of the West Country in the late 1720s and at isolated dates in the 1730s and 1740s, and at Leeds in the early 1750s. Their geographical extent was very limited, as was the number of trusts affected. It was mainly the Bristol, Gloucester, Hereford and Ross Turnpikes that suffered. The severity of the penalties imposed on rioters by Acts passed at this time has misled

Table XV

Petitions Presented to Parliament Concerning New Turnpike Bills, 1696–1750

	Numbers of petitions	Number of bills affected	Total number of bills	Proportion of bills affected
Counterpetitions				
Up to 1720	22	10	52	19 per cent
1721–30	20	8	57	14
1731–40	7	3	20	15
1741–50	8	6	49	12
	57	27	178	15
Support petitions				
Up to 1720	7	5	52	10 per cent
172–30	17	12	57	21
1731–40	1	1	20	5
1741–50	26	8	49	16
	51	26	178	15
Extension petitions				
Up to 1720	5	4	52	8 per cent
1721–30	12	10	57	18
1731–40	5	3	20	12
1741–50	10	8	49	16
	32	25	178	14

Source: Journals of the House of Commons.

historians into assuming that riots were more widespread than was actually the case.[2] One scholar who studied the incidence of riots and disturbances of all kinds in the first half of the eighteenth century made particular note of their limited extent, despite the volume of turnpike legislation (Isaac 1953: 120).

It is not surprising that disturbances were rare as turnpikes meant nothing to the poor unless they possessed a horse or cart, for pedestrians were allowed to go free. In many places they provided work. At Ledbury, for example, in 1740 'the meaner sort of people' had so changed their opinion of turnpikes that 'they look upon them now as their chief support, and without the employment they find under them, they and their families would go near perish' (Isaac, 120). Landowners too were not adversely affected: the improvement of a road damaged very little property, and when it did, each turnpike Act ensured that adequate compensation was paid. On the whole, local inhabitants stood to gain from improving roads and the transfer of income resulting from the shift of the cost of road repair to the road user. The widespread exemption from tolls for local traffic meant that many people became free riders on their own roads.[3]

River improvements, however, were in a different category. Direct interests were often at stake if the proposed navigation threatened the livelihood of mill-owners or fishermen. The fear of flooding, and the loss of land and damage to crops caused by the creation of a towpath concerned the landowning classes. These sorts of problems did not arise with a turnpike road. The counterpetitions that were presented against turnpike bills cover a range of complaints, but there were two common themes. The first was that the roads were considered to be quite adequate without the need of a toll: this accounted for 20 of the 57 counterpetitions presented up to 1750. The stage-coachmen and wagoners of Chippenham, for example, objected to the proposed Brentford Trust in 1717 in the following terms:

> 'that the several Towns and Parishes, in which the said Highways do lie, and which do contribute to the repairs thereof, have for some years past, not repaired the said Highways, according to the Laws now in Force; but suffered them to become ruinous, with a Design to exempt themselves, and lay the Burden and Charge on the Petitioners and others who travel the said Roads.' (JHC 18: 575)

A second common theme of counterpetitions—accounting for nine of the 57—was that an improved section of road would divert traffic away from, or into, a particular settlement, to the detriment of the inhabitants. This was the fear of the tradesmen of Kingston-upon-Thames, who objected to the proposed Leatherhead to Farnham Turnpike in 1758:

> 'the main Road now used from London through Kingston to Guildford, which is the ancient and direct Road to Portsmouth, will probably be totally diverted, and the Town of Kingston, which is now principally supported thereby, will be greatly injured.' (JHC 28: 113)

In many other cases, the cause of complaint was not identified. However, there were no counterpetitions which would support Adam Smith's later claim that counties near London campaigned against the extension of turnpikes into more distant regions, on the ground that the spread of accessibility would undermine their agricultural prosperity (Smith 1904: 147–8).

Opposition, and the grounds for opposition to turnpiking outside Parliament was strictly limited. There was no reason why Members of Parliament should react differently. Those who had agricultural and trading interests would gain from a network of improving roads. Perhaps more important was the fact that the turnpike trust was a simple and convenient means of maintaining and improving part of the national transport infrastructure by the use of local money and initiative. It thus enabled a very real national need to be met without depleting the resources of central government.

The third factor proposed by the analysis, that of resistance or opposition to the innovation, cannot therefore explain the length of the leading sector. The reasons for this must be sought in the operation of the other two factors. It is suggested that before 1750 the motive for adoption was strictly limited, due to the localization of pressure on the existing parish repair system.

The routes covered by the leading sector turnpike trusts, detailed in Appendix 1 and illustrated in Fig. 27, show that before 1750 the innovation was limited to certain important roads. They were mainly the roads leading to, and within 100 miles of the capital, and those around growing provincial cities and within expanding industrial areas. The turnpike road network in 1750 therefore had a strong London orientation, demonstrating the dominance of the capital's position in the economy, but with other concentrations around Bristol, in the West Midland region, and into Yorkshire and Durham. These were the roads on which traffic flows were heaviest, on which there was a high proportion of wheeled traffic, and hence those along which the motive for adoption of turnpiking schemes was strongest.

There are, however, significant variations in the time series before 1750. The number of new trusts established in a year rises to a peak in the mid-1720s, with 13 in 1726 and ten in 1727. It then declined to the earlier level of three or four a year in the 1730s and 1740s (Fig. 19). This sudden upturn represents the spread of the innovation outside its early London framework to the rich agricultural counties of the lower Severn Valley, and the nascent industrial areas in the West Midlands. In a brief burst of popularity, trusts were established to repair the roads around Bristol, whose trade at that time was 'prodigiously encreas'd in these last thirty years' according to Defoe; around the competing agricultural markets of Gloucester, Worcester and Hereford; and those in and near Birmingham.

In contrast, the 1730s and 1740s certainly show a decrease in the expansion of the innovation, although the overall trend from 1720 to 1750 is upward if the brief upturn of 1726–8 is ignored. It would be convenient to relate this apparent lull to the conventional view of an agricultural depression in these decades (Chambers and Mingay 1966: 41–2). However, this is unrealistic, for two reasons. Firstly it is quite probable that there was no general agricultural depression at this time. Agricultural prices were stable between 1730 and 1745, when they began to rise rapidly,[4] which combined with the spell of good weather and large harvests in these years (Ashton 1959: 18–21) should have made farmers and landowners more, not less prosperous. There seems little reason why agricultural traffic and landowners' propensity to invest in turnpike schemes should have declined.

Secondly, turnpike schemes were not concentrated in non-agricultural areas in the 1730s and 1740s. The majority of new trusts were still in rural areas, and only 20 of the 57 established between 1731 and 1750 were on coalfields, in industrializing areas, or in the immediate vicinity of growing towns.[5] This is not to deny that some important new regional turnpike networks did develop in such areas. In the early 1740s, six new trusts were established in the Yorkshire textiles region, and between 1743 and 1750 seven were set up for roads in the South Durham coalfield. Most of the late new leading sector trusts were, however, in rural areas. It is unlikely that the ability to adopt the innovation before 1750 was impeded by agricultural depression. Direct resistance is not a suitable explanation either. It was rather the limited need for the turnpike trust which underlay its slow diffusion, the motive for adoption being restricted to the more important main routes.

The Turnpike Boom

After 1750, the rate of adoption increases rapidly, with between 15 and 20 new trusts being established each year (Fig. 19). This boom is closely related to a quickening of the pace of economic change in Britain at this time. Although the turnpike boom itself has previously been recognized in the literature (Webb 1920: 124, Albert 1972: 51), its relationship to the onset of sustained growth in the eighteenth century economy has not. From the end of the 1740s, however, both demand and supply forces were strengthened: the motive to adopt, and the ability to adopt both became more pronounced.

There were two turning points in the progress of eighteenth century economic growth: one in the late 1740s, the other—the traditional 'take-off'—in the early 1780s. Nearly every economic indicator shows a pronounced, and sustained upturn at both these times, but it is the earlier one that is of interest here. Strong demand-inducing forces were becoming operative within the British economy by 1750. Population began to increase: growth had been negligible before 1741, but then rose at a rate of 4–7 per cent per decade through to 1781. This growth was not evenly distributed: there was a marked rise in the proportion of the population living in urban areas. It is estimated that about 13 per cent of the people of England and Wales lived in towns of over 5,000 in 1701. By 1751, this proportion had risen to about 15–16 per cent, and in 1801, it reached 25 per cent. The important point is not the absolute accuracy of these figures, but the trend of increased urban growth after mid-century. Manchester, for example, grew from 7,000 in 1700 to 17,000 in 1750 and then 84,000 by 1801. Liverpool expanded from 5,000 to 20,000 and then 78,000, and Birmingham from 15,000 to 30,000 and 74,000. London also grew rapidly from 550,000 to 700,000 by 1750, and then at a slightly faster rate, to reach 900,000 by 1801. Increasing urban size was reflected in the growth of traffic flows to towns, providing fuel and building materials, as well as food. Even if output had been stable, this shift of population ensured that a greater proportion, and hence increasing volume, would enter into internal trade to towns, with much of it being carried overland.

Agricultural and industrial output did, however, increase very markedly in the second half of the eighteenth century. Although the statistical indicators are weak, the trend is again clear. There are no adequate measures of corn production, but the absence of large corn imports until after 1800, and of net imports at all until the late 1760s, suggests that production was keeping pace with the growth of population. Wool and mutton output certainly rose rapidly. The available industrial statistics conform to a similar pattern. The production of the West Riding woollen industry grew at a rate of about 8 per cent per decade between 1701 and 1741, and then at 13–14 per cent between 1741 and 1772. The output curve of textile printed goods is similar. Coal and the metal industries provide a wide-ranging support for the upturn. Iron production, for example, grew at a rate of about 4 per cent per decade over the long period from 1570 to 1750, virtually stagnating at 0·3 per cent per decade for the last 30 years, and then increasing remarkably to attain 50 per cent decadal growth from 1750 to 1820. There is also very definite evidence, from the Port Books, of a marked rise in the volume of British foreign trade between 1745 and 1760.[6]

The available evidence of eighteenth century British economic trends suggests, therefore, that growth was initiated in the 1740s, prior to the general expansion of the 1780s. But this growth did not follow a 'leading sector' pattern: it was not concentrated in a few industries and regions. It was a process of general expansion, of balanced growth, pervasive throughout the economy and country. It was reflected in the demand for transport, and the satisfaction of that need by increasing flows of internal trade—from country to town, within and between industrial areas, from producer to consumer and from port to hinterland. Hence a widespread motive for the adoption of the turnpike trust was not felt until the late 1740s and 1750s, a consideration which goes a long way towards explaining the shape of the diffusion curve.

The demand for turnpike trusts could not be met, however, without a favourable supply situation, i.e. the ability to adopt. This favourable supply situation existed, and improved from the late 1740s, as industrial and agricultural output rose. A marked feature of all the price indices that have been constructed for the eighteenth century is the rise in agricultural price levels from 1745. Farmers were becoming more prosperous because they sold their increasing output at a higher price, and because two important cost factors, wages and rents, climbed less quickly (Chambers and Mingay 1966: 110). Landlords gained from increased rents after enclosure, whilst those who did not enclose still gained from this source as rent levels followed prices after 1760. Those who had trade and manufacturing interests benefited from the increasing level of economic activity. Even though industrial prices did not rise until the 1770s, rising production still meant increased returns with the less rapid rise in wages and the generally low cost of capital equipment.

This general increase in wealth is significant. For the farmer, landlord or manufacturer as investor, the loan of money to a turnpike trust was a reasonably safe and attractive proposition, paying between four and five per cent interest. However, for the same men as producers, such loans represented an effective reinvestment of capital for infrastructure development, something which had to be financed by the local economy if it was to take place at all. Ward's systematic analysis of canal investment in the eighteenth century has shown that these companies drew on a far wider range of sources than has hitherto been supposed, with landlords playing a rather less important part than had been assumed (Ward 1974). It is evident that turnpike promoters and supporters were also drawn from a wide range of interests.[7]

Hence the period after 1750 saw the convergence of two sets of forces, on the supply and demand side, which were favourable to an increase in the rate of adoption and diffusion of the turnpike trust. The result was a large rise in the mileage of turnpike road, from 3,386 in England alone in 1750, to 14,965 miles in England and Wales by 1770. The number of trusts rose from 143 to 519 (Figs 19 and 20). Before concluding this discussion of the turnpike boom, however, some attention must be given to two other factors—for the sake of tradition, the rate of interest, and for continuity, the level of resistance to new trusts in this period.

The effect of changes in the rate of interest on the level of new turnpike schemes seems to have been minimal. From 1720 to 1780, rates were at a generally low level, between $3\frac{1}{2}$ and $4\frac{1}{2}$ per cent, with no discernible trend. They were as low in 1750 as in 1720, and this had little or no impact on the shape of the diffusion curve. The second factor, however, is of greater interest. It might be expected that the much increased volume of turnpike activity after 1750 would have resulted in some concerted opposition. This, however, was not the case. Between 1752 and 1754, for example, only three bills failed out of a total of 100 new trust and renewal bills. Between 1765 and 1767, 14 failed, out of a total of 94. None were defeated, and most were reintroduced within a very short time. Outside opposition by counterpetition was not as strong as before, whereas over a third of the successful new trust bills in a random sample received support or extension petitions (Table XVI).

Table XVI
Turnpike Bill Petitions, 1751–70

	Number of petitions	Number of bills affected	Total number of bills in sample	Per cent of bills affected
Counterpetitions	3	2	38	5
Support petitions	15	9		40
Extensions petitions	10	6		34

Between 1748 and 1772, a total of 687 turnpike road Acts were passed, both for new trusts and the renewal of the terms of established ones. This mass of legislation comprised a large proportion of the total amount passed by Parliament between those dates—in fact, over 18 per cent (Table XVII). This figure gives some indication of the quantitative importance of turnpike bills, the massive efforts made locally to improve roads, and the positive attitude of Parliament, which was prepared to spend the time considering each case. Although its direct influence was limited to the passage of the various general highway laws, the importance of a form of Parliamentary procedure enabling such prominence to be given to private bills should not be underestimated as a factor encouraging economic development in the eighteenth century.

The initiation and importance of the boom in turnpiking from 1750 is explained by the convergence of two sets of forces. It is the coincidence of strong 'directive' forces—demand-inducing forces providing a motive for adoption; and powerful 'permissive' forces, enabling capital to be released to support the adoption of the innovation, which is the critical point. Interest rates were favourable, but cannot be considered a driving force. Opposition in Parliament and from outside was negligible, with the result that a mass of turnpike legislation passed unhindered into the statute book. The resulting turnpike road network that developed was not localized, or limited to certain routes, as was the case up to 1750. The general nature of the forces involved ensured that it spread all over Britain, in waves of spatial diffusion which are examined more closely in Chapter 6.

The Lagging Sector

The underlying economic conditions which produced the turnpike boom continued to be favourable after 1770, and particularly as the rate of economic growth accelerated in the mid-1780s. Despite this there is a marked decrease in the number of new trusts established in the 1770s, although there were later some important increases, corresponding to · peaks in the trade cycle, in the 1790s, around 1810, and in the 1820s (Fig. 19). This lagging sector was long, and it accounted for 45 per cent of the eventual total of new trusts. The proportion of mileage involved, however, was lower—only 32 per cent (Figs 20 and 21). This was due to the smaller size of lagging sector trusts, many of which were responsible for the less used secondary roads linking the major arteries of the network. This does suggest that by 1770, the height of adoption of the innovation was being reached in many areas.

Table XVII

Turnpike Acts as a Proportion of all Legislation Passed by Parliament, 1748–72

	A	B	C	D	E	F	G
1748	65	34	31	7	3	4	11
1749	100	52	48	18	7	11	18
1750	94	40	54	7	3	4	8
1751	105	59	46	17	9	8	16
1752	101	60	41	27	23	4	27
1753	148	101	47	51	38	13	35
1754	81	42	39	19	12	7	24
1755	115	60	55	24	19	5	21
1756	148	94	54	36	24	12	25
1757	128	69	59	24	15	9	19
1758	130	78	42	25	17	8	19
1759	131	71	60	25	22	3	19
1760	127	59	68	21	14	7	17
1761	91	44	47	17	13	4	19
1762	156	87	69	38	27	11	24
1763	105	59	46	22	12	10	21
1764	176	93	83	33	21	12	19
1765	223	108	115	50	32	18	23
1766	196	102	94	28	19	9	14
1767	223	106	117	31	15	16	14
1768	135	63	72	20	11	9	15
1769	307	95	112	38	20	18	12
1770	210	114	96	45	25	20	22
1771	202	99	113	35	16	19	17
1772	255	110	145	29	14	15	13

Total number of Acts — 3752
Total number of turnpike Acts — 687
Proportion of the total = 18·3 per cent

A = B + C Total number of Acts passed each year
B = Public Acts
C = Private Acts
D = E + F Total number of turnpike Acts passed each year, for England, Wales and Scotland
E = New trust Acts
F = Renewal and amendment Acts
G = D as percentage of A, proportion of Acts passed each year which were turnpike Acts, expressed as percentage

In a classic case of the operation of the diffusion process, however, the decrease in adoptions would come closer to the eventual ceiling of penetration. The timing of the decrease in the early 1770s, rather than at a date closer to 1836, is thus critical. It may have been influenced by the financial crisis of 1772–3, when money was scarce and there was a run on the banks. However, the downward trend from 1768, and the continued fall in the 1770s and 1780s would suggest that, at the most, this was a minor contributory factor. The most probable cause was the diversion of resources and effort at this time towards competing projects: notably enclosure and canals. The former provided an important opportunity for agricultural investment, particularly in view of the rise of rents in the 1760s and 1770s, as landlords took advantage of the increased prosperity of their tenants. The latter diverted the attention, enterprise and resources of the urban and commercial communities towards a potentially more profitable and efficient innovation.

The number of enclosure Acts passed by Parliament rises to an eighteenth century peak of 660 in the 1770s, from 385 in the 1760s, and only 137 in the 1750s (Fig. 22). The amount of land enclosed varied in each case and not all the Acts were implemented immediately, if at all. Large areas were enclosed by agreement, for which an Act was unnecessary. Thus the graph is only a rough guide to the amount of land and investment involved in enclosure schemes. Even so, the sheer volume

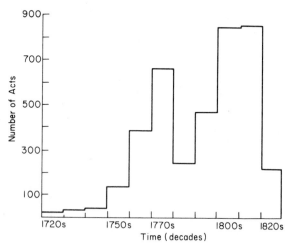

Fig. 22. The volume of the enclosure Acts, 1720s–1820s. *Source*: based on Deane and Cole 1962: 95.

of enclosure Acts passed in the 1770s is impressive evidence of a diversion of landlord capital into agricultural investment, augmented as it was by continuing expenditure on fencing, drainage, new buildings and other necessary improvements after the enclosures of the 1760s. It has been estimated that the cost of enclosure and subsequent improvement was between £1·8 and £2·4 million in the years to 1770, and between £3·4 and £4·7 million from 1770 to 1789 (Holderness 1971: 166).

There were sound economic reasons for the popularity of enclosure in the 1770s. Not only were returns to landlords increasing with rent rises, but a more efficient framework for agricultural production enabled farmers to take advantage of the accelerating rise in prices as population increased number of enclosure and turnpike schemes (Figs 19 and 22). terms, enclosure should follow turnpiking schemes. An improved road system eroded the position of farmers close to the market, and enhanced that of farmers in more remote places. In both cases, any improvement in efficiency was a sensible response. Although enclosure itself did not guarantee efficiency, it did provide a basis for more efficient farming.

The interrelationship of canal and turnpike road development is also of great interest. In the prosperous period of the 1790s, there was sufficient speculative capital to finance not only the 'Canal Mania', but also an increased number of enclosure and turnpike schemes (Figs 19 and 22). However, in the late 1760s and 1770s, this does not seem to have been the case. It was then that the widespread diffusion of the canal was initiated, with the start of the great trunk-canal building programme (Fig. 3).

Several large schemes were begun in the late 1760s, as the number of new turnpike trust establishments started to fall. The Staffordshire and Worcestershire Canal was under construction from 1766 to 1772, the Birmingham Canal between 1768 and 1772, and the Trent and Mersey between 1766 and 1777. The Coventry Canal was begun in 1768, although construction stopped in 1772 before being resumed in the 1780s, and the first part of the Oxford Canal was completed between 1769 and 1777. The first stages of the massive Leeds and Liverpool Canal were completed between 1770 and 1777. Both the Droitwich and the Forth and Clyde Canals were begun in 1768. A little later, in 1772, work started on the Chester Canal, which was finished in 1778. The Huddersfield and Stroudwater Canals were started in 1774, the latter completed five years later. The Birmingham system expanded in the mid-1770s, with the Dudley and Stourbridge Canals (1776) and the Birmingham and Fazeley of 1778. There was, therefore, a great deal of strategic canal construction, begun and continued as the turnpike boom was coming to an end.

The rate of growth of the economy, and hence internal trade, was maintained at a high level throughout the early and mid-1770s, not falling until the decline of foreign trade during the American War in the late 1770s and early 1780s. Turnpike toll receipts reflect the slackening of growth between 1775 and 1784, but do show a large rise in the volume of traffic on turnpike roads in the southern and midland counties between 1775 and 1779 (Ward 1794: 165). It was not, therefore, adverse economic conditions which ended the turnpike boom in the early 1770s—rather, most of the important routes had already been turnpiked, and attention was diverted to competing projects.

After the temporary recession of the late 1770s and early 1780s, the economy began to expand rapidly again as it experienced Rostow's 'take-off' into sustained growth. Internal trade expanded in step, and this brought new demands for an improved transport infrastructure. The heavy basic products of industrial expansion were those that were more efficiently moved in bulk by water, rather than by road and so a second canal building programme was started. Between 1780 and 1815, over £15 million was raised by canal companies, compared with only £2,149,000 by the earlier generation between 1755 and 1780 (Ward 1974: 74). In the 'Canal Mania' between 1791 and 1796, 51 new canal companies were established by Acts of Parliament, with an authorized capital of over £7·5 million (Dyos and Aldcroft 1969: 94). John Phillips, writing in 1803, claimed that 90 of the 165 canal Acts obtained since 1758 had been to serve collieries, and a further 47 for iron, lead and copper mines and works (1803: 598).

According to Dyos and Aldcroft, 'the boom of the 1790s was no more than an uninhibited acknowledgement by the investing classes that canals were the only form of transport that could accommodate this expansion . . .' (1969: 94). This was not so. From the mid-1780s, the number of new turnpike schemes also rose steadily, and although not achieving the levels of the turnpike boom of 30 and 40 years earlier, there was a significant upsurge (Fig. 19). Why, if a ceiling of expansion had been reached in the 1770s, should this have been so? The answer is partly that there was a genuine need for new trusts in all areas with the unprecedented level of economic activity. Once again turnpike schemes were initiated all over the country. However, a large proportion of new trusts were in those areas without an existing dense network, such as Lancashire, Yorkshire and Durham, where the new economic growth was concentrated, in the coal, mining and cotton textile industries. There were also a number of new trusts in Kent, linking the strategic war-time Channel ports to the existing turnpike roads.[8]

Two other indicators, the total volume of turnpike legislation and the investment by trusts in the turnpike system, do not follow the same course. In neither case did the general level of activity fall after 1770. Continued growth in the economy required the maintenance and development of existing highway resources. The total volume of turnpike legislation continued to rise unabated as existing trusts sought to renew their terms (Fig. 23). Total annual investment in the system did not fall either: it probably rose slightly each year after 1770, with a more rapid annual increase from the late 1780s. As traffic flows increased, and wheeled traffic became more prominent, continued investment in road improvements—widening, shortening, lowering and resurfacing—was all the more necessary.[9]

The last turnpike trusts, one in Lancashire, one in Yorkshire, and two short roads in Sussex, were not set up until 1836. In general a fairly stable level of new schemes prevailed throughout the first three decades of the nineteenth century, although there were marked cyclical fluctuations. The final downward trend came after 1830, as the maximum level of penetration was reached. There was relatively rapid economic expansion throughout this period, seemingly unchecked by the French wars. This is reflected in the high number of turnpike schemes sanctioned in the 1790s, around 1810 and in the mid-1820s. These peaks concur with peaks in the business cycle whereas the troughs of new trust adoptions coincide with downturns of each cycle: in the late 1790s, 1803–4, 1816, and the early 1820s (Gayer et al., 1953).

The diffusion of the steam railway began in the 1820s. The early lines were, like the early turnpike roads, short and disconnected, but in a remarkably short time, the railway spread widely. In the 1830s, long trunk lines were promoted and constructed (Fig. 3.) Nine hundred and fifty-five miles were sanctioned in 1836, and 1,023 miles were opened between 1839 and 1841 (Mathias 1969: 279–81). Already, in 1839 the Select Committee appointed to examine the effect of the railways on turnpike trusts was gloomy:

'. . . . although the lines of Turnpike Road running parallel to Steam communication are less frequented, it appears that nearly all Roads or Highways leading to stations . . . have increased in their traffic,

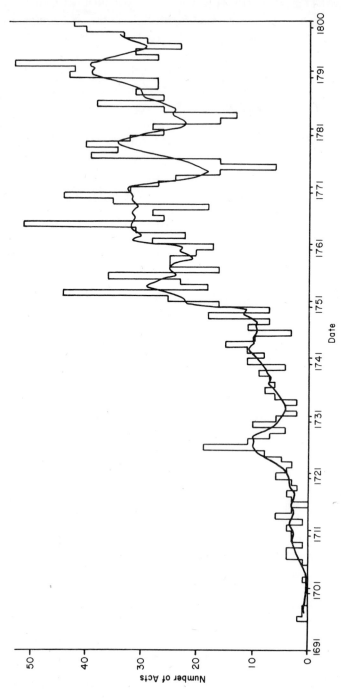

Fig. 23. Annual totals of turnpike Acts passed in the eighteenth century. This graph includes both new trust and renewal Acts. The annual totals have been smoothed by a five-year moving mean.

although the aggregate of this increase may not probably be found equal to the amount of the decrease on the lines of Road first mentioned.'

They concluded:

'This condition of the Turnpike Trusts is not likely to be improved by the Railroads already formed. There is every reason to believe that an extension of Railroads will take place every year. . . .' (BPP 1839 (295) IX 369: iii–iv)

5. Notes

1. The renewal bill was for trust 8 in 1726 (JHC 20: 693). The fourth new trust bill defeated was for the Bedford to Market Harborough road in 1750 (JHC 25: 993). Most of this road was turnpiked in 1752 (175).

2. Acts were passed in 1728, 1732 and 1735 to punish turnpike rioters. The most severe penalties prescribed by these Acts were respectively: three months imprisonment, transportation and death. (1 Geo. II, c. 19, 5 Geo. II c. 33, 8 Geo. II, c. 20.)

3. Toll exemptions are discussed in Chapter 8, pp. 204–6.

4. Deane and Cole's re-examination of the price indices does not reveal a significant decline between 1730 and 1745, and Dr P. K. O'Brien's new index shows a stable price level for both agricultural and industrial products over this period. I am grateful to Dr O'Brien for permission to quote his findings. His index is based on the original Beveridge data, but uses a wider range of commodity prices than the Schumpeter–Gilboy indices, and is reweighted.

5. Trusts nos 92, 93, 95, 96, 107–10, 112, 113, 120, 122, 123, 126, 129, 130, 132, 135, 139, 142.

6. These statistics are drawn from Chambers and Mingay 1966; Deane and Cole 1962; Mathias 1969. I am grateful to Mr Philip Riden for supplying me with the iron output figures.

7. Albert (1972) has examined this point in his sixth chapter: his preliminary analysis confirms that turnpike investment came from a wide variety of backers.

8. Figure 32 plots the location of lagging sector trusts. The new Kent trusts were nos 635, 645, 670, 674, and 703.

9. Ginarlis (1970) has made an ambitious attempt to estimate actual levels of investment in road and waterway facilities from 1750 to 1850. The turnpike road estimates are not entirely accurate, but the trend is plain enough. The efforts of trusts to improve their roads are discussed in Chapters 9 and 10.

6

The Spatial Diffusion of the Turnpike System

A spatial analysis of the spread of the turnpike system is a natural companion of the investigation of the time series. The interdependence of the temporal and spatial diffusion processes is already apparent. Various elements of the time series cannot be understood without reference to their location in space, whereas the spatial development of the system cannot be appreciated without first examing the temporal processes which underlay its construction. It is this interaction of process and form which is of great interest to geographers today (Harvey 1969: 129) and which provides, in this context, the meeting point between the fields of the economic historian and the historical geographer.

Several problems need to be considered. Where were the trusts in each sector of the diffusion curve located? Were the large number of trusts established in the turnpike boom evenly spread throughout the country, or were they concentrated in particular areas? How did the innovation spread from one area to another? Did it produce a diffuse and unconnected system, or did it form an integrated network of turnpike roads? Only this last question has been tackled before, and in this there is some disagreement. The Webbs took a 'pessimistic' line (1920: 125), and despite an uncharacteristic lack of evidence, their view has been accepted by many later authors (Smith 1968: 177, Mathias 1969: 165). Paul Mantoux, in his pioneer work on the Industrial Revolution, was far more 'optimistic'. His belief has been partially vindicated by Albert, who showed that turnpike schemes were well co-ordinated and almost continuous on the main roads to London by 1750 (1972: 30–56).

This conflict of views, as well as the remaining problems which have not been investigated, is good reason for a clear identification, analysis and interpretation of the spread of the turnpike trust in the eighteenth century. It is surprising that it has not been done before, in view of the complete record of the diffusion pattern that survives in the form of the turnpike Acts. The discussion will begin with the second of these three tasks. The analysis of spatial diffusion processes will provide a theoretical background to serve as a framework for the stages of identification and interpretation.

Spatial Diffusion Processes

There are two main types of spatial diffusion process: expansion and cascade or hierarchical diffusion. *Expansion diffusion* is a spatially continuous process, describing the spread of an innovation through a region or country from one area to another. The likelihood of adoption is a function of distance from the innovating centre or centres, because adoption is dependent upon contact with or demonstration of the benefits to be gained from adopters in close proximity to potential adopters. Such a pattern of adoptions is known as the demonstration or 'neighbourhood' effect. However, not all innovations diffuse in this manner. Some, such as those adopted by towns, follow a pattern of *hierarchical diffusion*. Innovations dependent upon a certain threshold size of population or urban area for their successful adoption and operation tend to diffuse down the urban hierarchy, from larger to smaller centres.

In the case of the turnpike trust, there is good reason for supposing that both these diffusion effects may have applied. The benefits of adopting a trust to maintain a section of road would have been most apparent to those parishes in proximity to an established trust: therefore expansion diffusion should have operated. However, as turnpiking was a response to the deterioration of road surfaces brought about by high traffic flows, such as those generated by towns, then a hierarchical diffusion pattern would become apparent as towns expanded, and parishes in proximity to them became less able to cope. Turnpiking would, therefore, spread from around the largest city, down the urban hierarchy, at the same time as being adopted around and between smaller centres in close proximity to the large towns. The size and distance effects in innovation diffusion must therefore be combined to provide a comprehensive analytical framework.[1]

Another point must be made. The deterministic approach implicit in these general models of the spatial diffusion process must be relaxed in favour of a probabilistic one. The processes described guided, rather than rigidly determined, the pattern of diffusion. Elements of randomness are always apparent in a diffusion process—the simplifying assumptions of the uniform plan and complete rationality are invalid in reality. Variations in the effectiveness of the parish repair system, due to factors additional to size of traffic flow, have already been highlighted.[2] Different sizes of parish and of population, and the uneven distribution of hills and deep clay stretches would partially upset the neat patterns predicted by this general analysis of spatial diffusion processes.

Identification and Interpretation

The spatial development of the turnpike road system in the years up to 1720 is shown in Fig. 24. At this date trusts were scattered fairly widely, but already a coherent pattern—although hardly a network—was beginning to emerge. The dominant influence of London is certainly apparent, with lines of turnpikes on the roads to the north, north-west and south of the capital. The scatter outside this pattern was due to the random elements of urgent cases of adoption elsewhere. The first 12 trusts, established between 1696 and 1708, were widely distributed and in all but one case (6), they were more than 18 miles from London. Only three were actually joined (8, 9, 13).

The Gloucester to Birdlip Hill Justice Trust of 1698 (5) had jurisdiction over the steep Birdlip and Crickley Hills on the Cotswold scarp. The Reigate to Crawley Trust of 1697 (4) and the Cherhill to Studley Bridge Trust of 1708 (12) were also established to repair hilly stretches on main roads. The busy cloth trade of Devizes, relying on wagons for transport, was the reason for the appearance of the trust there in 1707. (10). The Worcester to Droitwich Trust (25) and the Talke to Tittensor Trust in north Staffordshire (27), were both set up in 1714 to repair roads damaged by heavy industrial traffic: salt sledges from Droitwich to the River Severn at Worcester, and coal and iron ore carts around Newcastle. Both the Bath (11) and Tunbridge Wells (15) Trusts were a response to heavy seasonal tourist traffic.

The London-based orientation is, however, the most notable feature of this early map. Nearly a quarter of all new trusts established before 1720 were located within ten miles of London, half were within 30 miles, and two-thirds within 40 miles. The importance of London's external relations is the major theme underlying the pattern, with a marked distance–decay function in the rate of adoption from the capital clearly in evidence (Fig. 25). This pattern did not only develop in response to the greater quantitative flows of traffic: it reflected a qualitative factor as well. Wheeled

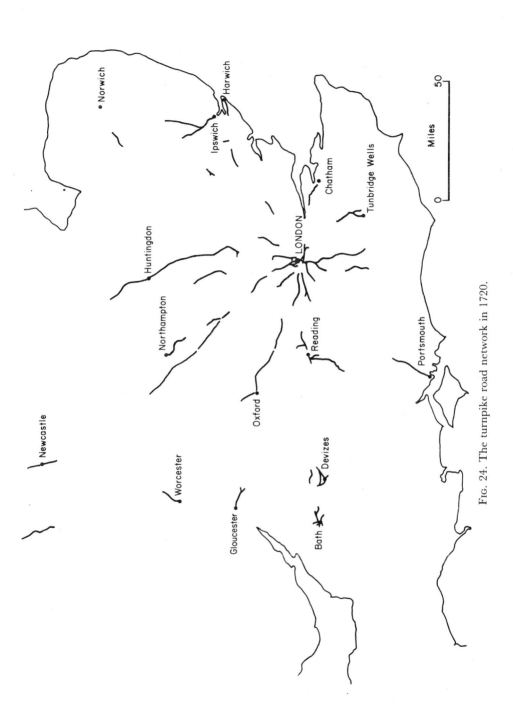

Fig. 24. The turnpike road network in 1720.

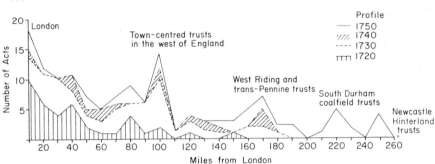

Fɪɢ. 25. Innovation profiles, 1720–50. This diagram plots the number of new trust Acts against distance from London. The Acts are aggregated into 10-mile interval groups. Distance from London is a straight-line measurement taken from the end of each trust that was closest to the capital.

traffic was widely in use in the south by this time, particularly in the vicinity of the capital and surrounding towns. Many turnpike petitions claimed that it was this type of traffic that was most damaging to road surfaces, or that the surfaces themselves inhibited the wagon trade.[3] Poor roads disrupted the intricate network of regular coach and carrier services to the capital, and delayed the wagons transporting manufactured and agricultural goods. The result was that the main roads to London formed the most important part of the early turnpike system.

The further development of the system up to 1750 is illustrated in two maps (Figs 26 and 27). In the three decades after 1720, the number of trusts and mileage of turnpike road around London increased, but the network spread over a far wider area, at the same time descending the urban hierarchy to surround cities such as Bristol, Birmingham, Manchester and Leeds. Both processes of spatial diffusion can be seen in operation.

In 1730, the London-based pattern is still clearly dominant, but a considerable amount of coverage by new trusts had formed a more articulate turnpike system. This system was best developed on the roads to the north of the capital, few routes to the south having been turnpiked. It was the important overland routes from the growing industrial areas of Yorkshire, Staffordshire and the Birmingham plateau, and those from the ports of Liverpool, Bristol, Harwich and Portsmouth, that had attracted the innovation. Road traffic flows on these routes was of great importance, because of the lack of a substitute means of transport. To the south of London, there were not only few large centres of population or production, but there was also a short and reasonably safe sea passage to

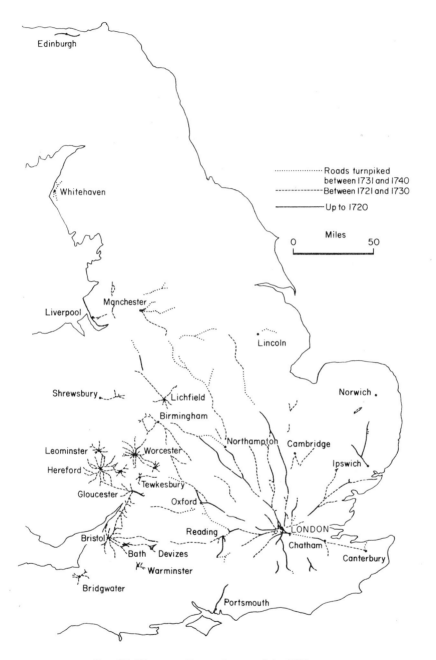

FIG. 26. The turnpike road network in 1740.

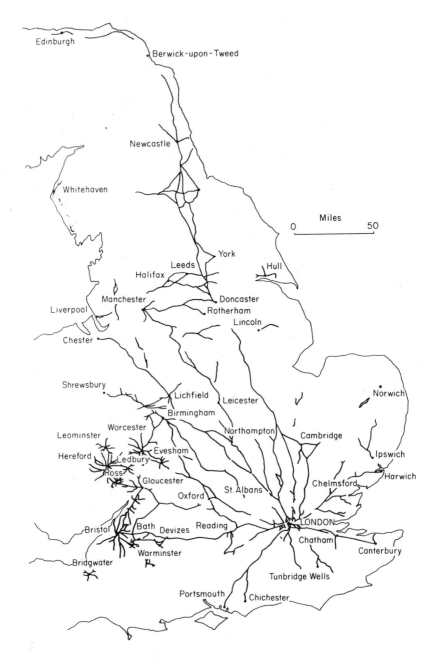

Edinburgh

Berwick-upon-Tweed

Newcastle

Whitehaven

Miles
0   50

York

Leeds
Halifax   Hull

Manchester   Doncaster
Liverpool   Rotherham
          Lincoln
Chester

Shrewsbury   Norwich
          Lichfield
          Leicester
          Birmingham
Leominster   Worcester   Northampton   Cambridge
Hereford   Ledbury   Evesham   Ipswich
Ross   Harwich
          Gloucester   Chelmsford
          Oxford   St. Albans
          Bristol   Bath   Devizes   Reading   LONDON
          Warminster   Chatham   Canterbury
Bridgwater
          Tunbridge Wells
          Portsmouth   Chichester

FIG. 27. The turnpike road network in 1750.

the Thames. Although towns within 15 or 20 miles of London, such as Tonbridge, Dorking and Reigate were well provided with land carrier services, those nearer the sea coast relied heavily on coastal shipping (Andrews 1954: 145–6). Much of the corn grown in eastern Kent, for example, was shipped by hoy to London (Baker 1970).

In the mid-1720s, a second important centre of turnpiking emerged in the west of England, in the Severn Valley. In 1726, trusts were established to repair the roads around Gloucester (59, 64), Tewkesbury (62) and Worcester (60). Trusts for Bristol (69) and Warminster (73) followed in 1727, for Evesham in 1728 (78), Leominster in 1729 (81) and Bridgwater (88) and Hereford (85) in 1730. These were all extensive 'town-centred' trusts controlling all the main routes of each town. They formed instant local networks, covering many miles of highway. The three largest were the Worcester Trust with 76 miles, the Bristol Trust with 109 miles, and the Hereford Trust with 118 miles. In this respect they were far bigger than the average (Table XII). They were also true urbanocentric innovations, and followed a roughly hierarchical diffusion pattern, but within a limited geographical area.

The spread of turnpiking into this region represents the growth of an important secondary innovation centre on the fringe of the first wave of adoptions. It is shown on the innovation profile for 1730, as a second peak between 90 and 110 miles from London (Fig. 25). It also composes a significant temporary upturn in the time series (Fig. 19). The Severn Valley was an important trade artery from the Birmingham Plateau, where several trusts were established at the same time (54, 71, 72), to the ports of Gloucester and Bristol. It was a rich agricultural area, with a number of competing markets in towns such as Hereford, Leominster and Worcester that adopted town-centred turnpike trusts. The innovation was thus spreading away from its original centre around London, down the urban hierarchy to Bristol and Birmingham.

Bristol, at this time, was England's second and Britain's third largest city, described by Defoe as 'the greatest, the richest, and the best port of trade in Great Britain, London only excepted'. Its external relations were, like those of the capital, of wide extent:

'. . . the shopkeepers in Bristol who in general are all wholesale men, have so great an inland trade among all the western counties, that they maintain carriers just as the London tradesmen do, to all the principal counties and towns from Southampton in the south, even to the banks of the Trent in the north.' (Defoe 1962 Vol. 2: 36)

F

Its trade was growing, and two new quays were completed in December 1725. In 1712, there were 4,311 houses in the city, and by 1735, 5,701 (Latimer 1893: 149). Its population reached about 50,000 by 1750. This growth was reflected by an expansion of road traffic in and around the city, encouraging the development of a local turnpike network, but the reason for the prominence of some of the other town-centred trusts is less obvious. Although Worcester was a city of over 10,000 people by 1750, and an important river port on the Severn, Hereford was less than half the size. Hereford was, however, an important market for an intensively farmed agricultural area. Overland communication in the country had long been dificult, and its turnpiking scheme was an attempt to accommodate the heavy local wagon traffic in hops, fruit, corn and cider, and prevent the loss of this trade to neighbouring markets at Ledbury, Leominster, Ross and Worcester.[4]

Another interesting feature of the 1730 map is the northward extension of turnpiking. Several new trusts were established on important interregional routes, ultimately leading to London: on the Great North Road in Nottingham (61), the future A6 road to Manchester in Leicestershire (53) and Derby (50), the Chester and Carlisle road in Staffordshire (80) and Lancashire (66, 67) and the Holyhead road in Shropshire. The Liverpool to Prescot Trust (63) was the result of pressure by the Liverpool merchant community after the price of coal from the big Prescot Hall colliery had risen sharply during the wet winter of 1725 because of carriage difficulties on bad roads (Barker and Harris 1954: 14). Their petition to Parliament, however, stressed the regional rather than the local interest:

> '. . . the Road from Liverpool to Prescot aforesaid is very much used in the carriage of coals to the Towns of Wigan, Bolton, Rochdale, Warrington and Manchester, and the counties of York, Derby, and other Eastern Ports of the Kingdom, in the carriage of Wool, Cotton, Malt and all other Merchants Goods; whereby the several Parts of the said Road are so very deep, and other Parts so narrow, that coaches, waggons and other Wheel-carriages cannot pass through the same. . . .' (JHC 20: 508)

In contrast to the 1720s, the 1730s was not a decade of much new activity (Fig. 19). Nevertheless by 1740, a certain amount of expansion had taken place within the turnpike network of the south, especially on the main London routes. A second route through Oxford had been turnpiked (98), a final connecting link had been made in the Coventry to

Northampton road (106), and the renewal Acts of two trusts on the Kent road had completed the turnpike route to Canterbury (22, 34). More significant were the extensions to the network in the north, on the A6 route through Derbyshire (102), and on three trans-Pennine roads (93, 95, 96). The effect of the trade between east and west described in the Liverpool petition, and the growth of local coal traffic, was also being felt by the parishes and trading communities in the hills. In 1735, the 'Principal Gentlemen, Owners, Occupiers of Lands and inhabitants of Manchester, and the several Townships of Newton, Failsworth and Oldham' claimed in a petition to Parliament that:

> 'the Roads . . . are very much travelled through, being Part of the Common Highway from Manchester to the trading Towns of Huthersfield and Wakefield; and that by Reason of the Nature of the soil, and of many heavy carriages frequently passing through the same from the several Coal and Canned Pits contiguous thereto, to the said Town of Manchester, the said Roads are become so ruinous that in the Winter season, and often times in Summer, many parts thereof are unpassable for Waggons, Carts and other Wheel Carriages, and very dangerous for Travellers. . . .' (JHC 22: 372)

In the 1740s, these trans-Pennine turnpike routes extended considerably (108, 112, 113) as the textile industries of Lancashire and Yorkshire developed (Fig. 27). A petition supporting the Doncaster to Saltersbrook turnpike bill in 1741 gives some indication of the traffic on these roads:

> '. . . great Quantities of manufactured Goods, Cheese, Salt and Potatoes are carried from Manchester, Barnsley and Parts Adjacent to Doncaster on Horses, and return loaded with Hemp, Flax, and German Yarn, for Manufacture.'[5] (JHC 23: 613)

In Yorkshire, six new trusts were set up in the same year, all within the textile area (108–13). These trusts, like the Liverpool example, were the result of pressure from the merchant community, the immediate stimulus being the delay to navigation on the Aire and Calder caused by the hard winter of 1740–1. The underlying reason, however, was the expansion of trade caused by the growing importance of cloth production in the area, and the generally unsatisfactory service provided by the Aire and Calder proprietors (Wilson 1971: 145–9).[6] Turnpike development was co-ordinated and planned, linking the main trading towns of Halifax, Leeds and Wakefield to ports on the Ouse, Aire and Don.

By 1750, the Great North Road had been turnpiked almost as far as the Scottish border, and an extensive network of turnpike trusts had come into existence in the North Riding, Durham and Northumberland. After the Doncaster to Boroughbridge Trust of 1741 (111), two more trusts quickly followed in 1743. The Boroughbridge to Pierce Bridge Trust (115) carried the turnpike system to the edge of County Durham. The Bowes to Brough Trust (114) set up in the same year was responsible for a remote 13-mile section of the London–Carlisle post road. It is a good example of a trust established due to the lack of population to operate the traditional parish repair system. One of the witnesses who testified before the Commons Committee examining the bill said:

> '. . . a great Part of the Road leads over a Moor, called Stainmore, which is a barren Country, and but few inhabitants live thereabouts; which inhabitants are not able to repair the same, as the Law requires. . . .' (JHC 24: 363)

In 1744, this turnpike was joined to the Great North Road by the Middleton Tyas to Bowes Trust (119), and a second north–south route, from Durham City through Northallerton to Boroughbridge, was tunpiked (124). The main reason given in petitions for the need for turnpikes on these north–south routes was the heavy traffic in 'Scotch cattle' (JHC 24: 363). The landing of the Pretender, and the revolt in the north, was not the critical factor promoting interest in their improvement, as has been suggested elsewhere (Mantoux 1961: 117, Vigier 1970: 24): it could not have been, as they were all turnpiked before Charles set foot in Derby. But the penetration of trusts into County Durham did stimulate the growth of a network of new trusts in the coalfield in 1748 (130, 132–4, 136). A year earlier, the turnpike link to the Scottish border was all but completed (128, 129). All these roads were within the hinterland of the port of Newcastle, at that time England's fourth largest town.

The southern half of the country was overshadowed by turnpike road development in the north in the 1740s. The innovation did not spread outside its existing geographical limits in the south, but the turnpiking of several important routes was completed. The Hastings (137) and Portsmouth roads (143) were taken over by trusts, and the last links in the Great Western Road to Bristol (116), and the Gloucester to London road (131) were made. Important links were added in two of the roads out of Birmingham, by the Stone Bridge Trust (126) on the Coventry road, and the Buckingham to Warmington Trust on the Banbury road (121).

Lastly, the old Great North Road through Cambridge to Godmanchester was added to the growing network (118, 127). Nevertheless, on the whole, turnpike development in the 1740s was firmly located to the north of the Wash: nearly 800 miles were added in the north, but only 400 in the south.[7]

The Turnpike System in 1750

In 1750 there was a reasonably coherent turnpike road network in central southern England, but it also extended far into the north, particularly through the West Riding to the Durham coalfield. The line of trusts on the Great North Road had even penetrated Scotland, with the Haddington Trust, in East Lothian, established that year (144).[8] It was a coherent system because it was reasonably well connected, and because of this, it is justifiably called a network. As early as mid-century, therefore, the strictures of the Webbs are seen to be unfounded:

'If, during the eighteenth century, anyone had taken the trouble to make a turnpike map of England, this would have shown, not a system of radiating arteries of communication, but scattered cases of turnpike administration, unconnected with each other, appearing at first as dots on the map, then gradually increasing in number and size so as to form continuous lines; and only at the end of the century beginning . . . to be so multiplied and extended as to form almost a universal plan of communication throughout the Kingdom.' (Webb 1920: 125)

With the exception of the Norwich and Exeter roads, the main routes from London to important provincial centres were almost completely turnpiked by 1750. A near continuous line of trusts stretched down the Dover road as far as Canterbury, down the Portsmouth road, along the Bath and Bristol roads, the Worcester and Gloucester roads, and the Birmingham, Manchester, York and Edinburgh roads. The Norwich road was half turnpiked, and the importance of this route is underlined by the establishment of two very early trusts—the Wymondham to Attleborough in 1696 (3), and the Essex Justice Trust in same year (2). The one major omission was, therefore, the Exeter road, an omission which may be accounted for in part by the gradual economic decline of Exeter itself in the first half of the eighteenth century, but also by the importance of the sea route to London for its cloth trade.

The orientation of the turnpike network in 1750 was still, as in 1720, very much towards London. The trade to London was a feature mentioned in many turnpike petitions, even those concerned with the trans-Pennine and North Country routes. However, in terms of route density, the western region of Hereford, Worcester and Gloucester was as important as the area immediately around the capital. This density pattern emerged in the 1720s with the development of the western town-centred trusts (Fig. 28).[9] Nevertheless, these western counties should not be regarded as a 'core' of equal importance to the London area. To do so would be to ignore the 'weighting' of the various turnpike links around the capital, due to the heavy traffic flows concentrated on relatively few routes.

The innovation profile for 1750 (Fig. 25) shows the effect of the spread of the turnpike trust into new areas. A clear secondary peak between 90 and 110 miles from London for the western town-centred trusts is still prominent, but it is complemented by a series of lesser peaks, corresponding to the northern extension of the network into the West Riding, the Durham coalfield and then the Newcastle area. In the development of the network up to 1750, the neighbourhood effect in expansion diffusion had been much in evidence. Hierarchical diffusion was also operative to a recognizable degree (Table XVIII). The hierarchical pattern had been tempered by distance. Towns high in the hierarchy, but some distance from London, such as Newcastle, Leeds and Chester and the Scottish centres, adopted later than those of similar size that were closer. Several lower in the hierarchy had, however, adopted relatively early. These were the towns such as Ipswich and Portsmouth near to the capital.

One final point to be gained from an examination of the turnpike road network in 1750 is the apparent unimportance of the influence of geology and topography. Although this factor has often been claimed, particularly by geographers, to be of importance in understanding the location of turnpike trusts, this was not so, except in a few cases of very early adoptions noted earlier. Even in 1720, the turnpike routes to the north and west of London showed little respect for the junctions between the clay and limestone belts. This is not particularly surprising: soil conditions varied far less than rock types. The turnpike system was a response to heavy flows of traffic brought about by the pressures of economic expansion, rather than by the pressures of geology. The development of this system was not illogical, or disordered, or disconnected, but coherent and well structured, forming by mid-century an extensive and connected network.

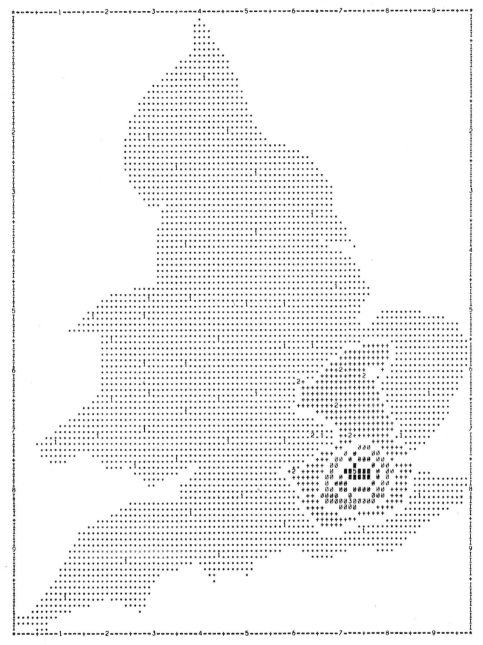

Fɪɢ. 28A. SYMAP of turnpike road density. 1720.

Key:

1	2	3	4	5

000	·030	·061	·091	·122
−·030	−·061	−·091	−·122	−·152

Miles of turnpike road per square mile, ranging from 000 to 0·152 miles.

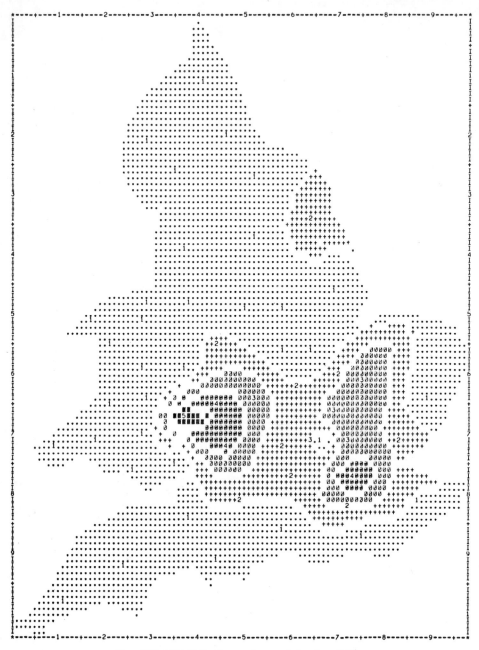

FIG. 28B. SYMAP of turnpike road density, 1730.

Key:

1	2	3	4	5
000	·050	·100	·150	·200
−·050	−·100	−·150	−·200	−·250

Miles of turnpike road per square mile, ranging from 000 to 0·250 miles.

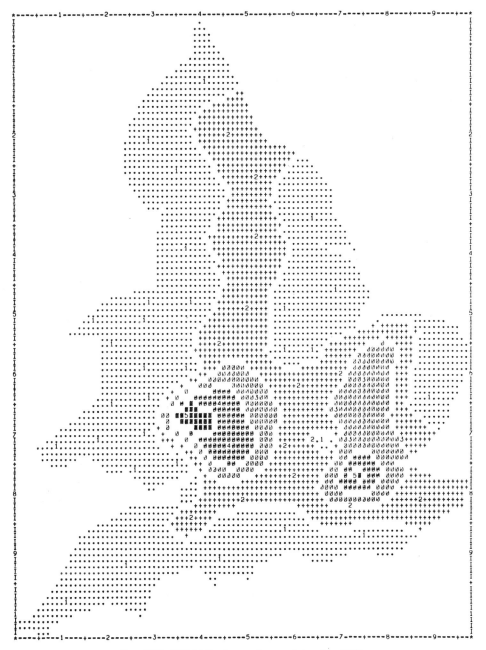

Fig. 28C. SYMAP of turnpike road density, 1750.

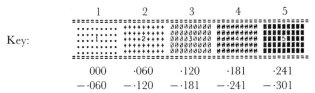

Key:

	1	2	3	4	5
	000	·060	·120	·181	·241
	−·060	−·120	−·181	−·241	−·301

Miles of turnpike road per square mile, ranging from 000 to 0·301 miles.

Note: These maps are produced by the SYMAP computer mapping programme. They show generalised isoline density surfaces.

TABLE XVIII
Rank Hierarchy of Towns in Britain
with the Date of First Turnpike Trusts, 1750

Rank	Town	Population	Date of first turnpike trust	
1	London	675,000	1696	(2)
2	Edinburgh	57,000	1714	(28)
3	Bristol	50,000	1727	(69)
4	Norwich	36,000	1696	(3)
5	Glasgow	31,000	—	
6	Newcastle	29,000	1747	(128)
7	Birmingham	23,700	1726	(54)
8	Liverpool	22,000	1726	(63)
9	Manchester	18,000	1725	(50)
10	Exeter	16,000	—	
11	Leeds	16,000	1741	(110)
12	Plymouth	15,000	—	
13	Aberdeen	15,000	—	
14	Chester	13,000	1706	(7)
15	Coventry	12,850	1724	(48)
16	Dundee	12,400	—	
17	Ipswich	12,100	1712	(20)
18	Nottingham	12,050	1738	(100)
19	Sheffield	12,000	1741	(112)
20	York	11,400	1741	(111)
21	Worcester	10,300	1726	(60)
22	Portsmouth	10,000	1711	(17)
23	Great Yarmouth	10,000	—	
24	Sunderland	10,000	1747	(130)

The numbers of the turnpike Acts are given in brackets. They refer to the first turnpike trust established in the vicinity of each town by 1750.

The Turnpike Boom

The best testimony to the effectiveness of the turnpike boom period in continuing the processes of spatial diffusion and interlinkage is the map of the network in 1770 (Fig. 29). It reflects the general pervasiveness throughout the country of the forces of economic growth from the late 1740s, and is powerful support for the thesis of balanced growth.

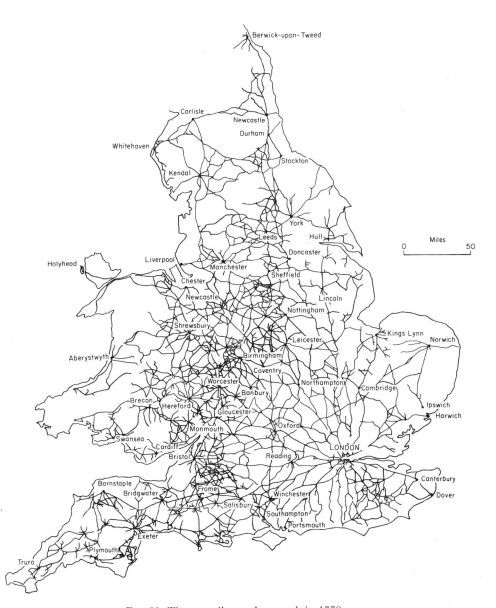

FIG. 29. The turnpike road network in 1770.

Turnpike schemes were implemented all over England, and the innovation spread into Wales and Scotland. The pattern of diffusion within this 20-year period was not, however, uniform. There were marked time–space concentrations of turnpiking as waves of diffusion spread into new areas in response to the forces of regional economic growth. These areas lay both within, and beyond the periphery of the innovation limits in 1750.

In the early 1750s, for example, a petition was presented to Parliament about the road from Keighley to Kendal, which crossed the Pennines from the West Riding into Lancashire. This area was one that saw a continuous number of new trusts, particularly between 1752 and 1756, and again in 1759–60. The reason for this was given by one of the witnesses testifying to the committee examining the Keighley to Kendal petition:

> 'the Woollen Manufacture carried on in the several Towns mentioned in the Petition, and the village adjacent, has of late Years considerably increased .. if the said Road was amended, the said manufacture might still be further extended, as such Reparations would facilitate the Carriage of the said Manufactures, as well as of local and of other Provisions necessary for the Manufacture. . . .' (JHC 26: 595)

At the same time, there was a marked growth in the number of trusts in Wiltshire and Somerset. Between 1751 and 1758, 16 new trusts were established in Wiltshire, many in the textile area of the north-west, around Bradford, Calne and Devizes. Eight were set up in the neighbouring part of Somerset, on the coalfield. Twenty-two Acts were passed for roads in Derbyshire, due in part to the increased traffic in minerals, particularly lead and iron, brought about by the Seven Years War (Scott 1973).

There were a number of new turnpike schemes in Staffordshire and Shropshire in the 1750s, as coal and iron output in these counties rose to meet the needs of the growing economy. Ten new trusts, controlling 310 miles of road, were set up in Shropshire between 1751 and 1758. In the south west, 19 new trusts were authorized for Devon between 1754 and 1766, covering 752 miles of road. Seven were set up in Cornwall between 1761 and 1763, partly in response to a rapid rise in the county's tin production (Deane and Cole 1962: 56). Similar waves of turnpiking occurred in the eastern counties in the 1760s. Kent received 14 new trusts between 1765 and 1770, and at the same time, seven new trusts were established in Sussex. However, the diffusion of the innovation into the fringe of East Anglia was the most sudden. Ten new trusts were set up in Norfolk between 1769 and 1772, six of these, covering 130 miles of road, in 1770 alone.

During these two decades, the innovation also penetrated deeply into Scotland and Wales. In 1753, five new trusts were established in Scotland, with responsibility for roads as far north as Perth (205-6, 213-14, 216). By 1770, there were 14 Scottish trusts confined, however, to the counties of the Border and the Central Valley.[10] In Wales by this time an almost complete network was in existence. Penetration into north Wales had been piecemeal, initially with extensions from trusts in Shropshire and Cheshire. In south and central Wales, however, a new type of trust had been established—the 'county trust'. Monmouth was the first to adopt such a trust, in 1758, under which all the main roads of the county were turnpiked together (288). Glamorgan followed in 1764 (412), Carmarthen in 1765 (428), Brecon (464) and Radnor (466) in 1767, Montgomery in 1769 (496) and Cardigan in 1770 (511). It was usual for the jurisdiction of these trusts to terminate at the county boundary. By their nature, they were very extensive: these seven controlled a total of 1,185 miles of road, an average of 169 miles each.

The spread of turnpiking into Wales was again a response to widespread pressures of growth. 'In many cases, roads were in a worse condition by the eighteenth century than in the Middle Ages for trade was increasing everywhere, not only on account of the improvement in agricultural output, but because of the increase in mining and quarrying activities. Coal was mined in increasing quantities in Cardiganshire and Flintshire; [and] iron was widely extracted.' (Sylvester 1969: 137.) Glamorgan was one county where these pressures were felt strongly. The Glamorganshire Trust was responsible for 192 miles of road in that county (Fig. 30), with the most important highway in its care being the post road to Haverfordwest. The trust looked after a 42-mile stretch from Rumney Bridge east of Cardiff, to Penllyr Castell on the Carmarthen border, near present day Ammanford. It also controlled a number of roads around Swansea, Cardiff, Bridgend and Cowbridge. Swansea was the biggest town in south Wales, with a population of 6,831 in 1750, and by that date, half the copper produced in Britain came from this area. Coal mining was developing at the same time, in the Neath Valley behind Swansea. Cardiff was then a much smaller town, with a population of only 1,087, but its turnpike road links also reflected the expansion of coal mining. Later, with the rapid growth of the iron industry around Merthyr from the mid-1760s, the roads to Cardiff

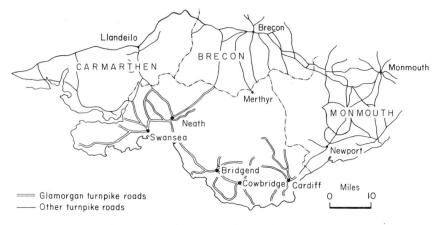

Fig. 30. The Glamorgan County Roads Trust.

became more important still, and were supplemented in the 1790s by the Glamorganshire and Aberdare Canals.[11]

The county trusts were limited to Wales, and to Scotland. A Berwickshire roads Trust had been set up in 1753 (206), and a comprehensive Ayrshire roads Trust in 1767 (478), but these Scottish county trusts became more numerous after 1770. The town-centred trusts of Western England were also still restricted in geographical extent in 1770, although they had spread into Shropshire in the north, and into Wiltshire, Somerset, Dorset, Devon and Cornwall in the south. The influence of these trusts on the structure of the network is clearly shown in Fig. 29. They were contained in this part of England due to the existence of a previously developed network to the east, and the large-scale Welsh county trusts to the west.

The Turnpike Road System in 1770

A well integrated turnpike road network had been developed by 1770, particularly in central England. Nearly all the counties of England and Wales at this date had received their greatest decadal mileage increase in the 1750s and 1760s. Nearly all had shared significantly in the turnpike boom. The exact mileages turnpiked per decade per county are given in Table XIX. It shows that there were only six counties which had not, at 1770, received their greatest decadal increase during the turnpike boom.

Three of these counties, Middlesex, Essex and Bedfordshire, were near

Table XIX
Mileages Turnpiked per Decade per County: England

	Up to 1720	1721– 30	1731– 40	1741– 50	1751– 60	1761– 70	Up to 1750	1751– 70
1 Beds.	17	41	—	4	38	17	62	55
2 Berks.	23	28	20	—	81	57	71	138
3 Bucks.	28	50	1	6	40	51	85	91
4 Cambs.	16	53	—	16	4	94	89	95
5 Cheshire	—	8	23	—	85	53	31	138
6 Cornwall	—	—	—	—	200	142	—	342
7 Cumberland	—	—	20	15	108	56	35	164
8 Derby	—	10	65	15	242	120	90	362
9 Devon	—	—	—	—	402	350	—	752
10 Dorset	—	—	—	—	212	134	—	346
11 Durham	—	—	—	113	20	—	113	20
12 Essex	46	94	3	47	—	88	190	88
13 Glos.	7	187	2	91	277	29	290	306
14 Hants.	24	—	14	6	276	132	44	408
15 Herefs.	—	211	—	43	146	34	254	180
16 Herts.	30	51	7	14	14	58	102	72
17 Hunts.	24	20	1	6	94	39	51	133
18 Kent	32	40	25	18	48	281	185	329
19 Lancs.	—	48	24	18	194	66	90	260
20 Leics.	—	27	12	—	196	74	39	270
21 Lincs.	1	10	26	1	179	217	36	396
22 M'sex	42	11	7	9	12	3	69	15
23 Norfolk	10	3	—	—	—	216	13	216
24 Northants.	31	21	16	15	108	46	83	154
25 Northumb.	—	—	—	77	213	—	77	213
26 Notts.	—	18	13	—	79	114	31	193
27 Oxon	21	29	32	—	67	63	82	130
28 Rutland	—	—	8	—	28	8	8	36
29 Shrops.	1	27	—	12	310	207	39	517
30 Somerset	13	66	6	35	426	130	120	556
31 Staffs.	10	71	—	49	115	324	130	439
32 Suffolk	30	—	3	—	4	99	33	103
33 Surrey	55	24	2	4	107	30	89	137
34 Sussex	1	3	—	22	112	181	26	293
35 Warwick	4	119	8	13	134	131	144	265
36 Westm'land	—	—	—	7	122	83	7	205
37 Wilts.	25	44	—	14	325	134	83	459
38 Worcs.	6	126	16	11	165	42	159	207
39 E. Riding	—	—	—	27	92	103	27	195
40 N. Riding	—	—	—	138	34	42	138	76
41 W. Riding	—	—	13	239	462	125	252	587
Decadal totals	495	1440	367	1084	5771	4170		
Running totals	495	1935	2302	3386	9175	13345		

(*continued*)

Table XIX (*continued*)
Mileages Turnpiked per Decade per County: Wales

	1751– 60	1761– 70	1751– 70
1 Anglesey	—	25	25
2 Brecon	19	210	229
3 Cardigan	—	164	164
4 Caernarvon	4	42	46
5 Carmarthen	—	119	119
6 Denbigh	106	29	135
7 Flint	76	44	120
8 Glamorgan	—	198	198
9 Merioneth	—	8	8
10 Monmouth	203	—	203
11 Montgomery	16	172	188
12 Radnor	8	177	185
Decadal totals	432	1188	
Running totals	432	1620	
England and Wales Totals	9607	14965	

the original diffusion centre, and it is to be expected that such areas would reach a high level of innovation penetration at an early stage in the diffusion process. Nevertheless, turnpike route densities were low in each of these counties, particularly against those of the west (Fig. 31).[9] Two factors help to explain this. Firstly the roads close to London were heavily 'weighted', there being relatively few arteries, each heavily used. Secondly, they were supplemented by important sea and river trade routes, such as the Thames, Lea and Wey. The Essex Justice Trust (2) controlled many of the roads in that county, having grown substantially in the 1720s and left little room for later expansion.[12] In Hereford, the fourth county, the Leominster and Hereford Trusts, set up in the late 1720s (81, 85), controlled 155 miles of road, limiting the scope for new trusts. Durham and the North Riding were the last of the group of six anomalous counties. Both were sparsely populated, with large areas of waste land, and had shared in the northward expansion of the turnpike road system in the 1740s.

The overall pattern of turnpike road density is revealed in Fig. 31. The

FIG. 31. SYMAP of turnpike road density. 1770.

Key:

1	2	3	4	5
000	·104	·209	·313	·418
− ·104	− ·209	− ·313	− ·418	− ·522

Miles of turnpike road per square mile, ranging from 000 to 0·522 miles.

greatest values were clearly in the west of England, where town-centred trusts predominated, and in the coal and mineral-producing counties of Staffordshire and Derbyshire. This 'core' is surrounded by a fringe of high densities including the town-centred trust region of the south-west, and the industrializing areas of Monmouth, Shropshire and Warwickshire. There was also a prominent arc of relatively high densities into the East Midlands, from Leicestershire to Cambridge, an area of increasing agricultural production after widespread enclosure. The lowest densities were in the east, the north and on the Welsh fringes, towards the geographical limits of the innovation. This pattern of density distribution was directly related to the distribution of population and varying levels of internal trade and economic activity. It would be foolish, however, to place too much significance in the pattern, which cannot take account, as shown, of the differential weighting of turnpike links and which reflects in large measure a structural feature, namely the localization of the town-centred trust in the West.

The Lagging Sector

The distribution of new turnpike trusts established in the last 30 years of the eighteenth century is shown in Fig. 32, for the two sub-periods 1771–85, and 1786–1800. In the first of these sub-periods the distribution is fairly even, with few counties gaining more than three or four new trusts. The apparent concentration in the West Riding is due largely to the size of the county, and less to regional economic growth. In fact, the woollen industry had its ten leanest years in the eighteenth century between 1772 and 1782 (Wilson 1966: 113). The new trusts were spread throughout the Riding, in agricultural as well as industrializing areas.

After 1785 the annual level of new turnpike schemes rose once more, with the general expansion of the economy in the traditional 'take-off' into sustained growth. The highest members of new trusts were in the industrializing counties from Staffordshire to Durham. Industrial output and urban growth began to increase rapidly in this group of counties. Broad-cloth production in the West Riding trebled to 9 million yards between 1781 and 1800. Retained cotton imports, reflecting the expansion of the Lancashire textile industry, increased sixfold from an average of £7·4 million per annum in 1775–84 to £42·9 million per annum in 1795–1804. The amount of coal shipped from Newcastle and Sunderland increased by 40 per cent to 817,000 chauldrons per annum

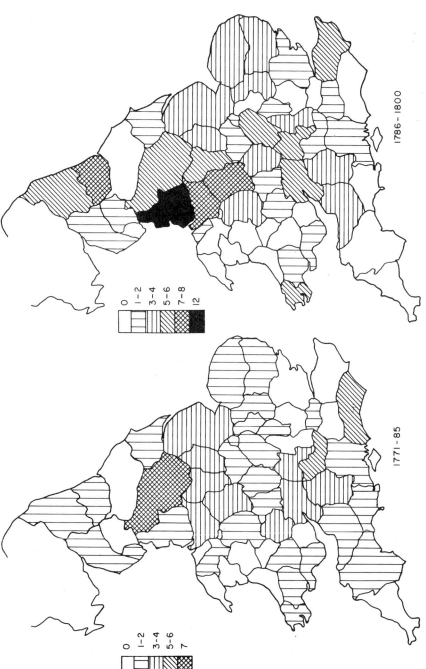

Fig. 32. The lagging sector, 1771–1800. This map plots the number of new trusts per county in each period. Trusts controlling roads in two counties are counted in both.

1786 – 1800

	0
	1–2
	3–4
	5–6
	7–8
	12

1771 – 85

	0
	1–2
	3–4
	5–6
	7

between 1780 and 1800 (Mitchell 1962). These increases were re-flected in the amount of internal trade and road usage in these counties.

The local response to these conditions was to create an improved transport network, partly by the building of canals, and by the readjustment of the turnpike road network. Twelve new trusts were set up in Lancashire, and eight apiece in Staffordshire, Cheshire and Durham. There were six new ones in Derbyshire and the West Riding. The late rise to prominence of Lancashire and Durham requires further explanation. Both had some of the lowest turnpike route densities in 1770, and were far less prominent than agricultural counties such as Devon or Hereford (Fig. 31). The roads in the coal producing areas around St Helens in Lancashire and Bishop Auckland in Durham had been turnpiked, but apart from the major through routes in each county, little else. In part this is accounted for by their large acreages which were not brought into farming use until the sharp rise in agricultural prices in the 1790s. In part it is also due to the early development of competing transport modes in both counties—of wooden railways in Durham, connecting the coalfields to the Tyne, Wear and Tees, and of navigable waters in Lancashire. Lancashire was very much the cradle of improved waterways, from the early schemes on the Mersey and Irwell and then the Weaver, into Cheshire, completed in 1733, the Douglas in 1742, the canalized Sankey Brook in 1757, and the famous Bridgwater and Leeds to Liverpool Canals in 1761 and 1774.

There were also a number of new turnpike schemes in other peripheral areas in the 1790s, as the wave of innovation diffusion spread outwards once again. Six new trusts were set up in Pembrokeshire, virtually the last part of Wales, apart from the mountainous core of Snodonia, with-out a turnpike network. With the gradual increase in accessibility and the development of South Wales, Pembrokeshire was being drawn out of its subsistence way of life and beginning to participate more fully in the economy. Northumberland, as well, had six new trusts in this period, as corn production rose on previously uncultivated land. This last part of the century also marks the consolidation of the innovation in south and central Scotland. Another 13 Scottish trusts were estab-lished between 1771 and 1800, including new county trusts for Peebles in 1771 (541), Lanark in the following year (552), Dumfries in 1777 (581) and Stirling/Dumbarton in 1790 (633). The northern rim of the Central Valley continued however to mark the northern fringe of the innovation.

Role of the State

The direct role of the State in the development of the eighteenth century turnpike road system, as in most other spheres of economic activity, was minimal. The only major exception to this was the military road building in the Scottish Highlands. Between 1726 and 1737, General Wade built 250 miles of road and 40 bridges, and later, after the rebellion of 1745, a further 800 miles of road, and 1,000 bridges were constructed (Hamilton 1932: 229). Such activity did not take place elsewhere, except in two special cases.

In 1751, 'the Nobility, Gentry, Clergy, Freeholders and Inhabitants of the Counties of Cumberland and Northumberland' petitioned Parliament about the road from Newcastle to Carlisle:

'. . . the Road between them is for the most part through a country uncultivated, or very thinly inhabited, frequently impassable, and at all times very inconvenient either for Troops or Carriages; and that it has been found by Experience, as well during the late Rebellion, as on former Occasions, that the said Passage cannot be properly guarded without a free and open Communication for Troops and Carriages at all Times of the Year . . . and that the Want of such a Communication has been attended with great Inconvenience and Danger to the Kingdom, and a Road proper for that Purpose cannot be laid out, or the Expence thereof defrayed, but by a National Assistance, and the Aid and Authority of Parliament.' (JHC 26: 87)

The petition was referred for the consideration of a Committee of MPs in the ordinary way, but evidence was taken from three Army Officers, the most important of these being Major General Cholmondely, who had led the march out of Newcastle to cut off the Pretender. He told the Committee of the exceptionally slow progress from the town due to the poor roads, and the total failure to intercept the other Army. The other two officers confirmed his evidence (JHC 26: 112). This would probably not have been a sufficiently good reason for direct assistance, however, had it not been for special local circumstances:

'. . . it is impossible to repair the said Road by the ordinary Course of the Law, or even by erecting turnpikes thereon, it being open in some Parts for twenty Miles together, so that the payment of Tolls might easily be evaded, but could they be collected, the Country having little

Commerce, and being uncultivated, a very small income would arise therefrom, the Inhabitants for Twenty Miles together, not being able to furnish Forty Carriages towards the Repair of the said Road, there being in some parts no Horse to be seen for Ten or Twenty Miles together.' (JHC 26: 112)

The matter was referred to a Committee of the whole House, for consideration with other questions of supply. Subsequently, Parliament voted 'a sum not exceeding £3,000 be granted to His Majesty for repairing the road from Carlisle to Newcastle.' (JHC 26: 188.) A bill was passed, establishing a turnpike trust for the road, with two bodies of Trustees, one for Cumberland and the other for Northumberland. The Act stipulated that 'such a Publick Road, when finished, may be supported, and kept in Repair, by proper Tolls and Duties to be raised and collected thereupon for that purpose.' (151.)

The Trust, which was known simply as 'the Military Road' started construction work on a new line of road immediately, but after two years, it had run out of money.[13] Both sets of Trustees then petitioned Parliament for a further grant, and subsequently, they were voted another £3,000 (JHC 26: 677). In 1754, they asked for more, but although the petitions were referred to a Committee of Supply, nothing further was heard about them (JHC 26: 901). In 1755, the Northumberland Trustees tried again, then in 1757, the Cumberland Trustees made another attempt (JHC 27: 100, 674). However, no further sums were ever granted, and construction of the road continued slowly using the proceeds of the toll on the completed sections.

The central authorities also took a limited interest in road building in the Royal Forest of Dean, attempting to facilitate the movement of ship timber. The main road from Gloucester to Chepstow along the southern fringe of the Forest had been turnpiked as part of the Monmouthshire Country Trust in 1758 (288). Parliament itself then spent £11,361 on the roads within the Forest between 1761 and 1786. However, the repairs were not satisfactory in the long term, and in 1796, most of the main roads in the Forest were turnpiked (695). Parliament advanced a further £10,654 to this trust in the next four years (Hart 1971: 392).

Elsewhere, however, state-sponsored activities had stimulated the establishment of several trusts through their effect on traffic patterns. One of the early trusts, the Petersfield to Portsmouth road of 1712, was set up as a result of 'the multitude of Carriages for Her Majesty's Service, and other Carriages travelling through that Road' to the Naval Dockyard in

Portsmouth (17). When the Act was renewed in 1742, part of the road was still in a bad condition 'occasioned by the Number of Heavy Carriages passing upon the same to the Docks with Timber' (JHC 24: 138). The Dockyard in Deptford caused similar problems, and several trusts were set up to cope with the heavy flows of traffic which it generated. In 1751, the people of Lewisham requested in an extension petition that some of their roads should be added to the proposed Surrey New Roads Trust. They had deteriorated:

'. . . particularly by Reason of the excessive loads of Timber which frequently pass out of Surrey and Sussex . . . over the . . . Road to His Majesty's Dockyard at Deptford, and to Wharves there, and at Greenwich . . . and of the excessive Carriages of Meal and Corn, which pass from Croydon . . . to His Majesty's Mill at Rotherhith. . . .' (JHC 26: 208)

Later, in 1757, a new trust was established for the Wealden road from Milford to Petworth (281), due to the heavy timber traffic to Dapdon Wharf in Guildford, on the River Wey, because:

'. . . for the said Roads . . . which are the principal Roads for bringing Timber out of the Wilds of Surrey and Sussex to Dapdon Wharf aforesaid, from whence it is navigated to London, to His Majesty's Yards on the River Thames, have from the Deepness of the Soil, and the very heavy Carriages passing thereon, become very ruinous, and, in the Winter Season, impassable for Coaches and Carriages, and in wet Summers, are impassable for Carriages loaded with Timber.' (JHC 27: 711)

In the early nineteenth century, the Government began to take a more direct interest, particularly in Scotland. In the first decade, Telford's Commission for Highland Roads and Bridges constructed 920 miles of new road and 1,117 bridges at a cost of £500,000, of which the government supplied over half (Campbell 1965: 85). Later Telford was employed on improving the Holyhead road, the Carlisle to Glasgow and Carlisle to Portpatrick roads, and that part of the Great North Road between Morpeth, in Northumberland, and Edinburgh. He was voted £50,000 by Parliament to reconstruct the Glasgow road alone (Jackman 1916: 269–74).

Road–Water Connexions

The interdependence of the land and water transport systems, discussed in Chapter 2, was reflected in the development of the turnpike road system. The first turnpike trust was established on a section of the Great North Road which was heavily used by malt wagons *en route* for Ware, on the River Lea.[14] As the network developed, first around London and then the other big towns, most of which were ports, it continued to show the importance of land–water connexions. Sometimes this was made explicit in turnpike petitions. The inhabitants of Yarm in the North Riding petitioned against the 1743 Boroughbridge to Pierce Bridge bill because, they claimed, their trade would be adversely affected:

'. . . the said Town of Yarum is a very ancient Market Town, and by its Situation upon the River Tees, which is a navigable River, great Quantities of Lead, Butter-firkins, Corn, Tallow and other Commodities, which are there brought and shipped for London, and other Places, are almost daily brought to Yarum aforesaid, by Land-carriage, from the several inland Market Towns of Richmond, Bedall, Middleham, Masham, Askrigg, Reeth and Hawes . . . and likewise great Quantities of Grocery Wares, Flax, Iron, Tar, Timber, Fir Deals, Salt and other Merchandizes, are sent by Land-Carriage from Yarum aforesaid to the above-mentioned seven several Market Towns, and other Places thereto respectively adjacent. . . .' (JHC 24: 394)

This interdependence of land and water, and the connexions of the turnpike road network to heads of navigation and ports, can be seen in all areas. The early trans-Pennine routes, and their links via the Rivers Ouse, Aire and Don to the Humber have already been noted. The coal routes further north, arrayed around the overland artery of the Great North Road, were connected to the river ports of Darlington and Stockton on the Tees, Newcastle on the Tyne, and North Shields and Sunderland on the coast (Fig. 27). In Kent, the relatively dense pattern of turnpike roads in 1770 in the Weald demonstrates the importance of the fruit and hop-producing areas around the head of navigation on the Medway (Fig. 29). Thus, although the independent land transport system encouraged the development of a coherent turnpike road network, this network was definitely influenced by the needs of interdependent land–water transport flows.

Microlevel Analysis

Some attention must now be given to the small-scale characteristics of the structure and spread of the system, at the level of the individual trust. Two points warrant further investigation. Firstly, how did the neighbourhood effect work in practice at the local level? Secondly, how was the choice of route determined, and what sort of qualities did these routes display?

It was unusual for the proceedings in Parliament on individual turnpike bills to make any reference to adjacent turnpike trusts. There are, however, some significant exceptions which reveal how the establishment of one trust directly stimulated the establishment of another. In a few cases it was claimed that the reconstruction of a road following its takeover by a trust had increased the flow of traffic, thereby further damaging the rest of the road. In 1741, Parliament was told that:

'. . . the Highway leading from Ealand to Leeds . . . being the great Road from the City of Chester, and from Liverpoole, Warrington, Manchester, Rochdale and other Towns in the County of Lancashire, to Leeds afores'd, for many Years last past, and especially since the amending the Highway from Rochdale to Ealand afores'd, pursuant to a late Act of Parliament for that Purpose, hath been and is very ruinous. . . .' (JHC 23: 561)

The Act to which this petition referred had set up the Rochdale to Ealand Trust (96), which looked after this trans-Pennine route over Blackstone Edge and through Halifax. That was in 1735, when it was claimed that trade was being disrupted 'by reason of the Narrowness thereof, in some Places and the Cragginess of the said Mountain, and the Morasses thereupon.' (JHC 22: 398.) The clear implication of the later petition, however, is that by 1741 the trust had so improved the part of the road in its care that there had been a considerable increase in traffic flow.

A similar problem was highlighted 20 years later, in 1761, when care of the Oxford Mileways was given to the Trustees of the Stokenchurch to Woodstock road (37). The seventeenth century statutes which required surrounding parishes to contribute to the upkeep of these Mileways by statute labour were repealed. A new system was necessary because:

'the Wear of the said Mileways has been greatly increased by the Number of heavy Carriages passing and repassing thereon since the establishment of Turnpike Roads at their several Extremeties.' (2 Geo. III, c. 41)

Thus, the improved turnpike road surfaces were not only encouraging wheeled traffic, but also the carriage of heavier loads.[15]

Sometimes the traffic flow along the route increased, not because part of it had been turnpiked, but because an adjacent route had been. Travellers then left the turnpike road to avoid the payment of tolls. The early turnpike system was particularly vulnerable in this respect, because of the number of alternative, toll-free routes, the lack of side-gates, and the openness of much of the country. The latter problems were gradually solved, after trusts had been given power to erect side-gates in 1741, and to impose heavy penalties on those who deliberately avoided the gates. However, the first problem was not easily overcome, until the turnpike network had developed sufficiently to cover most main roads.

The Brentford Trust was established in 1717 (32) because of the neighbouring Uxbridge to Tyburn Trust, which had been authorized a year earlier (30):

'. . . since the erecting of a Turnpike on that Road, many Cattle, and Waggons, and other Carriages, heavy laden, have come into this road, to avoid paying the Toll at the Turnpike on Uxbridge Road, which has made the Road about Hammersmith much worse than formerly.' (JHC 18: 520)

Eight years later, in 1725, the new Brentford Trust had caused a similar deterioration of a neighbouring road:

'[It] has occasioned most of the heavy Carriages which used to go from Hammersmith to London, upon the High Road, to now pass through a Bye-Road leading through Hammersmith to London, on purpose to avoid paying to the Turnpike.' (JHC 20: 405)

As a result of this petition, another trust was set up on the south-western outskirts of London to repair roads in Kensington, Chelsea and Fulham (65). Several other instances of such problems were brought to the attention of Parliament.[16]

There were also some cases of the actual operation of trusts being responsible for the creation of others. An additional reason for the establishment of the Brentford Trust had been that:

'. . . several of the Parishes, wherein this Road lies, are obliged to perform half their Statute Work in the Road leading to Uxbridge.' (JHC 18: 520)

Other main roads in these parishes were thus in a bad state because statute work resources were being concentrated on the Uxbridge road. However, when the Kensington Trust applied for a renewal Act in 1739, several roads were added as the result of an extension petition. One was the highway between the Brampton and Selwood Lanes:

> '. . . the Reason of it being in so ruinous a condition was the heavy Loads of Gravel continually passing through the same, for repairing The Roads directed to be amended by the Bill.' (JHC 23: 424)

The roads of the Devizes Trust were extended in 1725, and the Shoreditch to Mile End Trust (101) was set up in 1738 for the same reason (JHC 20: 402, 23:43).

In most cases, however, it is not possible to pinpoint such definite causes underlying the neighbourhood effect. The demonstration of benefits to be gained, in terms of income diversion to the local parishes, and improved roads for travellers and tradesmen, was usually the immediate factor. Sometimes this found its expression in the co-ordinated development of turnpike schemes in an area, under the guidance of one or several local leaders. This was the case in the West Riding in the early 1740s, when the wool merchants succeeded in implementing a network of turnpike schemes (Wilson 1971: 147). Around Oxford, Sir William Blackstone, a leading lawyer and Fellow of All Souls, was responsible for initiating several trusts in the 1760s and improving the Botley Causeway over the marshes to the west of the city (de Villiers 1969).

The actual choice of routes which turnpike roads followed was conditioned by the nature of the innovation. As the turnpike trust was a local affair, created to maintain existing highway resources, existing routes were used. In the upland parts of the country in particular, this often meant that turnpikes were really old pack-horse roads, following the high ground and steep inclines and avoiding the flatter valley bottoms. Davies, writing about the earlier turnpikes in South Wales, said, 'we frequently ascend an abrupt hillock . . . for no purpose other than to descend it on the other side.' (1814: 372–3.) They were thus not entirely suited to the new wheeled traffic, and were criticized for this. The Board of Agriculture Reports from these areas, published in the 1790s and 1800s, contain several such references.[17]

These deficiencies, however, were continuously being remedied— especially in the latter part of the eighteenth century and in the nineteenth century—as trusts took advantage of their powers to divert roads and construct new stretches. Hilly routes were replaced by more level valley-bottom roads, and distances were shortened as courses were straightened. It is not possible to illustrate this process adequately without the use of particular case-studies, and this task is reserved for Chapter 10.

Another criticism of the choice of route has been advanced by later writers. 'In the choice of roads that were to be benefited by turnpike Acts,' wrote Jackman, 'there was no security that the best routes would be selected, for there were so many diverse interests to be served.' Landowners, inn-keepers, villages and towns are all supposed to have manipulated turnpike schemes to their advantage (1916: 83–4; Webb 1920: 126). However, only nine counterpetitions were presented to Parliament before 1750 to protest that settlements would suffer by the diversion of a route one way or the other, and there is very little additional evidence.[18] Estate improvements and enclosure schemes did result in some realignments of turnpike roads—as at Sledmere in the East Riding in the 1770s (Harris 1961: 73–6) and at Maresfield in Sussex in the 1800s (Horesfield 1824: 376), but these were minor alterations.

The turnpike road network that developed in the eighteenth century was coherent, well ordered and, by 1770, fairly intensive. Although the turnpike trust itself was a local innovation, the network was not tailored solely to local needs. The early emergence of complete turnpike routes between major centres ensured that national transport needs were being attended to, but without any significant centralized direction. However, a network of turnpike routes did not in itself mean a network of radically improved roads. This depended on the efficiency with which trusts undertook their responsibilities, through their administration, their financial organization, and their approaches to road repair itself.

6. Notes

1. This is an important problem that has not been recognized sufficiently in the literature. But see Robson 1973: 137.
2. See above, p. 69.
3. Examples have been given in Chapter 3: for instance, the complaints of the Droitwich residents (p. 81) and those near the Kensington road (p. 79).

4. This seems the most likely reason (Lobel 1969: 10; Jones 1961: 33). The turnpike petitions themselves say little.

5. See also pp. 24–5 above.

6. The growth of West Riding cloth production is demonstrated in the output statistics for broad and narrow cloths, which is one of the few continuous series of production figures to survive for the eighteenth century. They are reproduced in Wilson 1971: 40.

7. 'North' here is taken as being that part of Britain to the north of the Wash. In the 1730s 167 miles of road were turnpiked in the north and 208 miles in the south.

8. There was also the 1714 Edinburgh roads Trust (28).

9. The density pattern on these maps has been derived using a computerized isoline technique, the SYMAP programme. I am most grateful to Mr Samir Shah for his help with this.

10. Nos 28, 144, 164, 205–6, 213–14, 216, 336, 410, 450, 478, 487–8.

11. Much of the information in this paragraph is derived from the introduction to Minchinton 1969.

12. See above, p. 105.

13. Military Road Minutes, 1751–91 (Cumbria RO).

14. See above, pp. 76–8.

15. There are several other examples, e.g. the extension of the New Cross Trust in 1738 (JHC 23: 118), of the Devizes Trust in 1725 (JHC 20: 402), and the Surrey–Sussex Trust in 1752 (33).

16. The Bermondsey road, included in the New Cross renewal Act in 1738 (JHC 23: 118); the 1753 Oundle to Alconbury Trust (212); the Epsom and Ewell Trust of 1755 (244– JHC 27: 90) and the Reigate Trust of the same year (230).

17. Clark (Brecon) 1794: 46–7; Bailey and Culley (Northumberland) 1797: 149; Bailey (Durham) 1810: 272–3; Vancouver (Devon) 1813: 368–9; Tuke (North Riding) 1800: 295; Marshall 1796 Vol. 1: 31.

18. See above, p. 120 for the information about counterpetitions. The Webbs' and Jackman's case is based on one article in the *Gentleman's Magazine*, one example given by Scott (1778) and a reference in the Board of Agriculture Report for Hereford.

Implementation

7

The Administration of Turnpike Trusts

The administrative structure of eighteenth century turnpike trusts was not complex, although it varied according to the size of the trusts, that is, their mileage of road or amount of toll income. It was also, as has been seen, rather more sophisticated or mature than that of the early Justice trusts.[1] Turnpike trusts were controlled by the Trustees or Commissioners appointed by each turnpike Act. Their decisions, however, were implemented by three Officers—the Surveyor, the Clerk and the Treasurer. These officers were responsible for the day-to-day running of the trusts and, in their turn, supervised the lesser officials, the toll collectors and the road labourers. The employees of the trusts carried out many of the trusts' projects and responsibilities, although when they had insufficient time or expertise, outside contractors were called in.

At the end of the turnpike boom in 1770, there were 519 individual trusts in England and Wales, and by 1800, there were no less than 689. The number of relevant units was even higher as a proportion of these were subdivided for management purposes. Consequently, the study of trust administration is not an easy task. Because of the number involved, it is necessary to resort to a sampling procedure to facilitate the collection of information. Two basic sources constitute the background material from which these samples can be drawn: the Acts of Parliament, and local trust documents. The former are of some value, if only to indicate the legislative limits within which trust operations took place. The latter— the trust documents— are the real focus of interest.

The discussion of trust administration in this chapter, and that of trust finances which follows in Chapter 8, is based on three samples drawn from these sources. Sample 1 is a random sample of 95 new turnpike Acts passed between 1696 and 1800. Sample 2 is a collection of 50 trusts' Minute Books, the administrative records of trust affairs kept by the

Clerk. Sample 3 is a collection of 50 trusts' Account Books, the records of trust financial affairs maintained by the Treasurer.

Trustees: Appointments

The men appointed to serve as Trustees of turnpike roads were named at the start of each turnpike Act. The number appointed varied from 34 for the 1714 Reading to Puntfield Trust (26) and 43 for the 1714 Talke to Tittersor Trust (27) to 250 for the Hereford Trust of 1730 (85) and 415 for the 1747 Durham to Tyne Bridge (129). On the whole, however, Trustee lists are distinguished by their length, as Table XX shows. They were

Table XX
Number of Trustees Appointed to Turnpike Trusts

	Number of trusts in sample	Mean number of Trustees	Coefficient of variation (V)
1696–1750	29	102·7	54 per cent
1751–70	36	216·5	59 per cent
1771–1800	30	183·2	40 per cent

Source: Sample 1.

made even longer by the inclusion of an indeterminate number of ex-officio members.[2] All the Aldermen and members of the Common Council could sit on the Hereford Trust, for example, and the Aldermen of no less than four towns—Durham, Stockton, Hartlepool and Newcastle were ex-officio members of the Durham to Tyne Bridge Trust. Turnpike trusts were not alone in this characteristic: size was a feature of eighteenth century public bodies. The early Commissions of Enclosure were very large (Beresford, 1946), as were river improvement Commissions. The 1751 Thames body had over 600 members. In 1844, the average size of the 42 Commissions of Sewers was 138, although they varied from 16 to 593 in strength. The same was true of the Improvement Commissions: the 1770 Plymouth body had 70 members, and that for Birmingham, appointed in 1773, had 77 (Webb 1922: 39, 235).

The names of Trustees were arranged in the Acts in simple socio-economic and occupational categories. Unfortunately this is not particularly useful because the majority of Trustees are described as

'Gentlemen' and 'Esquires', and by the mid-eighteenth century an increasing number of people has assumed these polite titles so that their original significance as indicators of the landed interest had diminished. Certain identifiable groups do, however, stand out in all cases. The upper classes and the Church both supplied large numbers of Trustees (Table XXI). The Reading to Puntfield Trust, a not untypical small provincial trust, had two baronets, two doctors, one clerk, the Mayor of Reading, 17 'Esquires' and 11 'Gentlemen' in its list. The Selby District of the 1741 Selby to Halifax Trust (113) had 205 Trustees, including three viscounts, 12 baronets, 12 clerics, 20 merchants, seven salters, three grocers, three wool-staplers, two mercers, two apothecaries, one linen-draper and a clothier. But as in every Act, the large residual group of 120 'Gentlemen' and 'Esquires' devalues the usefulness of this information.

Table XXI
Categorization of Trustees[3]

	1696–1750		1751–70	
	Number	Per cent	Number	Per cent
Viscounts, Barons and their heirs	86	2·8	104	2·5
Knights, Baronets	197	6·5	120	3·0
Gentlemen, Esquires	2,472	81·6	3,253	80·5
Clerics	249	8·2	512	12·6
Doctors of Medicine	26	0·9	55	1·4

Source: Sample 1.

It was usual for a number of Members of Parliament to be amongst those who were appointed. Only rarely were they ex-officio members,[4] but cross-checking of Trustee lists with lists of contemporary MPs[5] does reveal that the latter often named themselves for trusts in the vicinity of their seats, or within their constituencies. The number of MPs as a proportion of the total could be quite high (Table XXII). In addition, a large number of MPs served on more than one trust, as might be expected. They were joined in this by influential local landowners, JPs and the nobility. All but 19 of the 65 Lords, baronets and knights appointed to 16 trusts and districts in the north of England in the 1740s could sit on more than one trust, and some as many as nine or ten.[6]

Table XXII
Members of Parliament as Trustees

| Trusts | MPs named as Trustees | | | Proportion of |
	(sitting)	(retired)	(?)	the total (per cent)
59	12	1		18
62	10	1	2	15
64	17		7	9
218	40	2	10	16
445	20	5	2	10
454	47	6		24

Source: Sample 1.

However, overall the degree of 'cross-representation' should not be overemphasized. Two parallel turnpikes in Sussex, set up in 1765 and 1766 to repair roads south from Tunbridge Wells (445, 454) shared only one-third of their Trustees, and three Gloucestershire trusts of the 1720s, in close proximity, shared a smaller proportion still (Table XXIII). In fact, it appears that Parliament appointed a large number of Trustees from along the length of each road, so that as many local interests as possible could be represented if they so chose.

Table XXIII
Cross-representation on Gloucestershire Trusts in the 1720s

		1	2	3
59 Hereford to Gloucester	1	X	15 per cent	32 per cent
62 Tewkesbury	2	15 per cent	X	21 per cent
64 Gloucester–Stone	3	20 per cent	13 per cent	X

Source: Sample 1.

It should not be assumed, however, that large Trustee lists meant that an equally large number of Trustees attended most turnpike meetings. The Minute Books indicate that this was far from true, only a small proportion of Trustees ever being active.

Trustee Activity

The Clerk of each trust was responsible for taking the Minutes at every meeting. He also recorded the names of all the Trustees present, and listed them at the head of each entry. These lists of names can be used to assess the average level of attendance at trust meetings, and with the number of meetings themselves, give an indication of the level of Trustee activity. These two variables have been extracted from the Minute Books of the Sample 2 trusts, for two standard periods in each case.[7] The first covers the first three years of each trust's life, and the second is taken from about 20 years after.

The average attendance at meetings held in the first year of each trust's life was eleven (V = 47 per cent), and for the whole of the first three years, it was ten (V = 35 per cent). Even for the later three-year period it almost maintained this level, at nine (V = 35 per cent). Thus average attendances, although not nearly as high as the length of the trustee lists might suggest, nevertheless maintained a reasonable level. The number was large enough to ensure that trust affairs, in most cases, were not controlled by only one or two Trustees, but small enough to avoid serious management diseconomies. There was also no general decline in attendances with time. The data, however, are very general and do obscure significant variations.

The first two meetings held by trusts were usually much better attended than later meetings. Seventy-two Trustees came to the first meeting of the Brentford Trust in 1717, and 53 to the first meeting of the New Cross Trust in the following spring. A quite exceptional number—120—turned up at the Sparrows Herne to Aylesbury Trust's first meeting in 1762.[8] The average for the 50 trusts, however, was 29·4 (V = 70 per cent). Many basic managerial decisions were taken at these early meetings, which accounts for the interest shown in them. The Brentford meeting for example appointed two Surveyors and a Clerk, decided on the position of the two tollgates, and ordered that the Surveyor and two Trustees from each parish should make a report on the road, parish by parish, within a fortnight. They were to pay special attention to the availability of road gravel, and the state of drainage. These reports were evidently ready very quickly, as the minutes of the second meeting, held a week later, gave comprehensive details about the parts of the road to be raised, widened and resurfaced, and the location of new brick arches and drains. The 47 Trustees in attendance also ordered the Surveyor to widen the road to 30 feet, and provide a ditch alongside, and told the Clerk to advertise for 1,000 tons of stones.[9]

The first meeting of the New Cross Trust was less productive: the only decisions made concerned the appointment of Officers, and the position of gates. But the second meeting, attended by 28 Trustees and held ten days later, appointed a Committee of seven to consider various repair plans for the road. Two months later, this body was given Standing Committee status with power to enact the plans it had recommended. The 120 Trustees at the first meeting of the Sparrows Herne to Aylesbury Trust had time to do no more than take the oath, and appoint a Clerk-Treasurer. The more important business of selecting a Surveyor and positioning the gates was settled at the second meeting a week later, when the attendance had fallen to a more manageable level—16![10]

Similarly, when important matters were discussed at later meetings, attendances rose. The Old Street Trust in London, established in 1753, attracted about 12 Trustees to each meeting. However, when a proposal for building a new extension road, and application to Parliament for the necessary Act, was discussed in the summer of 1755, over 50 Trustees attended the two meetings. This number was again attained in the spring of the following year, after the Act had been obtained and the Trust was buying land and letting contracts. The passage of a renewal Act often had the same effect—55 Trustees came to the first meeting of the Stokenchurch Trust after its 1740 renewal. The appointment of new Trustees also boosted attendances. The New Cross Trust, drawing a steady 18 Trustees per meeting in the 1740s, had double that number when a proposal for erecting a weighing engine was accepted and new Trustees appointed in June 1745 and when the tolls were leased and new Trustees appointed in June 1746.[11]

In some areas, Trustees took a more active interest in the affairs of their Trusts than elsewhere. The highest averages for the first three years were 22 per meeting for both the Liverpool to Prescot and Old Street Trusts, whilst the lowest were 6·5 for the Burford to Preston and Harrogate to Boroughbridge Trusts. The London trusts were better attended than the provincial trusts, although not markedly so. Small trusts, responsible for less than 10 miles of road, were also better attended than the larger ones. These smaller trusts included five of the London trusts, and eight in rural areas (Table XXIV). The proximity of Trustees' residences to the meeting places of these small trusts encouraged a higher number to attend regularly.

There were several reasons for the general fairly low level of

Table XXIV
Trustee Attendances—Average per Meeting

	First 3 years	Later 3 years	N.
London trusts	14	15	6
Industrial	10	7	8
Rural	9·5	8·5	36
			50
Small trusts (< 11 miles)	12·4	10·3	13
Medium (11–20)	9·2	8·4	23
(21–30)	9·1	7·6	8
Large (> 30)	8·8	7·6	6
			50

Source: Sample 2.

attendances. Many of the Trustees were not interested in serving actively: often they had other time-consuming responsibilities, either in business, or in public service as Justices, Aldermen or at Westminster. Many who belonged to the big trusts lived too far from the regular meeting place to make the journey. The 1711 Royston to Wandesford Bridge Trust (16), which maintained 40 miles of the Great North Road, had to be divided into three separate districts in 1714 because it had proved impossible to meet the original Act's requirement of a minimum quorum for meetings of three Trustees, each from Cambridgeshire and Huntingdon (JHC 17: 572).

Another problem was that of qualifications. Property or income qualifications were generally required of all who served in public office in the eighteenth century (Webb 1922: 386–9) and were prescribed for turnpike Trustees in the 1753 General Highways Act, although there are some cases of earlier individual examples.[12] This requirement, confirmed by the General Turnpike Acts in 1767, 1773 and 1822, was the result of the recommendations of a Commons Committee, which had investigated the affairs of four trusts in 1752, and discovered mismanagement by a clique of Trustees in one of them, the Cranford Bridge Trust (JHC 26: 490–3). Trustees were required to take an oath, or sign the Minute Book or a separate 'Qualification Book' to assert their eligibility to serve. That many never did so reflects the foregoing factors, but may also indicate that some were not eligible.

The active Trustees came from a variety of backgrounds. The Justices, due to their traditional concern with road repair, and their control of the

Justice Trusts, were active in some areas, as in Gloucestershire (Moir 1969: 125). Often the county families were very interested. Lord North attended 13 of the Ilminster Trust's first 30 meetings. The Duke of Northumberland went to several of the Isleworth Turnpike's meetings, apparently being involved in road alterations concerning his estate.[13] In many areas, however, the merchants or manufacturers were more important. The ironmasters were among the active Trustees of the Shropshire trusts (Trinder 1973: 444), and in north Staffordshire the coal-masters and potters, including Wedgwood, took a leading role (Thomas 1934: 63–73). The merchants of Liverpool were the moving force behind the running of the first Lancashire trust (63) as were the merchants of Hull in the three trusts around that port.[14] In the West Riding, the trusts were largely established and controlled by the woollen merchants and the landowners took little interest (Wilson 1971: 146–7). A different type of entrepreneur, the banker, was widely interested by the end of the eighteenth century (Presnell 1956: 374–6). Many trusts were, however, in the hands of the local gentry, small farmers and tradesmen, including those near London, such as the Brentford and Marylebone Turnpikes (JHC 26: 490–3).

Trust Meetings

Turnpike Acts placed few restrictions on trust meetings. The level of the quorum was always fixed, usually at four or five, in addition to the time and place of the first meeting. This was normally held at an inn, except in the case of the Justice Trusts, when it was to be during the next meeting of Quarter Sessions. Most trusts continued to meet at inns, except for those that were able to use official rooms. In 1761, the Birdlip Hill Trust accepted the offer of the Grand Jury Room in Gloucester. The Taunton Trust met regularly at the Guildhall there, and the Wells Trust at the Common Council House.[15]

It was unusual for Acts to give any further direction about the number or location of meetings. Despite this, most trusts maintained a regular pattern of meetings. This was particularly so in their early years, when there was a lot of business to transact in connexion with initiating the trust's activities. The average number of meetings held by Sample 2 trusts in their first three years was 30·6 (V = 58 per cent)—almost a monthly frequency. In many cases, regularity was maintained later on in the trust's life. The average number of meetings called falls to 11·6 (V = 63 per cent) in the later three-year periods, although a quarterly frequency was kept up. But there were some bad cases of lack of management, where Trustees left their Officers solely in charge. Dr Richard Burn's observation of 1764 was certainly not unfair:

'I have known a Turnpike Meeting advertised, from Three Weeks to Three Weeks, and never a competent Number of Trustees attended for a Year together.' (Quoted in Webb 1922: 210)

The Chippenham Trust held no meetings between November 1739 and March 1743, nor did the Doncaster to Wakefield Trust between April 1745 and February 1748. There was an even longer gap, of nine years from 1764, on the Knaresborough to Pateley Bridge Trust, and another of three, from July 1776, on the Seend Street to Box Trust.[16] The failure of the Trustees to act in these cases should not, however, be taken to mean that the trusts themselves were inoperative.[17] All four later reverted to Trustee management and meetings were resumed.

On the whole, however, regular Trustee management was maintained, although the frequency of meetings varied between groups of trusts. It was highest in the London trusts, and the small and large—rather than medium-sized—trusts (Table XXV). Apart from the large trusts, this pattern confirms the evidence of Trustee attendances, and is attributable, in part, to the same causes. In addition, the London trusts faced problems of a different order and scale than those elsewhere. Despite being small in mileage, they had very large incomes which had to be continuously channelled to meeting the problems of very high traffic

Table XXV
Number of Meetings Held By Trusts

	First 3 years	Later 3 years	N.
London trusts	56·4	24·5	6
Industrial	24·5	12·5	8
Rural	28·1	10·5	36
			50
Small trusts (< 10 miles)	34	15	13
Medium (11–20)	27	10·2	23
(21–30)	26·4	10·9	8
Large (> 30)	40	14·7	6
			50

Source: Sample 2.

flows, and urban development. Their task was further complicated by the multiplicity of civil and commercial authorities with which they had to deal, and so the London Trustees had to hold a large number of meetings.

The London trust figures are reflected in the figure for small trusts, although the rural trusts in this group faced less complex management problems and hence held less meetings, depressing the overall figure. But it was the large trusts in the sample which held the most meetings—an average of 40 in their first three years. The figure, however, should be regarded with caution, because only six trusts were involved. The best records of these belonged to three town-centred trusts in Somerset (173, 198, 306).

Districts

Some trusts were formally divided by their Acts into more than one management unit. These units were called 'districts' and operated effectively as separate trusts for different parts of the road. Six per cent of the trusts established up to 1750 were divided in this way, and $7\frac{1}{2}$ per cent of those set up between 1751 and 1770. The number of districts was normally only two, but it could be much higher. The most complex divisions occurred in the county and town-centred trusts, the 1758 Monmouthshire Trust, having as many as seven (288). The 1763 Glamorgan Trust had five—one for each major town: Cardiff, Cowbridge, Bridgend, Neath and Swansea (412). More common was the simple division of a long country trust, such as the 1755 Ryton Bridge to Oxford Trust, divided in half at Banbury (237).

Districts appointed their own Officers, formulated their own repair plans and raised their own money. Co-operation between them was usually limited to the positioning of tollgates, and sharing the expense of high cost items, such as weighing engines or renewal Acts. An interesting example of this is provided by the Preston–Hering Syke Trust. In 1774, the Southern District proposed to the Northern District that they should share the cost of a weighing engine, one paying the contractor, the other donating £20. The Northern Trustees, given the choice, sensibly chose to make the donation, leaving the Southern District, who had apparently not sought an estimate of the cost beforehand, with a bill for £67 10s.[18] There were also many instances of districts co-operating with renewal Act costs.[19]

These formal, statutory divisions were not the only method used to divide large trusts. Often the Trustees themselves devised a similar system, using Committees to look after separate stretches of road. Seven of the Sample 2 trusts did this, and in each, the structure was of some permanence.[20] The Taunton Trust was an extreme example. It had nine Committees, one for each of the following roads: Lydeard, Norton, Kingston, Hestercombe, Wellington, Pitminster and Blagdon, Bridgwater, Langport and London. A larger number of trusts used a less permanent Committee structure, establishing them on an *ad hoc* basis when the need arose. It was common for Trustees to appoint several of their number to oversee the construction of a new bridge, the widening of a particular stretch of road, or the auditing of the accounts, for example. This system of management was used at various times by 24 of the Sample 2 trusts.

Trust Officers

The routine business of the trusts was undertaken by a small group of officials or 'Officers'. Each turnpike Act allowed:

'the said Trustees . . . present at their first or any succeeding Meeting . . . [to] choose and appoint One or more fit Person or Persons to be Treasurer or Treasurers, Receiver or Receivers, Collector or Collectors of such Tolls and Duties . . . and also One or more fit Person or Persons to be Surveyor or Surveyors of the said Road, to view the Condition thereof, and to see that the same is repaired and amended, and that the Money raised by virtue of this Act is duly applied; and also one or more Clerk or Clerks for the said Road, and such other Officers as shall be necessary in order to put this Act into Execution.'[21]

It was these three Officers—the Treasurer, Surveyor and Clerk—who formed the basic links in the administrative structure under the Trustees.

The precise role of each Officer varied between trusts. The Treasurer was generally responsible for collecting the toll money from the Gatekeepers, and meeting items of expenditure, either directly, or through the Surveyor. The Surveyor himself was in charge of the road repair labourers, and he usually recruited and paid them. But often he had wider powers, such as deciding which sections of road should be repaired. He was also sometimes required to enforce the statute duty obligation and remove nuisances. These latter tasks were more usually undertaken by the Clerk, however, the issuing of notices and serving of prosecutions being a natural extension of his post in charge of routine administrative matters. He drafted letters and documents, such as mortgages and contracts, and arranged, publicized and minuted meetings.

There was not always one person for each office. Low-income trusts sometimes combined the Clerk and Treasurer's post, whilst those with a large mileage or income, such as the London trusts, often had more than one Surveyor. Table XXVI records the details of Officers in Sample 2 trusts, during the first three years of their existence.

Table XXVI

Trust Administrative Structure

	Number of trusts
Clerk plus Treasurer plus Surveyor	29
Clerk/Treasurer plus Surveyor	13
Clerk plus Surveyor, no Treasurer	3
Clerk/Surveyor plus Treasurer	2
Clerk plus Treasurer/Surveyor	2
Clerk/Treasurer/Surveyor	1
	50

Source: Sample 2.

The last case, of one combined Office, was in the 1741 Wakefield to Halifax Trust. Later this post increased in popularity amongst the rural West Riding trusts. The Knaresborough to Pateley Bridge, the Knaresborough to Green Hammerton, and Grassington to Wetherby Trusts all had a Clerk/Treasurer/Surveyor in the 1770s and 1780s.[22]

The *Treasurer's* post was a most responsible one. His authority was easily misused as he was in control of trust funds, so it was important to appoint a reputable person. Such an appointment would also be more likely to encourage investment in the trust. But there were some unfortunate experiences. The Cranford Bridge Trust lost £857 after its Treasurer, a brewer, absconded in 1752. The Basingstoke to Hartfordbridge Trust lost £90 in the same way (JHC 26: 490–3). Most trusts therefore either appointed a Trustee to this position, or required a high surety. The 1773 General Turnpike Act made the latter requirement general.

The Treasurer of the Islington Turnpike was a Trustee, as was the Treasurer of the Fulham, Hockerill and Preston to Garstang Trusts.

Nevertheless, this did not stop unfortunate incidents. The Islington Treasurer resigned in mysterious circumstances a year after the trust had been set up, in 1717, at the same time as all four of the trust's Surveyors were relieved of their posts. The Fulham Treasurer, a Mr Ewer, had to resign after three years in office, when he was declared bankrupt in 1734. The Hockerill Trustees had better luck and retained the services of one of their Treasurers, Sir Conyers Jocelyn, for 30 years until his resignation in 1774.[23]

There was a tendency from the 1790s to appoint bankers as Treasurers. This helped trusts in two ways—by reputation, and direct financing. Although in the last quarter of the eighteenth century 'Treasurers of turnpikes were not, as yet, chosen preponderantly from bankers . . . they might be used for the collection of capital.' However, by 1834, 'at least 419 out of the 1,039 Trusts employed private bankers directly as treasurers.' (Presnell 1956: 269–70.) Treasurers were drawn, however, from a wide variety of occupations. It is rare for details to be noted in Minute Books, and only three examples have been found. In 1726, the Liverpool to Prescot Trust appointed Henry Homer, a linen-draper, and in 1755, the Yeovil Trustees chose John King, a bookseller. The Grassington to Wetherby Trust appointed Abraham Ogden, a grocer, as Clerk/Treasurer/Surveyor in 1775.[24] None of these men were Trustees.

The Treasurer's post was normally not remunerated, or carried only a small gratuity, particularly if it was held by a Trustee. Turnpike Acts forbade Trustees holding any 'place of profit'. In other cases, a salary of £20 to £30 per annum was paid. Some of the bigger trusts made the office less onerous by appointing two Treasurers—for example, the Hockerill Turnpike, or by hiring a Treasurer's Clerk. The Marylebone and Kensington Trusts both did this (JHC 29: 647).

The *Clerk* was a part-time official, hired by trusts, again at a salary of £20 to £30 per annum. The duties were not particularly heavy, except in some of the London trusts, where the Clerk was often involved in protracted correspondence with parishes over the issue of composition money, or with water companies about their pipes. The Clerk of the Marylebone Trust was relieved of his post in 1742, when it was discovered, in the middle of a dispute with local parishes, that orders to pay composition money had not been received.[25] But this was the only dismissal noted in any of the Minute Books examined; turnover was low. Some Clerks were employed by more than one trust. In the 1780s and 1790s, 26 of the Derbyshire trusts and districts were served by 19 Clerks.

Four of them worked for two trusts, and one for four. William Edwards was Clerk to the Derby to Risley, Derby to Duffield, London and Brassington and Derby to Uttoxeter Trusts in the early 1780s, and was still employed by the two latter trusts in the early 1790s.[26]

The *Surveyor* was an important Officer, as he was responsible for the maintenance and improvement of the trust's roads, although the Trustees were in overall charge of trust policy. In many cases, however, the Surveyor effectively assumed this managerial role as well. Inevitably, it is difficult to make exact assessments of the way in which individual trusts worked from the evidence in their Minute Books, but often it appears that the Surveyor was working unsupervised. In many of the Sample 2 trusts, the lack of interest in repair schemes shown by the Trustees at their regular meetings, or by their lack of regular meetings, indicates this. Entries in the Accounts, and sporadic references in the Minute Books confirm that repairs were proceeding in every case.

A general assessment of trust policy in this respect is given in Table XXVII. The evidence refers to the first three years of each trust's life, when Trustee interest in repair programmes should have been high. This was so in more than half the Sample 2 trusts, where the Minute Books indicate that the Trustees, working by direct orders at their meetings, or through Committees, were in control of the Surveyor, directing his activities. However, in 23 of the trusts, such direction was absent and there is little evidence of direct Trustee interest, if the blank record of the Minute Books is to be accepted.

There was a great difference between the energetic organization of the New Cross or Kensington Trusts, whose Minute Books are full of repair

Table XXVII
The Organization of Trusts

	Trustees	Surveyor	
Trustees directing the Surveyor			27
Surveyor apparently in complete charge			23
			N. = 50
London trusts	5	1	6
Industrial	7	4	11
Rural	15	18	33
			N. = 50

Source: Sample 2.

orders, and the Preston to Garstang Trust, which made only one recorded order in its first three years in existence, or the Blackburn to Burscough Bridge Trust for which none are recorded. The London trusts were certainly more concerned, on the whole, with direct supervision than were the provincial trusts. Nevertheless it would be a mistake to identify the small provincial trusts as those where repair supervision was generally minimal,[27] although admittedly this was true in about half the cases examined. So, although it is not possible to reach definite conclusions because of the nature of the Minute Book evidence, it does appear that the Surveyor's post was a very responsible one in many trusts.

What sort of people, then, were appointed as Surveyors? James MacAdam, in witness before a Parliamentary Committee in 1819, gave a list of those who had preceded him in the six trusts to which he was then General Surveyor. They included four old men, one of whom had been bedridden, two carpenters, two publicans, a baker, a coal merchant and a former Lloyd's Coffee House underwriter (BPP 1819 (509) V. 339: 35). Such diversity was to be expected when there was no tradition of professional road repair. In some trusts, the Trustees even appointed Surveyors from their own number. Both the Liverpool to Prescot Trust's first Surveyors, in 1726, were Trustees, although they resigned their Trusteeship on appointment. The two Trustee-Surveyors of the Fulham Turnpike, however, did not.[28]

Until the emergence of a widespread turnpike road system, there were few opportunities to become a 'professional' road surveyor. The previous experience of a new appointee was likely to be limited to that of parish surveyor, estate worker, or of County Surveyor in charge of bridge repairs. The Minute Books are silent on the experience and previous occupations of Surveyors, but press advertisements indicate that the qualifications were not high:

WANTED

A PERSON who understands the method of making and repairing Turnpike Roads, and can be well recommended, to superintend the Road from Chesterfield to Worksop; it is expected that he shall confine himself to this Business solely, and reside as near the Centre of it as possible: Any who are desirous of engaging in this Employment, may apply to Mr Richard Wilkinson.

12 January 1770.
(*Derby Mercury*, 19 January 1770)

By the early nineteenth century, however, professional Surveyors acting as consultants had emerged in different parts of the country. Some of them looked after the roads of several trusts at once. The MacAdam family were certainly the most famous. By 1819, J. L. MacAdam had been consulted by 34 trusts, in 13 counties, covering 637 miles of turnpike road. He had instructed all those sub-surveyors who had worked under him in his own method of road repair, and had taught many trust Surveyors who had come to see roads he was reconstructing (BPP 1819 (509) V 339: 19).

This assessment of eighteenth century Surveyors should not be taken as support for the conventional condemnatory view of them. The improvement of road repair techniques pioneered by Telford and MacAdam in the early nineteenth century is no reason to criticize eighteenth century Surveyors who had no knowledge of such methods. There is no evidence to show that, by the standards of the time, Trustees were dissatisfied with their Surveyors. The general improvement in road surfaces justifies their attitude.[29] Only eight examples of the dismissal of Surveyors were found in the Sample 2 Minute Books. As Trustees had no hesitation in removing unsatisfactory Gatekeepers, recorded in nearly every Minute Book, it seems unlikely that they would have been unwilling to dismiss Surveyors if there was good cause.

The Yeovil Trust did dismiss its Surveyor in 1754 because he was 'not good enough'. The Islington Trust sacked its General Surveyor and his three Under-Surveyors in 1718, the implication being that there were some irregularities in the Accounts. One of the replacements was removed some months later 'upon several representations being made of Mr Griers injudicious ordering of the Repair of the Roads under his Survey'. It was 'Resolved that he is incapable of performing the Office of a Surveyor.' The Cranford Bridge Trust sacked its Surveyor in 1729 for spending £219 without authority—the only one of the five remaining cases for which a cause of dismissal was recorded.[30]

It was common for trusts to appoint more than one Surveyor. Ten of the Sample 2 trusts originally appointed two, four appointed three, two appointed four and one appointed eleven. This last example was the 1727 Chippenham Trust, which chose the eleven to look after four different sections of the road. The Islington and Ilminster Trusts both appointed a General Surveyor and three Under-Surveyors.[31] However, none of these three trusts maintained this structure for very long, and they soon reverted to the employment of two Surveyors.

Trusts paid their Surveyors between £20 and £30 per annum, but there is not much evidence to show whether or not the job was generally full-time. In the London trusts, it certainly was, and the Surveyors were paid more. In the 1760s, the Hackney, Surrey New Roads and Marylebone Surveyors were receiving £60 per annum, and the Stamford Hill and the two Kensington Surveyors, £50 each (JHC 29: 646–8). John Marsh, Nicholas Halstead and Gilbert Edwards, the three Islington Under-Surveyors appointed in 1717 were paid £30 each, whilst Jonathan Norris, the General Surveyor, received £100. When Edwards appeared before the Trustees on 18 February 1718 to ask if he could take two days off work later that month because of some 'extraordinary Business', his request was granted on condition that he 'take care to appoint some other person he can confide in to see the Labourers do their Duty in his absence.'[32] Evidence from some other trusts shows that daily supervision of labourers was also necessary.

In some cases, however, the Surveyor's post was evidently not full-time. Not all trusts repaired their roads in the winter, and the Surveyor would have required a second occupation to support himself.[33] At the December meeting of the Tadcaster to York Trust in 1745 it was decided that 'as Mr. Duffield ye Surveyor cannot possibly attend at this Meeting by reason of his Serving under General Wade, this Meeting be adjourned to the third day of February next.' By the middle of that month, Mr Duffield had returned.[34]

Lesser Officials

The lesser officials of the turnpike trusts were responsible to the Officers. Trusts employed a number of these officials, but the two most important groups were the *Gatekeepers* (or Collectors) and the road labourers.

The collection of the tolls was sometimes quite a problem for the Trustees. There are frequent references in the Minute Books to the dismissal of Gatekeepers. Often no reasons were given, but when they were, fraud and disorderly behaviour feature most commonly. In July 1742, the Doncaster to Tadcaster Trust ordered that none of its Collectors were to sell liquor at a tollhouse, and subsequently, a week later, three were sacked for doing this. The Islington Trust Minutes record a colourful case in 1718:

'William Edge, Collector, appearing according to the Order of the last General Meeting and upon Examination it was found that he had Received Seventeen Pence and not brought to Acct. and that he had been frequently in drink and in company of Lew'd women and not capable of his business and therefore he was unanimously discharged from his Employ.'

Similar cases elsewhere occurred frequently.[35]

Fraud was a big problem. The Kensington Trust seems to have suffered from it continually, and its experience was revealed to several Parliamentary Committees investigating the affairs of various trusts. In 1732 MPs heard that the gates of the trust had been controlled by a clique of six Collectors between 1727 and 1730, who had pocketed money for which no tickets had been given, and caused a fall in toll yields from £2,016 to £1,674 per annum. After they had been dismissed, the tolls rose again to £2,226 (JHC 21: 837). In 1752 a Parliamentary Committee was told that the Dunstable to Hockcliffe Trust had experienced a similar increase, after their old Collector had died. And the Kensington Trust had again increased its tolls by changing the Collectors from gate to gate and employing 'an Officer on purpose to be a Cheque' at a cost of a guinea a week (JHC 26: 490–3). The Islington Trust regularly used the same technique.[36]

However, it would be wrong to assume that the experience of some trusts was shared by all. The London trusts did suffer a high turnover rate, but this was not repeated everywhere else. Some unusual records from the Ticehurst Turnpike in Sussex show a remarkably stable employment pattern, the average term its Collectors served being nine years, with some staying for over twenty (Table XXVIII). Eight of the trust's 22 keepers in this period were women. Several keepers worked in families, passing on a gate through generations, or controlling separate gates at the same time. Most of them held their gates singly, and in rural trusts this was the general pattern, as is shown by the entries in the receipts columns of the Sample 3 Account Books. It was a full-time occupation, and accommodation was provided in the tollhouse. There are frequent references in Account Books to the purchase of coal and candles.

In those trusts controlling busy routes, the pattern was more complex. The Kensington Trust employed 12 keepers at its six gates at first, to work alternate 24-hour shifts. After a short while, however, the shifts were reduced to 12 hours (Ffooks 1955). The Islington Trust was employing 17 keepers in the 1760s, three of these on the Paddington New Road. Earlier, it had established eight hour shifts for its keepers. The Kensington Trust still had 12 keepers, and the Marylebone Trust had eight (JHC 29: 647).

The Collector's task was not an easy one. He was responsible for

Table XXVIII
Collectors of the Ticehurst Town
Turnpike, 1756–1800

Gate	Collector	Dates of Service
1. Flimwell Vent Gate	Richard Friend	1757–59
2. Hurst Green Gate	Thomas Marchant	1778–1800
3. Northumberland	Elizabeth Myles	1777–82
Street Gate	Nicholas Myles	1782–85
	Elizabeth Swadling	1785–90
	Thomas Myles and	
	Elizabeth Swadling	1790–91
	John Lamb	1791–99
4. Robertsbridge Town	William Elphick	1763–65
Gate	Tim Jannings	1765–70
	Sarah Jannings	1770–82
	Thomas Marchant (jun.)	1782–99
5. St John's Cross	Mary Thomas	1763–87
Gate, Mountfield		
6. The Level Gate,	Samuel Cannan	1753–56
Battle	William Elphick	1756
	Elizabeth Blundell	1777–99
7. Marly Lane Gate	Jane Hyland	1768–87
8. Lake Gate	Sarah Gibbs	1778–81
	Mary Ticehurst	1781–92
	John Sneath	1794–98
9. Northern Cross	Richard Stace	1756–58
Gate, Ore		
10. Hastings Gate	Edward Raggett	1778–93
	Edward English	1795–99

Source: Dunn MSS 52/19 (East Sussex RO).
It is evident that these ten gates were not operative together over the whole period. The trust repositioned them often.

enforcing the schedule of tolls, and the complex general regulations covering wheel widths, numbers of horses and wagon weights. He had to issue tickets to all who passed through his gate, and record the details. He had to allow all those who were exempt, who had already paid, or who had compounded to pass without payment. When the trust bought a weighing engine, he had to operate this too. Neither was it the safest of jobs. The Collector was the first in line to receive any discontent directed at the turnpike. He could suffer abuse or injury in the hands of disaffected travellers. And he was vulnerable to robbery. In 1719, the Islington Trustees were told that:

> 'Whereas the Turnpike at Tottenham Court has been attempted to be robbed several times, it is found necessary to have casements above stairs to enable the Collector to discover the thieves and defend themselves from such attempts . . . and an iron bar by the door.'

In 1759, one of the Collectors of the neighbouring Marylebone Trust was knifed and robbed, and in 1763, one of them was murdered (Clarke 1955: 280–2). Cases resulting in prosecution by the Trustees are sometimes recorded in the Minute Books.

Turnpike labourers have left an even less informative record than the Gatekeepers. They were usually hired by the Surveyor or, on occasion, by the Trustees themselves, but often their only trace is in the entries of 'day labour' in the Accounts. The Surveyor, or his Under-Surveyors, were responsible for supervising the labourers. Sometimes the Trustees made orders about this. The Taunton and Yeovil Trustees were both concerned that:

> 'The Workmen be allowed only half an hour at Breakfast and One hour at Dinner and that their Wages be deducted in proportion for every loss of time.'

In 1742, the Doncaster to Tadcaster Trust ordered its Surveyor to supervise his labourers from 6 a.m. to 6 p.m. In the same year, the Trustees of the Great North Road in Huntingdonshire decided:

> 'for ye future that . . . the Surveyor . . . do not employ any Labourers, but such as are strong able bodyed men, and who are willing to do their work and not allow above 10d per day and give ye preference to ye parishes upon ye road.'[37]

Some of the labour employed was casual, some seasonal, and the rest more or less permanent. Trusts which repaired their roads throughout the year had a permanent work force. In London, the Kensington Trust employed about 30 men a week, and two Yorkshire trusts, the Rotherham to Wentworth and Wakefield to Sheffield used between ten and 15 in summer and five in winter. Detailed wage accounts survive for these trusts,[38] but these are unusual. Casual labour was paid a little less than permanent road labour. Rates varied between 9d and 1s 6d per day in the 1760s and 1770s, but were everywhere lower than those received by labourers in other trades.[39]

Contractors

It would be a mistake to assume that all the trust's work was carried out by their own employees. Contracting was a widely used device, but this term had a more flexible meaning than just the 'farming of the roads' which received such outright condemnation from John Scott (1778: 344–6) and subsequently from the Webbs (1920: 132). It is as a result of the opinions of these authors that the purpose of contracting as a whole has often been misunderstood.

Contracting was used in five main areas of trust activity. Nearly all trusts contracted the construction work for particular projects, such as tollgates, tollhouses, bridges, causeways and drains. Secondly, nearly all entered into contracts of a less formal nature for the delivery of repair materials. Thirdly, a much smaller proportion contracted the actual construction of stretches of road when the trust was first established. Fourthly, some did farm their roads, making the contractor responsible for maintenance over a specific period, but usually only for certain stretches of the road. Lastly, additional responsibilities, such as the paving, lighting and watering of urban routes was normally undertaken by outside labour.

The evidence for the first two types of contract can be found in nearly all Minute and Account Books, often with separate sums identified as payment to masons, carpenters, glaziers or blacksmiths. When Voucher Books have survived, as for the Marylebone and Islington Trusts, this is particularly clear.[40] However, the detailed contracts, with design specifications, are rarely found. The purchase and carting of repair materials was usually undertaken by contract, particularly after it became difficult to find sufficient close by the road—although some, such as the Chalk Trust in Kent, or the Marylebone Trust, had their own pits. Trusts frequently advertised in local newspapers, and the 1773 Act, which regularized the procedure, required that the Surveyor give ten days public notice of his intention to contract, and that he was to have no personal interest in the matter.

Construction contracts, the third type, are less common, but can be found in the Minute Books and local newspapers. In 1765, the Worcester Trust advertised for:

'An able and experienced Surveyor, who is capable and willing to undertake the Construction of a NEW ROAD, from Cotteridge Hill, within four miles of the City of Worcester, to Broadwas Town, in Length 2492 Yards. Any Person willing to undertake it may view the Ground, now staked out, and deliver his Proposals to Mr. William Giles, Treasurer, at Worcester, on or before Wednesday the fifth of June next, being Commission Day. It is expected to be stoned 16 Feet wide. . . .'

(*JOJ* 4 May 1765)

Sixteen of the 50 Sample 2 trusts used the same procedure, either to construct entirely new routes, as in the case of the Military Road, or to reconstruct, widen and improve existing roads. Some of these contracts were very small. The Hagley Trust paid £50 for the repair of a short section in 1753, and the Hockerill Turnpike paid £75 to its Surveyor, under contract, for the repair of the Hollow Way in Thorley in 1747. On the other hand, some contracts were on a far larger scale. The Knaresborough to Pateley Bridge Trust paid £506 to contractors for reconstructing 13 miles of road in 1759 and 1760, the Harrogate to Hutton Moor spent £1,252 on 3,500 roods, about 16 miles, between 1752 and 1755, and the Ripon to Boroughbridge Trust spent £506 between 1752 and 1754.[41]

These contracts were usually recorded in the Minute Books, and outlined in some detail. An especially good example is given in Appendix 3. The width of the road, its depth or height, the materials to be used, and the terminal date are normal details, although there are often surprising omissions, such as the price to be paid, or the means of inspection. Nearly all trusts seem to have been satisfied with the quality of their work. Only one recorded dismissal was found, when the Stourbridge to Colley Gate Trust relieved its contractor, James Wilders, in 1765.[42] Most of these contracts date from the middle years of the century, when the practice became widespread. It was particularly popular amongst the trusts of the West Riding.[43] But there are some earlier examples. The Gloucester to Birdlip Trust contracted repairs in 1706, and the Loughborough to Harborough and Kensington Trusts did so in the 1720s.[44]

The fourth type of contract, for maintaining turnpike roads, was not unusual, but often affected only short sections of road, sometimes as the result of clauses in the original construction contract. 'Farming' of the whole road was uncommon, and was resorted to by only seven of the Sample 2 trusts, for short periods each. The earliest case was the farming of the Tyburn and Edgware roads by the Marylebone Trustees in the 1720s, but this failed and the contracts were discontinued in 1735

(Sheppard 1958: 58–9). In the 1760s, two West Riding trusts, the Wakefield to Weeland and the Doncaster to Tadcaster both entered into seven-year agreements. Although the latter apparently had no trouble, the Wakefield Trust had to replace one of its two contractors 'by mutual consent' after three years, and sacked the other after four, thereafter taking a more direct interest in the road itself. The Liverpool to Prescot Trust farmed to a number of different contractors in the 1750s, but found it necessary to supervise them closely after complaints were received about the state of parts of their roads.[45]

In some trusts, the Surveyor himself was a contractor. This was so in the Sparrows Herne Trust in Hertfordshire, and the Chippenham Trust in Wiltshire. In 1750, the latter's contract was renewed for 14 years. He was to repair all the trust's roads at £19 per mile per annum. The last example was another Yorkshire trust, and Toller Lane End to Colne Turnpike. John Gott and Abraham Rhodes were first hired to construct several miles of road in 1755, and 20 years later, in 1775, they were still maintaining them.[46] Other examples of farming can be found without difficulty, and local newspapers often contain advertisements inviting tenders, but the practice does not seem to have been as widespread as has been assumed.

The main criticism levelled at farming—apart from it being widespread and inefficient, of which there is not much evidence—is that it involved jobbery. Trust Acts forbad Trustees to profit from their position in any way, and there is little indication that they did. This is despite the conclusions of several contemporary Parliamentary investigations. The 1764 Commons Committee examined the affairs of seven trusts and concluded that 'Mismanagement was chiefly owing to the acting Trustees having been employed or interested in the Works carried on under the Trust' (JHC 29: 1007), a judgement based solely on the activities of the Marylebone Trustees. But significantly, the historian of this trust found no evidence of overcharging when Trustees were involved in contracts (Clarke 1955: 307). The Kensington Trust was criticized on the same grounds in the following year (JHC 30: 429), but again there was no evidence of undue profits being made. Indeed, there seems little reason why jobbery should not have been widespread, but equally the grounds for assuming that this led to high prices and mismanagement are far from convincing.

This mature administrative structure of Trustee managers, professional Officers, paid employees and outside contractors, was in marked contrast to the impressed and amateur organization of the parish repair system. Road repairs could be carried out on a more intensive scale, in a co-ordinated manner, with some regard for the future transport needs of the area. However, before exploring in more detail the repair techniques used and the policies formulated by trusts, it is necessary to examine their financial resources and overall patterns of expenditure.

7. Notes

1. See above, pp. 87–94.
2. Thirty-nine of the Sample 1 Trustee lists included ex-officio members.
3. Trustee lists from Acts passed between 1771 and 1800 are excluded from the table because a large proportion of them no longer categorize Trustees in this way.
4. Only two cases have been found: Acts 141, 277.
5. These lists are given in: *The History of Parliament—The House of Commons, 1715–54*, Vols I and II, ed. Romney Sedgwick (HMSO 1970), and *The House of Commons 1754–90*, Vols I and II, ed. Sir Lewis Namier and John Brooke (HMSO 1964).
6. Trusts nos 108–13, 119–20, 122–5. Five could sit on eight trusts, three on nine, and one—Sir John Lister Kay, MP for York from 1734 to 1741—on ten.
7. The characteristics of the Sample 2 trusts are shown in the following Table:

Date of establishment:	Before 1750	20	(21 per cent)
	1751–70	29	(54)
	1771–1800	1	(23)
Size:	Under 10 miles	13	(19 per cent)
	11–20 miles	23	(33)
	21–30 miles	8	(22)
	Over 30 miles	6	(27)
Location:	London	6	(3 per cent)
	Industrial area	8	
	Rural area	36	

Source: See Appendix 2.

There are 50 trusts in the sample, hence percentage values are obtained by doubling these figures. The characteristics of the background population (i.e. all eighteenth century trusts) are given in brackets. It can be seen that early trusts—those established before 1750—are over-represented, as are small trusts and London trusts. These limitations should be borne in mind.

8. Brentford Minutes, 22 July 1717 (Chiswick Library).
   New Cross Minutes, 29 March 1718 (Kent AO).
   Sparrows Herne Minutes, 7 July 1762 (Herts. RO).
9. Brentford Minutes, 22 and 29 July 1717 (Chiswick Library).
10. New Cross Minutes, 29 and 31 March, 20 May 1718 (Kent AO).
    Sparrows Herne Minutes, 7 and 14 July 1762 (Herts. RO).
11. Old Street Minutes, 5 Aug., 2 Sept. 1755, March and April 1756 (Finsbury Library).
    Stokenchurch Minutes, 28 May 1740 (Oxf. CRO).
    New Cross Minutes, 28 June 1745, 27 June 1746 (Kent AO).
12. Acts nos 16 on renewal in 1727, 67, 95, 134, 210, for example.
13. Ilminster Minutes, 1754–61 (Somerset RO).
    Isleworth Minutes, 1767 (Hounslow Library).
14. Liverpool to Prescot Minutes (Lancs. RO).
    Hull trusts—120, 122–3 (MacMahon 1964: 23–5).
15. Gloucester to Birdlip Minutes 1761–73 (Glos. RO).
    Taunton Minutes, 1752–77 (Somerset RO).
    Wells Minutes, 1753–67 (Somerset RO).
16. Chippenham Minutes, 1727–68 (Wilts. RO).
    Doncaster to Wakefield Minutes, 1741–1830 (WR).
    Knaresborough to Pateley Bridge Minutes, 1759–1851 (WR).
    Seend St. to Box Minutes, 1753–91 (Wilts. RO).
17. Frequently the Officers continued to work, assuming a managerial role (see below, pp. 186–7).
18. Preston to Garstang Minutes, 1774 (Lancs. RO).
19. For example: trusts nos 59 (in 1747, 1760, 1769), 184 (in 1773), 195 (in 1773), 313 (in 1779).
20. Trusts nos 31, 42, 79, 173, 198, 277, 306.
21. Act 218. This was the standard clause in Turnpike Acts from about 1750. Before this date, the post of Treasurer was usually not mentioned, but this does not mean an appointment was not made. All the pre-1750 Sample 2 trusts had a Treasurer.
22. Knaresborough to Pateley Bridge Accounts, 1772.
    Knaresborough to Green Hammerton Minutes, 5 Aug. 1784.
    Grassington to Wetherby Minutes, 18 July 1775 (WR).
23. Islington Minutes, 20 and 27 May 1718 (Islington Library).
    Fulham Minutes, 14 March 1734 (Kensington Library).
    Hockerill Minutes, 4 May 1744, 12 January 1774 (Herts. RO).
24. Liverpool to Prescot Minutes, 15 Sept. 1726 (Lancs. RO).
    Yeovil Minutes, 20 June 1755 (Somerset RO).
    Grassington to Wetherby Minutes, 18 July 1775 (WR).
25. Marylebone Minutes, 1 July 1742 (Marylebone Library).
26. This information is taken from trust advertisements for letting the tolls, in the *Derby Mercury*, between 1780 to 1782 and 1790 to 1792 (Derby Borough Library).
27. This is the case argued by Albert (1972: 149).
28. Liverpool to Prescot Minutes, 20 May 1726 (Lancs RO).
    Fulham Minutes, 17 May 1731 (Kensington Library).
29. This point is discussed in Chapter 10.
30. Yeovil Minutes, 10 Aug. 1754 (Somerset RO).

Islington Minutes, 20 May, 30 Sept. 1718 (Islington Library).
Cranford Bridge Minutes, 3 March 1729 (M'sex RO).

31. Chippenham Minutes, 29 May 1727 (Wilts. RO).
Islington Minutes, 3 and 16 July 1717.
Ilminster Minutes, 17 July, 31 Aug. 1759 (Somerset RO).

32. Islington Minutes, 18 Feb. 1718. (Islington Library).

33. Doncaster to Tadcaster Minutes, 4 Nov. 1741 (WR).
Carlisle to Newcastle Minutes, 16 Dec. 1752 (Cumbria RO).
Yeovil Minutes, 11 Oct. 1753 (Somerset RO).

34. Tadcaster to York Minutes, 2 Dec. 1745 (WR).

35. Islington Minutes, 28 Jan. 1718 (Islington Library).
Liverpool to Prescot Minutes, 3 July 1756 (Lancs. RO).
Marylebone (Sheppard 1958: 69).
Kensington (JHC 21: 837).

36. Islington Minutes, summary accounts for 1763 (Islington Library).

37. Taunton Minutes, 7 May 1752.
Yeovil Minutes, 5 July 1753 (Somerset RO).
Doncaster to Tadcaster Minutes, 30 March 1742 (WR).

38. Kensington, Weekly Accounts of Cash Paid to Labourers (Kensington Library).
Rotherham to Wentworth, Account of the weekly labour employed.
Sheffield to Wakefield, Surveyor's Account (Sheffield City Libraries).

39. Albert 1972: 160–1.

40. Islington, Book of Cancelled Bills 1730–71 (Islington Library).
Marylebone Accounts 1736–53 (Marylebone Library).

41. Hagley Minutes, 4 Sept. 1753 (Birmingham Library).
Hockerill Minutes, 31 March 1747 (Herts. RO).
Knaresborough to Pateley Bridge Accounts, 1759–1880.
Harrogate to Hutton Moor Accounts, 1752–1814.
Ripon to Boroughbridge Accounts, 1752–1814 (WR).

42. Stourbridge Minutes, 4 March 1765 (Worcs. RO).

43. Among the Sample 2 trusts: 176 (Harrogate to Boroughbridge, Harrogate to Hutton
Moor, Ripon to Boroughbridge Districts), 210, 241, 325 (Knaresborough to Pateley
Bridge District), 535.

44. Kensington Minutes, 22 June and 19 July 1726 (Kensington Library), and Albert
(1972: 154).

45. Wakefield to Weeland Minutes, 11 Sept. 1760, 10 Jan. 1761.
Doncaster to Tadcaster Minutes, 9 April 1761, 3 Aug. 1764, 20 April 1765 (WR).
Liverpool to Prescot Minutes, 1755–8 (Lancs. RO).

46. Sparrows Herne Minutes, 14 July, 1 Nov. 1762 (Herts. RO).
Chippenham Minutes, 25 May 1750 (Wilts. RO).
Toller Lane End Minutes, 30 July 1755, 22 May 1777 (WR).

8
Trust Finances

The income and expenditure of turnpike trusts are matters which have never been examined in anything but a very general fashion. For the eighteenth century trusts this is not easy. The first records of the financial state of all trusts are not available until the nineteenth century. In 1821, and again in the 1830s, trusts were required to send their annual accounts, including a statement of debt, to Parliament. The 1821 Returns are averaged over the three years from 1818, whilst the 1830s Returns are annual, from 1834 to 1838. An examination of trust finances must rely heavily on this information. Although the actual figures are not relevant to the eighteenth century, the relative magnitude of values—for instance, in showing the variation of income between trusts, and overall patterns of expenditure—are of interest. Frequent reference is made, therefore, to these nineteenth century Returns, but they are supplemented, wherever possible, by eighteenth century information. In the discussion of trust expenditure, extensive use is made of information derived from the Account Books of the Sample 3 trusts.

Income

Turnpike trusts were financed by a number of different methods, but their primary means of support were the tolls granted by each Act. Toll income was normally supplemented by long and short-term borrowing, most commonly raised by mortgaging the tolls. The issue of shares was not a possibility, because of the peculiar nature of the turnpike trust. Its guardianship of a public resource, the King's Highway being a communal property right and existing facility, rendered the concept of private ownership innappropriate. However, this apparent limitation was not entirely disadvantageous, as it gave trusts the resources of the common law, namely the statute duty obligation of the parishes.

These sources of finance provided each trust with the money required to implement its policies. There was, however, considerable variation in the level of income between trusts, both in aggregate and income per mile terms. The Commons Committee of 1752 which investigated various trusts found that the Kensington Trust had a toll income of about £3,000 per annum, the Cranford Bridge about £900, the Dunstable to Hockcliffe about £600, and the Basingstoke to Hartfordbridge, only £300 (JHC 26: 490–3). The 1764 Commons Committee found similar variations between the income levels of the eight trusts it investigated (Table XXIX).

Table XXIX
Average Toll Income Per Annum of Eight Trusts, 1752–62

	Total	Per mile
New Cross	£2,108	£602·3
Marylebone	1,394	348·4
Islington	4,223	301·6
Kensington	3,559	296·6
New Road	484	161·4
Brentford	1,904	158·7
Surrey New Roads	1,006	125·7
Gloucester to Birdlip (1755–62)	382	54·6

Source: JHC 29: 1009.

Throughout the eighteenth century, toll income rose steadily as traffic flows increased, as Ward's work on traffic statistics has shown (1974: 165). By 1818–20, the total toll income for all trusts in England and Wales had reached £1,008,210 per annum, or £56 per mile (BPP 1821 (747) IV: 343). By 1838, it had risen to £1,527,297, or £69·5 per mile. There were large variations within and between counties. This is demonstrated by Table XXX, for a selection of ten counties.

These variations in toll income reflect differing rates of road traffic flow. In Surrey, for example, the highest toll incomes were those of the suburban Bermondsey Trust (£357·3 per mile) and the main road trusts (Croydon to Reigate: £277·1, Egham to Bagshot: £189·1, Gatton: £155·6). The Wealden trusts had the lowest incomes (Godstone to Highgate: £10·8, Godstone to Painshill: £23·3, Haslemere: £27·9). In Middlesex, the various roads consolidated under the Metropolis Roads

Table XXX
Toll Income of Trusts in Ten Counties, 1838

	Income per mile	V
	£	per cent
Berks.	88·4	64
Cambs.	55·3	49
Cumberland	50·6	35
Essex	98·9	129
M'sex	306·5	92
Merioneth	14·8	44
Monmouth	45·4	73
Oxon	60·2	77
Staffs.	73·0	112
Surrey	204·5	185

Source: computed from BPP 1840 (289) XLV: 391–531 (income).
1840 (280) XXVII: 15 (mileages).

Board in 1826 had a toll yield of £589·1 per mile, with the Highgate to Whetstone Trust exceeding even this, at £713·9. In distant Merioneth, however, the 15 mile long Barmouth Trust received only £6·3 per mile, and the Bala Trust with 72 miles, but £10·5.

This character and degree of variation was also typical of the eighteenth century, although the actual levels of toll income were lower. Toll income, however, was not entirely dependent on the volume of

Table XXXI
Average Income Per Annum of all Trusts in England and Wales, 1834–8

		per cent
Tolls	£1,498,287	85·9
Compositions (in lieu of statute duty)	32,119	1·8
Value of statute duty (estimated)	45,831	2·6
Fines	607	0·03
Incidentals	31,669	1·8
Money borrowed	135,968	7·8
	£1,744,481	

Source : computed from BPP 1840 (280) XXVII: 647.

traffic. And trust income, although largely derived from the tolls, was supported by other sources. Table XXXI shows the value of these sources over the period 1834–8.

The Tolls

The schedule of tolls chargeable by each trust was laid down in its Act. These varied considerably from trust to trust, and often between Acts for the same trust. The schedule itself was designed to cover all those categories of traffic which were considered to be a charge on road repair, differentiating to a certain extent on grounds of size and ability to pay. Each schedule was qualified by a list of exemptions and qualifications, the aim of which was to minimize the effect of the toll on local traffic and on categories considered to be beneficial to the maintenance of the road surface.

The variation in the level of tolls chargeable can be illustrated by extracting a standard list of charges, or 'toll standard', from the toll schedules of Sample 1 trusts. This toll standard has been defined as the sum of the tolls on a large and a small coach, a large and a small wagon (drawn by six horses and two horses in each case), a score of cattle, a score of sheep, and a single horse. The results are shown in Table XXXII, with large variations, illustrated by the high coefficients of variation, being immediately apparent. The toll standard for the 1721 Marylebone Trust was only 2½d (42), whereas that for the 1726 Tewkesbury Trust was 5s 8d (62). The 1752 York to Scarborough Trust charged no less than £1 2s (167) but the Bromyard Trust of the same year, only 4s 6d (174).

Table XXXII
Toll Standards

	Toll Standard	V
		per cent
1700–50	47·8d	47
1751–70	61·1d	32
1771–1800	76·8d	41

Source: Sample 1.

The general trend of toll standards over the century is graphed in Fig. 33. There was a gradual rise of 5·2 per cent per decade, but the clearest feature is the degree of overall variation. In the period up to 1750, the toll standard is significantly correlated with both the length of trusts' roads, and their distance from London.[1] The larger the mileage of road controlled by a trust, and the greater its distance from London, the higher the toll standard. This suggests there was some attempt to fix the level of tolls in line with the trusts' needs and the expected traffic flow. It is notable that all the heavily used turnpike roads around London had low toll standards, e.g. Marylebone—2½d, Highgate to Barnet—1s, Islington—1s 6d, Enfield to Shoreditch—2s 5d, Fulham—3s 1d. The highest toll standard applied on turnpike roads far from the capital, where the traffic flow was relatively light. On the Bowes to Brough road, it was 6s 9d, on the Manchester to Saltersbrook, 6s 10d, on the Wakefield to Pontefract, 7s 3d and on the Boroughbridge to Durham, 18s 5d. Such variations were still prominent between new trusts set up after 1750, but there is no simple explanation for them. There is no significant correlation between the toll standard and either of the two previous variables.[2]

Toll schedules were intended to last, not for the length of a trust's life, but only for the duration of the Act in which they were fixed. When Acts were renewed, the Trustees often asked for an increase in the level of tolls in order to raise their level of income. But these increases were not always granted, and if they were, it was not always as a result of a request from the trust. In a sample of renewal Acts, over half (53 per cent) maintained

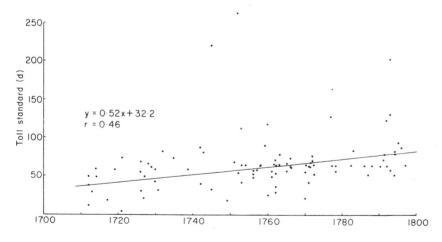

$$y = 0.52x + 32.2$$
$$r = 0.46$$

FIG. 33. Turnpike toll levels in the eighteenth century. Toll standards for Sample 1 trusts plotted against time. For an explanation of the derivation of the toll standard, see text.

tolls at the same level, 11 per cent actually reduced them and only 35 per cent increased them. Trust indebtedness does not seem to have been a decisive factor in this, being almost equal in the three sample groups.[3]

Toll Exemptions

The scale of tolls chargeable was not applicable to all classes of traffic. There was a range of general and particular exemptions, either listed in each Act, or allowed by general legislation. Those listed in each Act covered certain categories of local traffic, such as wagons used in agriculture, those used for the haulage of building and road repair materials, and people going to church. Certain special categories were also included, such as post-horses, the Army, wagons carrying vagrants, and people going to vote on election days.[4] The exemption of much local traffic was in keeping with the supplementary nature of the turnpike trust: to have charged these groups would have resulted in an inequitable form of double counting. The exemptions themselves cannot be seen as inequitable, as the Webbs claimed (1920: 136), and this helps to explain the minimal amount of opposition to turnpike schemes.

Regular users of particular turnpike routes, and those categories of local traffic which were not exempt, such as tradesmen, agricultural wagons carrying produce for sale, and passengers, were also favoured by the toll structure. On most turnpike roads, payment of toll at one gate secured a free passage at the next, if it belonged to the same trust. Payment at a gate also allowed the traveller to return through the same gate free of charge, providing he came back the same day. The situation around London had become so complex by the end of the century that John Cary produced a Road Book in 1790 covering all the major routes leading into the capital, showing the position of the tollgates and the extent of the validity of tickets purchased at each.

In addition to these general toll exemptions in each Act, there were often some special cases, making concession to the nature of the local economy, or to the promoters of the Act. Coal and lime were frequently carried free, or at only a quarter rate, on the turnpike roads in northern England and South Wales. This concession was subsequently made less favourable upon petition from many of the trusts concerned.[5] Very low rates were payable on iron products on the Talke Turnpike in Staffordshire (27) and green hop poles were carried free on the Rochester to Maidstone road in Kent (79).

Some interesting concessions were made on turnpike roads close to towns. The Bath Trust was to reimburse all those travellers who paid toll on leaving the town 'to take the air' and returned the same day, whilst grain wagons going to and from any of the mills within one mile of Bath were to be exempt (11). The Liverpool to Prescot Act of 1726 allowed all horses carrying corn, butter or cheese into the town to pass free (63), and the Reading to Puntfield Trustees could not charge any consignment of cloth and serge sent from any fulling mill under the renewal Act of 1728.

These special exemptions nearly always applied to categories of traffic, rather than to individuals or families. The Webbs' claim that 'invidious was the special privilege of exemption which influential inhabitants were sometimes able to secure for themselves, their families, their workmen, their servants and their agents, and for those of all successive owners and occupiers of their premises, as the price for abstaining from Parliamentary opposition' (1920: 137) is groundless. Very few cases of such 'privileged exemptions' can be found. The only examples which have come to light are the Royal Family itself on some of the London roads (57, 65, 92, 30 (on renewal in 1742)), the owners of Coley House in the 1746 renewal Act of the Reading to Puntfield road (26), and the Duke of Norfolk in the 1758 renewal of the Chesterfield to Worksop Act (105). Undoubtedly other examples exist, but they are very few in number.

It was also unusual for Trustees to accord themselves favourable rates: only two such cases have been found. In the 1750s, the Cranford Bridge Trustees had been doing this, prior to a reorganization of the trust, but this had cost less than 0·5 per cent of its annual income (JHC 26: 491). Earlier, the same trust had ordered that any Gatekeepers allowing a Trustee to pass without payment were to be sacked. The other case was the Hagley Trust, which in 1754 exempted its Treasurer and Surveyor, and its Trustees when passing to or from a trust meeting. [6]

In addition to these favourable rates and exemptions in each Act, some of the general Turnpike Acts made concessions to certain types of traffic to encourage general road policy. These applied on all turnpike roads. The Broad Wheel Acts ordered Trustees to lessen tolls on wagons with nine-inch wheels in 1753 and then to free them of toll completely for three years, in 1755. The toll on wagons with six-inch wheels was decreased slightly, and that on those with narrow wheels, of less than six-inch width, could be raised by not more than a quarter. The intention was to discourage the use of narrow wheels, which were considered to cut open road surfaces, so contributing to the formation of ruts, and stimulate the use of broad wheels, which supposedly rolled the surface, keeping it more even. To avoid damaging existing or future creditors, the latter Act granted all trusts an automatic five-year extension of their terms. Later, the details of the restrictions were altered, in 1757, and again in 1773, but always in favour of the broader wheels. The scale of the concession, however, led a few trusts to complain that their toll income had been considerably lowered as a result. [7]

Tollgates

The Trustees had rather greater freedom to decide the number and location of tollgates than they had with the structure and level of tolls. They were bound 'to Erect or cause to be Erected a Gate or Gates, Turnpike or Turnpikes across any part or parts of the said Highway'. Very few Acts were more specific than this, although some did fix the location of gates. [8]

Many of the rural trusts controlling just one stretch of road, required only one or two gates. However, those with a complex series of routes, such as the town-centred trusts, or some with big mileages, required several gates. The initial numbers of gates set up by the 50 Sample 2 trusts are given in Table XXXIII. The town-centred Ilminster and Wells

Table XXXIII
Initial Number of Tollgates

Number of gates	Number of trusts
7	1
6	1
5	3
4	3
3	11
2	17
1	9
?	5
	N. = 50

Source: Sample 2.

Trusts had seven and six gates respectively. The Kensington Trust with several different roads, and the Keighley to Kendal Trust, controlling 51 miles of turnpike, both had five gates.

Trusts frequently moved gates, or otherwise sought to stop evasion of the tolls. The Brentford Trust moved its Hounslow gate from the east to the west end of the town in 1719, because it was too easily evaded, after £2,000 had been offered on mortgage if this was done.[9] The Kensington Trust increased the number of its gates to seven after three years, often moving them to more advantageous positions (Ffooks 1955). The Oxford to Fyfield Trust petitioned Parliament successfully to alter a clause in its Act which restricted it to gates placed on the Fyfield and Eynsham roads alone, in favour of one unavoidable gate on the Botley Causeway (JHC 31:433). Side-gates, which were an immediate answer to the problem of evasion, were allowed by many Acts from the 1740s, although some trusts were permitted to use them considerably earlier (31, 37, 49). The privilege was extended to all trusts by the General Turnpike Act of 1773. The full toll was chargeable at these side-gates, although the tickets issued gave exemption at the next main gate, and traffic using the turnpike road for only a few hundred yards was usually totally exempt.

The result of this uncontrolled freedom in erecting gates was a profusion of the number of gates which travellers had to pass. In 1838, the only general count ever undertaken revealed that the 1,116 trusts and districts in England and Wales controlled a total of 7,796 gates and side-gates. Some of the bigger trusts had a very large number. The Worcester Trust had 48; the Coventry, 38; and the Cheadle, 37. The general position is shown in Table XXXIV.

Table XXXIV
Numbers of Gates and Side-Gates per Trust, 1838

	England	Wales
Trusts under 10 miles	3·4	2·8
10–20	5·6	4·6
20–30	8·4	7·5
over 30 miles	16·0	16·4
Average for all trusts (England and Wales)		7·0

Source : computed from BPP 1840 (280) XXVII: 631–46.

Cary's mapping of the high roads in and around London showed the large number of gates on the complex network of turnpike routes there. Within the city itself, the situation was made more complex by the addition of the Thames bridge tolls, and the Sunday tolls, chargeable at certain turnpike gates for the City Paving Commission. The numbers of gates which travellers encountered on various journeys from London are given in Table XXXV, along with the number of times that separate payments were required.

TRANSPORT AND ECONOMY

Table XXXV
Tollgates on Journeys from London, 1790

	Mileage	Number of trusts	Number of gates	Number of payments
London – Maidenhead	26	4	7	4
– High Wycombe	29	4	6	4
– St. Albans	21	3	6	3
– Hertford	21	2	5	2
– Chelmsford	29	2	3	2
– Maidstone	35	2	6	2
– Tunbridge Wells	36	4	5	4
– East Grinstead	29	1	4	1
– Guildford	29	2	5	2

Source: compiled from Cary (1790).

However, in some areas, outside interests ensured that trusts were less able to control the position of their gates. The merchants who had petitioned for the establishment of the northern trusts in the 1740s secured clauses in several of the individual Acts forbidding the erection of gates within a certain distance of some towns. The 1741 Doncaster to Wetherby Act did not allow gates to be positioned within one mile of Boroughbridge or Doncaster (111), and the 1745 Tadcaster to York Act (125) placed a limit of three miles on the proximity of gates to either town. Again, this meant effective exemption for local traffic, and many further instances occurred. The distances involved, however, were normally quite small, three miles being the usual maximum. The Selby to Leeds Trust, which was not allowed to place any gates within five miles of Leeds, petitioned against this clause, successfully, in 1751, on the ground that it means that 'the greatest part of the Tolls have been lost'. (JHC 26:56, 80.)

A further way in which local people might be favoured by the trusts was by the practice of compounding for the tolls. Amongst the Sample 2 trusts, this does not seem to have been a common practice, except in the West Riding. The Yorkshire trusts frequently allowed large numbers of local people, and sometimes whole townships, to make a small annual payment to cover all tolls. The Knaresborough to Green Hammerton Trust, for example, fixed a rate of five shillings per family for those living within three miles of Knaresborough and not working for hire. The Doncaster to Wakefield Trust allowed everyone living within three miles of a gate to compound, often at only sixpence or a shilling for a whole year. The agreements included some townships, for example Hassle for 15s and Hirmsworth for £1 15s.[10] There are several other examples from this area,[11] but elsewhere the practice was far more limited, being restricted to regular coachmen or wagoners.

Attempts to avoid payment of toll, either by deceiving the keeper, or avoiding the gate altogether, were potential sources of trouble to trusts. Acts generally made provision for the imposition of stiff penalties on those who tried to avoid gates, transfer tickets, or remove horses or part of their load before reaching the turnpike. The Act of 1773 fixed the fine at between 10s and 50s for drivers and £1 to £5 for owner-drivers. Landowners who encouraged travellers to by-pass gates by allowing passage over their fields could be fined between £1 and £2. Cases of prosecution are not common, but occur in most Minute Books.

Careful positioning of gates, and measures to contain traffic to the route were a better means of preventing evasion. The Wakefield to Halifax Trust appointed a sub-committee in 1742 to set up side-gates, as did the Wadhurst to West Farleigh Trust in 1765. The Salisbury to Eling Trust ordered its Surveyor to erect side-gates on any part of the road from Lopcombe Corner to Winchester in 1756.[12] Other trusts ensured that the road immediately adjacent to their tollhouses was secure, by locking farm gates and building fences. In this respect, the following newspaper notice is interesting:

Kidlington Turnpike

WHEREAS repeated Complaints have been made to the Trustees of the Kidlington Turnpike Road, That divers Persons, in order to evade the Payment of the Tolls at the Kidlington Gate, have made a Custom of passing through the Grounds towards Gosward Bridge; and in Consequence of such Complaints, the Gates adjacent to the Turnpike Road, as well as between the Cutslow and Water Eaton Estates have been locked up to prevent future Abuses of the like Nature: *This publick Notice is likewise given*, That whoever shall hereafter be convicted of Defrauding the said Trust of their Tolls, by illegally passing through the aforesaid Grounds, will be punished with the utmost Severity, according to the Power granted by the Law, and Actions of Trespass will also be commenced for watering Grounds, to the manifest prejudice of the several Tenants.

(*JOJ* 21 July 1770)

Farming the Tolls

The collection of the tolls was the responsibility of the Trustees, but they did not have to do this themselves. The practice of 'letting the gates' or 'farming the tolls' for a fixed sum over a certain period—usually one or three years—was regularized by the 1773 Act, although it was widespread before this. The Act laid down that the tolls were to be let to the highest bidder, after one month's notice of the auction had been given, and the net amount of the previous year's proceeds had been published. The tolls were to be put up at this level, and a three minute interval was to elapse after every bid. The highest bidder became the Farmer or Renter, upon provision of sureties. He was to pay the trust in monthly or quarterly instalments.

There is much evidence in the Minute Books, and local newspapers of the time, that trusts regarded the practice of farming as convenient. It relieved them of the need to employ and supervise Gatekeepers, and provided them with a steady, guaranteed income flow. At least 22 of the Sample 2 trusts adopted this practice at some time, particularly in the years after 1770. In the early 1760s, six of the trusts around Oxford were advertising toll auctions in *Jackson's Oxford Journal*, and in the *Derby Mercury* in the early 1780s and 1790s, respectively 15 and 19 trusts inserted auction notices.

There are much earlier cases. The Gloucester to Birdlip Hill Justice Trust first let its gate in 1702, and again, in 1710. The Maidstone to Rochester Trust let its two gates in 1730, the Gloucester to Hereford Trust did the same in 1726, 1727 and 1729, as did the New Cross Trust in 1746. Some let their gates very soon after establishment—for example, the Gloucester to Hereford Trust within five months, the Wadhurst to West Farleigh in 1765, within seven months, the Keighley to Kendal in 1754, within 12 months, and the Maidstone to Rochester within two years.[13]

Nearly all the newspaper advertisements indicate that gates had been let separately. This would suggest that most eighteenth century toll farmers were small-scale operators. In the nineteenth century, however, professional toll farmers emerged in some areas. The most notable of these was Lewis Levy, who claimed before a Parliamentary Committee in 1825 to be renting three quarters of the London tolls (BPP 1825 (355) V 167:30). In 1839, when his total rents were of the order of £100,000, he asserted that he had once controlled gates worth four or five times this amount (BPP 1839 (295) IX 369:13).

Long-term Borrowing

When it was necessary to supplement toll income to finance expensive projects, the Trustees arranged to borrow money. This was usually one of the first tasks of a new trust, although the Minute Books contain frequent references to subsequent borrowing. The money could be secured in three ways—by mortgage, against the security of the tolls; by bond, with the added personal surety of the Trustees; or by annuity. The second method had obvious drawbacks, and the third, whilst allowing Trustees to pay a higher rate of interest, was not to be preferred to a toll mortgage secured at a lower rate. The second and third methods were thus relatively uncommon and were used only by those trusts which had difficulty raising money on mortgage (Albert 1972:94). The 14 trusts of the Metropolis Roads Board, for example, had mortgage debts of £84,625 in 1827, floating debts of £16,395, but had issued only £3,800 worth of terminable annuities (BPP 1826–7 (339) VII:25).

The usual method of raising long-term finance was therefore by the use of the toll mortgage. These were interest-bearing loans, secured against the income from the tolls. Individual Acts specified the maximum rate of interest that could be paid, but usually not the total amount that could be borrowed, or in effect, the term over which the money could be borrowed. Most mortgages were undated, but they were understood to be valid for the length of a trust's legal term. The exact wording of the Acts was 'that the Trustees . . . [may mortgage . . . the said Tolls and Duties arising by virtue of this Act . . . for the Term for which the said Tolls and Duties are hereby made payable, or for any Part of the said Term, as a Security for any Sum or Sums of Money to be . . . borrowed . . .'. However, no provision was made in these Acts for the establishment of a sinking fund. Hence the presence of an outstanding debt guaranteed the extension of a trust's legal term (above, p. 103).

The toll mortgage was a flexible instrument and took a variety of forms. Trusts sometimes raised their borrowings on a single or limited number of large denomination mortgages. Subscriptions, raised before or after the establishment of a trust, offered the smaller investor the chance to lend money, whilst some trusts issued small mortgages in specific sums—usually £50 or £100—under the title of 'turnpike securities'. Each of these forms of mortgage were transferable, the only provisos being that the assignment should be executed in the presence of two witnesses, and notified to the Clerk of the Trust within three months. In the absence of a stated date of expiry, this was the only means by which creditors could recover their principal, although they could move an action for ejectment if the trust defaulted on its payments of interest.

A fairly detailed portrayal of the borrowing patterns of trusts is available elsewhere (Albert 1972:93–119), and only general points need be examined here. In the first half of the eighteenth century, trusts usually borrowed from a limited number of people after they had been established. In fact, it was common for there to be no more than one or two substantial creditors. The use of the subscription, raised to finance the Act as well as the trust itself, became increasingly common from the 1750s, thus broadening the basis of financial support. By the 1770s, pre- and post-enactment borrowing was usually done in relatively small amounts raised on subscription, or by the sale of low denomination securities.

Several cases of subscription borrowing occurred amongst the Sample 2 trusts. In Somerset, the Yeovil Trust opened a subscription at its first meeting in 1753, which raised £800. A few months later, a further £2,200 was raised in the same way. The Wells Trust was initially financed by a pre-enactment subscription and borrowed a further £850 on mortgage soon afterwards. The Taunton Trust opened a list in March 1753, after £2,000 had been secured on mortgage in the previous May. A further £1,000 was raised. In Yorkshire, the Keighley to Kendal Trust initially raised £3,600 on mortgage, and successfully sought £2,000 more on subscription three years later, in 1756, whilst in the middle of an extensive road widening and repair programme. Two years after, the Doncaster to Wakefield Trust opened a subscription to pay its creditors, and a third Yorkshire Trust, the Collingham to York, made 'proportionate calls' on all its creditors to raise £500 to pay for a renewal Act in 1791.[14] The six Sample 2 cases were thus limited to two counties.

Subscription borrowing had become sufficiently widespread for a clause to be inserted in the 1773 Act to enable Trustees to recover all sums subscribed in the list. The actual process of subscription is well illustrated by the case of the Oxford to Fyfield Trust:

'Whereas an Act of Parliament is now passed "for repairing and widening the Road from the West end of Thames Street in the City of Oxford, over Botley Causeway, to the Turnpike Road near Fifield in the County of Berks'', Such Persons and Societies as shall be pleased to contribute towards the repairing and widening of the said Causeway, and have not yet sent in their Names are requested forthwith to cause their Names, and the Sums which they severally intend to subscribe, to be entered in the Subscription-Roll, which now lies for that purpose in the Town Clerk's Office in Oxford: so that a complete Account of the Subscribers, and the Sums subscribed, may be laid before the Trustees at their first Meeting on the twenty second of April next.' (*JOJ* 7 March 1767)

In the event only £500 was raised, but when the toll income of the trust had been increased by the relocation of the gates, more money was forthcoming.

A further degree of flexibility was introduced into trust finance by the sale of negotiable turnpike securities, also referred to as 'bills' or 'deed polls', after 1750. Although these were technically no different to the other types of mortgage debt, they represented a more positive approach to the acquisition of credit. The securities were usually sold by direct advertising in local newspapers, or by auction to the highest bidder. The Wells Trust sold 42 deed polls, mostly in £50 and £100 units, in its first three years.[15]

The actual sums borrowed by trusts varied considerably. By 1838, the total mortgage debt for all English and Welsh trusts was £7,260,993, or £6,506 per trust. This sum was held in 42,637 mortgages, an average of £170 per mortgage (BPP 1840 (256) XXVII:9). The low level of this figure reflects the high number of small-scale creditors either on subscription lists, or holding bills.

Directly comparable figures are not available for the eighteenth century, but some indication of the level of trust borrowing can be gained from the indebtedness of the Sample 1 trusts when they applied for their first renewal Act. This information was given to Parliament, and is recorded in the Journals. The 29 pre-1750 trusts had average debts of £1,850 at this stage. But a comparison with the post-1750 trusts is not particularly meaningful, because after 1770 debts are most commonly cited in Parliamentary sources in a descriptive manner alone. Thus for the 36 1751-70 trusts, precise figures are available in only 13 cases, with an average of £3,115. Sometimes Parliament was presented with some very high debts. In 1764 the Surrey New Roads (155) owed £13,500, in 1767 the Tiverton Trust (289) owed £10,350, and in 1769 the Exeter Trust (201) was £23,250 in debt (JHC 29:773–4; 31:19; 32:272).

Short-term Borrowing

Although long-term borrowing was usually a planned operation, designed to meet specific needs, trusts also incurred short-term debts. Sometimes this was intentional, otherwise it was by default. Arrears of interest, and indebtedness to contractors and the trust's own Officers were the usual reasons. Some of these debts became long-standing, and were converted into principal, or long-term borrowing. In 1838, the trusts of England and Wales owed £1,123,623 in unpaid interest, £263,259 of which had been converted into principal. This figure represented a significant proportion of total debts, as is shown by Table XXXVI. Eighty-two trusts in England and two in Wales were said to have paid no interest 'for several years'.

Table XXXVI
Total Debts of All Trusts in England and Wales, 1834-8
(Average per annum, at the end of each year)

Bonded, mortgage debt	£7,179,313
Floating debt	237,072
Unpaid interest	1,045,425
Balance due to Treasurers	129,018
	£8,590,828
Balance in Treasurers' hands	316,193
Arrears of toll and compositions	88,800
Money in Government stock	7,399
	£412,392
Net	£8,178,436

Source : Computed from BPP 1840 (280) XXVII:647.

The problem of unpaid interest is not one that suddenly arose in the 1830s, although it grew appreciably worse from about 1820. In that year, the total interest owed by trusts was £384,314 (BPP 1821 (747) IV:343).

It rose sharply to £821,586 in 1829 (BPP 1840 (256) XXVII:9). Some trusts also had this problem in the eighteenth century. However, although it is difficult to gain an indication of the extent of interest debts, they do seem to have been limited. The Sample 3 Account Books reveal cases, but they are few in number. The Knaresborough to Green Hammerton Trust in Yorkshire agreed to pay off six years interest arrears in 1786, and the Leeds to Wakefield Trust liquidated several debts in 1771, some of which had been outstanding for nine years. In Berkshire, the Hungerford to Sousley Trust was four years behind by the 1790s.[16] Five of the pre-1750 Sample 1 trusts had interest debts upon first renewal, but in each case for less than £300. Albert's conclusion that it was the poor financial condition of the lagging sector trusts, particularly those formed after 1790, which contributed to the interest debt of the 1820s and 1830s, lends further support to this analysis (1972:90).

Trusts paid for contractors' work and road repairs upon completion, but some intentionally delayed payment by obtaining credit through the issue of turnpike bills. These were effectively the same as turnpike securities, except that the sums involved were often smaller, and of uneven amounts. Turnpike bills were of limited popularity—only three of the Sample 2 trusts used the system. Two of these were the Marylebone and Islington Trusts, which both issued them most frequently to pay tradesmen's and carter's bills. In 1719, the Islington Trustees decreed that all amounts under £10 were to be paid one-quarter in cash and three quarters in 'notes' at four per cent. In 1721, the Marylebone Trustees ordered 'notes to be issued for the payment of workmen repairing the roads.' These bills were numbered, and were redeemed in order of issue after notice in the press. The Marylebone Trust issued notes to the value of £5,061 between 1721 and 1727, but repaid the value of only £1,377. By 1742 it had a debt of £9,935 in outstanding bills. The Stevenage to Biggleswade Trust used the same system, both in borrowing money and in payment of carters' bills. It issued 120 'Promissory Notes' between 1722 and 1726, but seems to have reverted to direct payment after this.[17]

Some cases of trust indebtedness were not arranged formally in this way. In 1734, the Islington Trust was £8,073 in debt, £6,500 of this amount being held in mortgages. A further £405 was owing in bills, but £1,100 was due for work done over the previous year (JHC 22:250). By 1753, the situation had worsened, with the trust owing £7,617 to its mortgagees, and £1,577 to tradesmen, a total of £9,194 (JHC 26:571). Within six months of its establishment in 1718, the New Cross Trust owed £2,000 to workmen and agreed to borrow money on mortgage to pay this off.[18] The Brentford Trust was nearly £9,000 in debt within seven years of being started, the total including £2,500 for gravel received (JHC 20:258). However, all these trusts were high income earners (Table XXIX).

A more serious case involved one of the earliest trusts, the 1707 Fornhill to Stony Stratford road. Although it had a toll income at that time of only £400, it had spent £7,000 on road repairs in its first year, and by 1710 still owed £6,448 to local tradesmen and farmers for carriage, materials and work. In that year, the Act was extended for seven years at their request. But as money could still not be borrowed to cover the debt, the creditors advanced further services and materials, amounting in value to 20 per cent of their original debts, so that the road could be kept in repair. However, the money was still outstanding in 1717 and in 1738, when the creditors again petitioned Parliament (JHC 23:107). Nothing seems to have happened during this period to liquidate the debts, and the trust was re-established in 1740, having been apparently inoperative for some years.

Creditors could take direct action against a trust, if a formal agreement had been violated. They could foreclose if the terms of a mortgage had been contravened and interest not paid. They could take possession of the tollgates and use the proceeds to cover the arrears, as well as their expenses. The procedure was formally recognized in the 1773 Act, but had been used on several occasions before this.

In 1724, the Justices in charge of the Thornwood to Woodford road petitioned Parliament for a renewal of its term. The road was in a bad condition because:

'. . . there being owing to the Mortgagee the Sum of £700 and upwards, he took Possession of the said Toll; and the Money arising thereby being chiefly applied towards payment of the said Debt, which, we find, is lately paid off, very little, for three Years past, has been laid out in repairing the said Road.' (JHC 20:248)

Three years earlier, the creditors of another Justice trust, the Bath Turnpike, had obtained a decree in Chancery ordering the toll money to be used to repay their principal and interest (JHC 19:417). One of the mortgages of the Evesham Trust obtained a similar decree in 1741, but after two and a half years in possession of one of the gates, he had received less than £200 of the £1,950 due to him (JHC 24:491). But again, such actions were not widespread. These were the only examples brought before Parliament between 1700 and 1770.

Statute Duty

A third source of income, after the tolls and credit, was the statute duty. As the establishment of a turnpike trust did not relieve the parishes of their responsibility to maintain the roads, a proportion of their statute duty was allocated to the trust. Turnpike Acts either laid down the number of days which were involved, or directed the Justices of the Peace to decide. The 1773 Act also required them to apportion the duty in parishes which contained more than one turnpike road, where the total statute duty entitlement of these trusts exceeded three days. The Justices could remove the entitlement altogether and order all the duty to the parish, when the turnpike road was in a good condition, and its securities would not be endangered.

Many trusts actively enforced the statute duty obligation, as their Minute Books show. The Hockerill Turnpike in Hertfordshire would not employ any labourers who had not done their duty,[19] and the Shenfield to Harwich Trust had a Standing Order that no work was to be done on the road each year until the statute duty had been completed. This was 'punctually observed' (JHC 25:201). Other trusts adopted the same policy, particularly those in Kent. They regarded toll income as a supplement to the provisions of the common law—as technically it was— and made it their first task upon establishment, and in subsequent years, to enforce the parish obligation.[20] And, in addition, many trusts prosecuted parish Surveyors and individuals who failed to comply with the requirements.[21]

It is difficult to assess the value of the statute duty contribution to trust income, except when it was commuted for a cash payment. This was a growing practice in the eighteenth century, and was particularly common in the urban areas. It developed because individuals preferred to pay the standard fine rather than perform the six days labour, and was encouraged by many urban trusts, who often compounded with whole parishes. It was recognized by the 1773 Act. When figures for parish compositions are available, they contradict the conventional view that statute duty was an ineffectual source of income.

The Marylebone Trust received £838 in parish compositions between 1722 and 1727, £2,707 between 1739 and 1744, and £2,745 between 1753 and 1764. These sums amounted to 11, 21 and 15 of the trust's total income in each respective period.[22] The 1765 Commons Committee investigating the affairs of various trusts also found evidence of fairly

Table XXXVII

Toll and Composition Income for Six London Trusts, 1764

	Tolls	Compositions	Total	Compositions as a percentage of total
	£ s d	£ s d	£ s d	
Marylebone	1903 2 0	308 14 0	2271 16 0	13
Islington	4388 3 8	200 3 6	4588 7 2	4
Kensington	3919 5 6	326 0 0	4245 5 6	7
New Cross	2439 0 0	—	2439 0 0	0
Surrey New Roads	1460 10 2	—	1460 10 2	0
Stamford Hill	1962 3 6	183 1 0	2145 4 6	8

Source: JHC 30:431.

substantial income contributions from this source (Table XXXVII). Although these figures hide the annual variations in composition money yields, which was a feature of this income source, they do indicate a fairly high return for four of the six trusts. After statute duty had been abolished in 1835 by the General Highway Act, the 1839 Parliamentary Committee reported that a 'most intelligent witness' put the loss to trusts as high as £200,000 a year (BPP 1840 (280) XXVII:609). This was probably an over-estimate, however, as the Returns for 1834 and 1835 put the level of compositions and estimated value of statute duty performed at £130,000 in both years. Nevertheless, this still represented 7 per cent of total trust income in those years.

The London trusts had continuous problems with parish compositions and the receipts often fluctuated widely from year to year. The £2,475 which the Marylebone Trust collected between 1753 and 1764 was made up of annual totals ranging from £40 to £363. It had great difficulty in eliciting some parish contributions. In 1743, St James, Westminster owed £400, and St George, Hanover Square was £105 in arrears, despite a payment of £70 in the previous year following a threat of legal action. In 1735, the Middlesex Justices, enquiring into the operation of statute duty on the Islington Trust, found that 'the parishioners neglect their statute work and their compositions are greatly in arrears.' The two Islington parishes owed £145, their annual composition being £100, and Clerkenwell owed £40. Hornsey had not paid for ten years, and also owed £40. And Hampstead, which had refused to compound, had not done any work for ten years either. Although the Trustees successfully petitioned Parliament for an amendment Act to enable them to enforce the obligation more effectively, the trouble continued, and after 1769, most parishes refused to pay at all.[23]

The obligation to perform statute duty for the Marylebone Trust was ended by formal abolition in its Act of 1782. The Kensington Trust, however, continued to collect composition money into the nineteenth century, a new level of rates being set in 1811. But this hardly reflected the increase of population in the area over the preceding 90 years, during which time several of the compositions had actually fallen (Table XXXVIII).

Table XXXVIII
Kensington Trust, Parish Compositions

	1726	1811	1812
	£	£	£
Chelsea	50	34	55
Chelsea Hospital	8	8	13
Fulham	40	23	38
Kensington	35	72	122
St George, Hanover Square	100	100	170
St Margaret, Westminster	50	25	42

Source: Ffooks: 1955

Fines and Penalties

It was the responsibility of the Gatekeepers to enforce the table of fines and penalties for overweight wagons, excess number of horses, narrow wheels, and—if the offenders were caught—for evasion of the gates. It is difficult to know how much trust finances benefited from this, or even how prevalent violations were. Fines are usually integrated in the toll returns from Collectors, and not listed separately. There is also little evidence in Minute Books to suggest active prosecution of offenders by trusts, although sporadic examples can be found in most cases.

The restriction of the amount that wagons could carry had been a basic foundation of road legislation since the early seventeenth century. James I Proclamation of 1621 forbad the use of four-wheeled carriages and wagons weighing more than one ton, and the 1662 Highways Act set the maximum weights that could be carried at one ton in winter and 30 cwt in summer. There was no means of enforcing this, other than by restricting the number of horses that could be used to seven. This was the state of the law until an Act of 1741 gave Trustees authority to erect weighing machines, a provision which was made obligatory for trusts within 30 miles of London in 1751. In 1773, the obligation was removed by the General Turnpike Act but trusts were encouraged to erect weighing engines by an automatic five-year extension of their term if they did so.

The toll Collectors were obliged to weigh all wagons, under penalty of £5, and wagoners could be fined £2 for refusing to co-operate. Initially, under the 1741 Act, the scale of fines was very simple: a fine of £1 per cwt for all wagons over three tons in weight. But by 1773 the schedule had become extremely complex, as Table XXXIX shows.

Table XXXIX
Maximum Weights allowed by the General Turnpike
Act, 1773

	Summer	Winter
Wagon with 16 in. fellies	8 tons	7 tons
Wagon, 9 in. fellies, not over 4 ft 2 in. apart	6 tons 10 cwt	6 tons
Wagon, 9 in. fellies more than 4 ft 2 in. apart	6 tons	5 tons 10 cwt
Cart, 9 in. wheels	3 tons	2 tons 15 cwt
Wagon, 6 in. wheels, rolling 11 in.	5 tons 11 cwt	5 tons
Wagon, 6 in. wheels	4 tons 5 cwt	3 tons 15 cwt
Cart, 6 in. wheels	2 tons 12 cwt	2 tons 7 cwt
Wagon, wheels with fellies under 6 in.	3 tons 10 cwt	3 tons
Cart, wheels with fellies under 6 in.	1 ton 10 cwt	1 ton 7 cwt
Fines payable		
1 to 2 cwt over the limit	—	3d per cwt
3 to 5 cwt	—	6d per cwt
5 to 10 cwt	—	2s 6d per cwt
11 to 15 cwt	—	5s per cwt
15 or over	—	20s per cwt

Source: 13 Geo. III, c. 84.

Weighing engines were fairly widely used by trusts—at least 13 of the 50 in Sample 2 did so.[24] Some trusts shared an engine. The Doncaster to Tadcaster and Boroughbridge to Pierce Bridge Trusts constructed one at the junction of their roads in 1743,[25] and the investment of the two Preston to Hering Syke Districts has already been recorded (above, p. 184). The Kensington Trustees erected one in 1752, and replaced it in 1795 with one at Hyde Park Corner, and another in Pimlico (Ffooks 1955). The Islington Trustees originally built one on the Hampstead road in 1751, and supplemented it with a second at Battle Bridge (now Kings Cross) in 1774. In 1792–3, they built four more (Clarke 1955: 175–6).

There are some returns which show how much income these weighing engines provided. The Marylebone Trust, which had one engine next to its Tyburn Gate at the west end of Oxford Street, gained only £376 from it between 1753 and 1762. The annual yield fell from £118 to only £8.[26] The Stamford Hill Trust benefited even less, gaining only £198 from fines between 1752 and 1762, with nothing at all in the last four years (JHC 29: 659). It is possible that fewer wagoners abused the weight limits after a time, but the Collectors' or trusts' failure to use the engine seems equally likely. The Edgware Trust Ledger reveals details of overweight fines for 1772, and the sparseness of entries, particularly in the lower excesses, would suggest that the engine was not being fully used (Table XL).

Table XL
Edgware Trust, Overweight Ledger, 1772

March 25	John Skey Esquire	Wagon 400	Overweight	£4
27	Mr Cutter	100		1
April 25	John King	100		1
25	Mr Bliss	100		1
May 30	Lord Hyde	300		3
June 22	Mr Hudson	500		5
29	Mr Hurford	200		2
July 1	Ann Harrison	4,000		40
23	Mr Hunts	400		4
Sept. 11	Mr Keach	100		1
16	Mr Dodd	200		2
Dec. 15	Mr Dodd	100		1
15	Mrs Ann Mills	200		1
19	Mr Clark	100		1

Source: Accounts 1772–85 (Middlesex RO).
These fines are in pre-1773 rates.

Between 1772 and 1782, the total of fines collected by this trust amounted to 4·3 per cent of toll income, compared with 3·8 and 1 per cent respectively for the Marylebone and Stamford Hill series. The only other evidence found of overweight fines comes from the Kensington Trust, where the Hyde Park engine was used regularly, yielding £885 in fines between 1796 and 1798, or 4 per cent of total toll income.[27]

In the nineteenth century, weighing engines gradually fell into disuse. The Kensington machines were abolished by the trust's Act of 1824, and in 1828 they were removed throughout the trusts of the Metropolis Roads Board. In 1833, when a House of Lords Committee advocated their total abolition, there was only one left within 50 miles of London.[28] They were finally abolished, along with all other traffic restrictions, by the General Highway Act of 1835, as part of the post-Telford MacAdam reaction against making the traffic suitable for the roads.

Turnpike trusts were thus dependent on a variety of sources for their income, but by far the most important was the tolls. The number of trusts, and the number of gates they controlled were often the subject of complaint, and in the early nineteenth century, consolidation and amalgamation was frequently urged. Nevertheless, the local nature of the administration of the turnpike system was regarded as its greatest strength in raising income. Sir Henry Parnell, writing in 1833, said that:

'If rates on the land had been resorted to, the measure would inevitably have failed, because the landowners would, beyond all doubt, have preferred bad roads and low rates to good ones and high rates . . . If the roads had been vested in the hands of government, it may safely be said that this plan would also have failed, for government would never have been able to obtain the consent of Parliament to vote upwards of a million and a half a year for those roads only which now are turnpike roads. It is therefore to the turnpike system that England is indebted for her superiority over other countries with respect to roads.'   (Parnell 1833: 263–4)

Trust Expenditure

It must not be assumed that there was universal satisfaction with the way in which trusts disposed of their income, despite Parnell's comments. A series of Parliamentary Committees in the first half of the nineteenth century found defects in the management of trust expenditure. Adam Smith, although a strong supporter of the local rather than governmental control of road repair, thought that:

'. . . the abuses which the Trustees have committed in the management of [the] tolls, have in many cases been very justly complained of. At many turnpikes, it is said, the money levied is more than double of what is necessary for executing, in the completest manner, the work which is often executed in a very slovenly manner, and sometimes not executed at all.' (1904, Vol. 1: 217)

MacAdam, too, was a strong opponent of what he termed the 'misapplication' of funds. He argued before the 1819 Parliamentary Committee that more highly paid and qualified Surveyors were needed, and they should be made directly accountable to the Trustees:

'Without this control and superintendence an end cannot be put to the waste of public money, and all the various modes that are injurious to the public interest, the amount of which would appear incredible, could it be ascertained, but which, I conscientiously believe to amount to one-eighth of the road revenue of the kingdom at large, and to a much greater proportion near London.'

Again, he was referring to the way in which money allocated to road repair itself was spent. Two particularly wasteful policies, he considered, were the excessive application of repair materials on road surfaces, and the use of horses, rather than the labour of men, women and children (BPP 1819 (509) V: 20–1).

Turnpike trusts did not only spend money on road repair. As organizations, they incurred the expense of management. As borrowers, they had to pay interest and repay principal. As owners of tollhouses and tollgates, they had to employ craftsmen for construction and maintenance purposes. And as institutions dependent upon Parliament and the magistracy for their successful and continued operation, they incurred legal costs. It was the proportion of trust income which was thought to be directed towards payment of these non-repair expenses that was frequently criticized, and often advanced as the prime reason for the need for trust consolidation. The attitude of the 1840 Parliamentary Committee is typical:

'the Reports and Evidence to which we have referred exhibit the evils of the present system of turnpike management, arising from the number of Trusts—the expense of renewing Acts of Parliament—the great amount of law charges—the number of officers and aggregate amount of salaries—the number and frequently unjust, position of toll-gates—the high rates of toll—the vast amount of bonded debt—the high rate of interest with the toll revenue, and leaving the burden of maintaining the roads on the parishes through which they pass—the total absence of all control over the power of Trustees to borrow and expend money—the want of sufficient check, and of authority, to compel the keeping of regular, correct and just accounts of the receipt and expenditure of funds—and the employment of incompetent, unskilful and inefficient persons as surveyors—and all the Reports express an opinion, in which we fully concur, that, in order to obtain a more economical and efficient management of the roads, it is necessary to resort to some system of consolidation.' (BPP 1840 (256) **XXVII**: 10)

This attitude has been supported by later writers, notably the Webbs (1920: 119, 141) and Jackman (1916: 240, 242, 257). It does, however, deserve more critical analysis.

The first national statistics for trust expenditure are not, unfortunately, available until the 1830s (Table XLI).

Table XLI
Average Expenditure Per Annum of all English and Welsh Trusts, 1834–8

Manual labour	£400,993	26·8 per cent
Team labour, carriage of materials	158,469	10·6
Materials	226,469	15·1
Land	19,145	1·3
Damages to land	9,457	0·6
Incidentals	62,001	4·1
Tradesmen's bills	66,911	4·5
Salaries	95,434	6·4
Law charges	33,700	2·3
Interest	301,687	20·3
Repayment of principal	122,505	8·2
	£1,497,058	

Source: computed from BPP 1840 (280) XXVII : 647.

But the figures are revealing. 'Management expenses', defined as salaries plus law charges, accounted for only 8·7 per cent of total expenditure. This figure is anyway over-stated, as 4·3 per cent of the total was allocated for Surveyors' salaries, which are more properly considered a repair expense. However, this is in part compensated by the inclusion of certain administrative costs—books, tickets, room hire—under the heading of 'incidentals'. Interest payments amounted to 20 per cent of total expenditure, with the repayment of principal accounting for another 8 per cent. A small proportion of the remainder was spent on maintenance of tollhouses, and construction of gates, fences, and drains. This was covered by the 4·5 per cent in 'tradesmen's bills' and part of the 4·1 per cent of 'incidentals'. Even so over half the total expenditure of trusts was available for direct road repair purposes—54·4 per cent, or including the Surveyors' salaries, 58·7 per cent.

It is possible, using the detailed trust returns in the Appendix to the Committee Report of 1839, to categorize trusts according to their financial state of health. This was done by Albert (1972: 89–9). He decided that only those trusts which devoted less than 20 per cent of their expenditure to interest payments, and more than 55 per cent to road repair (including 'incidentals' and tradesmen's bills) were in a 'favourable condition'. On these grounds, 41 per cent of trusts responsible for 48 per cent of the mileage qualified. But 57 per cent of trusts, responsible for 63 per cent of the mileage, satisfied the second criterion.

Again, no comparable expenditure figures exist for the eighteenth century, but a sample of surviving Account Books—Sample 3—was taken to obtain information for part of the system. Each Account Book was examined in detail, and expenditure patterns derived for periods of five years.[29] In some cases, more than one such 'expenditure run' was obtained. Thus, for the sample of 50 trusts, 66 expenditure runs were recorded. Fifteen of these were for new trusts, i.e. they covered the first five years of trusts' existence. The remaining 51 were for established trusts. The expenditure runs were then reclassified according to period. The results are shown in Table XLII.

The expenditure categories used are directly comparable with those in Table XLI. The items 'salaries', 'interest' and 'principal' are self-explanatory. 'Legal charges' cover not only the cost of local legal actions, but also the cost of the original and renewal Acts. 'Roads' covers the cost of labour, materials and land. It was not possible to extract the proportion spent on land alone, because in many trusts, payment was made directly to the Surveyor for repair of a certain section, or repairs over a certain length of time. These sums would have included the purchase price of any land bought. The 'miscellaneous' category is the equivalent of the 'incidentals' and tradesmen's bills of Table XLI.

Table XLII
Expenditure Patterns for Sample 3 Trusts

	Total (66)	New trusts (15)	Established trusts (51)
Roads	56·1 per cent	70·2 per cent	52·0 per cent
Miscellaneous	6·8	8·7	6·3
Salaries	11·1	6·9	12·3
Legal charges	21·8	6·9	1·1
Interest	21·8	6·6	26·3
Principal	1·6	0·7	1·9
	1700–50 (9)	1751–70 (24)	1771–1800 (33)
Roads	59·8 per cent	66·4 per cent	47·7 per cent
Miscellaneous	11·1	8·3	4·6
Salaries	10·4	8·5	13·3
Legal charges	4·7	2·6	1·7
Interest	13·0	13·8	30·1
Principal	0·9	0·4	2·7

Source: Sample 3.

The results presented in Table XLII can be used to make tentative assertions about the nature of trust expenditure in the eighteenth century, as well as some tentative comparisons with the pattern in the 1830s. The first point of note is that the amount spent directly on road repair is very similar for both periods—approximately 55 per cent plus the Surveyors' salaries. This rises to about 63 per cent for both periods if the 'miscellaneous' category is included. This is not unreasonable, because although some of this money was devoted to administrative expenses, a high proportion went on the provision and maintenance of necessary facilities, such as tollhouses, gates, fences, drains and bridges, and tools.

However, there is a marked difference in the proportion of expenditure on road repair made by the 15 new trusts and the 51 established trusts in Sample 3. This was partly due to the low level of interest repayments of the new trusts, but also reflects the importance of their initial repair and improvement programmes. It is this factor which has caused the noticeably lower proportion of expenditure on road repair in the 1771–1800 runs, compared with the two earlier periods. Only two of the 33 runs from this period are for new trusts, compared with three of the nine for 1700–50, and ten of the 24 for 1751–70. Therefore it is not reasonable to conclude, on the basis of this sample data, that there was a general worsening of the financial position of trusts in the latter part of the eighteenth century. The 1830s statistics support this.

A second interesting point is that management expenses (salaries plus legal charges) accounted for 13·5 per cent of the expenditure of sample trusts. This was appreciably higher than the 8·7 per cent of the 1830s Returns. In each case, the highest proportion of these expenses was due to the payment of Officials' salaries, notably that of the Surveyor which would, as stated, be more appropriately included in repair expenditure. The fall in the proportion of expenditure devoted to salaries between the Sample 3 data and the 1830s Returns was due to the rapid overall increase in toll income in the last part of the eighteenth century. Salaries rose less quickly over this period, thus falling as a proportion of the whole. In the light of this, Jackman's claim that consolidation was widely favoured because it would do away with 'a host of parasitic officials who were drawing the Trusts of their funds' (1916: 257) it has little validity. And, as the analysis of trust administrative structure showed, the 'host' was not large.

Legal charges, however, were of similar proportions in both periods. This is in spite of the exemption of trusts from Private Bill charges for renewal Acts in the latter period, with the introduction of the Annual Turnpike Continuance Acts. But the high cost of obtaining the initial Act does show very clearly in the relatively high proportion of expenditure— nearly 7 per cent—of new trusts in Sample 3 on legal charges (Table XLIII). Obtaining an Act was expensive, because it was a complex process. Trusts had to pay Parliamentary fees, the fees of the firm of Parliamentary solicitors which guided the bill through both Houses, and the fees of a local solicitor, or the trust's own Clerk who drew up the petition and took it to London. An interesting breakdown of the cost of obtaining the Collingham to York Trust's renewal Act of 1791 is given in Appendix 4.

Thirdly, the proportionate spending on interest repayments by the Sample 3 trusts, and the entire system in the 1830s, is very similar. Again, there is a big difference between new and established Sample 3 trusts on this point. This reflects an increase in the level of mortgage debt after the first few years. But the 1830s evidence shows that the situation did not worsen progressively. Even though trusts were devoting 8 per cent of their expenditure to repayment of principal by then, in addition to the 20 per cent spent on interest, this did not affect the overall proportion spent on

Table XLIII
Cost of Turnpike Acts

New trusts Act		Date	Cost
31	Islington	1717	£152
32	Brentford	1717	£336
34	New Cross	1718	£121
42	Marylebone	1721	£218
63	Liverpool–Prescot	1726	£361
77	Hounslow Heath–Bagshot	1727	£194
91	Chapel–Bourton	1731	£364
108	Wakefield–Halifax	1741	£112
138	Newcastle–Carter Bar	1749	£219
176	Harrogate Roads	1752	£529
184	Stourbridge Roads	1753	£321
195	Salisbury–Eling	1753	£360
210	Keighley–Kendal	1753	£750
270	New Road	1756	£900
313	Oxdown Gate–Winchester	1759	£487
374	Stourbridge–Cradley	1762	£496
413	Wadhurst–West Farleigh	1765	£210
425	Tonbridge–Maidstone	1765	£206
535	Collingham–York	1771	£302
553	Hungerford–Soulsey Water	1772	£336
706	Wellingborough–Northampton	1797	£311
Renewal and amendment Acts			
	New Cross	1720	£100
	Edgware	1748	£180
	Wakefield–Halifax (bill lost)	1756	£289
		1757	£607
	Harrogate (Amendment)	1757	£181
	Doncaster–Wakefield (bill lost)	1757	£289
		1758	£618
	Gloucester–Birdlip	1761	£248
	Brentford	1767	£502
	Leeds–Wakefield	1771	£167
	White Cross–Beverley	1782	£280[a]
	Collingham–York	1792	£292
	White Cross–Beverley	1805	£359[a]

In 1833, the average cost of 128 renewal Acts was £436 3s (BPP 1833 (703) XV 409: 57).
Source: Minute Books and [a]MacMahon 1964.

road repair, largely because of the fall in the relative importance of salaries.

The pessimistic view of trust finances is not supported by this evidence. The remarks of the 1840 Parliamentary Committee quoted earlier, and the interpretation of this and the Reports by earlier Committees by Jackman and the Webbs, seem to be out of all proportion to the situation which actually existed:

'By the end of the eighteenth century the mortgaging of tolls had been carried to a great height, and many Trusts made default in the payment of interest on their bond debt . . . With the whole or greater part of the tolls thus alienated for payment of interest on past indebtedness—sometimes even with the mortgagees in possession, taking the whole money revenue for their arrears of interest and heavy legal expenses—the expenditure on the repair of the road was naturally reduced to a minimum.' (Webb 1920: 141–2)

This was undoubtedly true of some trusts, but it cannot be accepted as a mere general proposition.

Using Albert's criteria, 54·5 per cent of the Sample 3 trusts were in a healthy financial position, i.e. they were devoting less than 20 per cent of their expenditure to interest payments and more than 55 per cent to road repair. A higher proportion—68 per cent—satisfied the second condition. As many as 83 per cent were allocating over 45 per cent to road repair. The sample data also showed that there was no deterioration of trust finances with increasing age of trusts.[30] This finding lends support to the general argument that there was no marked change in the overall financial position between the eighteenth and nineteenth centuries, at any rate in respect of road repair expenditure.

There is also little evidence that the size of trusts affected the proportion of expenditure they allocated to non-repair expenses. For all Sample 3 trusts, the correlation is very low.[31] This is perhaps an unexpected finding, because of the traditional view that small trusts were very wasteful of resources. A constant concern of the nineteenth century Parliamentary Reports was that of consolidation, or amalgamation, of trusts. It was supported by MacAdam (BPP 1819 (509) V 339: 26–9), and by the early experience of the Metropolis Roads Board, under which 14 London trusts north of the Thames were consolidated in 1826. The Board made an immediate saving of nearly 40 per cent on salaries, and was apparently able to obtain its repair materials more cheaply with the ending of competition in the market (BPP 1826–7 (339) VII 23: 5). The case was again put by two of MacAdam's sons in 1833 (BPP 1833 (703) XV 409: 77, 142, 155–6). This Committee concluded that:

> 'One of the greatest evils in the present Road System is the Number of Trusts, as well as their limited Range and Extent . . . Consolidation would secure a more uniform and efficient Administration of the Trusts, by enabling the Trustees to employ more competent and skilful Officers, and a Reduction of useless Expenditure, by diminishing the Number of Clerks and other Officers, and the Outlays incurred by the Renewal of so many local Acts.'   (p. iii)

The Sample 3 expenditure pattern does not seem to support this view, with regard to 'useless Expenditure.' The sample does, however, overrepresent London trusts, as noted, and these, although small in mileage, were some of the biggest in expenditure terms. However, even with these trusts removed from the analysis, only 19 per cent of the variation in expenditure devoted to non-repair expenses by the sample trusts is 'explained' by variations in size.[32] The experience of the Metropolis Roads Board was, anyway not a good basis on which to make comparisons. The 40 per cent saving on salaries amounted to £2,000, or only 2·7 per cent of total Board expenditure in 1827.[33] It is interesting, too, that general trust consolidation never did come about, despite the widespread support for it. It became increasingly inappropriate, as the financial problems of the turnpike system from the late 1830s stemmed basically from railway competition, and not from the efficiency of individual trusts.

Actual levels of trust expenditure on road repair, including the 'miscellaneous' category, were highest for those trusts in London and on the main routes. Table XLIV shows the expenditure per mile levels adjusted to 1700 prices for each of the 66 expenditure runs in Sample 3. The mean level for all expenditure runs was £261·8 per mile, but because of the very high spending of the London trusts, only 12 of the runs exceed this figure. The median level was £77·6 per mile. The repair procedures of the London trusts, as these figures imply, differed both in intensity and scope from those of trusts elsewhere.

It does not seem reasonable to accept the traditional pessimistic view of turnpike trust finances. The pattern of expenditure of the Sample 3 trusts, and of the 1830s Returns, does reveal bad cases, but on the whole, a high proportion of expenditure was devoted directly to road repair. Even where a significant proportion went on interest payments, this cannot be

Table XLIV
Trust Expenditure on Road Repair

Trust	Expenditure per mile	Dates of expenditure run	Road
New Road	£1594·9	1756–60	London
Marylebone	1492·5	1721–6	London
Marylebone	1313·6	1739–44	London
New Cross	1210·5	1718–23	London
Marylebone	1175·6	1759–64	London
Islington	1085·6	1760–4	London
Edgware	917·8	1772–6	London
Kensington	781·6	1772–6	London
Stamford Hill	571·3	1752–6	London
St Albans–S. Mimms	465·7	1759–64	Watling Street
Edgware	463·5	1729–33	London
Edgware	382·0	1744–8	London
Gloucester–Birdlip	357·7	1761–6	London–S. Wales
Devizes	207·8	1763–8	Great West Road
Biggleswade–Alconbury Hill	200·8	1780–5	Great North Road
Leeds–Wakefield	191·3	1769–73	Yorks.
Sparrows Herne–Aylesbury	138·0	1764–9	Bucks.
Windsor Forest	176·6	1759–64	Berks.
Old Stratford–Dunchurch	157·7	1765–69	London–Birmingham
Ripon–Boroughbridge	154·7	1752–7	Yorks.
Ipstones	153·9	1770–4	Staffs.
Maidenhead–Sonning	152·1	1728–32	Great West Road
Harrogate–Hutton Moor	151·6	1752–7	Yorks.
Wadhurst–West Farleigh	144·0	1765–70	Kent
Liverpool–Prescot	141·8	1753–7	Lancs.
Taunton	133·5	1752–7	Somerset
Kippings Cross–Flimwell Vent	127·7	1795–1800	London–Hastings
Dover–Sandwich	110·4	1797–1802	Kent
Trentham	98·1	1772–6	Staffs.
Devizes	94·1	1707–8	Great West Road
Knaresborough–Pateley Bridge	89·3	1759–64	Yorks.
Leatherhead–Guildford	83·4	1758–63	Surrey
Wellingborough–Northampton	81·4	1797–1802	Northants.

(continued)

Table XLIV (continued)

Trust	Expenditure per mile	Dates of expenditure run	Road
Canterbury–Barham	73·9	1799–1802	London–Dover
Wrotham Heath	73·5	1768–73	Kent
Leatherhead–Horsham	65·0	1772–6	Surrey
Kneesworth–Caxton	61·6	1780–5	Cambs.
Chapel–Bourton	59·9	1731–6	Oxon
Cambridge–Ely	58·3	1791–6	Cambs.
Gosport–Chawton	57·4	1775–80	Hants.
Taunton	47·2	1773–8	Somerset
Doncaster–Wakefield	46·7	1768–72	Yorks.
Blackburn– Burscough Bridge	46·0	1760–4	Lancs.
Northampton– Old Stratford	40·9	1785–90	Northants.
Harrogate– Hutton Moor	40·0	1772–7	Yorks.
Wetley Rocks	39·4		Staffs.
Doncaster– Saltersbrook	37·6	1764–8	Yorks.
Blackburn– Burscough Bridge	36·7	1760–64	Lancs.
Hungerford– Sousley Water	32·9	1775–80	Berks.
Duffield–Wirksworth	29·4	1784–8	Derbys.
Winchester– Southampton	29·2	1775–80	Hants.
Banbury– Ryton Bridge	28·9	1755–60	Warwicks.
Doncaster– Wakefield	27·9	1744–8	Yorks.
Leatherhead– Guildford	27·0	1782–7	Surrey
Gloucester–Hereford	22·9	1788–93	Glos.
Oakmore	22·4	1770–4	Staffs.
Ripon– Boroughbridge	21·4	1771–6	Yorks.
Stockbridge– Winchester	20·6	1775–80	Hants.
Burford–Preston	18·5	1771–5	Oxon
Duffield–Wirksworth	15·7	1793–7	Derbys.
Banbury– Ryton Bridge	12·4	1782–6	Warwicks.

(*continued*)

Trust	Expenditure per mile	Dates of expenditure run	Road
Banbury–Lutterworth	5·5	1770–5	Warwicks.
Wetley Rocks	3·7	1796–1800	Staffs.
Skipton–Colne	1·4	1787–91	Lancs.
Hungerford– Sousley Water	0·6	1795–1800	Berks.
Banbury–Lutterworth	0	1790–5	Warwicks.

interpreted necessarily as 'bad management'. It represented the cost of past construction and repair projects, which may well have been delayed or never carried out by those trusts paying little interest.

This analysis has not, however, touched on the basis of Adam Smith's complaint, namely that the money spent on road repair itself was not disposed of in the best possible way. To do this, it is necessary to understand the nature of, and assess the efficacy of, trust road repair programmes.

8. Notes

1. $r_s = 0.47$ and 0.58 respectively, (significant at 0.01 per cent level).
2. $r_s = -0.04$ and 0.18 respectively.
3. There were 79 Acts in the sample, being all the renewal Acts of Sample 1 Acts passed before 1770. The recorded procedure in Parliament did not always reveal the exact indebtedness of a trust. Figures are available in only 58 of the 79 cases. The Table below shows the average indebtedness of the 58 trusts at the time of their renewal Act, arranged in three groups, according to the movement of the toll schedule in that Act:

	Tolls decreased	Tolls stable	Tolls increased
No. of Acts	9	42	28
No. for which figures are available	5	33	20
Average debt	£1,900	£2,438·2	£2,437

4. The exemption for the Army was made general in 1778 (18 Geo. III, c.63), and that for post-horses in 1785 (25 Geo. III, c.57).

5. These Acts gave concessionary coal and lime rates: 89, 66 (on renewal in 1731), 69 (1731), 108, 109, 111, 112, 115, 124, 134, 141, 149, 154. Subsequently many trusts petitioned against the concession: 115 (JHC 25:755–6), 124 (JHC 25: 722), 134 (JHC 27: 358, 433), 149 (JHC 27: 356), 154 (JHC 27: 464/5).

6. Cranford Bridge Minutes, 3 March 1729 (Middlesex RO).
Hagley Minutes, 1 April 1754 (Birmingham Library).

7. Trust no. 1 (JHC 29: 163), 86 (JHC 28: 63).

8. For example, Acts 2, 10, 54, 66, 80, 465.

9. Brentford Minutes, 3 Oct. 1719, 21 May 1720.
(Chiswick Library.)

10. Knaresborough to Green Hammerton Minutes, 1 June 1752.
Doncaster to Wakefield Minutes, 25, 27 May 1741 (WR).

11. Wakefield to Weeland Minutes, 11 May, 4 June 1741.
Harrogate to Boroughbridge Minutes, 27 May 1752.
Ripon to Boroughbridge Minutes, 24 Aug. 1752.
Doncaster to Tadcaster Minutes, 11, 27 May, 3 June 1752 (WR). This last trust was exceptional. It compounded with 73 people in 1742, 147 in 1743, 53 in 1744; 196 in 1749, 228 in 1750, 224 in 1751, 258 in 1752 and 283 in 1753.

12. Wakefield to Halifax Minutes, 19 Aug. 1742 (WR).
Wadhurst to West Farleigh Minutes, 13 June 1765 (Kent AO).
Salisbury to Eling Minutes, 13 Feb. 1756 (Wilts. CRO).

13. Maidstone to Rochester Minutes, 6 Aug., 31 Dec. 1730.
New Cross Minutes, 27 June 1746.
Wadhurst to West Farleigh Minutes, 18 Nov. 1765 (Kent AO).
Gloucester to Hereford Minutes, 8 Nov. 1726, 19 Dec. 1727, 3 Jan. 1729 (Glos. RO).
Keighley to Kendal Minutes, 27 June 1754 (WR).

14. Yeovil Minutes, 12 June, 11 Oct. 1753.
Wells Minutes, 14 July, 15 Sept. 1753.
Taunton Minutes, 6 March 1753 (Somerset RO).
Keighley to Kendal Minutes, 19 July 1753, 6 Jan. 1756.
Doncaster to Wakefield Minutes, 1758.
Collingham to York Minutes, 19 Aug. 1791 (WR).

15. Wells Minutes, 1753–6 (Somerset RO).

16. Knaresborough to Green Hammerton Minutes, 27 Aug. 1786.
Leeds to Wakefield Accounts, 1771 (WR).
Hungerford to Sousley Accounts, 1775–1800 (Berks. RO).

17. Marylebone Accounts, 1721–36 (Marylebone Library), and Clarke 1955: 103–4.
Stevenage to Biggleswade, Register of Promissory Notes (Herts. RO).

18. New Cross Minutes, 25 Sept. 1718 (Kent AO).

19. Hockerill Minutes, 30 July 1745 (Herts. RO).

20. Kippings Cross to Cranbrook Minutes, 1, 29 June 1765.
Tunbridge to Maidstone Minutes, 10 June 1765, 28 April 1766.
Wadhurst to West Farleigh Minutes, 20 May 1765 (Kent AO).
Salisbury to Eling Minutes, 11 June 1753, 17 Feb. 1755 (Wilts. RO).
Burford to Preston Minutes, 17 July 1753, 13 Nov. 1747, 29 Jan. 1748 (Glos. RO).

Keighley to Kendal Minutes, 8 Aug. 1753, 14 Jan. 1755 (WR).
21. For example:
    Tadcaster to York Minutes, 17 Dec. 1746.
    Harrogate to Boroughbridge Minutes, 1 Dec. 1753.
    Harrogate to Hutton Moor Accounts, 1754.
    Keighley to Kendal Minutes, 14 Jan., 20 Nov. 1755 (WR).
    Gloucester to Hereford Minutes, 3 Dec. 1728 (Glos. RO).
    Salisbury to Eling Minutes, 17 Feb. 1755 (Wilts. RO).
    A number of trusts also sought amendments to their Acts in order to be better able to
    enforce statute duty (above, note 23, p. 109).
22. Marylebone Accounts, 1721–36, 1736–53, 1753–64 (Marylebone Library).
23. Marylebone Minutes, 6 May 1740, Nov. 1741–Dec. 1743, and Clarke 1955: 132.
24. This is a minimun figure: 32 (1742), 111 and 115 (1743), 34 (1745), 31, 49 (1751), 19,
    23, 42, 65 (1752), 59 (1755), 203 (1773), 150 (1774).
25. Doncaster to Tadcaster Minutes, 2 May 1743 (WR).
26. Marylebone Accounts, 1753–64 (Marylebone Library).
27. Hyde Park Gate Weighing Machine Receipt Book, 1745-8 (Kensington Library).
28. BPP, HL 1833, (703) XV, 2nd Report: iv, 436, 496. The Metropolis Roads Board, an
    amalgamation of the trust in north London, is discussed below, p. 229.
29. The characteristics of this Sample are shown in the following Table:

Date of establishment:	Before 1750	20	(21 per cent)
	1751–70	26	(54)
	1771–1800	4	(23)
Size:	Less than 10 miles	17	(19 per cent)
	11–20 miles	20	(33)
	21–30 miles	9	(22)
	Over 30 miles	4	(27)
Location:	London	7	(3 per cent)

Source: Appendix 2

   For an explanation of this Table, see note 7, p. 196. The Sample over represents pre-
   1750 trusts, but there is little reason why this should make the results
   unrepresentative. The imbalance in the number of London trusts in the Sample is
   more serious, and is discussed in the text.
30. Correlation coefficient (r) between percentage of expenditure devoted to expenses of
    management, interest and principal (i.e. non-repair expenses) and age of trusts in
    years = 0·17.
31. Correlation coefficient between non-repair expenses and size in miles = 0·15.
32. $r = 0.44$, $r^2 = 19$ per cent (0·01).
33. Total expenditure was estimated at £74,746 (BPP 1826-7 (339) VII 23: 10).

9

Trust Road Repair

The approach of turnpike trusts to their fundamental responsibility for road repair was the key to the success or failure of the innovation. This approach varied greatly between trusts, according to their location, size of income and differing managerial structures. Some trusts followed more intensive repair schemes than others; some were very traditional whereas others were more prepared to experiment and adopt new ideas; some took vigorous steps to modify and improve their routes, whilst others simply maintained the existing line. There were notable regional variations in attitudes and policies, and distinct differences in the nature of the problem between urban and rural trusts.

A number of sources, local and general, can be used to build up a picture of trust road repair in the eighteenth century. The Minute and Account Book samples form the basic local material. On the whole, these are an invaluable source of information although some, particularly from those trusts run by their Surveyors, are not very revealing. They can be supplemented by reports and trust advertisements in local newspapers, and by the recorded procedure on trust renewal bills in Parliament. Careful interpretation of the remarks of contemporary travellers, for example, Young (1771) and writers such as Phillips (1737), and Scott (1778) adds much to these basic records.

Repair Plans

A distinguishing characteristic of turnpike trusts, compared with later, more modern enterprises such as the canal and railway companies, was their lack of concern with initial planning. Very few detailed route maps, as evidence of professional surveys, survive. Only two have been found. One of these was for the proposed Peterborough to Northampton turnpike, dated 1753, but when the Act was obtained in the following year, the section from Wellingborough to Northampton was omitted (JHC 26: 851). The other was carried out for the Tadcaster to Otley Trustees in the same year.[1] It seems that few were made, as there were only two references to such surveys at the beginning of the 50 Sample 2 Minute Books. Oxford Street was surveyed for the Marylebone Trustees in 1724 (Clarke 1955: 213), and the York to Collingham Trustees ordered a plan to be made at their first meeting.[2]

It was thus uncommon for trusts to obtain a professional road survey before enacting their repair programmes. The advantage of such surveys was that they enabled a thorough assessment to be made of repair and improvement needs, so that priorities could be established, and some coherence and direction be given to the trust's programme. However, a significant proportion of trusts did attempt to make such surveys themselves. Eight of the 50 Sample 2 trusts formed small Trustee Committees for this purpose,[3] and another four charged their new Surveyor with this responsibility.[4] It was normal for these surveys to be carried out after the first or second meeting, and a report to be made one or two meetings later.

Road repair usually began straightaway, with or without a clearly defined plan. Often the earliest repair directions were concerned with immediate action on particularly bad parts of the road. A few Acts, in fact, specified the order of repair. Some of the town-centred trusts were required to attend to the heavily used roads nearest the centre before progressing outwards.[5] In only four of the Sample 2 trusts was action delayed for any length of time. The Wells Trust took three months to appoint a Surveyor and the Ringwood to Wimborne District in Hampshire took as long to erect its gates and five months to make its first repairs. The Liverpool to Prescot Trust took eight months, whilst it was almost a year before the Doncaster to Wakefield appointed its Surveyor and began operations.[6] Nevertheless the remaining 46 sample trusts began to tackle their task immediately.

In some trusts, the production of detailed plans and subsequent repair activity was a feature of their later life. The Northampton to Harborough Trust commissioned a plan of its road in 1740,[7] two years after the New Cross Trust had employed Charles Sloane of Gravesend to survey its route. He was paid £16 15s 6d by the Trustees, for a plan showing the length and width of the roads, the inclines, ditches, and adjacent features (Elliston-Erwood 1956). The Gloucester to Birdlip Hill Trust received a new lease of life in 1760, after its renewal Act. It appointed a new

Surveyor, made two surveys of the road, and for some years afterwards produced an annual 'State of Affairs' report which gave details to the public of the repairs carried out in the previous year. The Stokenchurch to Woodstock Trust, after several years of inactivity whilst the whole road was farmed, found a new interest in 1770, when the Trustees took responsibility into their own hands again. The two Surveyors made surveys of the road, and on the basis of these, detailed repair orders were again issued. The same happened in the Doncaster to Tadcaster Trust in 1765 after it had relieved its contractors of their obligation. [8]

Repair Methods

The discussions recorded in the Minute Books, and the repair orders made, indicate that there were several common matters of concern to trusts in their repair activities. The state of the road surface and its width occupied most attention, but foundations, drainage and the shape of the road were also important.

The state of the *road surface* was the subject of the most numerous repair orders, the highest proportion of repair expenditure, and the largest number of complaints from contemporaries. Trusts made full use of their free access to, and compulsory purchase powers of, local gravel and stone, and applied these materials to the road surface to even out the ruts. This was a predominant and continuous concern in many trusts. The Brentford Trust, for example, advertised for 1,000 tons of stone at its second meeting in 1717, and the Fulham Trust ordered its Surveyor to lay up to 1,000 loads of ballast on the roads soon after it was set up in 1731. The Old Street Trust, on the other side of London, made orders for the deposition of no less than 5,100 loads in its first two years on just over one mile of road. It specified that each load was to weigh at least 25 bushels, and be inspected by the Surveyor upon delivery. The Islington Trust, with 12 miles of road, used 4,378 loads in its first 14 months, [9] whilst the Stamford Hill Trustees laid 3,630 loads on four miles of road in 1744 (JHC 24: 563). The Kensington Trust, which received severe criticism from Parliamentary Committees in the 1760s, managed to lay, in 1765 'in all 11,445 Loads, which . . . is owing to some of it not lying above one Month before it is taken off, and others not above Two or Three Months' (JHC 30: 429).

A high proportion of road repair expenditure was, in consequence, devoted to the expense of obtaining materials. Frequently these had to be bought under contract, because there was insufficient suitable material adjacent to the road in commons and waste ground. But the major cost was undoubtedly that of transporting, or carriage of these materials. This had to be met whether or not the materials themselves were obtained free of charge. Table XLV gives detailed breakdowns of the expenditure on road repair made by six trusts from Sample 3. Deriving this information from the Account Books is a laborious process and is often not possible because even the general itemization adopted here is incomplete. Hence the Table is limited in scope. Nevertheless, it does show that in nearly all cases, the purchase and carriage of materials accounted for around or over half of the total repair expenditure. With one exception, the amount spent on road labour was very much less.

This primitive policy of superficial repair, rather than sound road construction, had unfortunate consequences for those roads on which it was applied. Robert Phillips, writing in 1737, complained that many of the turnpike roads in and around London had been raised between five and eight feet above their original level. The surface of Oxford Street was three to four feet higher than formerly: it had been in the hands of the Marylebone Trustees since 1721 (1737: 2, 46). This was not too serious, however, as the 1724 Survey had shown that most of the houses were set

Table XLV
Percentage Breakdowns of Expenditure on
Road Repair for Six Trusts

Trust	Date	1	2	3	4	5	6
St Albans	1759–64	69·3	(1)	23·9	—	—	6·7
Edgware	1729–33	23·0	45·4	(1)	—	—	31·6
	1739–43	39·2	45·6	(1)	—	—	15·2
	1772–6	27·9	37·9	24·0	—	—	10·2
	1777–81	26·9	35·0	26·9	—	—	11·3
Gloucester to							
Birdlip	1761–6	7·5	48·1	40·6	—	—	3·8
Islington	1760–4	8·7	11·4	47·4	1·7	6·2	24·3
Kensington	1772–6	31·1	12·8	16·5	22·8	4·8	12·0
Marylebone	1721–6	56·5	(1)	9·2	10·2	—	24·0

(1) The value for this column is incorporated in Column 1.

1 = Materials, 2 = Carriage, 3 = Labour, 4 = Paving, 5 = Contractors' road repairs, 6 = Miscellaneous

Source: Sample 3.

about 18 feet back from the edge of the road (Clarke 1955: 213).
Nevertheless, the householders had complained in 1728, suggesting the
road should be paved (Sheppard 1958: 58). The inhabitants of
Hoddesdon, in Hertfordshire, were less fortunate. A similar policy
pursued by the Cheshunt Trustees forced them to protest in April 1751
that 'the continual laying on and heaping up Gravel' in the main street
had meant that the pavements had had to be raised to stop water entering
their houses. The ground floors had become 'in great part laid under
ground and became a kind of Cellars and thereby rendered so damp and
wett as not only to injure and Spoil their Household Goods and Effects
but even to indanger their Health'. The Trustees ordered the road to be
'sinked', and five to six inches of gravel was removed over the next two
months with ditches being dug to improve the drainage. The same had to
be done the following year, after similar complaints from people living in
Wormley Street, but this time, three feet of gravel was taken away.[10]

In Islington, the result of the Trustees' policy of 'raising the roads' over
the last century was revealed in 1808 when:

> 'On digging the foundation of the tollhouses, the ballast and other
> materials appear to have been laid upon the road to the depth of six
> feet. Its thickness in the Lower Street is about five feet, and it averages
> the same in several parts of the Upper Street.'[11]

This policy was far more widespread than these examples would suggest,
as the evidence of the Minute Books demonstrates. However, the high
level of toll income of trusts in and around the capital encouraged, or at
least permitted them to follow this policy. The 1764 Commons
Committee, in its investigation of the Kensington Trust, recommended
that its tolls should be lessened, and the Hyde Park and Westminster
gates removed, or else:

> '. . . a considerable annual sum should be taken from the Trust to
> prevent the amazing Quantities of matter, which . . . the present
> Trustees [are] continually putting on and taking off the Road, whilst
> they are in possession of so large an Income.' (JHC 29: 1006)

In fact, the 1767 Kensington Trust renewal Act removed the paving from
Piccadilly to Hyde Park Corner from the care of the Trustees, and
transferred it to the Commissioners of Paving for Westminster. For this
privilege, the Trustees paid the Commissioners £1,000 per annum.

It was evidently this sort of repair policy which led Adam Smith to
complain that England's turnpike roads could be effectively repaired

with only half the current toll income (above, p. 223). MacAdam, in an interesting observation made before the 1819 Parliamentary Committee, agreed. He had found that the roads east of Bridgwater in Somerset, around Kendal in Cumbria and near Northallerton in Yorkshire were 'in a much better state than in other parts of the Kingdom; and there is a striking difference in the moderate rate of their tolls, which I have always found most moderate where the roads are best managed' (BPP 1819 (509) V 339: 18). The success of MacAdam's repair policies in the second and third decades of the nineteenth century was partly due to the low cost of reconstructing the road surface by sorting and breaking the mass of materials already there. He claimed that 'all the roads of the Kingdom contain a sufficient quantity of materials to last for a number of years' (BPP 1810–11 (240) III 855: 28).

The policy of 'raising the roads' indiscriminately was not however universal in the eighteenth century, although it was common. As MacAdam's examples showed, some trusts were less able to afford such a generous expenditure on materials and were so more sparing in their approach. Some others were actually using reconstruction methods many years before MacAdam popularized them. John Metcalfe carried out reconstruction work for several trusts in Yorkshire, Lancashire and Derbyshire between the 1750s and the 1790s. His method was to dig out the surface material in the road, ensure that the foundation was firm and well drained, and then construct a convex road surface using sorted, well broken stone. Some of his earliest work was for the Harrogate to Boroughbridge Trust in 1753, and the Wakefield to Halifax Trust in 1757. The latter contract, for four miles of road just outside Wakefield, specified that the road was to be 'stoned' 20 feet wide, in a convex shape, 18 inches deep in the middle and six inches at the side. It was to be made of eight inches of 'strong stone', six inches of 'middle broke stone' and four inches of 'small broke and the hardest stone'.[12]

Metcalfe was not the only professional surveyor operating in the West Riding, although this is the popular impression. Several other trusts were employing contractors at the same time. The example of Joshua Parsons' agreement with the Keighley to Kendal Trust in 1753 shows the general methods adopted (Appendix 3). They were very similar, but less elaborate than Metcalfe's—several inches of compacted, well broken stone, covered with hard gravel, and formed in a convex surface. The Harrogate to Hutton Moor Trust employed Joseph Mountain, and a partnership of Messrs Rea, Robinson and Storey. The two Robinson brothers also worked for the Knaresborough to Pateley Bridge Trust, and

Storey for the Ripon to Boroughbridge Trust. John Gott and Abraham Rhodes worked for over 20 years on the Toller Lane End to Colne road. [13] All these examples are drawn from the 1750s, 30 years before MacAdam's first work on the Ayrshire Trust, and 60 years before he first began to publicize his methods widely.

This more modern approach to road repair spread through the work of these professional contractors and with the willingness of trusts to experiment. The Tadcaster to York Trust did just this in 1767. Its Trustees ordered:

> 'That the Surveyor cause about Twenty Yards of the Road at the Hill at the South Side of Copmanthorpe Gate to be hacked up, the Stones broke small and the old materials formed again into a Turnpike Road in order to try whether this Method will not sufficiently repair certain parts of the Road where the old Gravel and Materials lay thick without any new Gravel being laid on. . . .' [14]

The method was obviously the accepted wisdom in this region by the late 1760s. But it was also used by the Gloucester to Birdlip Trust in its reconstruction programme between 1761 and 1766. This trust spent less than 8 per cent of its road repair money on new stone, but a further 8 per cent did go on lifting existing material out of the road, with another 33 per cent being spent on breaking and relaying it. [15] Yorkshire contractors were also employed further north to construct the new Military Road east of Carlisle in 1751. [16]

Therefore the approach of trusts towards maintaining a reasonable road surface was not entirely traditional and unscientific. Some were forced to adopt a more cautionary policy, whilst others—particularly in the West Riding—were prepared to experiment with reconstruction methods. It was these trusts that were effectively adopting a long-term policy of tackling the cause, rather than the more common short-term policy of attacking the symptoms of poor road surfaces.

The *materials* used in road repair varied from area to area. The trust records, however, are rarely very informative in this respect, often referring simply to 'loads', sometimes of 'stone' or 'gravel'. But until the last quarter of the eighteenth century gravel and stone from the adjacent commons and fields were the main materials in use. The land around London, for example, was scarred with gravel pits used by the building trade and the turnpike trusts. The New Cross Trust had to pay £60 in compensation to Lord Trevor in 1718 for damage caused by diggings on his land, and in 1728, the Welwyn Trust had to buy a field for £50 after its owners, the Free School in Welwyn, complained that it had been ruined by gravel digging. Several trusts found it necessary to remind their Surveyor to fence diggings and give due notice to owners beforehand.[17]

The West Riding repair contracts specified that 'stone' and a 'gravel' covering was to be used. The success of this policy depended in part on the quality of the materials themselves, here as elsewhere. The trusts in Hampshire used a pebbly gravel which produced roads 'as good as any' (Vancouver 1813: 392), whilst in Bedfordshire and Oxfordshire, the gravel roads were of a high quality by the end of the century (Batchelor 1808: 587, Young 1809: 324). In many places, however, and particularly around London, the use of gravel was far less satisfactory. MacAdam, in 1825, observed that the Middlesex turnpike road surfaces were 'floating in a kind of porridge', an opinion repeated in various forms by writers from Phillips onwards.[18] The fineness of the gravel, and its dirtiness in a clay–loam mixture, produced an infirm, muddy and easily rutted surface in winter, and a hard, dusty one in summer.

In 1798, Middleton complained that the Edgware road was very flat, with loads of gravel being heaped on 'the slop', which was four inches deep after heavy summer rain, and nine inches deep all winter. The Uxbridge road was six inches deep in mud in the centre, with between a foot and eighteen inches of 'adhesive mud' on the outside. The Kensington road to Hounslow—the main Bristol road—was just as bad (1798: 395–7). In 1819, several big coachmasters, and the Superintendent of the Post Office mail coaches, made very similar complaints to the Select Committee on Highways (BPP 1819 (509) V 339: 11–17).

The policies of many of the London trusts encouraged these conditions. Either the gravel was not properly washed, or 'screened', so that it remained effectively embedded in clay, or materials such as brittle flints were used. These pulverized under the weight of traffic, producing a thick layer of dust, which was settled in the summer by watering the roads, and in the winter, by rain. Middleton wrote about Middlesex:

'The turnpike roads . . . are, generally, very bad; although at the tollgates of this county there is collected a very large sum of money, probably not less than £40,000 a year; a considerable portion of which is uselessly expended in sinking wells, erecting pumps, building carts, and hiring horses and men, to keep the dust down, by watering, instead of more wisely removing it.' (1809: 517)

The early Marylebone and Islington Trusts cleaned out their drains and ditches in the spring, and then threw the mud back into the middle of the road.[19] This led Phillips to exclaim that:

> 'If all the turnpikes were taken down, and the roads not touched for seven years, they would be a great deal better than they are now.' (1737: 15)

Some trusts did try to remedy the deficiencies of the local gravel by screening it before use. This procedure was recommended by authorities such as Scott, MacAdam, and Phillips himself. The Islington Trust was an early example, although its resolve evidently made no difference to its later policy. In 1717, the Trustees decided that:

> '. . . those Persons that have brought great quantities of Sand and Gravel and laid the same in the Roads to the great Prejudice thereof shall be Order'd to fetch it away again, or be indicted at the next Session of the Peace to be holden in this County.'[20]

The Kensington Trust had continual trouble with the local waterworks company, part of the difficulty being that the company replaced clean road gravel with an earthy mixture when repairing its pipes under the road (Ffooks 1955: 42). In 1763, the Trustees found it necessary to remind its two Surveyors:

> 'That in future, all Gravel for the use of this Trust be screened for Ballast, with Wire Screens above Half an Inch wide.' (JHC 29: 652)

The material that both trusts used was just not suitable. The gravel was too fine for the clay to be extracted and Middleton had cause for complaint about the roads of both trusts in 1798.

Experimentation, however, was common. Some trusts tried alternatives to gravel from the start, and by the end of the century, a wide variety of materials was in use as trusts sought cheaper and better ways of repairing their roads. River gravel was very suitable, as it was clean. In 1792, the Islington Trustees decided that:

> 'It appearing that ballast can hardly be gotten from any of the lands adjoining the roads and the trust being in great want of such articles, ordered that the Clerk publicly advertise for Thames and pit ballast.' (Clarke 1955: 242)

The Kensington Trust had been using Thames gravel in the 1770s, but by the 1790s, was experimenting with a variety of hard materials. Mr

Blizard, the Surveyor, advertised for 'dross, stone clippings, clinker, bricks or bats, damaged polling, or similar hard refuse material' (Ffooks 1955: 44). But Middleton considered the river gravels were best. They could:

'. . . be had in almost endless quantity in the bed of the river Thames, where, if the Trustees would resort for them, they would improve the navigation, and avoid spoiling land by making gravel pits.' (1809): 524)

Flint and ragstone were also widely used on the London roads. The Marylebone Trust was doing this as early as 1724, but it laid 400 tons of flint on top of 1,200 loads of gravel, without any attention to road construction (Sheppard 1958: 50). The Kensington Trust started to use flint in the 1750s, and was making widespread use of it by 1800 (Ffooks 1955: 33). The Islington Trust used field flints, of about one cubic inch in size (Clarke 1955: 244), whereas the Bermondsey Trust employed a combination of flint and Purbeck marble (Payne 1956: 132). The practice became so common that by the end of the century:

'Every road in the vicinity of London is repaired with gravel or stones of flint, which, although it be hard, is so brittle as to be unable to bear any considerable weight without being crushed to powder.' (Middleton 1809: 524-5)

Outside the capital, a wide variety of materials was in use, depending on what was available locally. According to Scott, 'picked stones' taken off the fields were commonly used in central and southern England. He described the Newport Pagnell to Olney road in Buckinghamshire as an example of how poor the surface could be when newly laid, if the stones were not properly broken. Here, the cubes were of four or five inch diameter (1778: 335). Arthur Young had noticed a similar deficiency in the Oxfordshire roads in the 1770s:

'The two great turnpikes which crossed the county . . . were repaired in some places with stones as large as they could be brought from the quarry; and when broken, left so rough as to be calculated for dislocation rather than exercise.' (1809: 324, and 1771: 435)

These three roads probably used flint, being in chalk country, but some flint roads were good, as in Dorset and Sussex (Stevenson 1812: 439, Young 1808: 416). But in Bedfordshire, Batchelor complained of the flint roads being 'loose and heavy' (1808: 587), because the stone was mixed with sand. The Dunstable to Hockcliffe Trust did this because it 'had few stones except Flints, which ground to Powder, but if mixed with Sand, they cement' (JHC 26: 492). Other trusts used chalk itself as a binding material, with flint or gravel. The New Cross Trust in south London owned a chalk pit, and applied it extensively, and the Chalk Trust, further down the Kent Road, was so called for this reason. The Chalk Trust was praised for the quality of its road surfaces (JHC 23: 120). In Hertfordshire, the Cheshunt Trustees experimented with a mixture of chalk and screened gravel in 1744, although it is not recorded whether they continued with its use. [21]

Limestone itself was a popular material, as on the turnpike roads around Gloucester. Limestone chippings were used as a cover when gravel was not available (Rudge 1807: 334). It was also used in parts of Dorset, Bedfordshire, northern Lancashire, Cumberland and Northumberland. [22] The turnpike roads of Cornwall were made of hard quartzstone, and Charnwood Forest granite was popular in Leicestershire, where it was used in small chippings. Whinstone was in use in Northumberland and Durham, and even as far south as Sussex. [23] But, as in Oxfordshire, there were complaints about the size of some of this material, particularly in parts of Bedfordshire, Huntingdon, Cumberland, Northumberland, and on the main road between Durham and Newcastle. [24]

The use of industrial waste was not restricted to the Kensington Turnpike. It was popular in clay areas, and in industrializing districts. Copper slag, from Liverpool and Ravenshead, was used to make 'excellent roads' on the Prescot and Manchester Turnpikes (Holt 1795: 187). Forge cinders were bought for the Sheffield to Wakefield road in the 1770s, and they were also used on some of the Wealden clay roads (Scott 1778: 336). [25] But around Gloucester, slag had been replaced by limestone by the early nineteenth century:

> 'Slag or scoria, from the copper works in the neighbourhood of Bristol was much used, and tended to greatly improve the roads . . . This material, however, being found unpleasant for travelling, ruinous to the feet of horses, and in the case of a fall, dangerous to the horses and rider, is now out of use.' (Rudge 1808: 334)

The city of Gloucester had contracted with William Nicholls, who had a monopoly agreement to buy slag from the Copper Company in Bristol, for 500 tons at 3s 6d a ton in 1781 (Spry 1971). The Gloucester to Birdlip Hill Trust had first used slag in 1768. [26]

In some areas, the roads were *paved*. Slabs of flat quarry sandstone were used on the Horsham to Dorking road, one of the main routes across the Weald (Scott 1778: 336). Stone from North Wales and Scotland was used to pave some of the roads of southern Lancashire and Staffordshire, but the causeways were very narrow, being barely wide enough for one carriage. They attracted Arthur Young's often repeated criticism in 1771 (Vol. 4: 430–5), but by the 1790s had been greatly improved and widened, those around Manchester, for instance, costing £1,500 to £2,000 per mile to construct. In the Weald, Boys advocated the use of clay bricks to pave the roads, citing the success of these new Lancashire pavements, although they were made of North Wales coast stone (Boys 1796: 168).

Several of the London trusts had begun to pave their roads rather earlier than this. The Islington Trust had made a pavement of 'the largest pebbles secured with timber' in 1719.[27] The Marylebone Trustees started to pave Oxford Street in 1724 using between seven and nine inches of Jersey pebbles on a gravel bed. The pebbles were 'of middling size and all of one size', bought at 10s per ton and laid at 3s 9d per yard. The pavement was extended to cover the whole of Oxford Street after the trust's renewal Act of 1735, which enabled the Trustees to raise a paving rate for that purpose.[28] The Kensington Trust paved Piccadilly almost immediately after it was set up in 1726, with pebbles to a width of 36 feet, at a cost of 4s 4d per square yard. They used Guernsey pebbles in the road to the east of Kensington Town in 1738, as did the Old Street Trustees for their new road in 1753.[29]

At the end of the century, more substantial materials were being used for the London pavements. The Kensington, Marylebone and Islington Trusts had all laid Aberdeen granite on the busiest parts of their roads (Ffooks 1955: 34, Clarke 1955: 246–7), and a mixture of granite and Purbeck marble was used on the Bermondsey Turnpike (Payne 1956: 132). However, the heavily used central turnpike roads had passed into the hands of independent Paving Commissioners by this time. Oxford Street was given to the St Marylebone Street Commissioners in 1770, who then repaved it with granite at a cost of £20,000. The Paving Commissioners of St James, Clerkenwell, took over the upkeep of the St James Street pavement from the Islington Trust in 1773, the Trustees paying them £100 per annum in exchange (Clarke 1955: 216, 291). The Kensington Trust lost control of Piccadilly in 1767 to the Westminster Paving Commissioners.

Foundations do not seem to have been of great concern to many trusts.

MacAdam himself, unlike Telford, did not believe that a solid stone foundation was necessary, but he did insist that the road bed should be dry, firm and well drained. Many of the London trusts, in particular, did not fulfil these conditions, laying gravel on a foundation of muddy gravel, merely accentuating the problem of drainage and rutting. Some trusts preferred to use a solid hard core of stone, then cover this with gravel, and dig drainage ditches along the sides, rather than lay foundations. Most of the West Riding road contracts required this to be done (Appendix 3).

Nevertheless a foundation of some sort was necessary to overcome the problem of clay bottoms, or springs under the road. Faggots, and wood, were popular for this. The Kensington Trust purchased 36,257 bavins in 1726, and used an additional 38,000 in the next four years. But there is no mention of bavins being used after this, and the trust evidently changed to a solid stone core. Timber and green faggots were laid as a foundation under parts of the Great North Road in Huntingdon in 1729, and the Gloucester to Birdlip Hill Trust was using furze in the 1760s. In its second printed 'State of Affairs' it reported that 2,300 faggots had been laid in places where springs had been bursting through, and there was a danger of quicksands forming.[30] John Metcalfe sometimes used heather under his moorland roads (Jackman 1916: 268, Lowe 1798: 136). However, this policy was not very wise. The faggots eventually decayed so the road had to be relaid, and without the use of clean materials on top, the faggots acted as a sponge under the road surface. Phillips claimed that the Kilburn road had been very good after the Edgware Trust had reconstructed it, for two or three years, there having been laid 'a great quantity of Bavins or Faggots below the Gravel'. Then, as the dirt in the gravel had been washed downwards, the bavins had become saturated until 'the Loom spued out' (1737: 11). There is, however, no evidence of faggots being used widely on the London roads, probably for this reason, and harder materials of flint or waste were used for the standard 'core'.

Some roads were constructed on wooden foundations. General Wade used tree trunks as a base for his Highland military roads when they crossed boggy ground (Hamilton 1963: 229–30). The Islington Trust used timber under its paving in 1719, and the Welwyn Trustees ordered their Surveyor at their third meeting in 1726 to buy 'such Timber as is necessary for preserving the roads'.[31] The Worcester to Droitwich Trust claimed to need £500 in 1726 to buy enough timber as a foundation for four and a half miles of road (JHC 20: 619).

The trusts used these materials to form a variety of cross-sectional *shapes*. Many of the complaints about turnpike roads were derived from this. However for most of the century, the most common shape was flat—the 'Ploughman's Road'—which came about simply as the result of the steady accretion of materials (Scott 1778: 316). It was actively encouraged by legislation. The 1691 Highway Act stated that roads were 'to be as near as may be even and level'. The 1755 Act ordered that 'Trustees cause Roads to be levelled and put in good Condition'. There is not much in the trust documents, with some notable exceptions, to indicate that Trustees were concerned with anything other than flat surfaces. Some actually ordered their Surveyors to carry out 'levelling' and 'beating down'.[32]

A few trusts—Scott gave the example of the Stamford Hill road into London—built 'Angular Roads', constructed on a slant, so that the water drained away to one side (1778: 319–20). Although this was not a popular construction principle, many roads were angular in parts, as in Lancashire, often being so steep that there was some danger of carriages overturning (Dickson 1815: 609). Phillips' advocacy of the 'Concave Road' does not seem to have attracted widespread attention, although it was used in north-west Leicestershire (Pitt 1809: 309), and many hill roads, because of heavy rainfall, became this shape by default (Scott 1778: 320). When Scott was writing in 1778, the 'waned surface', constructed in a series of waves 'till of late was very fashionable'. It had been used in Leicestershire, and on the Whitechapel road before 1750, and was also used by the Hackney and Kensington Trusts for a short time (1778: 322). But it was naturally very unpopular with travellers, and this probably prompted the insertion of the clause in the 1755 Act. The Kensington Trust certainly abandoned its experiments with this form of surface at about that time (Ffooks 1955: 33).

When a preferred, constructed shape emerged, it was convex. It was used by Telford and MacAdam, and most of the West Riding contractors, and advocated by many writers.[33] Repair contracts frequently specified that stone was to be laid more deeply in the centre than at the edges. The Piccadilly paving constructed for the Kensington Trust in 1726 was to be 36 feet wide, with a fall of one foot from the centre to the sides.[34] The Marylebone Trustees made similar specifications for the paving of the eastern end of Oxford Street in 1724 (Clarke 1955: 213). The Keighley to Kendal contract of 1753 directed Joshua Parsons to make the road 'in a Turnpike like manner' with it 'stoned five Yards broad and two Yards in the middle to be twelve inches thick after sufficiently broke and to decrease in thickness gradually to each side to four inches' (Appendix 3). Young later referred to it as 'the better sort of Turnpike method' (1771, Vol. 4: 423). Sometimes trusts' own Surveyors were told to 'throw up' the road, and form sections into 'Turnpike Roads'.[35]

The rationale of the convex shape was the ease of drainage it allowed when laid on a firm surface and supplemented with lateral drainage channels. Hence the remedy for the Cheshunt Turnpike's problem in Hoddesden and Wormley Street in 1751 and 1752 was to remove some of the excess gravel, provide the road with a degree of convexity and dig new ditches. Later, however, it seems that sometimes this functional property had been forgotten, and the shape became an end in itself. Several of the Board of Agriculture Reports claimed that some roads were dangerous, being far too high in the middle.[36] Many of the witnesses before the 1819 Select Committee, particularly coachmasters, condemned the dangerous degree of convexity on the roads near London. Telford's new Holyhead road was praised because of its moderate degree of convexity (BPP 1819 (509) V 339: 13–16), and he, MacAdam and Scott all advocated a very gentle degree of slope. But this particular problem was localized and many Board of Agriculture observers, and travellers such as Young, found no cause for complaint on this score.

All trusts recognized that *drainage* was an important matter. Each turnpike Act empowered the Surveyor to make drains and ditches, and if necessary, to carry them into adjacent grounds. There is much evidence in trust records of this being done, usually through the enforcement of the common law obligation of land-holders to maintain their own ditches.[37] Some trusts, however, entered into contracts for the construction of drains and 'arches', these usually being brick or wood channels constructed under the road surface to house streams.[38] The Brentford Trust employed George Downs under contract in 1718 to keep its ditches clear for £40 per annum. About the same time the Islington Trust decided that two men shall be 'constantly employed . . . to fill the Rutts and let the water out of the Roads' between Grays Inn Lane and Battle Bridge. This policy was also adopted elsewhere.[39]

Sometimes, there were drainage problems of a different order. In 1725, flooding from Cheshunt Wash was causing difficulties for the Cheshunt Turnpike, which were not solved until permission was obtained from Lord Bingley, the landowner, to build an overflow channel and floodgate. The neighbouring Hockerill Turnpike set up a Committtee to inspect Henlow Mill Water in 1746, and find ways of stopping excessive flooding.[40] The Dunstable to Hockcliffe Trust had expensive trouble with continual flooding from a watercourse (JHC 26: 492). Many trusts built bridges to overcome this problem, paying the construction and maintenance costs themselves, although this was the traditional responsibility of the parish or County. Twenty-two of the Sample 2 trusts erected new bridges in their first three years of operation, whilst some enforced the local obligation to maintain pre-existing structures.[41] The Marylebone Trustees, for example, had continual disputes with the City of London over its responsibility for the Banquetting House Bridge in Oxford Street. After a ten-year struggle in 1731, the City finally gave £100 for immediate repairs and £20 per annum for maintenance. The trust then paved the road at the bridge and doubled its width to 40 feet (Sheppard 1958: 62–6).

A very important part of trust repair programmes was their concern with the *width* of their highways. The 1691 Highway Act had directed that 'the Surveyors shall make every cartway leading to any market town eight foot wide at least'. The General Highways Act of 1773 contained a similar clause, but ordering the minimum width to be at least 20 feet. Turnpike trusts were encouraged to do this by clauses inserted in most of their Acts before 1740, and all of them after that date, permitting the Trustees to buy land for road widening purposes. Some of the Acts laid down maximum widths,[42] whilst several trusts established their own minimum widths. These were usually in excess of the eight feet minimum set by the Hagley Trustees in 1753—e.g. 24 feet by the Islington Trustees in 1718, 30 feet by the Brentford Trustees in 1717, 20 feet by the Cheshunt Trustees in 1751, and 36 feet, with 16 feet being gravelled, by the Hockerill Trustees in 1744.[43] One of the first acts of the latter trust was to set up a Committee 'to view the narrow roads'. In 1746, the New Cross Trust had three Committees working on this problem, so that by 1753, a correspondent in the *Gentlemen's Magazine* could write that they had 'widened several places in the road to Dartford, being perhaps the first who began to widen and make the roads straight'.[44] This, in fact, was far from true. At least eight of the Sample 2 trusts, for example, had implemented road widening schemes before this.[45]

Road widening was thus actively pursued by many trusts. At least 31 of the Sample 2 trusts bought land for this purpose in their first three years in operation, and it is possible that in some further cases, the purchase was not recorded. Those trusts entering construction contracts usually specified the width of the new road: these varied between 21 and 36 feet, and between 15 and 36 feet for the gravelled section. Some of the road wideners were very active. The Watton Turnpike in Hertfordshire purchased land from 84 owners in its first year, requesting the Sheriff of the county to impanel a Jury of 25 persons to fix fair prices. The Stevenage to Biggleswade Trust bought nine messuages and tenements, with 88 shops in Baldock in 1778, in order to widen the Great North Road. The net cost was estimated at £1,168 2s 6d after the furnishings and materials had been auctioned for £185 16s 0d. The Keighley to Kendal Trust bought land from more than 50 owners between 1753 and 1756, twice having to resort to the Sheriff to impanel a Jury.[46]

Improvements of this nature were widespread, especially in the second half of the century. Only one of the Board of Agriculture Reports—that for Devon—complained of the narrowness of a county's turnpike roads (Vancouver 1808: 8–9, 368). Scott in 1778 had been less impressed, stating that the roads to cities should be between 60 and 80 feet wide, a standard by which the main roads to London were, he thought, a disgrace (1778: 314–15). Arthur Young, in his Northern Tour in 1771, had found the road from Henley to the capital too small, especially the section from Brentford which was 'much too narrow for such vast traffic'. He had also criticized the paved roads of Lancashire and Cheshire on the same grounds, but significantly he found only two other turnpikes, responsible for only 21 miles of road, in the same condition in nearly 1,000 miles of travel on turnpike roads (1771 Vol. 4: 423–36).

Apart from road widening, trusts carried out a number of related improvements. Some trusts were established to build completely new roads, notably in the London area, whilst nearly all trusts were involved in shortening routes, and lessening gradients, particularly towards the end of the eighteenth and in the nineteenth century.[47] The land taken in usually had to be fenced or 'quicked' in order to contain the route. The Sparrows Herne Trust, for example, spent £134 on land for widening schemes, and £202 providing fencing along the new sections, between 1764 and 1769. Part of this was accounted for by two payments of £92 and £72 to contractors, who were to maintain the fencing for ten years.[48] Trusts also had to erect milestones, and direction posts. The requirement to provide milestones was inserted in turnpike Acts from the early 1740s, and this, along with the order providing for direction posts, was made general in 1767.

London Trusts

The management task confronting the London trusts in the eighteenth century was rather different, both in scale and scope, to that of the provincial trusts. Not only were their roads very intensively used, but there was a high proportion of damaging coach traffic. They faced particular difficulties because of the unsuitability of the local road gravel, whilst they had a range of problems resulting from urban development around, and encroachment upon, their turnpike roads. But to deal with these problems, the London trusts had higher incomes than those elsewhere (Table XXX), and were able to spend far more money per mile of road (Table XLIV).

Some of these problems, and the solutions adopted, have already been examined. The size of the management task necessitated frequent meetings, and particular areas of responsibility were delegated to Committees. The intensity of traffic flow produced intensive repair measures, initially in the form of overgenerous treatment, rather than sound construction. Gradually harder materials were brought into use, and the busiest streets and roads were paved. However, the Middlesex gravel and flint that remained in use elsewhere was unsuitable, and the roads had to be watered to keep down the dust. Also, in a growing city, they had to be cleaned, watched and lit as well.

In 1721, when the Marylebone Trust took over what is now Oxford Street, St Marylebone was a small village a mile over the fields from London, and the road was undeveloped. By 1800, the New Road had been built to the north of the village to relieve Oxford Street, and estate building stretched between the two thoroughfares, and away to the north. When the Kensington Trust was established in 1726 to repair the road from Piccadilly to Countersbridge, Knightsbridge, Kensington and Hammersmith were small communities well separated from Westminster. But in 1782, when Carl Moritz visited England, he found that 'before you well know you are out of London, you are already in Kensington and Hammersmith; because there are, all the way, houses on both sides, after you are out of the City' (1924: 100). This expansion brought with it a proliferation of local authorities and bodies responsible for new urban services. The trusts' task was not made any simpler by the need to deal with the parishes, the City, Paving Commissioners, and the water companies, whose functions and activities all impinged on one another.

It is possible to make a fairly detailed assessment of the history of these trusts, because many of their original records are preserved in local history libraries around London. In fact, these records have already produced some of the best local turnpike studies, notably Clarke (1955) and Sheppard (1958), which are concerned with the Islington and Marylebone, and the Marylebone Trusts respectively. Other useful works include Ffooks' study of the Kensington Trust (1955) and Payne's study of the Bermondsey Trust (1956). Relying heavily on these works, this account examines further some of the extra functions which the London trusts had to perform.

Middleton's complaints about the dustiness of London roads have already been noted. Obviously the inconvenience was very real in dry weather, as Pehr Kalm visiting the city in 1748 had observed:

'From the sun and strong west wind, the roads are now so dry that when vehicles and horses went on them there rose from them so much dust, that it was very difficult to get along, for both eyes, mouth and nose were filled with it. Trees and plants by the wayside were covered with it.' (1892: 37)

The general remedy for this was to *water the roads* to keep down the dust. The Kensington Trust was empowered to water the road from Hyde Park Corner to the end of Piccadilly by its original Act of 1726 (65). The Trustees sank a special well in Piccadilly, and contracted with Abraham Odell to water the road in summer. He used two carts and two horses, and started each morning at four o'clock (Ffooks 1955: 35). But most trusts did not receive such powers until the 1750s, and after.[49] The Old Street Trust was one of these. It established a special Committee in February 1754 to supervise the construction of two wells and pumps, and bought two water carts. It later contracted with a Mr Eldridge for £22 to water the roads that summer.[50] The Islington Trustees, by the end of the century, were paying considerably more than this. In 1800, their watering contract was worth £319, and by 1810, as much as £626 (Clarke 1955: 294).

Watching and *lighting* were even more expensive. In these two years, the Islington Trustees had to spend £1,425 and £1,617 on both services. Their renewal Act of 1776 had given them power to levy a sixpenny rate on properties of over £10 rental value, but this rate raised only £400 and £600 in both years. Between 1762 and 1766, the Marylebone Trustees devoted 11 per cent of their expenditure to paying for lighting and the watch, on average £224 per annum.[51] They were not given rating powers until 1808, when they were empowered to levy fourpence on properties of over £10 in rental value within 200 yards of the turnpike road (Clarke 1955: 286–90). The Kensington Trust spent £165 on lighting alone in 1772: this was 3·5 per cent of its total expenditure.[52]

Lighting and watching was essential in a growing city to protect citizens and their property. John Spranger stated in 1754 that 'streets can never be laid out in such a manner as to make them safe for passengers by night, without being well lighted'. He contrasted the smaller number of robberies in the well lit city with the very large numbers in Westminster (Sheppard 1958: 87). Since an Act of 1662 householders in both places had been responsible for hanging lamps outside their homes from Michaelmas until Lady Day, but only until midnight. The City Corporation had obtained powers in 1736 to compel householders to pay a lamp rate, so that permanent lamps could be constructed. Their example had been followed by some of the surrounding parishes, but Westminster did not do the same until 1761.[53]

About this time, the turnpike roads were also being permanently lit. Some parishes did this themselves, as on Newington Green in 1767, and in Grays Inn Lane in 1769. But the main roads were lit by the trusts.[54] The Hackney Trust was empowered to erect lamps in 1756, and had completed this task by 1757 (JHC 29: 657). Ten years later, the Kensington Trustees were able to light the Great West Road, Tyburn Lane (now Park Lane) and Grosvenor Place. By 1785, they had 592 lamps, which they farmed out for eight months of the year at a cost of 15s 6d a lamp (Ffooks 1955: 46). The Islington Trustees farmed theirs at about the same time for 11s a lamp (Clarke 1955: 288). As a result of all this activity Charles Moritz exclaimed as he travelled into London in 1782:

'The road from Greenwich to London is actually busier, and far more alive, than the most frequented street in Berlin . . . and on each side of the road [there are] well-built and noble houses, whilst all along, at proper distance, the road was lined with lamp posts.' (1924: 20)

And Monsieur D'Auchenholz, another foreign visitor was very impressed:

'In Oxford-street alone, there are more lamps than in all Paris. The great roads within seven or eight miles of town are also illuminated in the same manner; and as they are very numerous, the effect is charming. . . .' (1791: 85)

Powers to provide a watch were usually given to trusts at the same time. Watchmen were employed on beats. The Marylebone Trustees appointed seven watchmen in 1763 to guard both Oxford Street and the New Road, between sunset and midnight during the winter months. They were armed with blunderbusses, and carried horns (Sheppard 1958: 100). The Kensington Trust did not obtain the necessary powers until 1798: then they employed 12 men to guard the Great West Road (Ffooks 1955: 46). The Islington Trust had the most sophisticated system for its network of roads on the northern side of the city, stretching out towards Hampstead and Highgate. In 1789, they had five watch Supervisors, paid £1 per week, 11 horse patrols, paid 18s each, and no less than 64 foot patrols, at seven shillings a week. The trust provided the horses, and watchboxes at intervals, and armed its men with carbines and cutlasses (Clarke 1955: 286).

Urban expansion, however, brought further problems. The newly built-up areas had to be supplied with water, and the *water companies* were a continual source of trouble to the turnpike Trustees. The Chelsea Water Company was set up in 1723 to supply the West End, and from the start, the Kensington Trust was complaining about its pipes. In July 1726, the Company agreed to make drains under these pipes where they lay in the trust's roads. But leaks continued to spoil the roads, and when mains were dug up, or new ones laid, as in Pimlico in 1728, earth was mixed with the clean gravel.[55] In June 1731, the Trustees complained that:

'. . . the pipes belonging to the Chelsea Water Works lying in the road from Hyde Park Corner to Mr. Green's back gate (in Pimlico) are a very great nuisance to the publick, and very dangerous to passengers, great numbers of holes being in the road occasioned by the ouzings of their pipes, Several gentlemen having been thrown from their horses and Stage Chaises overturned.'

The Secretary of the Company replied that they had no responsibility for the holes, but after the Clerk of the Trust produced the Act setting up the Company (8 Geo. I, c. 26), which specified that the Company was to repair any damages caused to any road, there was no more trouble (Ffooks 1955: 42–3).

The Islington Trust experienced similar difficulty with the New River and Hampstead Companies which supplied the northern side of London with water. As early as July 1717, the Trustees complained of the damage that leaky pipes were causing, and in September of that year they resolved that:

'The Proprietors of the Hampstead Aqueducts forthwith move their pipes that lie in Watery Lane and the road from the Halfway House in Hampstead Road to Kentish Town.'[56]

In January 1768, the trust's paving in Goswell Street was damaged by the New River Company's pipes. The Company refused to do anything about it, and did not do so until the case had been in and out of court for three years. The same company spoilt the paving in Oxford Street in 1743, after the Marylebone Trustees had paved it. Their new pipes leaked and heaps of gravel were left behind. The damage was still unrepaired in 1745 (Clarke 1955: 295–6). Later, in 1770, the same happened again, when the company's paviours filled a hole with the old pebbles instead of the new granite laid down by the Paving Commission (Sheppard 1958: 136).

Street cleansing was not a service that was usually undertaken by the trusts. The 1662 Act required householders in the City and Westminster to sweep the street outside their houses twice a week, and parishes to appoint an unpaid Scavenger, in the same way as they appointed a Surveyor. Rates were to be levied to pay the wages of a raker, who actually cleaned the streets and removed the rubbish. In 1691, these powers were extended to all parishes within the Bills of Mortality (2 Wm & Mary sess. 2, c. 8). But outside the Bills, responsibility still fell to the Surveyor himself. St Marylebone successfully persuaded the Marylebone Trustees to accept an annual composition to clean Oxford Street. The Trust brought its own team of four horses, two carts and a wheelbarrow, and performed the task between 1728 and 1745. The collection of the composition proved so difficult, however, that the trust gave up for that reason, and by 1740, they had asked the parish to resume cleaning the street.[57]

Other London trusts did not take such a direct interest as this, but they did not hesitate to use the law to make sure that their roads were kept clean. In August 1719, a Committee of Trustees inspected the Islington road and ordered that 'those inhabitants of Islington that annoy the Road by throwing filth and other Annoyances into the same be forthwith prosecuted'. Their Accounts for 1762 record a payment of £3 12s 0d to the Clerk for bringing an action against a householder for 'shooting Night Soil' into the road. The Marylebone Trustees offered a reward of £1 for information leading to the conviction of people doing the same in Oxford Street in 1742. The Kensington Trust also prosecuted for this reason, and offenders were fined between £1 and £2.[58] In the rapidly expanding industrial suburbs of Bermondsey and Deptford, the Bermondsey Trustees waged a vigorous campaign against such nuisances. They cleaned and arched over many hundreds of feet of common sewer, and pressed the Commissions of Sewers of Surrey and Kent to remedy the defects in the local drainage system. Tanners who hung skins to dry across the road were prosecuted, as were those who threw ashes, waste, water and filth into the streets. The trust even pressed those who had 'privies or boghouses' within ten feet of a footway 'much to the Annoyance of the Public' to remove them to a less offensive position (Payne 1956: 140).

Most turnpike trusts, both within and outside London, seem, therefore, to have taken their responsibilities seriously. In the best tradition of the eighteenth century, many unpaid Trustees expended much energy on road repair and improvement, and in London, on street maintenance too. Although their methods were initially entirely traditional, and in many respects remained so, they were prepared to experiment and adopt more advanced ideas. Road repair was gradually supplemented by sound construction, road maintenance by deliberate improvement, whilst in London, the trusts effectively assumed the mantle of Improvement Commissions.

It remains to examine the effect of this activity on the quality of turnpike road surfaces and route networks, and to assess the impact of trusts' improvements on economy and society.

9. Notes

1. Peterborough to Northampton Plan, unmarked MSS (Northants. RO). Tadcaster to Otley Plan (WR).
2. York to Collingham Minutes, 20 June 1771 (WR). Unfortunately the first volume of the Marylebone Trust's Minutes has been lost since Clarke completed his research in 1955. Hence he is the only source of information about this trust between 1721 and 1740 (Marylebone Library).

3. Trusts nos 32, 34, 65, 118, 203, 277, 301, 32 (new Isleworth District in 1767).
4. Trusts nos 42, 49, 63, 535.
5. Trusts nos 40, 60, 62, 81, 85, for example.
6. Wells Minutes, 20 Sept. 1753 (Somerset RO).
   Ringwood to Wimborne Minutes, 19 Sept., 16 Nov. 1759 (Hants. RO).
   Liverpool to Prescot Minutes, 2 Jan. 1727 (Lancs. RO).
   Doncaster to Wakefield Minutes, 15 Feb. 1742 (WR).
7. Northampton to Harborough Plan (Fisher/Sanders MSS 61/68, Northants RO).
8. Gloucester to Birdlip Minutes, 1761–73 (Glos. RO).
   Stokenchurch to Woodstock Minutes, 1770 (Oxford CRO).
   Doncaster to Tadcaster Minutes, 1765 (WR).
9. Brentford Minutes, 29 July 1717 (Chiswick Library).
   Fulham Minutes, 6 Sept. 1731 (Fulham Library).
   Old Street Minutes, 24 July 1753, 3 Sept. 1754, 2 Sept. 1755 (Finsbury Library).
   Islington Minutes, 16 Sept. 1718 (Islington Library).
10. Cheshunt Minutes, 1 April, 6 June 1751; 31 Aug., 20 Nov. 1752 (Herts. RO).
11. The History, Topography and Antiquities of the Parish of St Mary, Islington (London 1811: 21).
12. Harrogate to Boroughbridge Minutes, 15 Dec. 1753.
    Wakefield to Halifax Minutes, 18 June, 11 Aug. 1757 (WR).
    Both these contracts were well before the date of 1765 that Jackman named for Metcalfe's earliest work (1916: 267).
13. Harrogate to Hutton Moor Minutes, 20 May, 17, 29 June 1752.
    Knaresborough to Pateley Bridge Minutes, 11 June, 7 Nov. 1759.
    Ripon to Boroughbridge Minutes, 24 March 1753, 24 June 1754.
    Toller Lane End Minutes, 30 July 1755, 22 May 1777 (WR).
14. Tadcaster to York Minutes, 22 May 1767. The Surveyor was later paid for doing this, but there is no record of whether the trust then implemented it more widely (WR).
15. Table XLV, and Accounts, 1761–6. These items were listed separately (Glos. RO).
16. Military Road Minutes, 16 and 18 July 1751 (Cumbria RO).
17. New Cross Minutes, 1 Dec. 1718, 12 Jan. 1719 (Kent AO).
    Welwyn Minutes, 2 Dec. 1728, 3 Feb. 1729.
    Watton Minutes, 5 Oct. 1759 (Herts. RO).
    Islington Trust (Clarke 1955: 236).
18. MacAdam's quote: BPP 1825 (355) V 24–8, and Phillips 1737: 3, 5; Middleton 1798: 399–400; BPP 1819 (509) V 339: 11–19.
19. Sheppard 1958: 58; Islington Minutes, 5 July 1720.
20. Islington Minutes, 16 July 1717 (Islington Library).
21. Cheshunt Minutes, 3 June 1751 (Herts. RO).
22. Stevenson 1812: 439, Batchelor 1808: 587, Holt 1795: 186, Bailey and Culley 1797: 149, 219.
23. Worgan 1815: 161, Pitt and Parkinson 1813: 309, Bailey and Culley 1797: 149, Bailey 1810: 271, Young 1808: 416.
24. Batchelor 1808: 587, Parkinson 1811: 274, Bailey and Culley 1797: 149, 219, Bailey 1810: 271.
25. Sheffield to Wakefield, Surveyor's Accounts 1774 (Sheffield Libraries).

The use of slag in Sussex was in part the result of the 1585 Wealden roads Act (27 Eliz., c. 19), which required ironmasters to donate loads of slag to the parishes for road repair. See above, p. 75.

26. Gloucester to Birdlip Minutes, 27 Aug. 1768. (Glos. RO).

27. Islington Minutes, 7 April 1719 (Islington Library).

28. This rate was almost unique amongst turnpike trusts. The only other cases which have been found were lighting and watching rates granted to the Islington Trustees in 1776 (see below, pp. 254–5) and the Marylebone Trustees in 1808. The Marylebone paving rate was levied annually at 1s per yard of pavement outside each house, plus 9s on houses of less than £20 rental value, and 18s on those worth over £20. It raised £100 in 1745, £130 in 1752 and £154 in 1761 (Clarke 1955: 213–15).

29. Kensington Minutes, 13, 22 June 1726 (Kensington Library), and Ffooks 1955: 33. Old Street Minutes, 7 Aug. 1753 (Finsbury Library).

30. Kensington Minutes, 1726–34.
    Great North Road, Huntingdon Minutes, 29 March 1729 (Hunts. CRO).
    Gloucester to Birdlip Minutes, 11 July 1763 (Glos. RO).

31. Welwyn Minutes, 16 May 1726 (Herts. RO).

32. Liverpool to Prescot Minutes, 2 Jan. 1727 (Lancs. RO).
    Hagley Trust Minutes, 23 Sept. 1754 (Birmingham Library).

33. For example, Defoe 1697: 91, Homer 1767: 30, Scott 1778: 325.

34. Kensington Minutes, 13 June 1726 (Kensington Library).

35. For example:
    Worcester to Droitwich Minutes, 2 May 1757 (Worcs. RO).
    Knaresborough to Green Hammerton Minutes, 11 May 1752.
    Harrogate to Boroughbridge Minutes, 16 May 1752.
    Tadcaster to York Minutes, 22 May 1767 (WR).

36. As in Devon (Vancouver 1808: 272).

37. Such orders occur in nearly all Minute Books, e.g.:
    Doncaster to Tadcaster Minutes, 22 Nov. 1743.
    Tadcaster to York Minutes, 4 Oct. 1745 (WR).
    Gloucester to Hereford Minutes, 27 Nov. 1754 (Glos. RO).

38. For example:
    Brentford Minutes, 29 July 1717 (Chiswick Library).
    New Cross Minutes, 30 April, 30 Aug. 1718 (Kent AO).
    Salisbury to Eling Minutes, 20 June 1753 (Hants. RO).
    Stourbridge to Colley Gate Minutes, 8 Nov. 1763 (Worcs RO).

39. Brentford Minutes, 8 Dec. 1718 (Chiswick Library).
    Islington Minutes, 5 Nov. 1717 (Islington Library).
    Cheshunt Minutes, 3 June 1751.
    Hockerill Minutes, 4 Jan. 1773 (Herts. RO).
    Gloucester to Birdlip Hill Minutes, 11 July 1763 (Glos. RO).

40. Cheshunt Minutes, 2 Oct. 1725 to 9 May 1726.
    Hockerill Minutes, 1 Feb. 1746 (Herts. RO).

41. Liverpool to Prescot Minutes, 6 Dec. 1755, about Berry Bridge in Knotty Ash (Lancs. RO).
    Hockerill Minutes, 25 June 1772, about Littlebury Bridge (Herts. RO).

42. 11, 234 (20 yards); 45, 46 (15 yards).

43. Hagley Minutes, 23 Sept. 1754 (Birmingham Library).
    Islington Minutes, 4 Jan. 1718 (Islington Library).
    Brentford Minutes, 29 July 1717 (Chiswick Library).
    Cheshunt Minutes, 3 June 1751.
    Hockerill Minutes, 26 March 1745 (Herts. RO).
44. Hockerill Minutes, 17 July 1744 (Herts. RO).
    New Cross Minutes, 28 Feb. 1746 (Kent AO).
    Gentleman's Magazine, May 1753 (quoted in Webb 1920: 134).
45. Brentford Minutes, 3 Oct. 1717 (Chiswick Library).
    Islington Minutes, 9 Dec. 1718, 5 July 1720 (Islington Library).
    Chiswick Minutes, 7 March 1726.
    Hockerill Minutes, 17 July 1744 (Herts. RO).
    Liverpool to Prescot Minutes, 2 Jan. 1727 (Lancs. RO).
    Maidstone to Rochester Minutes, 31 July 1729 (Kent AO).
    Wakefield to Halifax Minutes, 18 May 1741.
    Wakefield to Weeland Minutes, 7 March, 4 June 1741, 5 Oct. 1742 (WR).
46. Watton Minutes, 22 July, 1 Aug. 1757.
    Stevenage to Biggleswade, MSS notes, TP6/74 (Herts. RO).
    Keighley to Kendal Minutes, 8 Dec. 1753, 10 Sept. 1754 (WR).
47. This is discussed in Chapter 10.
48. Sparrows Herne Accounts, 1764–9 (Herts. RO).
    See also:
    Knaresborough to Pateley Bridge Accounts, 1759–64.
    Harrogate to Hutton Moor Accounts, 1752–7.
    Ripon to Boroughbridge Accounts, 1752–7 (WR).
49. Powers to water the streets were normally given at the same time as power to provide
    a watch, and lighting (see note 54).
50. Old Street Minutes, 5 Feb., 2 July 1754 (Finsbury Library).
51. Accounts 1762–6 (Marylebone Library).
52. Accounts 1772 (Kensington Library).
53. Acts: 1662 14 Car. II, c. 2; 1736 9 Geo. II, c. 20; 1761 2 Geo. III, c. 21.
54. The renewal Acts of the following trusts gave such powers. In 1756—42, 101; 1762—
    44; 1764—155; 1765—226, 342; 1767—32, 65; 1774—23. A few trusts outside
    London also had lighting powers—Bath in 1708 (11), Shepherd's Shore to
    Marlborough in 1743 (116) and Shepton Mallet in 1791 (200).
55. Kensington Minutes, 19 July 1726, 1 July 1728 (Kensington Library).
56. Islington Minutes, 10 Sept. 1717 (Islington Library).
57. Marylebone Minutes, 4 June 1740, 5 Nov. 1741, 3 March 1742 (Marylebone
    Library), and Sheppard 1958: 61–2, Clarke 1955: 264.
58. Islington Minutes, 18 Aug. 1719.
    Accounts, 1762 (Islington Library).
    Marylebone Minutes, 3 Feb. 1742.
    Kensington Accounts, 1796–7: 3 entries (Kensington Library).

Impact

10

The Quality of Turnpike Roads

Squire Western's sister, upon completing her long journey from Somerset to London in 1749 declared: 'Well, surely no one ever had such an intolerable journey. I think the roads, since so many turnpike acts, are grown worse than ever.' (Fielding 1962: 182.) And she was not alone in her opinion. Twelve years earlier, Robert Phillips had written:

> 'The general complaints of the Badness of the Roads, especially some near London, is very much increas'd of late years: And those that frequently travel have a double Reason to complain; first they pay a great deal of Money to the Turnpikes; and then, as they find the Roads daily grow worse.' (1737: A3)

It is easy, though, to find very different views. Defoe was most impressed:

> 'Several of these turn-pikes and tolls have been set up of late years, and great progress had been made in mending the most difficult ways, and that with such success as well deserves a place in this account . . . it must be acknowledge they are very great things, and very great things are done by them.' (Defoe 1962, Vol. 2: 119–20)

A foreign visitor, travelling a few years after Defoe, in 1726, wrote home to his family that:

> 'The journey on the highroads of England and more especially near London, is most enjoyable and interesting. These roads are magnificent, being wide, smooth and well kept.' (de Saussure 1902: 146–7)

And near the end of the turnpike boom, in 1767, an Oxford writer forecast:

'That there is no one circumstance, which will contribute to characterise the present Age to Posterity so much as the Improvements, which have been made in our publick Roads.' (Homer 1767: 3)

Nevertheless, complaints about individual trusts, and the turnpike system in general, persisted after this date. In 1819, when the network was almost at its maximum extent, a Select Committee reported that:

'The concurrent testimony of all the witnesses examined by your Committee established the fact that the general state of the Turnpike Roads in England and Wales is extremely defective.' (BPP 1819 (509) V 339: 4)

Earlier in the nineteenth century other Parliamentary Reports had said very similar things.[1] Yet, at the same time, many commentators were favourably disposed. Such conflicting evidence is, however, inevitable. The horse rider and the coach traveller saw things differently, as did the pamphleteer and the local historian. The Londoner, used to a long period of turnpike road repair, could well be less charitable than a foreigner seeing British roads for the first time. Those who were impressed by changes over a long time could produce a more favourable report than those commenting on the state of the roads at a particular date.

A fair assessment of the success or failure of the turnpike trust system in its primary task of improving the quality of the road surface, alignment and network can, however, be made fairly easily. There are three basic methods. Firstly, individual reports, journeys and histories can be sifted to build up a general overall picture. Secondly, those sources which give a more general coverage can be used to obtain an idea of the situation at a particular date. Thirdly, the improvements in the road network in particular areas over time can be seen, objectively, in contemporary maps.

It is not necessary to pursue the first method in detail. This was done by both the Webbs and Jackman half a century ago. Both concluded from the evidence they examined that a favourable view was correct:

'. . . all the contemporary evidence indicates that . . . the mileage of useable roads was, by the eighteenth century Turnpike Trusts, very greatly extended. . . And we have the significant fact that the most eminent observers of, and participants in, the local government of the latter half of the century—Sir Henry Hawkins, Dr Richard Burn,

John Scott, and Arthur Young—all expressly assert, or at least unequivocally imply, the expediency of the Turnpike Trust and its toll.' (Webb 1920: 144–5)

'The truth of the matter seems to lie in a moderate view so that before the end of the eighteenth century, it was possible, for those who took a wider retrospect of the preceding fifty years, to note great improvements within that time, such as made the English roads "the admiration of foreigners".' (Jackman 1916: 301)

This was certainly so. For a writer in the *Gentleman's Magazine* in 1792, 'the great improvements which, in the memory of man, have been made in the turnpike roads throughout this kingdom, would be incredible, did we not actually perceive them.'[2] About the same time, the historian of Derby commented that:

'Eight roads proceed from Derby to adjacent places; all are turnpiked. . . . These are all excellent and used with pleasure. . . . But I knew them when the best was incommodious even in summer and scarcely passable in winter.' (Hutton 1791: 10–11)

In Somerset, in 1798, the Board of Agriculture writer stated 'that nothing so much contributes to the improvement of a county as good roads; before the establishment of turnpikes, many parts of this county were scarcely accessible.' (Billingsley 1798: 104.) In the Gloucestershire Report, in 1807, it was said that the restraints on farming 'are now in a great measure removed by the state of the roads.' (Rudge 1807: 333.)

In Staffordshire, at the same date, 'the roads . . have been very much improved in the last forty years, by the introduction of tollgates upon most of the public thoroughfares.' (Pitt 1808: 281.) And Arthur Young, a famous commentator, and the first Secretary of the Board, remembered 'the roads of Oxfordshire forty years ago, when they were in a condition formidable to the bones of all who travelled on wheels. . . . A noble change has taken place. The turnpikes are very good, and where gravel is to be had, excellent.' (Young 1809: 324.)

The opinions of these writers are confirmed by reports from other parts of the country.[3] They clearly indicate a belief in the improvement of the state of the high roads under the turnpike system in the second half of the eighteenth century—since, in fact, the widespread adoption of the system between 1750 and 1770. But whilst such a general improvement may have been most noticeable in the second half of the century, there is no reason to suppose that the more limited turnpike network of the first half did not bring about its own improvements. Defoe's enthusiasm confirms this, as do the independent indicators examined in more detail below.

The second method can be used, with the very limited number of sources available, to make more systematic assessments of the state of the turnpike roads at particular dates. The first of these sources is Arthur Young's Northern Tour, published in 1771. It contains some valuable information, because Young travelled nearly 1,500 miles, 1,000 of these on turnpike roads. He did so at about the time from which many of the Board of Agriculture writers dated the 'great improvements' in turnpike road quality. He was a discriminating observer, generally travelling by chaise, and noting the state of the roads, and whether they were cross or turnpike, between each of the points on his journey. Each stretch of road is described with labels ranging from 'vile' to 'excellent', so that it is possible to arrive at a quantitative assessment of his opinions (Table XLVI).

Table XLVI
Arthur Young's Assessment of the Roads
on his Northern Tour, 1771

	Turnpike mileage	Cross road mileage
Excellent	19·9 per cent	3·7 per cent
Very good	9·4	—
Good	24·3	17·3
Pretty good, middling	18·1	9·4
Indifferent	1·2	8·3
Bad	8·2	28·5
Very bad, vile	18·8	32·8

It is notable that he found the turnpike roads consistently better than the cross roads, except where the latter had been mended by private means. This is strong evidence for improvement in the quality of turnpike roads before the last part of the eighteenth century. But, secondly, he was sufficiently impressed by over half the turnpike road mileage to describe it as 'good', 'very good' or 'excellent': a suitable antidote to counter the views of those who accept Young's condemnation of some turnpike roads, particularly those in Lancashire and Staffordshire, as representative of his opinions.

A second systematically compiled source is the collection of County Reports of the Board of Agriculture. Although some go into detail about changes in the eighteenth century, as has been seen, each Report also has a description of the roads—turnpike, and parish—at the time of compilation. Although this is a general assessment, rather than a detailed mile-by-mile analysis, it provides a picture of the quality of each county's turnpike roads at the end of the century. The Reports for 33 English counties have been examined, and the results are consistent with Young's earlier findings (Table XLVII). The turnpike roads were nearly always described as being much better than the parish roads, and the majority of county networks—two-thirds—were described as being in a 'good', 'very good' or 'excellent' condition. Only three were condemned as 'bad'— those of Shropshire, Buckingham and Middlesex. And Middleton, who compiled the latter Report, still spoke of 'great improvements' in the preceding 40 or 50 years (1798: 394).

Table XLVII
Assessment of the State of 33 County Turnpike Networks at the end of the Eighteenth Century from Board of Agriculture Reports[4]

Excellent, very good	11 counties	33 per cent
Good	11	33
Middling, could be better	4	12
Variable, good in parts	4	12
Bad	3	9

The third source of information about the state of turnpike roads at a particular date is considerably later than the other two, but it is the most detailed available. The Appendix to the Report of the 1840 Parliamentary Committee records the condition of the roads under every trust in England and Wales, with very few exceptions. The Appendix was compiled from detailed returns made by the Clerk of each trust in answer to a list of questions about trust size, management and finances. One of these questions was:

'What is the present condition of such Road, and is any part under indictment for want of Repair?'

The answers were, in nearly every case, given in sufficient detail for trust mileage to be classified into 'good', 'bad' or 'indifferent'. Because the information came from the trusts themselves, rather than independent

K

observers, its usefulness may be open to question. However, the willingness of Clerks to use the full range of descriptions suggests the results have some validity.

The Returns have been examined in detail.[5] Roads described as 'indictable', 'founderous', 'low', 'very indifferent', 'much in need of, or out of repair' and 'bad' are taken as 'bad' roads, and the mileages involved assessed as a proportion of the whole for each county. This was done successfully for every county of England and Wales, except Brecon and Glamorgan, where the returns were insufficiently detailed. The results are shown in Fig. 34. In only eight counties was more than 12 per cent of the turnpike mileage described as 'bad'. In several of these— Pembroke, Carmarthen, Hereford, Leicester and Huntingdon—this was because of only one or two trusts.

The second part of the question requested information about current indictments before Quarter Sessions. Very few parishes were under indictment, or had been in the recent past, for failing to repair a turnpike road. Forty-three cases were recorded, on account of 27 turnpike trusts. These were limited to 12 counties. Hence only 2·4 per cent of the trusts in existence in 1840 were affected and most of the indictments were for short half-mile or mile-long sections only.

Information in Quarter Sessions records about presentments and indictments of turnpike roads could, however, prove a useful indicator of their quality at earlier dates. This has been argued by Lewis, in his study of Carmarthenshire trusts (1967). In the period 1792–1800, he found 66 presentments of highways in the county, and 40 of these were for turnpike roads, with 20 alone against the roads of the Kidwelly Trust. Even in 1840, this was a poor area for turnpikes (Fig. 34). The roads were hilly, and the traffic light, with coal and lime carriages, which contributed the bulk of the traffic, being partially or totally exempt from toll. The Kidwelly Trust itself supervised 80 miles of road, including the post road to Milford Haven. But in 1840, the Returns indicated that none of its roads had been indicted for the past 20 years.

The Carmarthenshire example is thus likely to be exceptional, but this source of information itself requires more detailed local examination. Dowdell, in the only general county study available, found a considerable decrease in the volume of highway fines imposed by Quarter Sessions in Middlesex, as turnpike trusts gradually took over the more important roads (1932: 93–7). Jackman also noted a general decline in highway business, although he did not specifically refer to fine under indictment (1916: 79). It is interesting, however, that the detailed

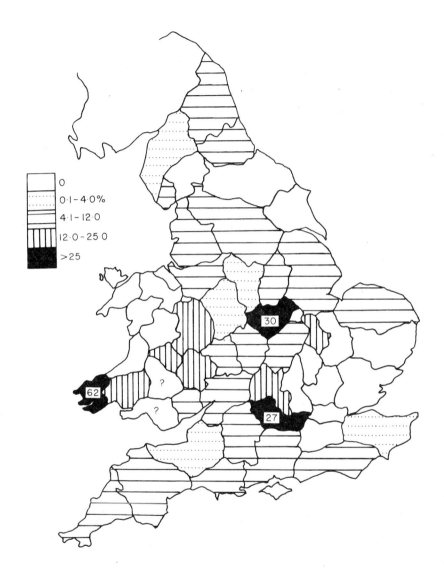

FIG. 34. The quality of turnpike roads in 1840. This map shows the proportion of turnpike road mileage considered 'bad' in the Appendix to the Report of the Commissioners for inquiring into the State of the Roads in England and Wales (BPP 1840 (280) XXVII: 15).

research in the Sample 2 Minute Books revealed only one recorded indictment against a trust. In 1796, Holgate Parish was indicted for part of the Collingham–York Trust's road 'it being in a very bad state and insufficiently wide in several parts'. The trust's Surveyor was given authority to buy sufficient land, and to request the township to keep the road in repair once it had been widened.[6] However, the lack of further examples in the Minute Books suggests that indictment of parishes on account of bad turnpike roads was not common in the eighteenth century.

The third method that can be used to assess the impact of turnpike trust management on the quality of roads in their care is by detailed examination of changes in road networks and alignments in particular areas. This method has the advantage of producing objectively based results, unmarred by impressionistic assessment or observer bias. Three areas have been chosen—the immediate vicinity of London, and the Oxford and mid-Sussex regions.

A writer in the *Gentleman's Magazine* in 1798 exclaimed:

'To turn our eyes back on the state of this Metropolis only half a century ago, it is with wonder and delight we view the improvements on every approach to the great city.'[7]

And the improvements which had been made were not only to the existing road network—a series of new links had also been opened up as the city grew. Although this process started in mid-century, it was by no means finished in 1798, and the nineteenth century saw a further wave of new road construction (Figs 35 and 36).

The two most important eighteenth century schemes were the construction of the Surrey New Roads south of the river in 1751–2, and the opening of the New Road, in 1756, extended in 1761 by the City Road into the core of the built-up area. The Surrey New Roads, sanctioned by Act of Parliament in 1751 (155) were built after the opening of Westminster Bridge in that year, to provide new avenues to the main turnpike routes into Kent and Sussex. The avenues were to be at least 42 feet wide, across the open land of St George's Fields. The specifications were laid down in detail (JHC 26: 199), and the scheme was enacted immediately, taking little more than six months to complete.[8] It was extended in 1769, after Blackfriars Bridge was finished, by the construction of an 80-foot wide carriageway—Blackfriars Road—southwards to Westminster Bridge Road, the modelling of St George's

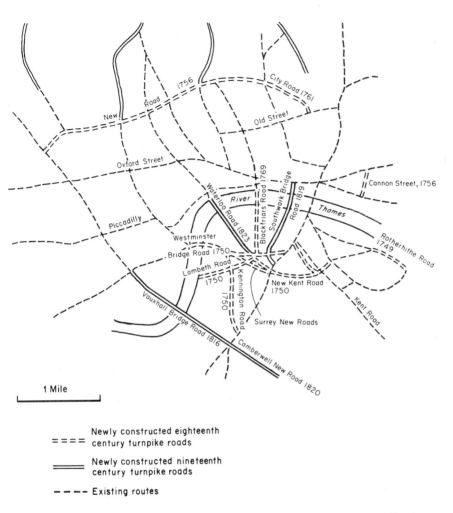

FIG. 35. Newly constructed turnpike roads in central London. *Source*: Turnpike Acts. Cary 1790, Hall 1964.

Circus, and another link from this to the Surrey–Sussex Turnpike (509).

The purpose of the New Road, now the Marylebone, Euston and Pentonville Roads, was rather different. It provided a by-pass from the Edgware Turnpike round the north side of the city as far as the Angel, Islington, but primarily for cattle on their way to Smithfield, not carriages. The Act was passed in 1756 (270), and enabled the Marylebone and Islington Trusts together to construct a 40-foot wide

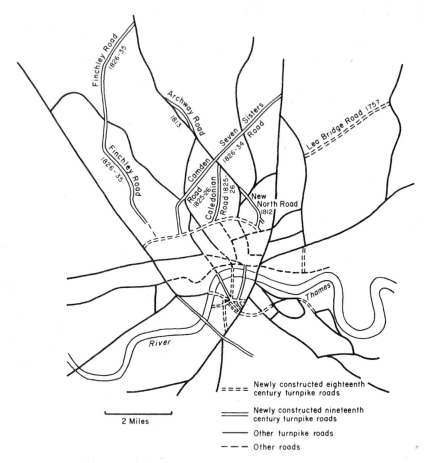

Fig. 36. Newly constructed turnpike roads in the London area. *Source*: see Fig. 35.

roadway, respectively to the west and east of Tottenham Court. The Act specifically forbad paving, and so the road simply had to be staked out through the fields. It was open within two months (Sheppard 1958: 99). In 1761, the construction of the City Road was authorized under a separate Trust, to carry the New Road into Old Street (342). It was opened in June 1761 'and continues at this day one of the finest highways leading from the Metropolis'. [9]

There were some further eighteenth century schemes. The Bermondsey and Rotherhithe Trust was set up in 1749 (142) to take over various roads in those parishes, and build a new link between

Bermondsey and the dockyard at Deptford, to save a four-mile journey up to London Bridge, down the Kent Road, and up Back Lane (JHC 25: 726–7). In 1754, Cannon Street was opened on the eastern side of the city, to provide a connexion between the docks and wharves and the Whitechapel Turnpike (226). Three years later, in 1757, an Act was passed which enabled Trustees to build a new road and bridge over the River Lea (the Lea Bridge Road) to relieve some of the congestion of this turnpike, and provide more direct access for traffic from East Anglia (282).

Some of the most spectacular turnpike schemes in the London area belonged, however, to the early part of the nineteenth century. More new roads were built in South London, after the Vauxhall, Waterloo and Southwark Bridges were finished in 1816, 1817 and 1819. In North London, some ambitious by-pass schemes were completed. Islington High Street was skirted by the New North Road (1812) to the east, and the Caledonian Road to the West (1826). The Archway Road (1813) took an easier route round Highgate main street, whilst Finchley High Road (1826–35) provided a new exit route for much north-bound traffic, avoiding the Hampstead and Highgate Heights altogether. At the same time, a new north-easterly link was constructed and opened, from the New Road as far as Tottenham on the Stamford Hill Turnpike (Hall 1964: 53–6).

This history of new road building, new bridge construction, the avoidance of old settlements and the choice of easier routes can also be seen in the Oxford region (Fig. 37). It was in this city that Homer wrote his enthusiastic pamphlet in praise of turnpike roads, quoted above. It is no coincidence that notable improvements were being made on the western approach roads to Oxford at the same time.

The main carriage route into Oxford before 1769 was from Witney, though Long Hanborough to the Woodstock road, and then south into the city. This was a 14-mile circuit, three miles longer than the horse road through Eynsham and over Wytham Hill. Both these roads had been turnpiked in 1751 (152), but the Wytham route was never properly improved, because—being dependent on the ferry at Swinford—it could never be used by carriages. It remained like this until the Swinford Toll bridge was built by the Earl of Abingdon in 1768, when the road was transferred to the Oxford-Fyfield Trust and legally upgraded to a carriageway (465). The first stage-coach was able to use this route in the following year (de Villiers 1969).

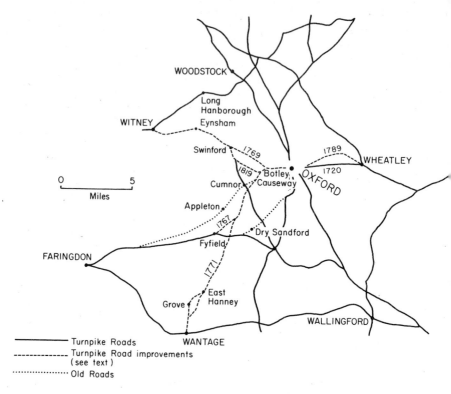

Fig. 37. Turnpike road improvements in the Oxford region. Based on: Rocque 1764, Cary 1787, Mavor 1809, Greenwood 1823, Bryant 1824 and Chapter 6.

This improvement was part of a wider scheme promoted by Sir William Blackstone. In 1767, he succeeded in obtaining an Act establishing the Oxford–Fyfield Trust, which not only enabled a better route to be made into the city from the south-west, but also sanctioned the improvement of Botley Causeway. The subscription opened for this latter purpose was not too successful, and Blackstone and one of his friends between them had to provide £5,800. The causeway was widened from its existing 14 feet and new bridges and walls provided. Subsequently, the road to Fyfield, which was described as only a horse road, was similarly improved. It provided an effective by-pass of the villages of Appleton and Cumnor, which were on the old road. It was also shorter by one mile than the alternative route through Dry Sandford and Foxcombe Hill.

    There were, in addition, several later improvements on the turnpike roads around Oxford. The first trust to be established in the area in 1719 was on the road from London. It had responsibility for the road from Stokenchurch on the Chilterns to Woodstock, with a branch from Wheatley, over Shotover Hill, to the end of the Mileway in Headington (37). In 1789, this branch was replaced by an easier route, involving the construction of a new road from the end of Cheyney Lane, round the northern flank of Shotover, and into Wheatley. A similar improvement was carried out on the Eynsham road in 1819. The improved horse road over Wytham Hill was not popular, because of the steep inclines involved, and in that year it was replaced by a low level route to the south.

The final example in this area is from the Wantage road. This was turnpiked in 1771, from Besselsleigh through Wantage to Hungerford (548). The turnpike followed an existing line of country lanes, which were gradually straightened to form the present route. At the end of the century, between 1787 and 1809, a major improvement was made to the north of Wantage, between the villages of East Hanney and Grove. A straight route was cut through the fields to avoid both settlements. The old road can still be seen through the line of the village streets and the connecting public trackway.

In the third area chosen, the mid-Sussex region, a similar range of improvements to the road network took place, but here it was in response to the growth of the new resorts of Eastbourne and Brighton. Its history is one of the turnpiking of successive routes, as the new resorts gradually displaced older centres in the settlement hierarchy (Fig. 38).

In 1775, the largest centre in this area was Lewes, the county town. It had a population of about 3,600, compared with 2,900 in Brighton and less than 1,500 in Eastbourne. The first turnpike roads were thus centred on Lewes. In 1752, it was connected by turnpike to London with a link to the existing Surrey–Sussex Trust near East Grinstead (170). In 1766, this new trust took over two of the high roads into East Sussex—those to Battle and Burwash. But neither Brighton nor Eastbourne could be reached directly by turnpike road. The usual route to both towns was through Lewes, and then by hilly downland road. There was a more westerly alternative to Brighton, on the Horsham–Beeding Turnpike, set up in 1764 (393), and then over Beeding Down, or a more easterly alternative to Eastbourne on the 1754 turnpike to Langley (218). But this was primarily a drove road from Pevensey Marshes.

With the growing prominence of both resorts, more direct roads were turnpiked. Brighton's population increased to 3,600 in 1788 and 8,500 in

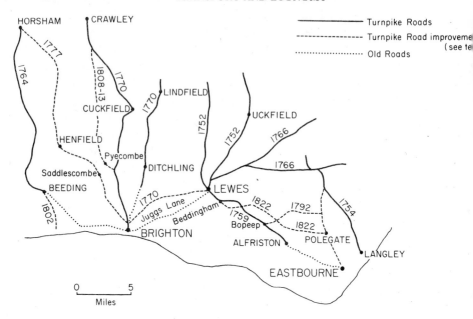

FIG. 38. Turnpike road improvements in mid-Sussex. Based on: Cary 1787, Gream 1799, Greenwood 1823 and Chapter 6.

1801, and by that date, there were no less than five turnpike roads to the town.

In 1770, three routes were set up—one from Lowell Heath through Cuckfield (528), one from New Chapel through Lindfield to Ditchling (520), and one to directly connect Lewes and Brighton (515). The latter road, in fact, provided an improved low level route up the Winterbourne Valley, avoiding the hill road through Juggs Lane and over Newmarket Hill. But the Cuckfield and Ditchling roads both climbed steeply over the scarp face of the South Downs at Clayton Hill and Ditchling Beacon.

The subsequent history of improvement reflects the desire to avoid these steep hill routes. In 1777, the Horsham to Brighton road through Henfield was turnpiked. This was in one respect better than the Cuckfield road, as it climbed the scarp gradually through the Saddlescombe Gap, although it still entailed a hilly ride from there onwards into Brighton, which the Cuckfield road, following the Pangdean Valley, avoided. In 1802, the Beeding Trust built a completely new road from the village to the coast down the Adur Valley, so providing, with the Lewes road, a second low-level, but nevertheless indirect, way into Brighton. The problem was not completely overcome until 1808, when the Lowell Heath–Brighton trust started to improve existing trackways from Pyecombe to Handcross, which not only straightened considerably the most popular coach route into the town, but avoided the climb over Clayton Hill.

The roads into Eastbourne underwent similar modifications. In 1759, the road from Lewes to Alfriston, under the Downs, was turnpiked. It stopped eight miles short of the resort, the road becoming a hilly downland track (321). But in 1792 the section from Bopeep to Alfriston was disturnpiked, and a flatter route, over Chilver Bridge, and eastwards to the present A22, was turnpiked under the same trust. This new route, following existing lanes, was about three miles north of the scarp. It was extended southwards into Eastbourne, and also northwards to join the 1754 turnpike to Langley at Hailsham (JHC 43: 598). Eastbourne now had a direct turnpike connexion to London, and a flat, if circuitous route to Lewes. This latter route was further improved in 1822, when the trust came under the guidance of MacAdam. A completely new road, almost straight, was built from Beddingham to Polegate. Although the western five miles followed old lanes, the eastern five miles were laid out across the fields.

The history of the turnpike system in these areas shows the nature and extent of improvements brought about by trusts in the road network. It is useful factual material to support the impressionistic, but widespread evidence of qualitative improvement in the state of the high roads in the eighteenth century. But immediately, a further question arises. If this was so, how was it reflected in the provision and quality of transport services, and in a broader context, in change in economy and society as a whole?

10. Notes

1. BPP 1808 (225) II 333: 6–7; 1810–11 (240) III 855: 5–6.
2. *Gentleman's Magazine* 1792, part II: 1161.
3. For example; Hutton 1795: 398, Lowe 1798: 135, Middleton 1798: 394, Hutton 1803: 168, Young 1804: 227, Duncomb 1805: 142, Holland 1808: 302.
4. Table XLVII includes all the Board of Agriculture Reports listed in the Bibliography, except those marked with an asterisk. These either gave insufficient detail, or were duplicates.

5. The County Summaries in the Appendix to the 1840 Report are best ignored. These are inconsistent, in many cases, with the individual trust mileages and descriptions (BPP 1840 (280) XXVII 15).

6. Minutes, 25 Feb. 1796 and 13 April 1797 (WR).

7. *Gentleman's Magazine* 1798, part II: 647–9.

8. *Gentleman's Magazine* 1753: 207–9.

9. The History, Topography and Antiquities of the Parish of St Mary, Islington (London 1811: 22).

11

Direct Benefits

The most immediate impact on economy and society of a successful transport innovation are the 'direct benefits' of the lower cost of carriage of goods and persons. But the resources saved need not be limited to the money savings of lower fares; in fact there may be no savings of this sort. Of great importance in the eighteenth century were any savings in travel time that could be effected, as well as the elimination of seasonality in travel schedules and a lessening of the risk of loss or accident. An improvement in any of these respects effectively lowered the cost of transport.

The transport services system in the eighteenth century underwent gradual modernization, with a concurrent increase in the number and range of services available. The immediate causes of this development were innovations within the transport services themselves, stimulated by the impact of growing national demand for these services. But the state of the roads was a critical permissive factor. Without improved road surfaces, it was not possible for the amount of organized travel to increase. Nor was it possible for wagons to supplant pack-horses, for stage-coaches to supplant the post-horses, or for lighter, faster conveyances to supplement these coaches.

This modernized transport services system was able to effect certain resource savings over the more traditional system it replaced. Paramount amongst these were the savings in travel time, and the gradual elimination of seasonality. In part, this was due not to improved road surfaces *per se*, but to the competition between transport operators which improved surfaces made possible. The effect on transport charges, or fares, is less clear, but again it does seem that the gradual destruction of monopoly provision brought about by increased competition, and the control of carriers' combinations by the Justices[1] enabled firms and passengers to save resources over time.

The role of the turnpike roads in the production of direct benefits for those who used transport services was therefore permissive, rather than directive. The benefits gained were not a result of direct action by the turnpike Trustees, as they were not themselves the suppliers of the transport services. It was rather the action of the turnpike Trustees in improving the state of the roads which enabled the operators who did supply these services to do so at a lower cost. The case is thus not as simple as with the railways, which provided both an improved transport network, and improved services on that network. Paradoxically, the direct benefits that resulted from the introduction of the turnpike road system were indirectly induced through the actions of those who controlled the transport services of the period.

The Modernization of Transport Services

The seventeenth and first half of the eighteenth centuries were the era of the horse, in both goods and passenger traffic. Even in 1800, the pack-horse was still widely used in some areas, such as the Pennines and the West Country and travelling post on horseback was still common. Although wheeled traffic had been widely used in and around London by the mid-seventeenth century, it was not until after 1750 that many of the big towns outside the Home Counties, and most of the smaller ones within them, gained a wagon or stage-coach service. The use of wheeled traffic both encouraged, and was encouraged by, the development of the turnpike road network. The early prominence of the London-based network was due, in part, to the use of wheeled traffic on the main roads leading to the capital. [2]

Some of the important towns of seventeenth century England did have coach services by 1660. The routes to St Albans, Hatfield, Hertford and Cambridge were recorded by Taylor in 1637, and by 1650, Bath and Bristol had services. In 1658, there were coaches running to Exeter and Salisbury in the south, and Chester, Doncaster, York and even Edinburgh in the north. But the towns which grew to prominence as trading and manufacturing centres in the eighteenth century did not gain a stage-coach connexion until after the surrounding roads had been turnpiked. The first direct coach from Nottingham and Derby to London was advertised in the *Derby Mercury* on 27 March 1735. Manchester's first service to the capital did not start to run until 1754, and Liverpool had no link until the Warrington Flying Stage Coach was started in 1757 (Baines

1852: 434). Neither Leeds nor Sheffield had a London coach until 1760 (Leader 1901: 90). Three years later, Brecon and Monmouth were connected by a weekly coach to London. In 1774, Carmarthen, and then Haverfordwest received a service.[3] By 1776, there was also a Holyhead to London coach (Dodd 1925: 142).

The timing of the emergence of services to smaller towns is of similar significance. Many places of only 1,000 or 1,500 in population size had their own direct stage-coach to London by 1800. Inevitably, these used roads away from the main turnpike routes of 1750, and were dependent on those lesser turnpike roads that were established between 1750 and 1770. Many of the small town services of England and Wales were established at this time (Fig. 39).

This general coincidence of the spread of wheeled traffic and turnpiking can also be illustrated with examples from goods services. After the Manchester–Buxton road was turnpiked in 1725 (50), the trust ran into financial difficulties for this very reason:

'. . . the greatest part of the Toll has been raised by Horses, carrying Malt from Derby, and the parts adjacent, into Cheshire; but Malt has, since the Road was in part repaired, been chiefly carried by carts, drawn with two Horses, which has very much lessened the Profit of the Toll.' (JHC 21: 435)

In Kendal, extensive wagon services were available in 1790, which the historians of Cumbria dated from the establishment of turnpike roads in the area. In 1753, before most of the local roads were turnpiked, carriers used pack-horses.[4] And in 1798, it was said of Somerset:

'Before the turnpike roads were established, coal was carried on horses' backs . . . each horse carried about two hundred and a half weight. Now one horse, with a light cart, will draw ten hundredweight, or four times more than the horse could carry. Can an insignificant toll be put in comparison with this saving?' (Billingsley 1798: 104)

In many of the peripheral and upland parts of the country, where the pack-horse remained in use longer than elsewhere, local observers and historians noted the same change in the nature of traffic as the roads were improved by the turnpike Trustees. In Wales, Clark wrote of '. . . the misfortune attending the original making of the turnpike roads throughout the whole kingdom'—the old route over, rather than round the hills, being generally chosen, because 'when carriages were not then

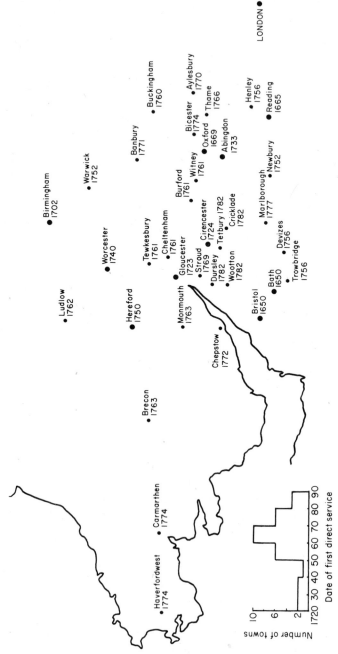

FIG. 39. Towns in western England and South Wales with a direct stage-coach service to London by 1782. The map shows the date of the first regular direct coach service to London from the towns of this region. *Source: Gloucester Journal* (from 1722), *Jackson's Oxford Journal* (from 1753), and Jackman (1916) for earlier dates.

so common as they are at present the advantages of level roads were but faintly seen.' (Clarke 1794: 29.) In South Wales, wheeled traffic was rare in the 1750s and 1760s when the main roads were first turnpiked, but by the end of the century, it was considerably more common (Lewis 1968: 32). A similar transformation occurred in North Wales (Dodd 1925: 142), and in Scotland. In Ayrshire, for example, it was unusual for carts to be used in agriculture in the 1750s but by 1790, they were more general (Goodwin 1970: 53). The roads of this county were turnpiked under a County Trust in 1767 (478).

In Lancashire, the Board of Agriculture reporter wrote despairingly in 1795 that 'from the vast increase of carriage in this county, and the general use of waggons, carts &c with excessive weights, it is become almost impossible, by any means, and at any expense, to support the public roads' (Holt 1795: 191). And in Devon, where Celia Fiennes had met great trains of pack-horses a century before, wheeled traffic was now commonplace on the main roads (Vancouver 1813: 368). Indeed, the general, and growing importance of wheeled traffic in England always caught the attention of foreigners such as Guy Miege in 1699, Pehr Kalm in 1749 and Charles Moritz in 1782.[5]

The innovations in transport services were not limited to the substitution of wheels for horseback. There were many minor improvements, which were introduced independently of the turnpiking of the roads. The general adoption of steel springs for stage-coaches from about 1760—after which date this innovation is frequently recorded in coach advertisements in local newspapers—enabled coaches to travel more safely at speed. It also allowed more passengers to be carried, it being feasible to seat people on the top of the coach. The old stage-coach without springs, carrying four or six inside passengers, was replaced by the 'flying coach' with seats for up to four people on the outside. Similarly, changes in the design of mail coaches in the early nineteenth century, incorporating a lighter body hung on elliptical springs, allowed still greater speeds.

These innovations were accompanied by an increasing range of transport services—both in terms of the number and types of services available to particular destinations, and in the range of destinations. This was due to the increasing demand for, and competition amongst services, but the latter improvement also owed much to the better state of the cross-roads under the turnpike system. Before 1750, there was often no choice for producers but to send goods by pack-horse, particularly if they were situated in one of the more peripheral areas. But after this date, stage-wagons, faster services known as 'flying wagons' or 'vans', and for small parcels, the stage-coaches themselves, were increasingly common. Travellers, who had been limited to posting on horseback, or a standard stage-coach service, could now choose between high and low-quality travel, at a fast or slow rate, and a cheap or expensive fare. Flying machines and flying stage-coaches appeared, as well as smaller and more exclusive post coaches and diligences. Post chaises were available for fast, high-quality travel, and stage-wagons for a cheap, slow journey. Even within the limits of a single service, passengers often had the choice of 'inside' or 'outside' travel, the latter at half the price.

The number and type of services proliferated as competition between firms intensified. Webb (1922) has provided an account of this on the Bath and Bristol road, but the files of any local newspaper in the 1760s, 1770s and 1780s are full of evidence with advertisements in every issue for rival firms. The complexity of the networks which emerged has already been emphasized: choice and range were continually widening. Bristol, for example, had regular services to London, Gloucester and Bath at the beginning of the eighteenth century. It extended its direct links to Salisbury in 1730, Oxford in 1743, Birmingham in 1759, Exeter in 1764, Leicester in 1772, and Plymouth, Holyhead, Liverpool, Weymouth and Portsmouth in 1782. By 1784, apart from a daily mail coach service to London at 4 p.m., there were also daily post coaches leaving for the capital at 2, 4, 5, and 6 a.m., and 2, 3, and 4 p.m. There were two machines daily at 8 p.m. All these services took less than 24 hours, but there were still four two-day services for those who preferred to break the journey: two thrice-weekly post coaches, a daily post coach and a daily machine. [6]

These services were well integrated. After the introduction of the mail coaches in 1784, travellers into London could leave for their final destinations by one of the 8 p.m. mails to the more important provincial centres. In addition, the capital had stage-coach routes to most towns (Fig. 39). Cross road services made connexions at important inns with other provincial and London services. The stage-coach from Leicester, through Coventry to Bristol, for example 'meets the London coaches from Birmingham, Liverpool, Warrington, Lancaster, Chester and Kendal at Coventry; the Worcester at Moreton, and the Gloucester and Oxford at Cirencester—by which Passengers and Parcels will be forwarded to the above places, with the utmost Care and Expedition.' Goods services were similarly integrated. [7]

Travel Times

The most noticeable benefit brought about by these modernized transport services was the general saving in travel times. A correspondent in the *Gentleman's Magazine* for 1792 wrote:

'The great improvements which, in the memory of man, have been made in the turnpike roads throughout this Kingdom, would be incredible, did we not actually perceive them: when it is considered that Windsor, not long since, was a day's journey for a stage-coach, which stopped to dine on the road, one instance is as good as a thousand.'[8]

A few years earlier Charles Moritz, who was touring England, for most of the time on foot, gave a graphic picture of two of the journeys he did undertake in a stage-coach:

'From Oxford to Birmingham is sixty-two miles; but all that was to be seen between the two places was entirely lost to me, for I was again mewed up in a post-coach, and driven along with such velocity from one place to another, that I seemed to myself as doing nothing less than travelling . . . The journey from Northampton to London I can hardly call a journey, but rather a perpetual motion, or removal, from one place to another in a close box.' (Moritz 1924: 161, 214)

Jackman estimated, from a wealth of evidence, that coach travel had speeded up so dramatically by 1830, that travel times were only one-third to one-fifth of what they had been in the 1750s (1916: 339). Further research confirms his estimates.

The fall in travel times was due to the variety of factors already identified. Innovations in coach design were important, as was the reorganization of travel schedules under the stimulus of competition. But of more direct interest here was the effect of improved roads. It is the exact timing of the general increase in travel speeds which is of significance: this provides one of the most critical indicators of the beneficial impact of turnpiking.

A series of time-space convergence curves has been constructed, using evidence from original and secondary sources [9] (Fig. 40). These show the decline in travel times by coach from several provincial towns to London in the period 1660 to 1840, and the gradual convergence, in time-distance terms, of these towns with the capital. The times used are expressed in hours, and are those for the fastest regular service available at any date. Hence they

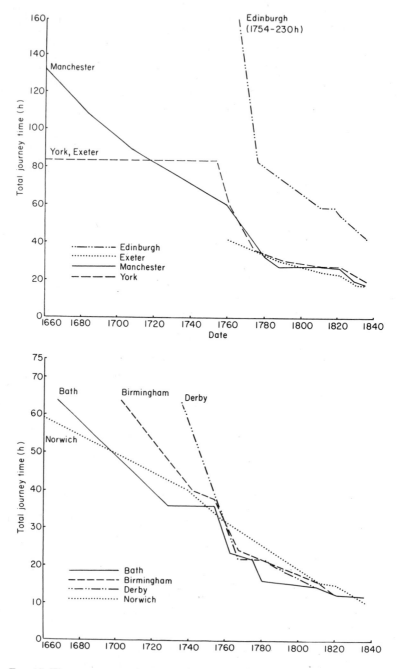

Fig. 40. Time-space convergence curves, 1660–1840. These curves show the decline in total journey time between these four towns and London, using the fastest available coaches. *Source*: see text.

represent minima, rather than averages. They are total travel times, including overnight stoppages, rather than journey times on the road. It was the former that were important from the traveller's point of view.

The shape of these curves is generally similar, with each showing a sharp decline between 1750 and 1780. This coincides exactly with the period of the maximum rate of turnpiking and its aftermath during which the new trusts were making immediate repairs. But for those towns nearest to London (Fig. 40b), there was a fall in travel times before 1750, paralleling the development of the leading sector of trust diffusion in the first half of the century. After 1780, there was no marked further improvement until about 1820, when turnpike trusts came increasingly under the influence of MacAdam, and on the Holyhead road, of Telford.

Part of the fall in travel times up to 1780 was due to the reorganization of schedules, so as to increase the journey time on the road. The coach from Edinburgh to London, for instance, took ten days for the regular summer journey in 1754, but only four days by 1776. This improvement was brought about partly by cutting the amount of time spent overnight at inns, but, being of such magnitude, an increase in speed on the road must have been the basic reason. It is notable that by 1750, the road to Berwick was almost completely turnpiked (Fig. 27), and as these trusts carried out their repairs, and as the rest of the road was turnpiked (206, 421, 447, 526), road surfaces improved. The Edinburgh curve is paralleled by the York curve, which shows rapid decline from a time of 4 days up to 1754, to 3 days in 1761, and only 36 hours in 1776.

In 1750, many of the major provincial towns of England and Wales were more than 24 hours travel time away from London (Fig. 41a). Bristol, Bath, Gloucester, Birmingham and Norwich all ran two-day coach services to the capital. The standard two-day Bath stage-coaches left at 6 a.m. and arrived in London at 6 p.m. the following day, with an overnight stop of about eight hours. Journey time on the road was thus about 28 hours. The first one-day flying machines, which started to run in 1763, dispensed with the overnight stay, by leaving at 11 p.m. and travelling right throught the night to arrive the following evening. The effect of improving roads is reflected in the fall in journey time on the road from 28 to 24 hours, yet total travel time fell more dramatically from 36 to 24 hours. Similarly, the first Gloucester one-day flying machine of 1767 left at 10 p.m. and arrived the next day in London at 10 p.m. The old two-day coach, meanwhile, left at 3 a.m., and stopped overnight at the New Inn, Oxford, making the journey in about 40 hours. The standard three day Manchester–London machines took two days from Derby, leaving at

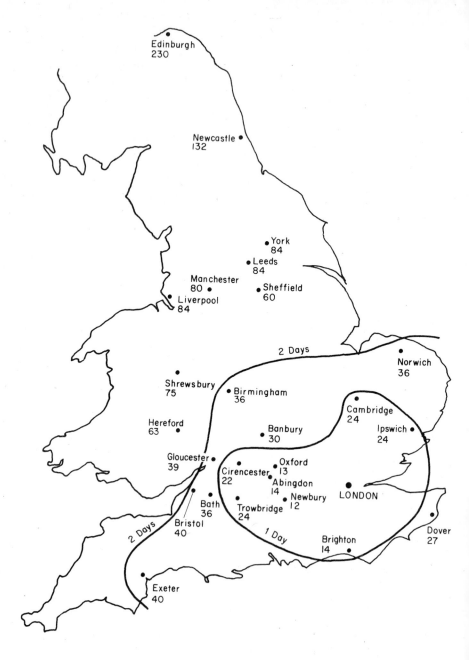

Fɪɢ. 41a. Journey times from London in 1750. This map shows the journey time in hours by the fastest stage-coach between London and selected towns. *Source*: Jackman 1916, and local newspapers.

Fɪɢ. 41b. Journey times from London in 1811. This map shows the journey time in hours by mail coach between London and selected towns. Mail coaches left London at 8 p.m.— their arrival times are plotted. *Source*: Paterson 1811: 521–37.

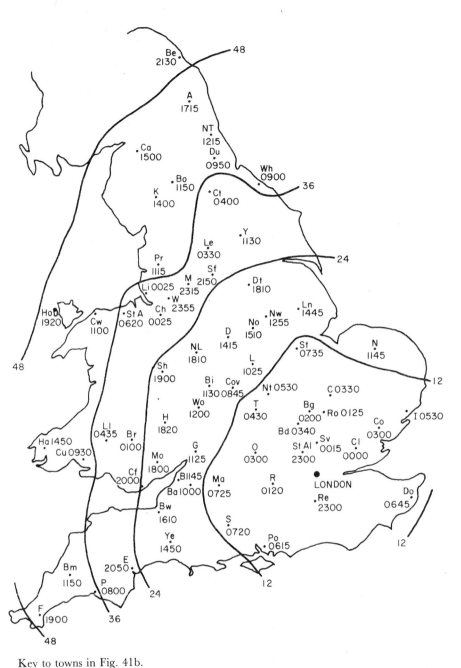

Key to towns in Fig. 41b.

A. Alnwick; B. Bristol; Ba. Bath; Bd. Bedford; Be. Berwick; Bg. Biggleswade; Bi. Birmingham; Bm. Bodmin; Bo. Bowes; Br. Brecon; Bw. Bridgwater; C. Cambridge; Ca. Carlisle; Cf. Cardiff; Ch. Chester; Cl. Chelmsford; Cm. Carmarthen; Co. Colchester; Cov. Coventry; Ct. Catterick; Cw. Conway; D. Derby; Do. Dover; Dt. Doncaster; Du. Durham; E. Exeter; F. Falmouth; G. Gloucester; H. Hereford; Ha. Haverfordwest; Ho. Holyhead; I. Ipswich; K. Kendal; L. Leicester; Le. Leeds; Li. Liverpool; Ll. Llandovery; Ln. Lincoln; M. Manchester; Ma. Marlborough; Mo. Monmouth; N. Norwich; NL. Newcastle-under-Lyne; No. Nottingham; NT. Newcastle-on-Tyne; Nt. Northampton; O. Oxford; P. Plymouth; Po. Portsmouth; Pre. Preston; R. Reading; Re. Reigate; Ro. Royston; S. Salisbury; Sf. Sheffield; Sh. Shrewsbury; St. Stamford; Sta. St Asaph; StAl. St Albans; Sv. Stevenage; T. Towcester; W. Warrington; Wh. Whitby; Wo. Worcester; Y. York; Ye. Yeovil.

5 a.m., and stopping overnight on the way. By 1767, however, a one-day post-coach was in operation, which left Derby at 9 p.m., and arrived in London the next day at 7 p.m. The one-day Leicester machine left at 2 a.m., arriving the same night.[10]

The increasing speed of journeys was not accomplished, therefore, without a tightening of schedules. Nevertheless, journey times on the road were considerably cut. But the reorganization of schedules itself could not have been carried out without the assurance of good roads. It would not have been possible to run a stage-coach service through the night, or early hours of the morning, in darkness, unless the roads were well maintained. The fall in travel times up to 1780 was therefore largely dependent on improvements brought about by the turnpike trusts.

After 1780, the increasing speed of mail coach services indicates that travel times continued to improve. In 1765, the new Post Office Act specified that post-boys were to carry the mail at a speed of 6 m.p.h., a rate seldom maintained. The first mail coach, from Bath to London in 1784, covered the 110 miles in 16 hours, at a speed of 7 m.p.h. By 1821, the average was almost 8 m.p.h., and in 1836, it had reached 9 m.p.h.[11] These improvements were in part due to the use of lighter coaches, but again this indicated the existence of smooth roads. Passenger loads increased, but the number of horses used did not. In 1836, nearly all mail coaches were permitted to carry four inside and four or more outside passengers. Before the 1800s, only one outside passenger could be accommodated. It was standard for mail coaches and stage-coaches to use only four horses, but these were changed at regular intervals to ensure that speeds were maintained. By the early nineteenth century, therefore, travel times had been cut considerably, and the range of places within a day's journey of London was much more extensive than in 1750 (Fig. 41b).

A parallel improvement with the fall in travel times was the gradual elimination of seasonality in schedules. In the first half of the eighteenth century, many stage-coach services apparently did not run in the winter months. Advertisements in local newspapers for coach services are not common before 1750, but those which do appear always do so in March or April, at the start of the summer season. The *Gloucester Journal*, for example, advertised the start of services to Exeter and London on 10 April 1733, and the annual start of the Gloucester to Bristol stage on 9 May in 1744 and 17 April in 1754.

However, from 1750, many routes began to run throughout the year, but on a less exacting schedule in the winter months. Throughout the 1750s, 1760s and 1770s, advertisements regularly appear to announce the start of the 'flying' service in March or April, and the winter service in October. In 1762, for example, the Gloucester and Hereford coaches to London began flying on the 12th and 13th of April respectively, and left off flying in the 4th October. The summer schedule allowed the Gloucester coach a day, and the Hereford coach a day and a half to reach London: the winter schedule lengthened these to two and three days respectively. But by the 1770s, the summer times were operated throughout the year.[12] This became increasingly common on other routes about the same time. The mail coaches, from the 1780s, ran on non-seasonal schedules, and by the early nineteenth century, their arrivals could be timed within minutes. This was also true of standard stage-coach services, and was a necessary precondition of the increasing integration of services.

Transport Charges

The evidence regarding the trend of transport charges for the movement of goods and passengers is not as conclusive, nor as easy to interpret as that for travel times. There were a number of factors encouraging a decline in the level of rates charged. However, there were other factors working in the opposite way.

The greater efficiency of the transport system itself led to a decline in costs, for both coachmen and carriers. The increased speed of travel meant that coaches and wagons could be used more intensively to make a larger number of journeys in a given time than previously. The return on the original investment was thereby increased, although this was offset to a certain extent by increased maintenance charges. Similarly, as it became feasible to take outside passengers, coach owners were able to carry larger loads: although whether or not they did so depended on actual coach loadings, something about which little is known. But it is certainly true that they were able to use fewer horses. Early depictions of stage-coaches in advertisements placed by their proprietors indicate that six or eight horses were used on many routes before 1750. In the latter part of the eighteenth century, however, four became the standard number.

Carriers could also convey goods more effectively. The capacity of a wagon hauled by six horses was legally, by 1765, anything up to six tons.

In fact, Kalm in 1748 was surprised that 'the waggons which are used here are frightfully large, with very high wheels, and are loaded with an astonishing weight . . .' (1892: 12). Six pack-horses, on the other hand, could manage at the most, a ton between them. That carts and wagons themselves could be used more efficiently as the roads improved is implicit in the gradual rise in the size of the maximum permitted loads.[13] It is also demonstrated by the complaints of turnpike Trustees and parishes that heavier loads were being carried, hence making their task of repairing the roads that much more onerous.[14]

Sometimes turnpike Trustees also complained that their tolls were being reduced as wagoners were able to use fewer horses. The Pierce Bridge–Boroughbridge Trustees claimed, in 1749, that coal wagons, which travelled free on their road in the summer half of the year, did much damage, and should be forced to pay toll since:

'. . . (they) receive great Advantage from the Repair of the said Roads during the Summer as well as the Winter Months, since they draw as great a weight now with two Horses as they could have done before with three. . . .' (JHC 25: 766)

The Stump Cross Trustees were suffering from the same problem in 1755 (JHC 27: 131).

These factors, along with the competition between coach owners, were encouraging a long-term fall in the level of transport charges. However, upward cost pressures elsewhere were tending to compensate for this. The rising trend of agricultural prices from the 1740s inevitably increased the cost of horse-feed. The requirements of the general highway legislation meant extra expenditure—for instance, on broad wheels—to conform with the law. Carriage and excise duties were not inconsiderable. Carriage duty, for wagons and coaches, stood at £4 per vehicle per annum from its introduction in 1747 until 1776. It was then raised to £5, in 1785 to £7, and in 1798 to £9 12s. Excise duty, introduced in 1779, involved the purchase of a 5s licence, and the payment of a mileage charge—initially ½d, then in 1783, 1d, and in 1797, 2d.[15] In addition, there was the burden of an increasing number of turnpike tolls as the number of trusts spread.

In view of these increased cost factors, it is not surprising that coach owners sometimes combined together to raise the level of transport charges. One such notice appeared in the *Gloucester Journal* for 15 April 1782:

'The Proprietors of the different STAGE COACHES on the North Road, finding themselves materially injured by the present Price paid by Passengers between Bristol and Gloucester, as being inadequate to the Expences of Duty etc attending the said Coaches, beg leave to acquaint the Public, that they are necessitated for the future to charge Eight Shillings for each Inside Passenger and Four Shillings Outside, from Bristol to Gloucester, and in Proportion for any part of the Road.'

Carriers, however, were often prevented from combining in such a manner, particularly after mid-century, because the Justices of the Peace had authority to settle rates for goods carried. The Highway Act of 1691 enabled magistrates to fix the rates for goods carried into their jurisdictions, although, as the number of surviving assessments is very low, it is not possible to know whether they did so effectively. But in 1748, another Act extended these powers to include assessments on goods leaving their areas of control, and required magistrates to send these annually to the Clerks of the Peace for Middlesex and Westminster, and to the Lord Mayor of London.

This second Act was effective, and the assessments, which survive in some numbers, are a valuable source for the study of the movement of land carriage rates. Most of the assessments refer to rates between London itself and provincial towns. The willingness of magistrates to alter them, rather than keeping them at a stable level over long periods, suggests that an attempt was made to ensure that the assessments reflected prevailing conditions. The validity of this source has been fully discussed by Albert, and much of the original data has been reproduced by him (1972: 168–87, 260–2). It can be supplemented by advertised land carriage rates and passenger fares in contemporary local newspapers. A substantial amount of such information was collected by Jackman, for the period after 1750 when it became plentiful. This has been supplemented by further examples. All this material, reduced to per-mile rates, is reproduced in Table XLVIII.

Defoe, in his enthusiastic praise of the early turnpikes, claimed that the cost of carriage for goods 'is abated in some places, 6d per hundredweight, and in some places 12d per hundred' whilst a later writer, in the 1750s, put a figure of 30 per cent on the fall in rates since turnpike trusts had began repairing the roads. In the absence of sufficient data it is not possible to test these assertions. From the 1740s, however, an increasing amount of evidence enables more certain conclusions to be made.

Table XLVIII
Changes in Transport Charges in the Eighteenth Century

Passenger fares:
Averaged per mile fares for various routes computed from information given in Jackman[a] (1916)

1752/3	—	2·2d	1786	—	3·2d
1756/7	—	2·7d	1787	—	3·1d
1760/1	—	2·8d	1788	—	3·7d
1774/5	—	2·8d	1789	—	3·3d
1776/7	—	2·7d	1790	—	3·2d
1778/9	—	2·9d	1791	—	2·7d
1780/1	—	2·8d	1795	—	4·5d
1782/3	—	3·0d	1796	—	3·9d
1784/5	—	3·2d	1808	—	4·5d

Goods charges:
Averaged per ton–mile charges for various routes computed from information given in Jackman (1916) Appx 7.

1754	—	10·7d	1784	—	9·6d
1760	—	11·5d	1792	—	12·9d
1766/7	—	11·6d	1793/4	—	9·3d
1770/1	—	12·0d	1796	—	11·0d
1773/4	—	12·5d	1808	—	13·8d

Justices' assessments of goods charges:[b]
Averaged per ton–mile assessments from provincial centres to London computed from the Returns given in Albert (1972) Appx I.

1690s	—	14·8d	1760s	—	13·2d
1700s	—	16·4d	1770s	—	12·0d
1710s	—		1780s	—	11·7d
1720s	—	14·5d	1790s	—	12·4d
1730s	—	13·5d	1800s	—	14·0d
1740s	—	14·3d	1810s	—	15·3d
1750s	—	13·3d	1820s	—	14·9d

[a] The years given are those for which Jackman provides information. In the first column years have been combined in pairs so that a minimum number of routes—at least 4—is represented in each case.

[b] Justices of the Peace were empowered under Acts of 1692 (3 Wm & Mary, c. 12) and 1748 (21 Geo. II, c. 28) to fix the maximum rate that carriers could charge. Albert (1972: 176–87) has fully discussed the validity of these assessments. The figures given here are averaged winter/summer rates. The value for each decade has been decided by averaging the individual assessments for different routes recorded by Albert in each decade.

The trend of land carriage rates is remarkable for one thing—its stability. Advertised rates in local newspapers show a general, but slow rise from the 1750s to the 1800s. The Justices assessments show a slight fall from the 1740s to the 1780s, rising thereafter to the 1820s. The difference between the two series reflects the shortcomings of the samples, but is not significant in the absence of a marked trend in either case. In both series, the rise in the level of rates between 1750 and 1800 was considerably less than the 100 per cent rise in agricultural prices, and the 50 per cent rise in industrial prices. In real terms, therefore, the cost of land carriage fell. The elimination of the differential between winter and summer rates on many routes by the early years of the nineteenth century was also a significant gain (Albert 1972: 175).

In the case of passenger rates, the evidence tells a different story. The newspaper data indicate an approximate doubling of the level of inside passenger fares per mile over the 50-year period from 1750. This trend is confirmed by a recent local study: in South Hampshire, by the 1820s, fares were almost double those of the 1770s and 1780s (Freeman 1975: 277–8). There were, however, considerable variations in fares on any one route, according to the quality of the service. A selection of fares on the Oxford to London route is shown in Table IL. An outside coach passenger, or those who travelled by stage-wagon, paid half the price of an inside coach ticket. But those who wished to go in the faster, or more exclusive diligences or post-coaches often had to pay 25 or 50 per cent more. And those who wanted to travel by post-chaise, so combining both these advantages, paid a considerable premium. It is significant that post-chaise charges were generally between 7d and 9d per mile on the turnpike roads, and 9d to 1s, or up to a third more, on the unturnpiked cross routes.[16]

Nevertheless, the fare charged by the operator did not represent the real cost of the journey to the traveller. He had to pay for overnight stoppages, and for meals taken en route. It was here that a substantial money saving was made as journey times decreased. Quicker journeys meant fewer, or no overnight stops. Less meals were consumed, as a lower number of hours was spent in travelling. The coachmen and guards also expected tips, and shorter journeys meant fewer changes of staff. The cost of meals alone could amount to seven shillings for breakfast, dinner and supper in the late eighteenth century—with drinks and tips, the total of extras could rise to twelve shillings or thereabouts. This would have doubled the cost of a single day coach journey to London from Oxford in the 1770s. Nevertheless, a two-day journey, necessitating further

Table IL
Level of Passenger Fares from Oxford
to London, 1754–78

The major advertised services in *Jackson's Oxford Journal:*

Service	Single fare	Date of advertisement
Stage-coach (Kemp's)	12s 6d	7 Sept. 1754
Stage-coach (Sandeford's)	10s	4 Oct. 1754
Machine (Kemp's)	12s 6d	20 March 1756
Wagon (Pitt's)	3s 6d	25 Jan. 1757
Machine (Kemp's)	12s 6d	1 April 1758
Flying machine (Sandeford's)	10s	12 May 1759
New post-coaches	15s	30 March 1765
Machine (White's)	10s	24 Aug. 1765
New post-coaches	15s	3 Jan. 1767
Machine (Whiten's)	10s	30 Oct. 1762
Wagon (Redhead's)	8s	20 Feb. 1773
New post-coaches (Kemp's)	15s	18 March 1775
Machine (Whiten's)	10s	8 April 1775
Dilly (Gevaux')	15s	18 April 1775
Dilly (Taylor's)	14s	30 Sept. 1775
Machine (Taylor's)	12s	6 Jan. 1776
Dilly (Taylor's)	14s	6 Jan. 1776
Post-coaches (Kemp's)	12s 6d	26 July 1777
Old coach (Whiten's)	12s 6d	14 Feb. 1778
Fly (Boulton's)	14s	28 Sept. 1778
Post-chaises:		
Borton's (6d per mile)	30s	21 July 1753
Borton's (9d)	45s	25 Sept. 1756
Borton's (7d)	35s	20 Oct. 1764
Kemp's (1s)	60s	25 Aug. 1764
Borton's (7½d)	39s	26 Aug. 1769

expenditure on the overnight stay, could add another third or half to the total cost.[17]

Thus there is certainly evidence of direct resource savings in transport charges brought about by the modernized road transport system that emerged in the eighteenth century. Of equal significance were the gains in speeds, so cutting travel times, and the gradual elimination of seasonality. The accessibility of places one to another was increased in relative terms, whilst in some of the remote areas, such as North Wales and the Fens, there was a provision of absolute accessibility in the winter months, which had previously been impossible (Dodd 1925: 125, 142. Grigg 1966: 44).

It was the translation of these direct benefits into tangible social and economic advances, however, that was of great and continued significance to the progress of the Industrial Revolution in Britain. The gains to agriculture and industry of faster and relatively cheaper goods transport, the effect on home–workplace patterns of easier passenger movement, the change in settlement structures with the channelling of traffic along particular routes and the breakdown of regional characteristics: all these things need to be examined further.

11. Notes

1. See below, p. 295.
2. See above, pp. 136–8.
3. *Gloucester Journal*, 31 Oct. 1763, 29 Aug. and 7 Nov. 1774.
4. See above, p. 46.
5. Kalm 1892: 10–14, Moritz 1924: 20, 125. The reference to Guy Miege is from *The New State of England under our present Monarch, King William III*, part II, London (1699), 22, in Thirsk and Cooper (1972), 428.
6. This information has been taken from advertisements in contemporary Bristol newspapers, listed in the Bibliography.
7. The Leicester coach advertisement appeared in *Jackson's Oxford Journal* in 1772, for example on 1 Aug. The integration of goods services has been discussed in Chapter 2, pp. 48–52 and is exemplified by Fig. 14.
8. *Gentleman's Magazine* 1792, part II: 1161.
9. These sources include all the local newspapers listed in the Bibliography, Paterson (1811), BPP 1836 (364) XLV: 450–1, Joyce 1893: 399–401 and Jackman (1916).
10. The Bath coach times are from *Felix Farley's Bristol Journal*, 2 Feb. 1754 and *Bristol Journal*, 9 April 1763; the Gloucester times from *JOJ*, 21 March 1767 and *Gloucester Journal*, 28 Aug. 1753 and 21 March 1767; the Derby times from the *Derby Mercury*, 21 March 1761 and 3 April 1767 and the Leicester times from the same paper, for 16 March 1764.
11. The 1765 Act was 5 Geo. III, c. 25. The 1821 speed is derived from Joyce 1893: 399–401 and that for 1836 from BPP 1836 (364) XLV: 450–1.
12. *Gloucester Journal*.
13. See above, p. 22.
14. See above, pp. 165–6.

15. BPP 1857 (2199) IV: lix, clvii).
16. These differentials were stressed in newspaper advertisements, for example, *JOJ*, 5 March 1763, 22 Oct. 1764, 22 Feb. 1766; *Derby Mercury*, 3 July 1761.
17. Little evidence survives about the cost of these extras. These estimates are based on those of Hart 1960: 155, although he used few original sources.

12

The Wider Impact

'The many important advantages to be derived from amending the Highways and Turnpike Roads of the Kingdom, need hardly be dwelt on. Every individual in it would thereby find his comforts materially increased, and his interest greatly promoted. By the improvement of our Roads, every branch of our Agricultural, Commercial and Manufacturing Industry, would be materially benefited—Every article brought to market, would be diminished in price—The number of Horses would be so much reduced, that by these and other Retrenchments . . . the Expense of Five Millions would be annually saved to the Public—The Expense of repairing Roads, and the wear and tear of carriages and Horses, would be essentially diminished; and thousands of Acres, the produce of which is now wasted in feeding unnecessary Horses, would be devoted to the production of food for Man. In Short, the public and private advantages which would result from effecting that great object, the improvement of our Highways and Turnpike Roads, are incalculable; though from their being spread over a wide surface, and available in various ways, such advantages will not be so apparent as those derived from other Sources of Improvement, of a more restricted and less general nature.' (BPP 1810–11 (240) III 855: 3–4)

So reported one of the many Committees established in the early nineteenth century to investigate the workings of the turnpike road system. They were concerned, as were successive Parliamentary enquiries at this time, that the quality of turnpike roads was not as good as it could have been. This was certainly true: the sharp fall in travel times in the 1810s and 1820s, as the influence of MacAdam and Telford spread, shows it to be so (Fig. 40). Nevertheless, the pessimistic tone of this Report does obscure 'the many important advantages' which had already been derived from a century of improving roads and road transport facilities.

In one respect, this Report was most pertinent. It is very true that the extent of the improvements brought about by an innovation such as the turnpike trust are incalculable, and because they were so generally pervasive, they are not even easily identifiable. The extent of the direct benefits it did produce indicates that the wider impact must have been significant. However, the difficulty of establishing the ways in which a transport improvement was used by producers and consumers, and the problem of separating transport induced effects from those brought about by changes in other sectors, has not encouraged research into this area.

'The role of turnpike roads in economic development is often underestimated', wrote Flinn (1966: 96). It is underestimated partly because the case for the extensive and fundamental importance of road transport in the eighteenth century has not been clearly articulated in works concerned with this period, something which the second chapter of this book has endeavoured to remedy. It has also been underestimated precisely because the lack of previous research into the topic, something which is symptomatic of this aspect of all transport innovations, has obscured its significance. There has, for instance, been no clear statement of the interrelationship of transport and the eighteenth century economy, such as was provided for agriculture by Jones (1967: 1–48).

This last chapter attempts to make good this omission. It is divided into four main parts, examining firstly the impact of improving roads on industry, secondly on agriculture, then on urban change and lastly on settlement patterns.

General considerations

The cost-cutting direct benefits of a transport innovation can be used by producers to widen the extent of the market, and enable them, because of the easier transfer of information, to respond more readily to those markets. Consumers gain from a cheaper, or wider range of goods, a range about which more is known as information services improve. Production benefits from the increase of market size, and as resources which were previously devoted to the payment of transport costs are released and made available for investment elsewhere in the manufacturing process. Consumption benefits as goods become cheaper or are made available over a wider area than previously. Production increases as consumption rises, and further increases as firms are able to make internal economies to take advantage of their larger scale of operation.) These are the *forward linkages* of a transport innovation (Fig. 2).

This is the traditional economic view of the impact of transport innovations. In reality, however, it is inadequate, for three reasons. Firstly, it is an oversimplification. Increased production may be the end result of a process of improving transport facilities, but often more than a simple reallocation of resources is involved. A modernization of the structure of industry consequent upon improving communications can be as important a moving force, and, indeed, it is the case argued here. In addition, however, an increase in production may well be accompanied by a change in the nature of production, or a change in its location.

Secondly, the framework within which a response is made to a transport improvement is behavioural, not deterministic. Improvements in one sector need not lead to any change in the other. The response is the collective result of many individual decisions. Single producers or consumers may not make any positive resonse at all, because of ignorance of, or prejudice against the transport innovation, or because of inability or unwillingness to take advantage of it. There may be a substantial time-lag. This is particularly likely when these producers and consumers are not the promoters of improvement in transport and transport services.

Thirdly, improved transport affects processes other than production and consumption. It affects modes of living and means of leisure. The fall in the cost of goods transport with the spread of the turnpike road network was accompanied by the increasing ease of passenger movement. This encouraged, in the eighteenth century, the development of suburbs and the outward spread of towns as home and workplace became more separated, the move of the urban elites into the country, and the early growth of the spas and seaside resorts.

Hence, the general advantages of improved transport, of the direct benefits of cheaper cost, quicker movement and more reliable, regular, better-integrated services, were translated into forward linkages in a complex and involved fashion. These effects are sometimes not easily identifiable, and the equifinality problem is forever present. Often many interconnected forces were working together, so that separating the effects of improved transport from those of improvements in other sectors of the economy is not possible, nor would it be realistic.

Forward Linkages: Industry

Eighteenth century industry was, in the main, small-scale and localized. There were few industrial concentrations, and production was spread widely throughout the country, in both towns and rural areas. It was largely dependent on organic raw materials, particularly wool, water and the products of agriculture, which were themselves widespread in distribution. It was characteristically concerned with the production of consumer rather than capital goods. Hence local industries produced textiles and cloth, ironwares and pottery for surrounding areas, whilst in towns, leather-ware, brewing and food processing were basic.

This is not to deny, however, the existence of large-scale businesses, or limited industrial concentrations, even in 1700. Both flourished where industry was more specialized, and concerned with either the luxury end of the market, or with government orders. There were important textile manufacture concentrations, producing high-quality cloths, in Devon and Norwich, whilst in the port cities of London and Bristol, industries based on the import trade, such as metal and sugar refining, tea, tobacco, and coffee production, were gathered together. There were also some substantial firms, often dependent on government ordnance orders, in the iron industry, which itself was beginning to concentrate in the West Midlands. These industries drew on factors of production from widely separated sources, and depended on effective and widespread market penetration. For the luxury goods industries, however, this often meant sources and markets abroad, reached by water transport, and the internal land transport system was not of great significance.

Throughout the eighteenth century, the importance of industrial concentrations, and the big firms within them, grew as industrial output rose. The production of industry and commerce roughly quadrupled between 1700 and 1800, so that by the latter date, it accounted for approximately 41 per cent of total national income (Deane and Cole 1962: 78–9, 161). The nature of this output also altered. The home consumer market became increasingly important for the large-scale, capitalized industries. Many of the successful firms, and all the industrial concentrations of the later eighteenth century were dependent on quantity sales to a mass market in this country. Hence, the British market-orientated concentration of collieries in the north-east, owing their success to the demands of London, was replicated elsewhere—the growth of cotton textiles firms in Lancashire after 1770, the West Riding woollen industry, the north Staffordshire potteries around Stoke, and the iron founding and forging businesses of the West Midlands and South Wales.

Improved transport and road transport services became more important as the scale of industry increased and its organization became more sophisticated. Not only were assured and regular supplies of raw material necessary, but close and regular contact with markets was vital. In this context, the impact of the turnpike road system was obviously significant. Improving roads meant that supplies of raw material and shipment of finished products became both cheaper and easier: year round movement was possible, and delays became less frequent. Information flows between different parts of the firm, and between the firm itself and its markets, could be transmitted more satisfactorily, enabling a more rapid response to be made to changes in demand and supply. Improvements in the road transport services, particularly the carriers and the post, were thus of fundamental importance.

In the early eighteenth century, the road transport system had already reached a sufficient degree of advancement for such firms to exist and function in the home market. The ironworks in the Foley Partnerships, for instance, operated in four geographically dispersed groups, but these were closely interdependent. The largest of the four, formed in 1692, had works in the Stour Valley in South Staffordshire, in the Forest of Dean, and later in Monmouth and Sussex, as well as warehouses from which to supply customers at Bewdley in the West Midlands. John Wheeler, who was in charge of the operation of this group from the beginning, was also the 'managing director' of the second group of works in Staffordshire, and the third group in Nottinghamshire and Derbyshire (Johnson 1951). Although the raw materials and finished products of these groups were moved by water, particularly on the Severn to and from Bewdley, the business organization itself must have depended on an efficient postal service to co-ordinate such widespread activities.

The most remarkable organization of this period is undoubtedly the Crowley iron-making business, which was developed and controlled by one man, Ambrose Crowley III, from his house in Greenwich. Ambrose II, who was a successful West Midlands iron forger, had interests around Stourbridge and in South Wales in the 1690s, as well as in some Devon waterworks. But his son, who was apprenticed in London, had an even more extensive business. As early as 1682, he had opened an ironware factory in Sunderland, which developed into three factories on the Tyne west of Newcastle. These supplied his warehouses in London. In 1704, he built his own warehouse and slitting mill on the Tyne, bought the house in Greenwich, and built a warehouse and wharf there. By 1710:

'As well as the factories in the North, there was the warehouse at Blaydon-on-Tyne and a manager at Newcastle. In the south, there was the head office, wharf and warehouse at Greenwich, and the five warehouses in the City around the original property in Thames Street. At each of the six principal naval dockyards in the Thames estuary and on the south coast a stock of naval goods was held, and workshops for repair work maintained. Finally, there was a chain of warehouses in the provinces at Ware, Wolverhampton, Walsall and Stourbridge where stocks for wholesale distribution were held. In addition, the Stourbridge warehouse served as the hub of an extensive domestic nail manufacturing organisation, and was also used as a collecting centre for bar and rod iron purchased in the Midlands and sent on to the works in Durham for processing.' (Flinn 1962: 55)

The success of this impressive organization was entirely dependent on the postal service. The day-to-day operation of the Durham factories was the responsibility of a Council of Officials directed by Crowley through instructions sent in a weekly letter. This was posted on Thursdays, taking three days to reach the north-east. As it could not be acted upon until Monday morning, there was always a time-lag of four days for transmission of orders in one direction. It took over a week for the order to be given, and a reply to be received back in Greenwich. Orders for iron goods from branch warehouses to the factories were all directed through Greenwich too. It thus took considerably longer for branches to receive a reply. One consequence of this was that large stocks had to be held in the warehouses, so freezing a substantial part of the firm's capital. 'In 1728 the stock of finished goods in the seven Thames warehouses amounted to nearly £58,000 of ironware' (Flinn 1962: 139).

Nevertheless, the Crowley empire was a remarkable and most successful organization for its time. It shows, *par excellence*, the importance of the land transport system in the growth and development of big firms, enabling them to sustain a large-scale of operations and widespread market penetration. During the eighteenth century, more organizations of this nature began to emerge. The increasing ease and speed of the transfer of information was particularly important in their development. The Crowley business must itself have benefited considerably from the increasing efficiency of the Post Office. By 1811, it took a little over 36 hours for a letter to reach Durham. Orders for stock which were taking up to two days to arrive in London from the West Midlands warehouses in the 1700s were, by this time, reaching the head office in just over 12 hours (Fig. 41).

Wilson has defined the entrepreneur as a man with 'a sense of market opportunity, combined with the capacity needed to expoit it' (1957: 103). These flows of information were vital in determining the most profitable course of production, by providing a constant link with markets. An increasing number of firms were thus using outriders, an early form of commercial traveller, to provide direct contact with the consumer, as well as establishing warehouses and showrooms in the major urban centres to encourage sales.

One of the best known entrepreneurs in this tradition was Josiah Wedgwood. He ensured that he produced marketable products, to a certain extent creating the demand himself by seeking patronage amongst Royalty and the aristocracy, and so establishing a fashion. But he also devoted much attention to the marketing process. He set up a London warehouse and showrooms in Grosvenor Square in 1765, following this later with outlets in Bath, Liverpool and Dublin. He used newspapers as a means of advertising, and by 1787 had three travelling salesmen, who personally introduced his pottery to potential customers, by using samples, catalogues and pattern boxes.

This sophisticated marketing organization was very successful. Wedgwood, who started with virtually nothing, was worth £500,000 when he died in 1795. His pottery was known all over Britain, and throughout the world from America to China. But 'such fabulous success is not easily explained. It certainly cannot be explained in terms of Wedgwood's gift's alone. For Wedgwood was fortunate in the period in which he lived' (McKendrick 1960: 408). He was fortunate not just because the demand for his products was continually increasing, with the spread of tea and coffee drinking, and the rise in incomes, and not just because of technical advances in pottery making and the application of steampower. He was also fortunate because of the improving transport and information flow system of the period which enabled him to break out of the local markets of Staffordshire that had absorbed most of the production of the industry before his time.

Other firms followed Wedgwood's example. Boulton and Fothergill established showrooms in Pall Mall, Josiah Spode opened one in Fore Street, Cripplegate, and Minton also had a London outlet (McKendrick 1960: 420). Mathew Boulton used the outrider system to penetrate distant markets. In 1772, there were 1,470 designs in his pattern book

(Robinson 1963: 44). The orders gained in this way were transmitted back to the firm by the post and carriers. Where correspondence has survived, the importance of these services in the operation of these firms becomes even more evident. Samuel Oldknow, the Lancashire cotton manufacturer, relied on regular contact with his London agent for sales orders (Unwin 1924), and the cloth manufacturers of Devizes dealt with the London factors, the merchants of Bristol and Exeter, and their own shopkeeper customers all over the south of England directly by post and carrier (Mann 1964).

The Dowlais Iron Company of Merthyr Tydfil used a representative, who travelled widely all over the country, calling on small manufacturers, blacksmiths and shops. He reported his progress back to the company, along with orders, in a series of letters (Elsas 1960). That this company relied heavily on the postal services is shown by a petition that its managers sent to the Postmaster General in 1813:

> 'That your Memorialists being convinced that if a Daily Post was established between Brecon and Merthyr Tidfil, the Advantage to the Revenue would be great and the Country in general much benefited and that in addition a more direct communication between the Iron Works at Merthyr Tidvil and those in Staffordshire and the North of England would be the consequence . . . That the only Communication at present by post between these places is through Cardiff, Swansea and Carmarthen, a Distance of about One Hundred and forty Miles, and that a letter sent by such post cannot be delivered 'till the third day after it is despatched.'[1]

But perhaps the best known example of an outriding system is that of the Manchester men. Aikin, in 1795, identified an interesting change in the system of selling Lancashire textile goods as trade increased and roads improved:

> 'For the first thirty years of the present century, the old established houses confined their trades to the wholesale dealers in London, Bristol, Norwich, Newcastle, and those who frequented Chester fair. The profits were thus distributed between the manufacturer, the wholesale, and the retail, dealer. . . . When the Manchester trade began to extend, the chapmen used to keep gangs of pack-horses, and accompany them to the principal towns with goods in packs, which they opened and sold to shop-keepers, lodging what was unsold at small stores at the inns. The pack-horses brought back sheep's wool, which was bought on the journey, and sold to the makers of worsted

yarn at Manchester, or to the clothiers of Rochdale, Saddleworth, and the West-Riding of Yorkshire. On the improvement of turnpike roads waggons were set up, and the pack-horses discontinued; and the chapmen only rode out for orders, carrying with them patterns in their bags. It was during the forty years from 1730 to 1770 that trade was greatly pushed by the practice of sending these riders all over the kingdom, to those towns which before had been supplied from the wholesale dealers in the capital places before mentioned.' (Aikin 1795: 182–4)

The road transport system of the eighteenth century, and the information services it supported, were thus of fundamental significance in supporting the large-scale enterprises which were emerging in several branches of industry. These firms were able to function more efficiently as postal and carrier services speeded up, and became better integrated, as a result of the developing and improving network of turnpike roads. Significant time-savings in the transfer of orders from customer to manufacturer enabled a more rapid response to be made to market demand, thereby lessening the need for large stocks, or independent wholesale merchants. But undoubtedly, the point of greatest importance is that manufacturers were able to make a widespread market penetration. The friction of distance was being steadily overcome as firms were able to locate the different parts of their enterprises—marketing and production—in the most advantageous places, and control their labour forces, agents and salesmen from afar. A basic contribution of improved turnpike roads in the eighteenth century as a consequence of the direct benefits that they induced was, therefore, towards the greater sophistication of industrial structure and organization. Indeed Professor Willan has remarked, in reference to Abraham Dent of Kirkby Stephen that:

'Dent's activities as a hosier and a shopkeeper show that he operated in a national market, which was probably freer from impediments in the movement of goods than was the case elsewhere in Western Europe. The importance of this in fostering the development of factory production has not, perhaps, been fully appriciated.' (1970: 110)

A second major contribution of improving roads to industrial development was in assisting the expansion of the market for these new firms and their products. To a certain extent, these firms encouraged and fostered it themselves. But the increasing ease of movement and spread of ideas as travel and information flows increased was important in one major respect. It helped to create a receptiveness for new methods and new products by encouraging the spread of fashion and the imitation of new ways.

In 1814, this process had apparently already overtaken one of the more remote areas of Britain, the Lake District:

'The press of commerce towards Carlisle and Glasgow and the numerous visitors to the Lakes introduced a constant stream of travellers from the metropolis, and with them new ideas of human life. A stagecoach called the Fly commenced from London over Stanemore to Glasgow in 1774; and the Mail began to run along the Kendal and Shap road in 1786. After this the revolution in buildings, dress, furniture, food, manners and literature, soon attained its height, and the peculiarities of this country are now verging fast into oblivion.'[2]

Nearly 40 years before this, John Byng was regretting this aspect of regional change:

'I wish with all my heart that half the turnpike roads of the Kingdom were plough'd up, which have imported London manners, and depopulated the country—I meet milkmaids on the road, with the dress and looks of Strand misses.' (Andrews 1935: 6)

And earlier still, in 1761, in an essay entitled 'On the Country Manners of the Present Age', a writer commented:

'. . . the manners, fashions, amusements, vices and follies of the metropolis now make their way to the remotest corners of the land . . . along the turnpike road.'[3]

Carriers, coachmen, travellers and salesmen brought news and samples of new products. The latest consumer goods were publicized by the wealthy minority who could afford to go to London and the resorts for the season, then returning to their county towns and country estates. Provincial newspapers were an important influence, carrying news and advertisements from the capital and the bigger towns. Magazines circulated widely—even Abraham Dent, in Kirkby Stephen, sold five different issues, including the London, Universal, Royal and Gentleman's (Willan 1970: 16). In the bigger market towns, the new shops were instrumental in promoting new fashions and products. One of the most widespread indicators of the spread of ideas through the provinces from London and the bigger towns was in architecture. The simple Georgian buildings of the middle and later decades of the century, with their plain stone or stucco fronts, which can still be seen in many market towns, are a witness to the increasing standardization of styles, as the old vernacular designs were covered up or swept away. However, more basic than this to economic development was the increasing demand for the products of industry such as tea, coffee, clothing, buttons, pottery, and iron goods which became pronounced from the 1730s onwards (John 1961: 182–7).

This demand could be satisfied because of the marketing techniques of the larger manufacturers, operating through their own salesmen and showrooms, and because of the growth of permanent shops in the towns. These shops became more effective outlets as they were able to rely on a regularity of supply and variety of stock from many suppliers that was guaranteed by the improving road transport system. William Stout, the grocer of Lancaster, regularly bought in London and Liverpool, and had contacts in Bristol (Marshall 1967: 25). The extent of Abraham Dent's contacts was wider still. He was supplied with groceries, tobacco, spirits, stationery, cloth and pins by a reliable network of agents all over the north of England.[4]

If improving road transport fostered changes in industrial structure, and helped to bring about the creation of a national market for the products of industry, what were its effects on the location of industry? The seventeenth and early eighteenth centuries have already been characterized as a period of dispersed industrial location. The later eighteenth, and nineteenth centuries are traditionally the period of raw material orientation, and only in the twentieth century is industry said to become market based. But this view oversimplifies the real situation. It has been argued that the successful, large-scale firms of the eighteenth century were already market-orientated, because their aim was to satisfy a mass rather than a local market, and part of their stock of buildings was located to further this end.

However, if improved transport and communications enabled firms to be market-orientated in this way, the corollary is that it also enabled entrepreneurs to locate the production end of the manufacturing process in the more advantageous positions. As coal, the fuel of new industry, was expensive to carry—indeed Nef estimated that at the end of the seventeenth century, it may have doubled in price for every two miles it was moved, making land carriage over ten or 15 miles prohibitive (1930

Vol. 1: 102–3)—the coalfields became the natural location for large-scale, power-dependent industry. The successful, and reasonably central, craft based industries of the West Midlands, Lancashire and the West Riding thus formed the core of new industrial concentrations: of iron-making and manufactures in the West Midlands, and mass-produced textiles in the north. Birmingham, with a population of 15,000 in 1700, had grown to 74,000 by 1800. Manchester had grown from 17,000 to 84,000. New centres began to emerge around Sunderland and Newcastle on the north-eastern coalfields, and in South Wales at Swansea, and along the ironstone outcrop on the northern rim of the Welsh valleys.

The manufacturing, as well as the marketing operations of these new industrial concentrations were assisted by the development of the turnpike road system. Turnpike roads helped, before the canals were built, to ease the transport problem within the coalfields, and were actively promoted in these areas by industrialists and coalmasters (Albert 1972: 105–7). The coalmasters of Coventry, for example, gave enthusiastic support to local trusts, recognizing the opportunities of a wider regional market that would occur. The Coventry market itself, although important, was becoming increasingly volatile in the eighteenth century, as it became more dependent on a mass of luxury industries (White 1972: 177). Wedgwood's role in obtaining and supporting turnpike schemes in the Potteries is well known: but many other potters, and local mine owners were involved too (Thomas 1934). In South Lancashire, in the first half of the eighteenth century, over half the coal output was raised by collieries near Liverpool, in part dependent on the Liverpool to Prescot turnpike. Prescot Hall Colliery, which raised less than 3,000 tons in 1721, was producing 6,000 tons in 1731 after the turnpike trust had begun to improve the road, 15,000 tons in 1735 when it had finished, and 21,000 tons by 1750. The nearby Whiston mines were of comparable size, but both these collieries were far larger than the average for the area, which was about 2,000 tons per annum (Langton 1972: 42–3).

The success of the coalfields as production centres was due to fortunate resource endowments, and later, to cheap movement of bulk materials by canal transport. Nevertheless, they could not have become important manufacturing regions, catering for a national market, without two basic additional factors. The first of these was entrepreneurial talent which, building upon the skills and wealth of pre-existing craft industry, used it as a foundation for mass-production enterprise. The second was the connexion of these areas by the growing transport system and information services to the mass market: to London, the provincial towns and ports, and intervening rural areas. This enabled them not only to develop local locational advantages, but to break out of the local sphere of influence, and flourish at the expense of other regions.

The experience of the less well endowed regions, and those isolated because of poor roads, substantiates this argument. The Forest of Dean was one such example. From being an important iron-making centre in the early eighteenth century, it steadily declined, in both iron and coal production, despite its central location between South Wales and the Midlands. This was essentially because of the failure of the Crown, which controlled much of the Forest, to improve the roads adequately. Not until 1796 were the roads through the Forest turnpiked (695). Although the Office of Woods had spent some money on these roads in the preceding 30 years, it deprecated the spending of too much so as not to encourage the miners to take more timber under custom out of the woods in heavy wagons. The price of coal was thus kept at a high price in markets outside Dean, with repercussions on the pits themselves. In 1787, the total coal output of the Forest was less than 2,000 tons a week and iron output had dwindled to little more over the year. No new coke furnaces were set up until the 1790s, by which time Dean, from being pre-eminent amongst iron-producing regions in 1700, was completely overshadowed by South Wales and the West Midlands. And the South Lancashire coal-pits, encouraged by new canals and turnpike roads, were producing 10,000 tons of coal a week, five times the Dean total.[5]

Forward Linkages: Agriculture

Much of eighteenth century agriculture was market-orientated, which is shown by the notable regional specialization of production illustrated in Chapter 2. This was true even in the mid-seventeenth century. There were about 800 towns with functioning markets in England at that time, no less than 300 of which held specialized markets, selling products which people came from afar to buy (Everitt 1968: 119).

Nevertheless, there were many areas close to market towns and the big urban centres which did not participate in the market economy. In the first half of the eighteenth century, these included parts of the heavy Midland claylands, the undrained fens, the unreclaimed Wealden woodlands and the heaths of the chalk scarps. In contrast, many fertile parts adjacent to these areas were highly specialist producers, such as the sheep pastures of the east Midlands, the granaries of the northern Home

Counties, the dairylands of Wiltshire and Gloucestershire, and the fruit gardens of Hereford. A von Thünen model cannot effectively describe the pattern of agriculture: the uneven provision of transport facilities over the country ensured, amongst other things, that the simple principles of distance–decay, bulk to value ratios and perishability did not hold true.

However, a zoning model cannot be completely rejected. Three general zones of agricultural production can be recognized. Firstly, around cities, intensive agriculture predominated. The advantage of proximity encouraged the production of market garden goods, dairy produce and fat cattle for the urban markets. Market gardening had been carried on around London since the beginning of the seventeenth century, on the gravels to the north of Stepney, Hackney and Islington, and along the Thames valley west of Westminster. At the end of the eighteenth century, it was estimated that there were 8,500 dairy cows on land adjacent to Westminster and the City (East 1937: 160).

Secondly, the geographically peripheral parts of the country were mostly beyond the effect of market influences. Large parts of the extreme south west, of Wales, the north of England and Scotland were cultivated only at subsistence level, or lay in waste, not cultivated at all. In Northumberland, for example, Arthur Young thought that:

> 'It is amazing, that in a country, in which free exportation of corn was allowed for so many years, such tracts of land should remain in so desert a state.' (1771 Vol. 3: 81–2)

In Cornwall, in 1795, it was estimated that there were over half a million acres of waste, with the more accessible parts of the county being devoted to small-scale production of barley, beans and potatoes. Pembrokeshire, too, was primarily a pastoral county, producing little for the outside world, 'the character of the field produce [being] largely related to the domestic economy.' Oats and barley predominated (Dicks 1964: 73–7).

The third, or central zone, encompassed the area in between the inner zone of intensive urban production, and this extensive peripheral zone of subsistence and waste. It had characteristics of both the other two zones, with areas of specialist market-orientated agriculture and pockets of subsistence and wasteland. Where transport and communications were good, farmers could produce those products for which their skills, soil and situation were best suited. Where, however, accessibility was a problem, an alternative, non-optimal method of production was adopted. The influence of transport in this central zone could thus be clearly seen in those areas which were well served, and, in contrast, in those areas which clearly were not.

The most advanced area of agriculture in Kent, for example, lay along the Dover road, in the Faversham–Maidstone–Canterbury region. It was not only the most fertile area of the county, but was enclosed and cultivated intensively because of its good road and river links to the London market. It was an important corn, fruit and hop producing area, even in the seventeenth century. However, an area even closer to London, north-west Middlesex, between Uxbridge and Edgware, was notably backward agriculturally as late as 1800. Much of the land was still in open fields and poor husbandry prevailed, due to its heavy clay soils and relative remoteness, being away from the main turnpike roads (East 1937: 161).

Two contrasting areas slightly further from London were the Home Counties to the north and south of the city. The northern counties of Hertfordshire and Bedfordshire, in particular, were rich granaries, producing a lot of corn for the capital. It was transported to market along the main turnpike roads, which were established early in this region (Figs 24 to 27), and down the rivers Lea and Colne. There was a ring of important corn market towns between Enfield, Ware and Watford. But the Weald, equidistant to the south of London, was noted as a backward agricultural region until late in the eighteenth century with bad roads, inconvenient navigations and poor soils. It was heavily wooded with many small, poor farms:

'. . . the distance of the Weald from any considerable market, the badness of the roads, and the want of coal, all seem to have contributed to the preservation of the wood, and of course to have prevented the cleaning and cultivation of this district.' (Stevenson 1809: 425)

This distance, however, was relative, not physical, for most of the Weald was within 30 miles of London.

The effect of the improved transport and communication brought about by the eighteenth century turnpike road system was to extend gradually the advantages of market accessibility to most areas within this central zone, and to initiate the erosion of the subsistence farming and wastelands of the peripheral zone. The direct benefits to farmers of quicker, cheaper, more reliable, non-seasonal transport, were twofold. They were the same as for manufacturers: firstly, the advantages of better transport *per se*, and secondly, the benefits of improved communications and information linkage.

Better roads enabled farmers to use wheeled transport, and transfer from pack-horse to wagon carriage. Produce could be moved in greater

antities. Markets which had formerly been inaccessible in winter, or in
weather, could now be reached at all times. Basic production
requirements could be obtained with less difficulty: marl and lime could
be carried over greater distances, and supplies of winter fodder were more
easily bought when needed. The process of production thus became, in
itself, easier: greater stability and assurance were introduced into the
farmer's routine.

The information services were important for another reason. The new
local newspapers of the time always included regular reports of local
market prices. Knowledge of various market conditions came also from
the carriers, and by word of mouth from other travellers. With stability
and assurance, therefore, came choice. A farmer who was better informed
could make the choice between a high price market and a lower price
market. He could make the choice between producing those goods that
were in high demand, and those goods that were in lower demand. He
was able if he wished to make the rational adjustment to high prices.

These matters were important to the eighteenth century farmer, and
sometimes they featured specifically in the procedure on turnpike
petitions before Parliament. In 1730, when a trust was set up to mend the
road from Stratford-upon-Avon through south Warwickshire to Long
Compton Hill (82), one of the main cornmarkets in the area, at Shipston-
on-Stour, was unable to open in winter because of its inaccessibility (JHC
21: 440). And, in a successful plan of 1733 to extend the roads under the
Ipswich Trust (20) to include those around Eye, it was said:

> 'That the farmers carry Corn to Ipswich, and by the Badness of the
> Roads, their Cattle have received great Damage; but if the said Roads
> were amended, they would constantly return loaded, which they
> cannot do now, and would also fetch all Plank from Ipswich:
>
> That if the Farmers do carry Corn to Bungay, they must deliver 21
> Coomb, for a Score, and at Ipswich, only 20 Coomb. . . .' (JHC 22: 97)

The improvement in market accessibility as roads were mended had
two general results. The first was to strengthen the position of the larger,
more specialist markets where better services, and often better prices,
prevailed. The intervention of city merchants and factors was partly
responsible for this, introducing a powerful outside element into the local
economy of demand and supply. As farmers gained a better relationship
with the market, the market system was rationalized, with the expansion
of the bigger, better placed markets, and the decline of the smaller ones.
This process is discussed more fully below.[6] The second effect was on the

pattern of production and land use itself. Production increased, and sometimes altered in character completely, as farmers were better able to use their land to its full potential, and for the purposes for which it was best suited. Land which had been used only for livestock production because the roads were too poor to allow farmers to market anything else, could be profitably transformed into arable as corn prices rose and roads improved in the second half of the eighteenth century.

Arthur Young, in his Tour through the Southern Counties of England in 1769, made a valuable description of the variation in prices of agricultural products over space (1769: 301–18). He was not surprised to find that the demand for food in the great London market was reflected in increasing prices as the capital was approached, but concluded that:

'. . . in respect of the influence of great cities, I was never out of it. London affects the price of wheat everywhere; and though veal and butter were very cheap in Wales, yet the prices of them were by no means those which arose from a home consumption alone, as I plainly perceived by the great quantities of provisions bought up in all the little ports of the Severn, by the Bristol market boats . . . I found all the sensible people attributed the dearness of the country to the turnpike roads; and reason speaks the truth of their opinion. I can imagine many tracts of the country, and there are certainly such in this Kingdom, wherein provisions cannot be dear. The inhabitants of these tracts are in the right to keep their secret; make but a turnpike road through their country, and all the cheapness vanishes at once.' (1769: 317–18)

Turnpike roads gradually increased the accessibility of towns to agricultural areas, so channelling their rising demand for the produce of farms over wider areas. The vanishing cheapness as urban factors intervened in country markets, was certainly not beneficial for the rural non-farm population: for the inhabitants of market towns and villages who did not grow much food. But it did contribute to the increased prosperity of the farmers. As market accessibility improved, the farmer was able to respond more readily to increasing demand.

In many areas this increased prosperity was reflected in a rise in rental values. Sometimes this was quite dramatic, as along the Sleaford to Tattershall Turnpike in South Lincolnshire, established in 1793 (666). In this area as a whole turnpike road improvements, along with the drainage of farmland soils, enabled farmers to make a 'striking expansion' in the arable acreage. In Kesteven, it increased by almost 100 per cent between

1792 and 1801 alone (Grigg 1966: 70–1). Although this trend was motivated amongst individual farmers by high grain prices, here as elsewhere, for example in the East Riding (Harris 1961: 86–7), it could not have been accomplished without better roads. Indeed, where they remained poor, as in south-east Kesteven, grazing was still very much the predominant form of land use (Grigg: 69).

Young himself reported a similar increase in the value of land after the Horsham to Epsom road out of the Weald was turnpiked in 1755 (236):

'It was no sooner completed than rents rose from 7/– to 11/– per acre: nor is there a gentleman in the country who does not acknowledge and date the prosperity of the country to this road; and the people who were the greatest opposers of it, are now so convinced, that there is a general spirit of mending their cross roads by rates.' (1808: 418)

This account may well be somewhat exaggerated, particularly as it was written 60 years after the event it describes. Nevertheless, it does reflect the agricultural development in the Weald as it was opened up by turnpike roads from the mid-eighteenth century (Fig. 29). Several of these roads were improved to enable timber to be transported more easily: the Milford to Stopham (281) and the Guildford to Arundel roads (283) in 1757 (JHC 27: 714), and the Milford to Lippock road in 1764 (399) (JHC 29: 794).

By 1809, William Stevenson, the Board of Agriculture reporter for Surrey could write:

'the very trifling value . . . of wood, in a country thinly inhabited, cut off from other districts, and abounding in timber, necessarily led to the formation of better roads: and these again changed the face of the country, both by opening a market for the timber and for corn which as yielding a quicker return, was preferred to timber, now that the superfluity could be disposed of.' (1809: 425)

The new turnpike roads to the north of Lewes (170) similarly helped in the clearing of the woodland there. When Defoe passed between Tunbridge Wells and Lewes in 1723, he remarked that 'the timber I saw here was prodigious, as well in quantity as in bigness.' Sometimes, he claimed, it took two or three years for single trees to be moved overland to the Medway (1962 Vol. 1: 128–9). But by the 1790s, as Faden's map of Sussex shows, most of this woodland had gone and the formerly afforested areas of the Broyle, Laughton and Holland Park had been largely cut up into small farms.

The Wealden agricultural economy underwent a fundamental change in emphasis from livestock to cereals similar to that experienced in many other areas, as transport by land and water improved. As the wood was cleared, land was reclaimed from the heath and old grassland was converted to arable. In 1798, Marshall observed 'there is scarcely an acre of natural herbage or old grassland in a township.' Wheat and oats were the new crops (1798: 102, 139). Much heath land was reclaimed on the Forest Ridges of East Sussex between Heathfield, Battle and Burwash, and in the High Weald of Ashdown, Tilgate and St Leonard's Forest (Brandon 1974: 184–7). The Lewes Turnpike (170) had been extended along the Forest Ridges to Burwash and Battle in 1766, and about the same time, several roads had been turnpiked through the High Weald (393, 520, 528).

One aspect of Wealden agricultural improvement was the increased use of lime to neutralize the acidic sandstone soils. Marl had been used for this purpose since early medieval times, leaving a legacy of widely scattered pits. However, marling died out in the eighteenth century as lime, which was more effective, became popular. The improved roads enabled it to be transported more easily from the South Downs, on the north face of which are scores of old chalkpits, to the Wealden ridges up to 20 miles away (Brandon: 191). Marshall noted that kilns were to be seen on every common, with the bigger farms having their own (1798: 143). Another area in which the use of lime became common at this time was in Devon, although here the practice was already widespread by 1750. After 1770, as grain prices rose, nearly every Devon farmer began to use lime. The new turnpike roads in the county of the 1750s and 1760s (Fig. 29) undoubtedly encouraged this, as the material often had to be carried ten to 25 miles to the farm (Havinden 1974).

There are many other specific examples of agricultural improvements induced by turnpike roads. The hopes of the projectors of the Wallingford turnpike (161) were certainly realized.[7] As the road was improved, the production of malt in the town for shipment down the Thames increased dramatically. The average annual production of malt in the five years up to 1754 was 49,172 bushels; in the five years up to 1774, it had risen to 113,135 bushels (Jones 1967: 33–4). Agriculture improved in the heavy clay vale of north Wiltshire after the Great West Road through Devizes and Melksham, and surrounding routes, were turnpiked. Dairying became more prominent, with alternate pasturing and haying, and an increasing amount of cheese was made for the London market (East 1937: 165).

Intensive husbandry such as this could be adopted elsewhere, as better roads opened a rapid link to markets. The market garden products of the inner zone of agriculture could be grown in areas further away from major towns, taking advantage of peculiar local situations. Bicester, in Oxfordshire, became a notable butter market, and by 1800 it sent ten tons of butter by wagon to London each week. Thame, a neighbouring market centre, also supplied some, along with poultry and fruit (Lambert 1953: 51, 167). Around Sandy, to the east of Bedford, market gardening was well established by the end of the century. The area, with fertile terrace soils, was on the Old Great North Road. The section from Stevenage to Biggleswade had been turnpiked in 1720 (39), with the section through Sandy to Alconbury Hill being added five years later (52). These placed Sandy within two days wagon journey of London, which was short enough for the non-perishable, but nevertheless fragile, products of the area—onions, cucumbers and root vegetables. Much of the local produce was sold in the capital, but it was marketed widely in Bedfordshire and Hertfordshire (Beavington 1965).

The famous market gardening area in the Vale of Evesham also began to flourish in the eighteenth century, dependent on road transport to distant urban markets for its specialist produce. William Pitt, the Board of Agriculture's reporter for Worcestershire, noted 'considerable gardens and nurseries' near Worcester and Evesham, in which were grown 'garden plants, onions, cucumbers and asparagus . . . from sixty to eighty horses a day have formerly been laden with garden stuff for Birmingham market; the roads now being improved, it is sent in wheel-carriages, with a much fewer number of horses.' But asparagus was sent as far afield as Bath and Bristol by this means (Pitt 1813: 14).

Turnpike road improvement also encouraged development in the peripheral agricultural zone. A notable example of this was Northumberland, where several big landowners, such as the Culleys, Swinburnes and Blacketts were prominent leaders in the spirit and method of improvement. It was characterized by enclosure, reclamation of the waste, the introduction of improved breeds and better cropping systems, and a remarkable extension of wheat-growing (Butlin 1975: 228–34). This was accompanied by the improvement of roads, both under turnpike trusts, and within the estates themselves. Abraham Dixon, the owner of Belford, repaired the roads around that village, whilst Sir Walter Blackett had so improved the roads on his estate that Arthur Young, in his Northern Tour, was moved to describe them as 'a piece of magnificence which cannot be too much praised.'(1771 Vol. 3: 70–81).

The most significant highway improvement in Northumberland was the 'Corn Road', a new direct turnpike route between Hexham and Alnmouth (166). It was promoted by Lancelot Allgood of Nunwick Park in 1752, and ran through the estates of several improving landlords, such as the Swinburnes and Blacketts (Newton 1972: 224). Much of the reclaimed land in the country, enclosed by Parliamentary Act from 1720 onwards, lay immediately west of the line of this road. Many of the remaining eighteenth century enclosures were in the south of the county, near the Military Road (151) and the Hexham Turnpike (168).[8]

The exact relationship between turnpiking and enclosure, however, is something about which little is known. In areas such as central Northumberland, where landowners took a wide interest in improvement, then enclosure and turnpiking schemes were planned to proceed together. But often, such co-ordination was absent. Nevertheless, it does seem that enclosure activity generally increased after accessibility had been facilitated by new turnpike roads. This was the case in Northumberland as a whole, where there was a marked intensity of enclosure by Act in the 1770s (Butlin 1975: 229). This reflected the national pattern of diffusion of these two innovations, with the general rise in enclosure schemes in the 1770s coming after the turnpike boom of the 1750s and 1760s.[9] It was due, in large measure, to the rising tide of agricultural prices in markets—markets which were becoming more accessible as turnpike roads were improved.

In Leicestershire, as well, enclosure followed this pattern, as a recent reappraisal has shown. Schemes were heavily concentrated in the 1760s and 1770s, whilst many of the main routes had been turnpiked by 1760. Furthermore most of the enclosures in these two decades were within one to three miles of an existing turnpike road (Albert 1972: 115–16). In Oxfordshire, a county noted for its open-fields even in 1800, the pattern of enclosures by that date was largely related to their proximity to main roads. This is noticeable on Richard Davis' 1797 map of the county, which illustrates every closed and open field. The land adjacent to the Banbury, Chipping Norton, Burford, Dorchester and London turnpike roads was mostly enclosed. In between, however, lay large pockets of open-fields. The land to the west of the Cherwell along the Banbury road was enclosed, but land of a very similar character, on the same soils, to the east of the river in Garsington and Heyford parishes was still in open-field. These parishes lay between the Weston-on-the-Green and Banbury turnpikes, some distance from both. A large area to the north of Burford, between the Gloucester and Birmingham turnpike roads was still open, as were several parishes around Dorchester in the south of the county, between the turnpike roads to London and Reading.

Nevertheless, individual enclosure, improvement and turnpiking schemes were the outcome of many individual decisions, and often there was little co-ordination between them. Except where turnpiking and agricultural improvement were initiated together as part of a definite plan, as along the Corn Road, turnpiking was no more than a permissive factor in subsequent change. Other factors, notably agricultural prices and landlord attitudes, were important in the process of agricultural advance, and hence often very little happened immediately after a road had been turnpiked.

In Sussex, for example, it was over half a century after a trust had taken over the roads to the north of Lewes (170), that much of the land was finally enclosed into farms from the woodland. In Framfield, a large parish adjacent to the 1754 Uckfield to Langley Bridge Turnpike (218), enclosure did not take place until 1862 (Brandon 1974: 188–9). Young, in his Northern Tour, found that no more than three of the 12 miles of land along the Bowes to Brough road in Durham and Westmorland was cultivated, although it had been turnpiked 28 years before (114):

> 'The turnpike keeper in his little garden, which is taken in from the waste, shows what might be done with this land: He raises excellent potatoes, good garden beans, and admirable turnips. It is a country that calls for the industry to enclose: fertile fields loaded with corn, and giving food to numerous herds of cattle, ought to be the prospect in this tract, not whins, fern, ling and other trumpery! Shame to the possessors!' (1771 Vol. 2: 185–6)

Turnpiking, therefore, was certainly not a sufficient condition for enclosure. But outside the early enclosed regions, such as Kent, the Chilterns and Devon, the proximity of enclosure schemes to turnpike roads suggests that it may have been a necessary condition. In Arthur Young's mind it was, as he travelled in between Brough to Askrigg, in the North Riding:

> '. . . most of these fifteen miles, however dreadful the road, are tracts of very improveable land; if a good turnpike road was made from Askrigg to Brough, the first great step to cultivation would be over; for it is impossible to improve a country without spirit, the roads of which are impassable.' (1771 Vol. 2: 187)

✗ Urban Change

The effect of turnpike road development on urban change was both direct and indirect. It was direct in its effect upon marketing centres and the sorting of the market town hierarchy, and in its generation of facilities and employment in coaching towns. It was indirect in its effects upon the development of industry.

The development of industry is recognized as the most powerful force in eighteenth century urban growth (Chalklin 1974: 32). It has already been seen that the provision of improved road services was vital in increasing the efficiency of both the marketing and production ends of the manufacturing process. When entrepreneurial talent, suitable local resources and adequate transport facilities enabled industry to flourish, industrial concentrations began to emerge. These were further encouraged by internal economies of scale, as market areas widened, and by external economies as a pool of service industries and skills developed. Industrial towns became prominent, with centres such as Birmingham, Manchester, Glasgow, Leeds, Sheffield, Swansea and Dundee growing rapidly. Many of these industrial centres depended for their initial expansion mainly on road, river and sea linkages, with the canals not becoming important until the latter part of the eighteenth century.

This section, however, is concerned more with the direct effects of turnpike road development on urban change. In the mid-seventeenth century, there were about 800 market towns in England, functioning as centres of exchange. Although this was probably only one third to one half as many as in the early fourteenth century, the number nevertheless continued to decline. By 1770, only about two-thirds of the 800 survived.

Already in 1660, about 300 market towns were specialized, being noted for one or two particular products—corn, malt, horses, sheep— which people came some distance to buy (Everitt 1968: 120). The gradual provision of better transport and communications hastened this trend towards specialization in the bigger, well positioned markets. The smaller, less nodal markets, and those situated in poor hinterlands declined, with many dying out completely. They continued to exist as villages, but their trade was diverted away from them to the larger towns. Not only could these places offer a wider choice of goods and better market facilities, but as the roads improved, they became accessible over increasingly large areas. This growth and decline of market centres was reflected in their size of population. A comparison of population sizes to estimate rates of change is thus a good way of assessing the prosperity of markets over time. However, pre-1801 town populations are not easy to obtain, particularly for whole counties. For this reason, Chalklin's (1974) data for Lincolnshire and Dorset have been used. The Lincolnshire figures compare the number of families in a diocesan census of 1705 with the equivalent figure in the 1801 Census. The Dorset figures compare population estimates from the 1662–4 Hearth Tax Assessments with the 1801 Census. The rates of change of market town populations for these counties are shown in Figs 42 and 43.

Both counties show a definite pattern of differential expansion, with the biggest rates of increase coming in the largest and best positioned market towns. In Lincolnshire, Lincoln, Louth, Boston and Stamford all grew by more than 100 per cent between 1705 and 1801. These towns were well spaced, being 25 to 40 miles apart. They were at the centre of local turnpike road networks, and each was on or near a navigable waterway. In 1705, they had been amongst the six largest centres in the country and by 1801, they were the four largest. The other two big centres of 1705, Grantham and Spalding, had grown less rapidly, because of their proximity to the more successful markets. Spalding was within 15 miles of the port of Boston, and Grantham was without a navigable river. The two smallest centres, Bourn and Market Deeping, grew very slowly, being within but ten miles of Stamford and Spalding.

In Dorset, the three most rapidly growing towns between the 1660s and 1801 were the port of Poole, the resort of Melcombe Regis, now part of Weymouth, and Blandford. Each was a nodal centre on the county's turnpike road network. In addition, at about 12-mile intervals in a ring around the edge of the county, lay a series of expanding market centres from Bridport to Shaftesbury. But the slow growth, and even decline of several intermediate market towns is very noticeable. Dorchester, despite its apparently central position, had not only a hinterland that was largely poor heath, but suffered from competition from Bridport, Blandford and Weymouth. Its role, as county town, as a resort for the county's gentry was undermined by its proximity to Melcombe Regis. Cerne Abbas, having been by-passed by the main Dorchester to Sherborne turnpike, barely grew. Both Lyme Regis and Sturminster were on turnpike roads, but were smaller centres which suffered from their proximity to the bigger markets.

A similar pattern of market town expansion and relative decline can be seen in most other counties. In Oxfordshire, for example, the nodal and well spaced markets of Oxford, Banbury, Thame, Woodstock and

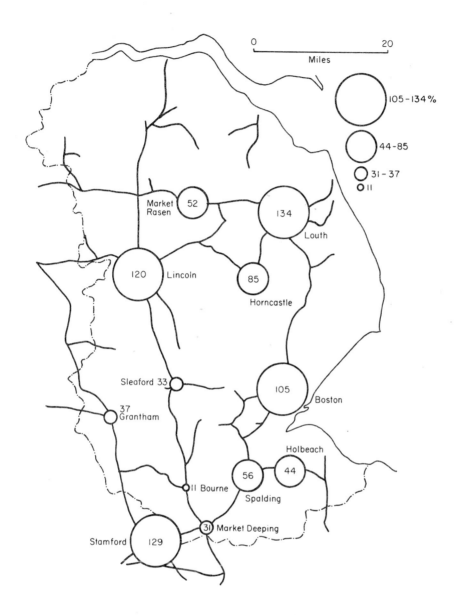

FIG. 42. Population increase in the market towns of Lincolnshire, 1705–1801. This map is based on Chalklin's data (1974: 320), superimposed on the 1770 turnpike road map. Population increase in the county as a whole as 34 per cent during this period.

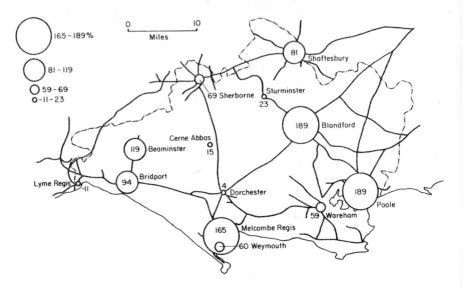

FIG. 43. Population increase in the towns of Dorset, between the 1660s and 1801. Based on Chalklin (1974: 322) and the 1770 turnpike road map. Population increase in the county as a whole was 63 per cent in this period.

Bicester flourished. The biggest market was at Banbury, which lay at the junction of the limestone uplands and the clay vale, at the confluence of several major turnpike roads. It was 'held to be the best market . . . within 30 miles' in the *Universal British Directory* of 1791. It dwarfed the local market at Deddington, and overshadowed that at Chipping Norton. In the centre of the county, Oxford's market had grown so much with the increasing accessibility of the city, that both Wheatley and Eynsham, six miles either side, had lost their markets by 1800, whilst those at Islip, Charlbury and Bampton were small, and in steady decline (Lambert 1953: 171–82).

In Essex, markets were in decline at the small centres of Rochford, Rayleigh and Chipping Ongar, and those at Kelvedon, Thaxted and Harlow had been discontinued by the end of the century. Growth was concentrated on the bigger centres of Colchester, Chelmsford, Dunmow, Witham, Malden, Epping and Romford. A town such as Chelmsford, which had a population of 1,725 in 1670, 2,151 in 1738 and 3,755 by 1801, offered a number of facilities which smaller market towns could not emulate. Most important of these were the new shops and inns, centres of private marketing outside the market place, which Everitt has called 'one of the most far-reaching developments . . . in the inland trade of England in this period.' (1968: 121). It was these which encouraged specialization, wider choice and an increasing clientele. Chelmsford had 18 shops in 1769, and 31 in 1794. It had 27 inns in 1703, 48 in 1769, and 31 in 1800, many having their own market rooms. The town's sphere of influence was increased by the provision of bookshops and coffee houses, by the use of its inns for the meetings of official bodies such as turnpike Trustees, and local societies, and in its role as county town, by the holding of the Assizes and Quarter Sessions. Chelmsford, like well placed towns in other counties, thus grew at the expense of the smaller centres (Brown 1969: 97–117).

Although the larger towns on turnpike roads, particularly those in nodal positions, often grew rapidly, such a location was not itself a means towards survival and prosperity. The improved accessibility afforded by better roads undermined the prosperity of the smaller markets, so that these, as well as those isolated away from turnpike roads, declined relatively. Dorchester, Lyme Regis, Bourne, Market Deeping, Eynsham and Wheatley were all on turnpike roads. In Cumbria, two new markets were founded in the late seventeenth century at Shap and Ambleside, and both received an initial stimulus from the turnpiking of the roads on which they were situated, the main Carlisle (181) and the Kendal to Keswick (377) routes. But by 1800, both markets were in great decline, suffering with the competition from Kendal (Milward 1964: 213–15).

The bigger markets flourished. Skipton for example, became the gathering centre for Craven wool after the road from Keighley to Kendal was turnpiked in 1753 (210) (Raistrick 1970: 157). Whitby, a seaport and fishing village, developed an important market after its landward connexions were strengthened when the road to Middleton was turnpiked in 1764 (403). Its neighbour, Egton, abandoned its own, whilst Whitby grew, becoming a resort and residential town. Patrington, a small port to the east of Hull, received a new lease of life when its inland link was turnpiked in 1761 (347). New warehouses were built, and the trade of the port increased (MacMahon 1964: 25–35). The success of the river port of Wallingford has already been noted. A writer in the *Gentleman's Magazine* in 1765 illustrated the growth of Dorking's trade:

'It has a good market on Thursdays, for all sorts of grain, the business of which has been very much increased since the completing of the turnpike road from Epsom, through the main street of the town to Horsham in Sussex; for by this road a much greater quantity of corn is brought out of that country than before; the water mills, which are very numerous in the parish and neighbourhood, have a great demand for corn, and the market is frequented by buyers a good way round many of whom send considerable quantities of meal to London.'[10]

The growth of coaching towns was closely related to the expansion of the bigger markets. This was not only because of the close connexion between markets, inns and coaching, but because the spacing of the prominent market towns, at distances of 15 to 35 miles, corresponded with the viable length of stages on coach and posting roads. The growth of coach services, and the generation of inns which this stimulated, was an additional contributory factor in the course of urban population change.

In the coaching towns, the inns and the coaching firms were important providers of employment. In Northampton, there were about 60 inns in 1777, and these employed, with their servants and coachmen, probably 250 people. This was not inconsiderable in a town with a population of about 6,000. The innkeepers were a wealthy class: an analysis of probate inventories showed that they held about one fifth of the town's wealth in the period between 1660 and 1750. In Canterbury, the number of innkeepers and wayfarers listed in the Poll Books almost doubled from 45 in 1790 to 79 in 1818—about 8 per cent of those listed at each date. The town was a major coaching centre on the Dover road (Everitt 1971: 31–3, 41).

Many smaller towns on main turnpike routes such as Burford and Enstone in Oxfordshire, and Towcester, Daventry and Dunstable on the Coventry road, were more dependent on the coaching trade. Dunstable, chiefly supported by 'the great passage of travellers' almost doubled its population to 1,300 people between 1760 and 1801 (Chalklin 1974: 30). And Defoe thought that the settlements along the Essex road, 'Brent Wood and Ingarstone, and even Chelmsford itself have very little to be said of them, but that they are large thorough-fare towns, full of good inns, and chiefly maintained by the excessive multitude of carriers and passengers, which are constantly passing this way to London . .' (1962 Vol. 1: 37).

The diversion of traffic away from such settlements, with the improvement of turnpike roads, often had serious repercussions on their prosperity. Wilton declined rapidly after an alternative road to Exeter through Salisbury was turnpiked in 1761 (348). East Grinstead, in Sussex, was affected when the Brighton coach traffic started to take the new turnpike route through Cuckfield (528) after 1770, in preference to the longer road via Lewes (170) (Jackman 1916: 275). Burford itself

declined when the Trustees of the Crickley Hill to Oxford Turnpike
constructed a by-pass round the town in 1812. It gradually lost the trade
of the 40 coaches a day that passed through in 1800, and its market
shrank. Between 1801 and 1821 its population fell from 1,516 to 1,409
(Lambert 1953: 291).

Turnpike road development thus had important effects on urban
change in the eighteenth century, stimulating the growth of markets and
coach traffic in some centres, and draining trade from others. But it was
only one of several forces, of which industry, as has been seen, was the
most important. The new industrial towns grew most rapidly, whilst the
market and coaching trade could not completely restore the prosperity of
declining industrial centres. Towns such as Norwich, Colchester and
Gloucester were regional trade centres, but suffered from the competition
of the new industrial towns. The population of Norwich in 1801 was the
same as 50 years previously. Tiverton, in Devon, had lost about 2,000
people between 1730 and 1770 (Chalklin 1974: 33–4). Colchester's
population declined steadily until the 1770s, with the loss of its cloth trade
(Brown 1969: 98–9), and Gloucester, overshadowed by Bristol, did not
begin to prosper until the canal to Berkeley was opened in 1827 (Lobel
1969: 13–14).

Changing Settlement Patterns

In addition to the direct effect of turnpike roads on urban prosperity and
population, the direct benefits of quicker travel times and increasing ease
of travel had a marked general impact on settlement patterns. The most
notable changes were in the nature and direction of urban growth, with
the development of suburbs and dormitory centres; in the pattern of rural
settlements along turnpike roads; and in the appearance of new resort
towns dependent on the increase in passenger travel.

Aikin, in 1795, wrote of Manchester:

'At each extremity of Manchester are many excellent houses, very
elegantly fitted up, chiefly occupied by the merchants of the town,
which may in some measure be considered as their country residences,
being from one to two miles from their respective warehouses.
Ardwick-green, to the south of the town, on the London road, is
particularly distinguished by the neatness and elegance of its buildings.

Some years ago it was regarded as a rural situation; but the buildings of Manchester have extended in that direction so far as completely to connect it with the town; and this quarter is principally inhabited by the more opulent classes, so as to resemble, though on a small-scale, the west-end of the city of London.' (1795: 205–6)

This separation of home and workplace was a direct consequence of the availability of quicker travel, and the desire for more comfortable residence in rural areas amongst those who could afford it. Similar patterns of growth could be seen around all expanding towns in the eighteenth century. In Leeds, Nottingham, Newcastle and Liverpool new housing was spreading along each of the main roads away from the original nuclear centre, with some infilling of streets and squares in between. Donn's map of Bristol revealed extensive ribbon development around the city by 1769, with attached suburbs spreading towards Clifton and Bedminster and more distant roadside growth around Long Ashton to the west and to the east on either side of Kingswood.

Ribbon development itself was not new. It had been a natural way for towns to expand once they had outgrown the confines of their medieval walls. But in the latter part of the eighteenth century, the process of suburban development on an unprecedented scale began. It was the start of the transformation of the nature and size of urban settlements that has continued ever since. The general rate of increase of urban growth provided the mechanism of expansion, but its direction was in large measure dependent upon improving passenger transport facilities and road surfaces.

London illustrates the process of suburban spread better than any other British city in the eighteenth century, partly because it occurred here on a scale much larger than elsewhere and partly because it is better documented. In 1782, Charles Moritz had commented on the line of suburban villas that stretched from Greenwich right into the City, and then out from Westminster through Kensington to Hammersmith (1924: 20, 100). At the turn of the century Middleton wrote:

'The turnpike roads in Middlesex bear evident marks of their vicinity to a great city. Scattered villas, and genteel houses, in the manner of a continued, and rather elegant village, are erected on one, or both sides of the road, for three, five or seven miles out of London. The footpaths are thronged with passengers, and the carriage-ways with horses, carts, waggons, chaises, and gentlemen's carriages of every description.' (1798: 393)

That Moritz and Middleton were describing accurately the suburban spread of London is shown clearly in contemporary maps, such as those of Paterson (1802) and Cruchley (1828) which illustrate the elongation of settlement up the major roads.

Summerson has recognized four types of development in London's suburban growth: village development, country villa building, roadside development and estate development (1962: 270). Village development, a form of suburban growth separated from the main city, was pronounced on all sides of London. Some of the earliest turnpike roads connected popular residential villages with the city: the Stamford Hill Trust to Tottenham and Edmonton in 1713 (23), the Islington Trust to Kentish Town, Hampstead and Highgate in 1717 (31), the New Cross Trust to Greenwich and Lewisham (34), and the Surrey–Sussex Trust to Peckham, Streatham and Clapham (33) in 1718. Harrison's *History of London* (1775) noted that at Peckham 'there are many handsome houses . . most of which are the country seats of wealthy citizens of London, or the fixed habitation of those who have retired from business', whilst at Kentish Town, 'the air being exceedingly handsome, many of the citizens of London have built houses.'

The more wealthy built detached villas in their own grounds, the second type of suburban development. Burlington's house at Chiswick is the leading example, but most were not in so grand a manner. In 1796, there were 36 country seats in Richmond, 13 in Wimbledon, 12 in Croydon, 11 each in Epsom and Clapham, and 10 in Bromley (Dyos 1952: 73), each of these settlements being on an early turnpike road into London. The third type, roadside development, emerged early in the eighteenth century in Islington, and earlier still in Southwark. It was considerable along all main roads from the city by the end of the century. One of the best areas of ribbon development and infill was to the south of the river, where the Surrey New Roads had been built in the early 1750s (155) (Fig. 35). This part of London became an increasingly popular residential area as the new Thames bridges were opened. As soon as 1753, the *Gentleman's Magazine* reported:

'These new roads, passing thro' gardens and meadows, were so frequented by the nobility and gentry, and all sorts of passengers, that schemes were talked of for building streets and squares in its neighbourhood, rooms erected for entertaining company, several handsome shops built and the country wore quite a new face.'

The extent of new suburban development here—particularly to the west of the main Surrey–Sussex Turnpike—is shown on Neele's large-scale map of London, published in 1797.

Such ribbon development was complemented by Summerson's fourth category, estate development, which helped to fill in the green spaces between the major roads. These estates were most prominent north of the river: Hans Town, begun in 1771 off Sloane Street, Somers Town (1786), Camden Town (1791), Pentonville, and in the 1820s, the great Regents Park estate to the north of the New Road (Summerson 1962: 281–3).

The growth of these suburbs was reflected in the increase of the number of short-distance coach services from London. In 1773, 37 daily suburban services left the City, and 37 left Westminster, for destinations south of the river. In 1805, the numbers had increased to 219 and 102 respectively, and by 1821, had reached 434 and 108. The pattern of destinations is shown in Table L. These increased suburban transport facilities generally indicated a rise in the number of workers of all kinds making the daily return trip to the City. These workers helped to swell greatly the populations of towns and villages in and near London. Table LI shows the increase over the century for several Essex settlements close to London. Several of these doubled in size, and some increased fourfold, whereas the general level of increase in Essex as a whole was between 55 and 68 per cent in the eighteenth century.

The evolving pattern of London-based settlement was not limited to these suburban developments within ten miles of the city. Some of the wealthier London inhabitants moved considerably further out. Reading, which had only 900 houses in the early eighteenth century, had a population, which had probably doubled, of 9,421 people by 1801. It was said then that the Reading man 'who leaves his house in the morning to transact what business he may have to do in London can return the same evening.' (Lobel 1969: 7, 9). And Cobbett wrote vitriolically of one of the new resorts in the 1820s:

'. . . the town of Brighton, in Sussex, 50 miles from the Wen, is on the seaside, and thought by the stock-jobbers to afford a salubrious air. It is so situated that a coach, which leaves it not very early in the morning reaches London by noon; and, starting to go back in two hours and a half afterwards, reaches Brighton not very late at night. Great parcels of stock-jobbers stay at Brighton with the women and children. They skip backward and forward on the coaches, and actually carry on stock-jobbing in 'Change Alley through they reside in Brighton.'
(Cobbett 1930 Vol. 1: 149)

Table L
Suburban Coach Services from London to Destinations South of the Thames

Destination	Date 1773	Date 1805	Date 1821
Barnes	2	11	see Richmond
Battersea	—	7	17
Blackheath	—	9	19
Brixton	—	—	31
Bromley	2	5	5
Camberwell	4	36	53
Carshalton	1	2	1
Clapham	4	14	40
Croydon	3	8	8
Deptford	4	33	27
Dulwich	3	3	10
Eltham	2	6	—
Epsom	4	11	—
Greenwich	14	33	54
Kennington	—	16	36
Kingston	2	12	—
Lewisham	—	13	8
Mitcham	3	16	9
Newington	—	15	5
Norwood	—	7	7
Peckham	2	21	44
Putney	7	15	—
Richmond	9	56	43
Rotherhithe	—	3	10
Streatham	1	7	13
Sydenham	1	3	1
Vauxhall	—	15	36
Walworth	—	17	11
Wandsworth	4	11	8
Wimbledon	—	4	6
Woolwich	2	11	9

Source: Dyos 1952: lxxvi.

M

The effect of turnpiking on rural settlements away from the influence of suburban development reflects in part the advantages of easier travel, and also the canalization of traffic along particular busy routes. Rural houses became more attractive to the urban gentry as second, or even main residences, with proximity to a turnpike road being an important contributory factor. Improved roads encouraged agricultural development, as has been seen, and this sometimes resulted in the growth of new roadside settlement in newly farmed areas. Thirdly, existing settlements which were by-passed by turnpike roads, often developed a second nucleus on the road, around inns and chapels, with the eventual abandonment of the former centre.

Table LI

The Increasing Populations of Essex Settlements near London, 1723–1801

	1723	1763	1778	1790	1801 houses	families
Dagenham	120f	150f		180f	207	219
Gray's, Thurrock	33f	51h	70h		83	113
East Ham	105f				156	221
Tilbury	17f		30h	60h	100	104
Walthamstow	130f	200h	400h		515	519
Wanstead	c. 40f	75h		125h	159	178
Woodford		80f	150h		273	295

Source: Brown 1969: 100.

h   houses
f   families

The importance of the increasing ease of travel in encouraging rural settlement by the urban gentry was noticeable early in the century to Defoe. It was reflected in the advertisement of country properties in the London and provincial newspapers. For example, 17 houses and two building plots were advertised in the London papers from April to June, 1704. Four of these were within two miles of the City or Westminster, but the rest were all more than seven miles out: seven within ten miles, another four within 16 miles, and four over 20 miles away.[11] Later in the century, when sales notices of country properties became more numerous, location close to a turnpike road was frequently specifically mentioned. This suggests that the value of such properties was thereby increased:

To be LET or SOLD

A very genteel modern-built HOUSE in perfect Repair, situate in ABBOTS BROMLEY, in the Co. of Stafford.

The above premises are pleasantly situated in an healthy and fine sporting country, between the Forests of Needwood and Cannock, on a good Turnpike road, six Miles from Uttoxeter, and 11 from Lichfield, by which, passeth a regular Post 4 days a Week, and a regular Coach three Times a Week.

(Derby Mercury, 19 Aug. 1790)

Sales advertisements for farms, woodland and inns[12] frequently mentioned similar locations, the latter obviously as an indication of trade prospects, and the former because of the ease of access and dispatch implied.

New settlements sometimes appeared around inns on turnpike roads, or more commonly, old village cores moved towards the attraction of traffic, with new inns, non-conformist chapels, stores and houses being built away from the old church and green. On the Lewes to Battle Turnpike in East Sussex, Gardner Street, a tiny settlement on the road, gradually usurped the service functions of the old village of Herstmonceux, a mile and a half to the south, to the extent of eventually taking over its name. By 1813, only the church and farm were left on the old site. A few miles away, to the north of Battle, the village of Salehurst declined as the new settlements of Northbridge Street and Robertsbridge grew on the London to Hastings Turnpike a mile to the west in the same parish (Fuller 1950: 207–12).

Similar examples can be found in many counties. Several small settlements developed around inns on the post road across Anglesey, at Crossgates near Llandrindod Wells in Radnor, and at West Felton, near Shrewsbury (Sylvester 1969: 145). In Cambridgeshire, Caxton, on the Great North Road, and Bottisham, near Newmarket, both grew away from their original cores towards the main road (Taylor 1973: 227–8). This process was also encouraged by the development of new agricultural settlements on turnpike roads, as land that had formerly been waste was taken in and reclaimed.

Several new settlements developed on the line of the Uckfield to Burwash turnpike, and the Heathfield to Battle road in the Weald. From the mid-1770s, plots of waste were gradually released by lords of the manor, and new villages emerged at Burwash Weald, Burwash Common, Broad Oak, New Heathfield, and at Cade Street and Punnetts Town. They were loosely built smallholders' communities, with their own non-conformist chapels, alehouses and small traders. Similar settlements grew around Ticehurst and Flimwell, on the London to Hastings Turnpike, and on the London road to the north of Uckfield at Nutley (Brandon 1974: 196–9). However, turnpiking sometimes had no noticeable effect on the rural settlement pattern. Very little new settlement was attracted to any of the new turnpike roads to Brighton in mid-Sussex (Fig. 38).

Finally, the development of the turnpike road system was important in the growth of a class of new eighteenth century settlements: the spas and seaside resorts. Two of the earliest turnpike trusts were set up to ease the problem of access to two of the earliest spas—Bath (11) and Tunbridge Wells (15). Later in the century, turnpike schemes were promoted to provide better roads to several seaside towns—Scarborough in 1752 (167), Whitby in 1764 (403), and the Sussex resorts (Fig. 38). Although the medicinal properties of seawater, believed to be beneficial by some, encouraged the growth of these resorts, they were stimulated by the increasing ease of travel, and the growing Romantic mood of the later eighteenth century. This became more prevalent as easier travel conditions made touring for pleasure a possibility, and eventually a fashion. The coastline, formerly wild and desolate, became pleasant and picturesque—and fashionable.

Nevertheless, the resort towns were never a large part of eighteenth century urban growth. Like the development of suburbs and the reorganization of rural settlement patterns, they were part of a trend which did not begin to gather its greatest momentum until the middle years of the nineteenth century, with the expansion of the railway network. Bath never attracted more than 12,000 people at the height of an eighteenth century season, but by 1801, its population was 32,000, making it the ninth largest town in England. The other inland resorts were far smaller. Cheltenham, Tunbridge Wells and Leamington Spa all had less than 3,000 inhabitants at this date. The seaside resorts were also small, the three biggest being Brighton (7,399), Scarborough (6,409) and Margate (4,706). But all these, apart from Margate with a direct link by coastal hoy to London, were dependent on turnpike roads for their prosperity and continued growth. Brighton, for example, had one London coach service three times a week in 1756. By 1811, there were 28 coaches each day, and by 1821, the number had reached 40 (Hart 1960: 147). The countervailing effect of this increase in traffic on the turnpike road of mid-Sussex itself has already been seen (Fig. 38).

Transport and Economy

The first turnpike trust was set up in 1663 to meet a particularly difficult local road repair problem on the Great North Road in Hertfordshire and Cambridgeshire. It was followed, from 1696, by a continuous series of new trusts, established as such problems became more widespread. The basic characteristic of this innovation was the internalization of the costs and benefits of road travel, through the levy of a direct toll on road users. It diffused slowly at first, but with gathering momentum from mid-century. By 1770, an extensive and coherent turnpike road network was in existence, supporting a wide range of transport and information services.

The pressures of change and growth which brought the turnpike trusts into existence, however, intensified in the latter half of the century. The transport problem of the new manufacturing areas made it necessary to find a cheaper means of moving one of the basic materials of industry—coal. A second innovation wave in the transport system developed from the 1760s, as the canal network was established on the coalfields, and expanded outwards to provide links between them.

The effect of the canals was to cut drastically the cost of transporting bulk goods, such as heavy manufactures and minerals. Overall, the cost of transport by canal was only one quarter to one third that of the land carriage cost (Jackman 1916: 446). The opening of the Grand Trunk Canal in 1777, for example, saved shippers in Liverpool and Manchester up to 75 per cent of the former cost of sending goods to destinations in the Midlands (Baines 1852: 439–40). The canals thus inevitably captured much bulk road traffic, and much new traffic that would otherwise have gone by road. Their trade was newly created, as well as in part diversionary. But the canal and turnpike road systems were, to an important extent, complementary. Not only did roads act as feeders for canals, but the entire passenger, local carrier and information road services were virtually unaffected. Road traffic continued to grow. Wilson's work on the West Riding economy has shown how turnpike toll receipts kept on rising until the 1820s, despite the existence of an extensive canalized river system in the area (1966: 115). Ward's traffic statistics provide evidence of the same increase, but on a more general scale (1974: 165).[13]

Toll income on the turnpike road system thus did not reach its peak until the 1830s. Thereafter it declined steadily in the face of the advance of another, and directly competing transport innovation, the railway.

The railway was a more efficient means of movement for bulk goods, passengers and information. Its impact was immediate. Already, by 1839, Parliament had set up a Select Committee 'To ascertain how far the formation of Railroads may affect the interests of Turnpike Trusts and the Creditors of such Trusts.' Where railway lines ran in direct proximity to turnpike roads, toll receipts fell dramatically. Then, over whole counties, the amount of road traffic declined.[14] It never dwindled completely, and continued to be important in the local economy right through Victorian times, as Everitt has shown in his study of Leicestershire (1973). Nevertheless, from the 1840s, the Annual Turnpike Continuance Acts began to omit, and specifically repeal certain trust Acts. In the 1850s, 1860s and 70s the bulk of the turnpike roads in Britain were formally 'disturnpiked'.

This book has been concerned with the relationship between transport and economy in eighteenth century Britain. It has endeavoured to show how changes in the eighteenth century economy affected and altered road services and the road network, and how these alterations themselves affected and assisted change in the economy.

At this point it may be useful to return to the discussion in the first chapter and the model with which the book began (Fig. 2). The bulk of the first part of the book (Chapter 2) dealt with the first part of this model: it showed why internal trade was expanding at this time, and how road transport services were organized and modified to meet this expansion. The second part (Chapters 3 to 9) dealt with the second part of the model, tracing the effects of the expansion on the road network, and discussing the emergence, diffusion and implementation of the innovation—the turnpike trust—that was adopted to meet the breakdown of the parish repair system. It was an emergence and diffusion which closely mirrored the regional and general growth of the economy; mirroring and accompanying, rather than preceding, the development of the London trade in the first part of the century and the more general booms of the mid-century onwards.

What of the other side of the equation—the effects of transport on economy? In the popular imagination, turnpikes mean one thing. 'Turnpikes! . . . yes, all those tollhouses and gates! . . . Do tell us about that delightful little one out on the Faringdon road. . . .' But the turnpike trust and the improved road system it developed, were responsible for far more than these architectural curiosities, and this has been the concern of the last section of this book (Chapters 10 to 12). The turnpike road system was a characteristically eighteenth century solution to an eighteenth century problem. It played a fundamental role in repairing and improving the existing road network for the needs of an industrializing nation. It helped to ensure that transport and communication became quicker, cheaper and more reliable. It fostered the extension of the market and the growth of the information services. In doing so, it played an important and necessary part in the development of agriculture, industry and settlement patterns, in structural change, specialization and expansion. The extent and visible magnitude of the forward and backward linkages produced by the railway were undoubtedly greater than those produced by the improved turnpike road system. But many of the changes which have been traditionally ascribed to the railways—coalfield industrial concentration, regional agricultural specialization, the destruction of small markets, suburban growth and the development of the resorts—were already in motion in the eighteenth century, encouraged by the modernization of road transport services and public highways. And, such are the vagaries of change, that with the continuing evolution of the relationship between transport and economy, the turnpike road network of the eighteenth century provided, only a century later, the basis of the modern highways system that has since served the next great transport innovation in British history.

12. Notes

1. Dowlais letters, 1813, fo. 137 Elsas (1960) 85.
2. J. Britton *et al.*, *The Beauties of England and Wales XV: Westmoreland* (1814), 42–3.
3. Quoted in Pratt 1912: 96–7.
4. See above, p. 30.
5. This account is based largely on Hart 1971: 267 and Langton 1972: 50.
6. See pp. 323–8.
7. See above, p. 81.
8. See the map in Butlin 1974: 230.
9. See above, p. 128.
10. *The Gentleman's Magazine Library*: a classified collection, Part XII, Surrey and Sussex (1900: 68).
11. This information is from property advertisements in the *Flying Post*, the *Daily Courant*, the *London Post* and *Post-Man*, between April and June 1704 (Burney Collection, British Museum).

12. Sales advertisements for houses, inns, woodland and farms which mention proximity to a turnpike road are very common in local newspapers such as *Jackson's Oxford Journal*. e.g. 15 Jan., 10 Dec. 1757; 1 April 1758; 17 Feb. 1759; 19 April, 20 Dec. 1760; 6 Feb., 15 May, 30 Oct. 1762; 14 Jan., 7 May, 7 July, 14 July, 29 Dec. 1764.
13. These have already been referred to above, p. 130 and p. 200.
14. This process has been well identified in Williams (1975) and Freeman (1975).

Appendix 1

This Appendix lists all the new trust Acts passed by Parliament between 1663 and 1800.

Each Act is given a reference number in the left column, which is used to refer to those Acts cited in the text. Acts are grouped according to the session of Parliament in which they were passed.

The name of each Trust refers to the main route it controlled— when several routes came under the same trust, only the main road is given. Modern place-name spellings are used throughout.

1	1663	Wadesmill–Stilton	15 Car. II, c. 1
2	1696	Shenfield–Harwich	7/8 Wm III, c. 4
3		Wymondham–Attleborough	c. 26
4	1697	Reigate–Crawley	8/9 Wm III, c. 15
5	1698	Gloucester–Birdlip Hill	9/10 Wm III, c. 18
6	1703	Thornwood–Woodford	1 Anne, c. 10
7	1706	Whitchurch–Barnhill	4/5 Anne, c. 9
8	1707	Hockcliffe–Woburn	5 Anne, c. 10
9		Fornhill–Stony Stratford	c. 21
10		Devizes	c. 26
11	1708	Bath	6 Anne, c. 1
12		Cherhill–Studley Bridge	c. 14
13		Old Stratford–Dunchurch	c. 15
14	1710	Stoke Goldington–Northampton	8 Anne, c. 2
15		Sevenoaks–Tunbridge Wells	c. 12
16	1711	Royston–Wandesford Bridge	9 Anne, c. 7
17		Petersfield–Portsmouth	c. 8
18		Dunstable–Hockcliffe	c. 9
19	1712	Kilburn Bridge–Sparrows Herne (EDGWARE)	10 Anne, c. 7
20		Ipswich–Pye	c. 9
21		Highgate–Barnet	c. 33

22	1712	Northfleet–Rochester (CHALK)	c. 34
23	1713	Enfield–Shoreditch (STAMFORD HILL)	11 Anne, c. 1
24	1714	Shepherds' Shore–Horesley Upright Gate	12 Anne, c. 2
25		Worcester–Droitwich	c. 3
26		Reading–Puntfield	c. 4
27		Tittensor–Talke	c. 14
28		Edinburgh	13 Anne, c. 30
29	1715	St Albans–South Mimms	1 Geo. I, c. 12
30		Uxbridge–Tyburn	c. 25
31	1717	Highgate–Hampstead (ISLINGTON)	3 Geo. I, c. 4
32		Kensington–Cranford Bridge (BRENTFORD)	c. 14
33	1718	London–East Grinstead, etc. (SURREY–SUSSEX)	4 Geo. I, c. 4
34		Kent Street–Lime Kilns (NEW CROSS)	c. 5
35		Maidenhead–Henley	c. 6
36		Reading–Basingstoke	c. 7
37	1719	Stokenchurch Hill–Enslow Bridge	5 Geo. I, c. 1
38		Beaconsfield–Stokenchurch	c. 2
39	1720	Stevenage–Biggleswade	6 Geo. I, c. 25
40	1721	Ledbury roads	7 Geo. I, c. 23
41		Wendover–Buckingham	c. 24
42		St Giles Pound–Kilburn Bridge (MARYLEBONE)	c. 26
43	1722	Brampton Bridge–Welford Bridge	8 Geo. I, c. 13
44		Whitechapel–Woodford	c. 30
45	1723	Dunstable–Shafford	9 Geo. I, c. 11
46		Gloucester–Birdlip Hill	c. 31
47	1724	Stump Cross–Cambridge	10 Geo. I, c. 12
48		Dunchurch–Meriden Hill	c. 15
49	1725	Enfield–Hertford and Ware (CHESHUNT)	11 Geo. I, c. 11
50		Manchester–Buxton	c. 13
51		Foulmire–Cambridge	c. 14
52		Biggleswade–Alconbury Hill	c. 20

53	1726	Market Harborough–Loughborough	12 Geo. I, c. 5
54		Birmingham–Edgehill	c. 6
55		Newbury–Marlborough	c. 8
56		Crackley Bank–Shrewsbury	c. 9
57		Lemsford Mill–Cory's Mill	c. 10
58		Horseley Upright Gate–Bath	c. 11
59		Hereford–Gloucester	c. 13
60		Worcester roads	c. 14
61		Grantham–Lower Drayton	c. 16
62		Tewkesbury roads	c. 18
63		Liverpool–Prescot	c. 21
64		Gloucester–Stone	c. 24
65		Kensington, Chelsea, Fulham (KENSINGTON)	c. 37
66	1727	Wigan–Preston	13 Geo. I, c. 9
67		Wigan–Warrington	c. 10
68		Cirencester–St. John's Bridge	c. 11
69		Bristol roads	c. 12
70		Studley Bridge–Toghill	c. 13
71		Birmingham–Great Bridge	c. 14
72		Bromsgrove–Birmingham	c. 15
73		Warminster roads	c. 16
74		Luton–West Wood Gate	c. 17
75		Cranford Bridge–Maidenhead Bridge	c. 31
76	1728	Chatteris Ferry–Somersham Bridge	1 Geo. II, c. 4
77		Hounslow Heath–Bagshot	c. 6
78		Evesham roads	c. 11
79		Maidstone–Rochester	c. 12
80	1729	Lichfield–Stone etc.	2 Geo. II, c. 5
81		Leominster roads	c. 13
82	1730	Bridgetown–Long Compton Hill	3 Geo. II, c. 9
83		Galley Corner–Lemsford Mill	c. 10
84		Chatham–Canterbury	c. 15
85		Hereford roads	c. 18
86		Rollright Lane–Enslow Bridge	c. 21
87		Wisbech–March	c. 24
88		Bridgwater roads	c. 34
89	1731	Lawton–Cranage Green	4 Geo. II, c. 3

90	1731	Godstone–East Grinstead	c. 8
91		Chapel-on-the-Heath–Bourton-on-the-Hill	c. 23
92		Fulham	c. 34
93	1732	Manchester–Saltersbrook	5 Geo. II, c. 10
94	1733	St John's Bridge–Fyfield	6 Geo. II, c. 16
95	1735	Manchester–Austerlands	8 Geo. II, c. 3
96		Rochdale–Ealand	c. 7
97	1736	Whitstable–Canterbury	9 Geo. II, c. 10
98		Henley Bridge–Oxford	c. 14
99	1737	Hartfordbridge–Odiham	10 Geo. II, c. 12
100	1738	Nottingham–Coates	11 Geo. II, c. 3
101		Shoreditch–Mile End	c. 29
102		Loughborough–Brassington	c. 33
103	1739	Grantham–Stamford	12 Geo. II, c. 8
104		Nettlam–Baumber	c. 10
105		Bakewell–Mansfield	c. 12
106		Dunchurch–Northampton	c. 18
107	1740	Whitehaven roads	13 Geo. II, c. 14
108	1741	Doncaster–Wakefield and Halifax	14 Geo. II, c. 19
109		Wakefield–Weeland	c. 23
110		Ealand–Leeds	c. 25
111		Doncaster–Wetherby	c. 28
112		Doncaster–Saltersbrook	c. 31
113		Selby–Leeds and Halifax	c. 32
114	1743	Bowes–Brough	16 Geo. II, c. 3
115		Boroughbridge–Pierce Bridge	c. 7
116		Shepherd's Shore–Marlborough	c. 10
117		Cirencester–Lansdown	c. 22
118	1744	Harlow–Stump Cross	17 Geo. II, c. 9
119		Middleton Tyas–Bowes	c. 22
120		Hull–Beverley	c. 25
121		Buckingham–Warmington	c. 43
122	1745	Hull–Kirk Ella	18 Geo. II, c. 4
123		Hull–Hedon	c. 6
124		Boroughbridge–Durham	c. 8
125		Tadcaster–York	c. 16
126		Birmingham–Stone Bridge	c. 19
127		Godmanchester–Newmarket Heath	c. 23
128	1747	Newcastle–Bucton Burn	20 Geo. II, c. 9

129	1747	Durham–Tyne Bridge	c. 12
130		Sunderland–Durham	c. 13
131		Cirencester–Birdlip Hill	c. 23
132		Stockton–Barnard Castle	c. 25
133		Catterick Bridge–Durham	c. 28
134	1748	Bowes–Sunderland Bridge	21 Geo. II, c. 5
135		Wolverhampton roads	c. 25
136		Pierce Bridge–Sunderland Bridge	c. 27
137	1749	Farnborough–Riverhill	22 Geo. II, c. 4
138		Newcastle–Carter Bar	c. 7
139		North Shields–Newcastle	c. 9
140		Wandesford Bridge–Stamford	c. 17
141		Ross roads	c. 26
142		Southwark and Bermondsey roads	c. 31
143		Kingston-upon-Thames–Petersfield	c. 35
144	1750	Haddington roads	23 Geo. II, c. 17
145		York–Boroughbridge	c. 38
146		Egremont–Salthouse	c. 40
147	1751	West Lavington–Seend etc.	24 Geo. II, c. 9
148		Crosford Bridge–Manchester	c. 13
149		Richmond–Lancaster	c. 17
150		Preston–Hering Syke	c. 20
151		Newcastle–Carlisle (THE MILITARY ROAD)	c. 25
152		Crickley Hill–Oxford	c. 28
153		Ludlow roads	c. 29
154		Darlington–West Auckland	c. 30
155		South London roads (SURREY NEW ROADS)	c. 58
156	1752	Wrotham Heath–Foots Cray	25 Geo. II, c. 8
157		Warminster–Bath	c. 12
158		Cirencester–Stroud	c. 13
159		Seend–Beckington	c. 17
160		Morpeth–Piercy's Cross	c. 18
161		Wallingford–Faringdon	c. 21
162		Shrewsbury–Wrexham	c. 22
163		Tinhead–Trowbridge etc.	c. 24
164		Edinburgh–Stirling	c. 28
165		Morpeth–Elsdon	c. 33
166		Alnmouth–Hexham	c. 46

245	1755	Manchester–Rochdale	c. 58
246		Addingham–Black Lane End	c. 59
247		Leeds–Blackburn etc.	c. 60
248	1756	Bethnal Green–Shoreditch	29 Geo. II, c. 43
249		Whiteparish–Southampton	c. 45
250		Basingstoke–Lopcombe Corner	c. 46
251		Wincanton roads	c. 49
252		Bruton roads	c. 50
253		Tewkesbury roads	c. 51
254		Poole roads	c. 52
255		Salisbury–Dorchester	c. 54
256		Towle Down Gate–Christian Malford Bridge	c. 56
257		Gloucester towards Cheltenham	c. 58
258		Ludlow roads	c. 59
259		Much Wenlock roads	c. 60
260		Shrewsbury–Church Stretton	c. 61
261		Shrewsbury–Shawbury	c. 64
262		Kington roads	c. 65
263		Welshpool–Oswestry–Wrexham	c. 68
264		Faringdon–Acton Turville	c. 77
265		Oxford–Chilton Pond	c. 81
266		Derby–Sheffield	c. 82
267		Ripon–Pateley Bridge	c. 83
268		Lincoln–Littleburgh Ferry	c. 84
269		Lincoln–Watton	c. 85
270		New Road, Paddington	c. 87
271		Presteigne roads	c. 94
272	1757	Tenbury roads	30 Geo. II, c. 38
273		Frome roads	c. 39
274		Melksham–Castle Combe	c. 41
275		Hitchin–Bedford	c. 43
276		Loughborough–Ashby-de-la-Zouch	c. 44
277		Hertford–Broadwater (WATTON)	c. 45
278		Corsham–Batheaston	c. 46
279		Towcester–Weston-on-the-Green	c. 48
280		Markfield–Snape Gate	c. 49
281		Milford–Stopham Bridge	c. 50
282		Walthamstow Marsh Road	c. 59
283		Guildford–Arundel	c. 60

284	1757	Bagshot–Hartfordbridge	c. 61
285		Spalding–Maxey	c. 68
286		Wrexham–Holywell etc.	c. 69
287	1758	Lyme Regis roads	31 Geo. II, c. 43
288		Monmouthshire roads	c. 44
289		Tiverton roads	c. 49
290		Donington–Wigtoft	c. 50
291		Brent Bridge–Plymouth	c. 51
292		Cirencester–Cricklade	c. 61
293		Sheffield–Sparrowpit	c. 62
294		Leeds–Sheffield	c. 63
295		Tetbury roads	c. 64
296		Christian Malford Bridge–Shillingford	c. 66
297		Shrewsbury–Westbury etc.	c. 67
298		Westbury–Market Lavington	c. 68
299		Chawton–Gosport	c. 73
300		Bishops Waltham–Odiham	c. 74
301		Stockbridge–Southampton	c. 75
302		Leatherhead–Guildford	c. 77
303		Guildford–Farnham	c. 78
304	1759	Mansfield–Chesterfield Turnpike	32 Geo. II, c. 37
305		Nottingham–New Haven	c. 38
306		Ilminster roads	c. 39
307		Bridgwater roads	c. 40
308		Macclesfield–Buxton	c. 41
309		Chesterfield–Hernestone Lane End	c. 43
310		South Molton roads	c. 45
311		Sonning–Virginia Water (WINDSOR FOREST)	c. 46
312		Wakefield–Austerlands	c. 48
313		Oxdown Gate–Winchester	c. 50
314		Ideford–Bittaford	c. 52
315		Grantham–Nottingham	c. 53
316		Dewsbury–Ealand	c. 54
317		Mold–Conway etc.	c. 55
318		Leadenham Hill–Newark	c. 57
319		Derby–Newcastle-under-Lyme	c. 60
320		Stretford Bridge–Leintwardine	c. 66
321		Lewes–Alfriston	c. 67

322	1759	Modbury–Plympton St Mary		c. 68
323		Nether Bridge–Dixes		c. 69
324		Barnsley–Cawthorne		c. 70
325		Wetherby–Grassington		c. 71
326	1760	Oakhampton roads	33 Geo. II,	c. 36
327		Chesterfield–Matlock Bridge		c. 39
328		Tamworth–Ashby-de-la-Zouch		c. 41
329		Halworthy–Wadebridge		c. 42
330		Hinckley–Tonge		c. 46
331		Burton-on-Trent–Hinckley		c. 47
332		Halifax–Littleborough		c. 48
333		Kidderminster roads		c. 50
334		Chester–Stone Bridge		c. 51
335		Bawtrey–Wortley		c. 55
336		Dearburn Bridge–Cornhill		c. 56
337		Maidstone–Cranbrook		c. 57
338		Brecon–Brobury		c. 58
339		Launceston roads		c. 59
340	1761	Buckland Newton–Osmington	1 Geo. III,	c. 24
341		Liskeard roads		c. 25
342		City Road		c. 26
343		Grampound–West Taphouse		c. 27
344		Martock–Somerton		c. 29
345		Falmouth–Marazion		c. 32
346		Ashburton–Highweek		c. 34
347		Thorngumbald–Patrington		c. 35
348		Salisbury–West Knoyle		c. 37
349		Stone and Wolverhampton roads		c. 39
350		Gatherley Moor–Staindrop		c. 41
351		Whitecross–Beverley		c. 42
352		Appleby–Kendal		c. 43
353	1762	Amesbury roads	2 Geo. III,	c. 39
354		Sandon–Bullock Smithy		c. 42
355		Saltash roads		c. 43
356		Bolton Moor–Newton		c. 44
357		Creed–Ruan Lanihorne		c. 46
358		Swindon–Everley		c. 49
359		Tavistock roads		c. 50
360		Kelsall–Highgate Warren		c. 53
361		Hinckley–Lutterworth		c. 54

362	1762	Bradford–Laycock		c. 59
363		Weyhill–Urshfont		c. 60
364		Winchester–Newton		c. 61
365		Ashbourne–Leek		c. 62
366		Sparrows Herne–Watton		c. 63
367		Bridgetown Pomeroy roads		c. 64
368		Cranbrook–Appledore		c. 65
369		Whitesheet Hill–Harnham Hill		c. 66
370		Flimwell Vent–Rye		c. 72
371		Deeping St James–Morcot		c. 73
372		Sudbury–Bury St Edmunds		c. 75
373		Faversham–Hythe		c. 76
374		Stourbridge–Cradley		c. 78
375		Cleobury Mortimor roads		c. 79
376		Burback–Coventry/Leicester Turnpike		c. 80
377		Hesket Newmarket–Kendal		c. 81
378		Sedbergh roads		c. 83
379		Cosham–Chichester		c. 84
380	1763	Heath Charnock–Bolton	3 Geo. III,	c. 31
381		Newmarket–Fulborne		c. 32
382		Kendal–Ireleth		c. 33
383		Mothvey–Tavernspite		c. 34
384		Barnstaple roads		c. 35
385		Cambridge–Soham		c. 36
386		Totnes roads		c. 38
387		Llangollen roads		c. 43
388		Halkin Mountain–Cornsillt		c. 44
389		Lawton–Burslem		c. 45
390		Penryn–Redruth		c. 52
391		Stafford–Sandon		c. 59
392	1764	Shillingford–Reading	4 Geo. III,	c. 42
393		Horsham–Beeding		c. 43
394		Romsey–Middle Wallop		c. 47
395		Callington roads		c. 48
396		Worksop–Attercliffe		c. 52
397		Spalding–Tydd St Mary		c. 53
398		Derby–Mansfield		c. 61
399		Milford–Lippock		c. 63
400		Tinsley–Doncaster		c. 64

401	1764	Rotherham–Wentworth		c. 65
402		Alfreton–Mansfield		c. 67
403		Whitby–Middleton		c. 69
404		Beverley–Kexby Bridge		c. 76
405		Spalding–Donnington		c. 80
406		Bucks Head–New Inn		c. 81
407		Ashbourne–Ripley		c. 82
408		Ilkeston roads		c. 83
409		Melton Mowbray–Leicester		c. 84
410		Scots Dyke–Haremoss		c. 85
411		Bideford roads		c. 87
412		Glamorgan roads		c. 88
413	1765	Wadhurst–West Farleigh	5 Geo. III,	c. 52
414		Dunham Ferry–Great Markham		c. 54
415		Porthaethwy Ferry–Holyhead		c. 56
416		Great Torrington roads		c. 58
417		Lymington–Eling		c. 59
418		Crewkerne roads		c. 61
419		Kippings Cross–Cranbrook		c. 63
420		Hurst Green–Burwash		c. 64
421		Balby–Worksop		c. 67
422		Wrotham Heath–Oxted		c. 68
423		Newton Abbot roads		c. 69
424		Woolborough–Torquay		c. 70
425		Tonbridge–Maidstone		c. 71
426		Birstall–Nunbrook		c. 72
427		Grimsby–Wold Newton		c. 73
428		Carmarthenshire roads		c. 76
429		Welford Bridge–Leicester		c. 78
430		Chatteris Ferry–Tydd Gote		c. 83
431		Newcastle-under-Lyme–Hassop		c. 84
432		Bawtry–Hainton		c. 85
433		Barton–Riseholme		c. 88
434		Mansfield–Tansley		c. 90
435		Minehead roads		c. 93
436		Romsey–Sherrill Heath		c. 95
437		Alford–Boston		c. 96
438		York–Kexby Bridge		c. 99
439		Stockport–Audenshaw		c. 100
440		Wisbech–Islington		c. 101

441	1765	Poole road–Wincanton Turnpike	c. 102
442		Banbury–Lutterworth	c. 105
443		Warwick–Northampton	c. 107
444		New Malton–Pickering	c. 108
445	1766	Tunbridge Wells–Maresfield	6 Geo. III, c. 56
446		Beverley–Great Driffield	c. 59
447		Bawtry–East Markham	c. 67
448		Wimborne Minster–Blandford Forum	c. 68
449		Cranford Bridge–Langley Mill	c. 69
450		Lauder–Kelso	c. 73
451		Ashbourne–Yoxall	c. 79
452		Brimington–Chesterfield Turnpike	c. 80
453		Haverhill–Shalford	c. 84
454		Tunbridge Wells–Uckfield	c. 85
455		Hursley–Chilton Pond	c. 86
456		9 Milestone, Mansfield–Ashover	c. 87
457		High Bridges–Uttoxeter	c. 88
458		Newcastle-under-Lyme–Nantwich	c. 89
459		Wareham roads	c. 92
460		Biddenden–Ashford Turnpike	c. 93
461		High Bullen–Bilston	c. 95
462		Dartford–Sevenoaks	c. 98
463		Huckley Corner–Bescot Brook	c. 99
464	1767	Brecon roads	7 Geo. III, c. 60
465		Oxford–Fyfield	c. 66
466		Radnor roads	c. 67
467		Northfield–Wotton	c. 68
468		Spernal Ash–Digbeth	c. 77
469		Hatton–Bell Broughton	c. 81
470		Carlisle–Skillbeck	c. 83
471		Tunbridge Wells–Etchingham	c. 84
472		Bromley Turnpike–Beggars Bush	c. 86
473		White Cross–Bridlington	c. 89
474		East Malling–Pembury Green	c. 91
475		Whitchurch–Nantwich	c. 92
476		Tenterden–Ashford	c. 103
477		Machwiel–Whitchurch	c. 104
478		Ayrshire roads	c. 106
479	1768	Goudhurst roads	8 Geo. III c. 35

480	1768	Huddersfield–Enterclough Bridge	c. 47
481		Reading–Hatfield	c. 50
482		Bishops Castle roads	c. 51
483		Northampton–Old Stratford	c. 52
484		Buckland Dinham–Timsbury	c. 53
485		York–Oswaldkirk	c. 54
486		Thetford–Newmarket	c. 55
487		Haremoss–Galashiels	c. 59
488		Selkirk roads	c. 60
489		Abingdon–Swinford	c. 61
490	1769	Cranbrook–Sandhurst	9 Geo. III, c. 43
491		Greenfield–Henllau	c. 45
492		Denbigh–Mold	c. 46
493		Wool Bridge–Dorchester	c. 47
494		Mereworth Cross–Wrotham	c. 49
495		Shawbury roads	c. 55
496		Welshpool roads	c. 56
497		Macclesfield–Knutsford	c. 65
498		Norwich–Scole Bridge	c. 66
499		Bury St Edmunds–Scole Bridge	c. 67
500		Norwich–Caister	c. 68
501		Bodmin roads	c. 69
502		Tal-y-Cafn–Pwhelli	c. 77
503		Maidstone–Key Street	c. 78
504		Beverley–Hessle	c. 79
505		Cheadle–Butter Moor End	c. 80
506		Darley Moor–Ellastone	c. 81
507		Tring–Bourn Bridge	c. 86
508		Woodstock–Old Stratford	c. 88
509		Blackfriars Bridge–Newington Butts	c. 89
510	1770	Norwich–Trowse	10 Geo. III, c. 54
511		Cardiganshire roads	c. 55
512		Aylesbury–Shillingford Bridge	c. 58
513		Westerham–Croydon Turnpike	c. 62
514		Upton–Wellesbourne Hastings	c. 63
515		Lewes–Brighton	c. 64
516		Barton Bridge–Brandon Bridge	c. 65
517		Tunstall–Bosley	c. 66
518		Norwich–Swaffham	c. 67
519		Bicester–Aylesbury	c. 72

558	1772	Burlton–Llanmynech		c. 96
559		Eccles–Eymouth		c. 97
560		Downham Market towards Swaffham		c. 98
561		Spalding–Peakirk		c. 103
562		Crickhowell–New Inn		c. 105
563		Cardington–Temsford Bridge		c. 107
564		Bewdley–Coalbrookdale		c. 109
565	1773	Newark–Bingham	13 Geo. III,	c. 90
566		Hampton–Staines		c. 105
567		Stamford–Durley		c. 108
568	1774	Southwell, Normanton roads	14 Geo. III,	c. 101
569	1775	Yarmouth Bridge–Gorleston	15 Geo. III,	c. 67
570	1776	Doncaster–Bawtry/Retford Turnpike	16 Geo. III,	c. 71
571		Clitheroe–Blackburn		c. 75
572		Ebdon–Red Swyre		c. 83
573	1777	Henfield–Ditchling	17 Geo. III,	c. 74
574		Henfield–Brighton		c. 91
575		Bedford–Woburn		c. 94
576		Bala, Dolgellau roads		c. 100
577		Skipton–Harrogate		c. 102
578		Crickrell–Bridport		c. 103
579		Asthall–Buckland		c. 105
580		Halifax–Sheffield		c. 106
581		Dumfries roads		c. 107
582		Loughborough–Cavendish Bridge		c. 108
583		Gateshead–Ryton Lane Head		c. 110
584	1778	Birches Brook–Tern Bridge	18 Geo. III,	c. 88
585		Barwick–Charminster		c. 95
586		Gloucester–Stroud		c. 98
587		Hexham–Alston		c. 116
588	1779	Maidenhead–Cookham	19 Geo. III,	c. 84
589		Gander Lane–Sheffield		c. 99
590		Ludlow Fach–River Amman		c. 102
591	1780	Horsley–Rodborough	20 Geo. III,	c. 84
592		Melton Mowbray–Grantham		c. 95
593	1781	Linlithgow–Hollhouse Burn	21 Geo. III,	c. 79
594		Wilmslow–Church Lawton		c. 82
595	1782	Parton–Monkland Hill	22 Geo. III,	c. 100

596	1782	Wrexham–Barnhill	c. 105
597		Tarporley–Weverham	c. 106
598		Clifford–Windmill Hill	c. 112
599		Brecon–Hay	c. 113
600	1783	Newnham–Littledean	23 Geo. III, c. 104
601	1785	Lutterworth–Bilton	25 Geo. III, c. 115
602		Ipswich–Bungay	c. 116
603		Cheltenham roads	c. 125
604	1786	Wiveliscombe roads	26 Geo. III, c. 135
605		Newton–Ashton	c. 139
606		Heage–Tibshelf	c. 151
607	1787	Gainsborough–Saundby	27 Geo. III, c. 71
608		Nottingham–Mansfield	c. 76
609		Berwick–Dunglas Bridge	c. 89
610		Chester–Birkenhead	c. 93
611	1788	Whitesheet Hill–Barford	28 Geo. III, c. 86
612		Walsall roads	c. 98
613		Blidworth–Normanton	c. 99
614		Foston Lane–Hinckley/Ashby Turnpike	c. 100
615		Saltney–Flint	c. 101
616		Merlin's Bridge–Pembroke	c. 102
617		Spann Smithy–Talke	c. 104
618		Staplebar–Walford	c. 105
619		Lampeter– Carmarthen and Llandovery	c. 109
620		Dumfries–Moffat	c. 114
621	1789	Glasgow–Ayr Border	29 Geo. III, c. 79
622		Bishop Wearmouth–Stockton	c. 81
623		Wakefield–Abberford	c. 86
624		Annan–Ayr Border	c. 87
625		Odiham–Farnham	c. 89
626		Congleton–Prestbury	c. 93
627		Overbury–Evesham/Alcester Turnpike	c. 102
628		Bury–Blackburn	c. 107
629		Rochdale–Prestwich	c. 110
630	1790	Newmiln Bridge–Craill	30 Geo. III, c. 93
631		Fosbrook–Cheddleton	c. 100
632		Dudley–Kingswinford	c. 102

633	1790	Stirling and Dumbarton roads	c. 109
634		Bromham–Olney	c. 114
635	1791	Canterbury–Barham	31 Geo. III, c. 94
636		Robeston Wathen–St Clears	c. 102
637		Bicester–Aynho	c. 103
638		Haverfordwest–Newport	c. 106
639		Milford–Merlin's Bridge	c. 109
640		Alcester Turnpike–Chipping Camden	c. 116
641		Haverfordwest–St Davids	c. 126
642		Buckingham–Banbury	c. 133
643		Great Marlow–Stokenchurch	c. 135
644	1792	West Auckland–Elishaw	32 Geo. III, c. 113
645		Folkestone–Barham	c. 117
646		Almond–Baillieston	c. 120
647		Lanark–Hamilton	c. 122
648		Aldeburgh roads	c. 126
649		Middleton in Teesdale–Bishop Auckland	c. 127
650		Chapel en le Frith–Enterclough Bridge	c. 128
651		Peterborough–Thorney	c. 129
652		Bradford–Bathford Bridge	c. 137
653		Saddleworth–Oldham	c. 139
654		Cornhill Burn–Lowick	c. 145
655		Lower Swell–Tewkesbury/Stow Turnpike	c. 146
656		Bury St Edmunds–Thetford	c. 148
657		Burford–Lechlade	c. 153
658		Llandeilo–Llandovery	c. 156
659	1793	Uttoxeter–Hardwick	33 Geo. III, c. 131
660		Lanvabon–Abernant	c. 133
661		Saddleworth–Thornet	c. 140
662		St Mary's Bridge–Rockingham	c. 143
663		Cockleton Bridge–Staindrop	c. 146
664		Gateshead–Hexham	c. 148
665		Hadley–Stifford Bridge	c. 149
666		New Sleaford–Anwick	c. 150
667		Wirksworth–Hulland Ward	c. 152
668		Stafford–Uttoxeter	c. 153

669	1793	Selby Ferry–Market Weighton	c. 159
670		Ashford–Romney Marsh	c. 162
671		West Harptrey–Marksbury	c. 165
672		Bawtry–Selby	c. 166
673		Wombourn–Prince's End	c. 167
674		Maidstone–Ashford	c. 173
675		Heage–Duffield	c. 177
676		Clay Hill–Bicester	c. 180
677		Odiham–Alton	c. 182
678		Kelso–Selkirk	c. 185
679	1794	Norwich–Aylsham	34 Geo. III, c. 114
680		Ticknall–Burton/Ashby Turnpike	c. 120
681		Rochdale–Edenfield	c. 124
682		Burtry Ford–Alston	c. 125
683		Oundle–Middleton	c. 126
684		Dunchurch–Southam	c. 128
685		Rawreth–Chelmsford	c. 137
686		Lyne Bridge–Scotch Dyke	c. 143
687	1795	Oldham–Ripponden	35 Geo. III, c. 137
688		Preston Condover–Alton	c. 138
689		Burnley–Tottington	c. 146
690		Bedford–Kimbolton	c. 148
691		Aylesbury–W. Wycombe	c. 149
692		Stamford–Greetham	c. 152
693		Towcester–Hardingstone	c. 153
694		Abernant–Merthyr–Rhyd y Blew	c. 156
695	1796	Forest of Dean roads	36 Geo. III, c. 131
696		Wearmouth Bridge–South Shields	c. 136
697		Little Yarmouth–Blythburgh	c. 142
698		Macclesfield–Congleton	c. 148
699		Old Trent Bridge–Nottingham	c. 152
700	1797	Rochdale–Bury	37 Geo. III, c. 145
701		Castleton–Bury	c. 146
702		Norwich–North Walsham	c. 147
703		Dover–Sandwich	c. 156
704		Holmes Chapel–Chelford	c. 157
705		Milnthorpe–Kirkby Lonsdale	c. 165
706		Wellingborough–Northampton	c. 167
707		Atcham–Dorrington	c. 172
708		Little Bolton–Blackburn	c. 173

Appendix 2

This Appendix lists the Sample 2 trusts whose Minute Books were used in the analysis in Chapter 7, and the characteristics of these trusts, summarized in the table in the Notes to Chapter 7. It also lists the Sample 3 trusts, whose Account Books were used in the analysis in the second part of Chapter 8, and the characteristics of these trusts, as given in the table in the Notes to Chapter 8.

Sample 2   Trust Minute Books

	Trust no.	Trust	A	B	C
1	247	Blackburn to Burscough Bridge	2	25	R
2	32	Brentford	1	12	L
3	199	Burford to Preston	2	16	R
4	151	Carlisle to Newcastle	2	16	R
5	49	Cheshunt	1	12	R
6	70	Chippenham	1	16	R
7	75	Cranford Bridge to Maidenhead Bridge	1	14	R
8	111	Doncaster to Tadcaster	1	54	R
9	108	Doncaster to Wakefield	1	20	I
10	92	Fulham	1	2	L
11	59	Gloucester to Hereford	1	30	R
12	184	Hagley	2	33	I
13	118	Harlow to Stump Cross	1	21	R
14	176	Harrogate to Boroughbridge	2	11	R
15	176	Harrogate to Hutton Moor	2	15	R
16	277	Hertford to Broadwater	2	9	R
17	77	Hounslow Heath to Bagshot	1	13	R
18	306	Ilminster	2	40	R
19	32	Isleworth (Brentford)	2	6	R
20	31	Islington	1	12	R
21	65	Kensington	1	9	L
22	210	Keighley to Kendal	2	51	I

Sample 2   **Trust Minute Books**

	Trust no.	Trust	A	B	C
23	325	Knaresborough to Pateley Bridge	2	15	R
24	172	Knaresborough to Green Hammerton	2	8	R
25	419	Kippings Cross to Cranbrook	2	17	R
26	57	Lemsford Mill to Cory's Mill	1	20	R
27	63	Liverpool to Prescot	1	10	R
28	79	Maidstone to Rochester	1	12	R
29	42	Marylebone	1	4	L
30	34	New Cross	1	8	L
31	211	Old Street	2	1	L
32	150	Preston to Garstang	2	11	R
33	313	Ringwood to Wimborne	2	11	R
34	176	Ripon to Boroughbridge	2	6	R
35	195	Salisbury to Eling	2	18	R
36	182	Seend to Box	2	10	R
37	366	Sparrows Herne to Aylesbury	2	28	R
38	301	Stockbridge to Winchester	2	10	R
39	374	Stourbridge to Colley Gate	2	5	I
40	125	Tadcaster to York	1	11	R
41	173	Taunton	2	64	R
42	241	Toller Lane End to Colne	2	25	I
43	425	Tonbridge to Maidstone	2	21	R
44	413	Wadhurst to West Farleigh	2	16	R
45	108	Wakefield to Halifax	1	17	I
46	109	Wakefield to Weeland	1	22	I
47	203	Wells	2	25	R
48	313	Winchester to Romsey	2	11	R
49	198	Yeovil	2	34	R
50	535	York to Collingham	3	16	R

Key: The trust number refers to those listed in Appendix 1.

        Column A: 1—Leading sector trust, established between 1696 and 1750.

                        2—Boom period trust, 1751–70.

                        3—Lagging sector trust, 1771–1800.

        Column B: Length of road controlled by trust, in miles.

        Column C: L—London trust, within 5 miles of London or Westminster.

                        R—Trust in a rural area.

                        I—Trust in an industrializing area.

Sample 3 — Trust Account Books

	Trust no.	Trust	A	B	C
1	29	St Albans to South Mimms	1	9	R
2	442	Banbury to Lutterworth	2	25	R
3	237	Banbury to Ryton Bridge	2	23	R
4	52	Biggleswade to Alconbury Hill	1	24	R
5	247	Blackburn to Burscough Bridge	2	25	R
6	199	Burford to Preston	2	16	R
7	385	Cambridge to Ely	2	22	R
8	635	Canterbury to Barham	3	6	R
9	91	Chappel to Bourton	1	12	R
10	354	Cheadle (Huntley Rocks)	2	8	R
11	365	Cheadle (Oakmore)	2	15	R
12	10	Devizes	1	10	I
13	112	Doncaster to Saltersbrook	1	45	I
14	108	Doncaster to Wakefield	1	20	R
15	703	Dover to Sandwich	3	14	R
16	266	Duffield to Wirksworth	2	10	R
17	19	Edgware	1	6	L
18	46	Gloucester to Birdlip Hill	1	7	R
19	59	Gloucester to Hereford	1	59	R
20	299	Gosport to Chawton	2	34	R
21	176	Harrogate to Hutton Moor	2	15	R
22	553	Hungerford to Sousley Water	3	18	R
23	505	Ipstones	2	10	R
24	31	Islington	1	14	L
25	65	Kensington	1	12	L
26	15	Kippings Cross to Flimwell Vent	1	9	R
27	325	Knaresborough to Pateley Bridge	2	15	R
28	16	Kneesworth to Caxton	1	9	R
29	302	Leatherhead to Guildford	2	12	R
30	236	Leatherhead to Horsham	2	22	R
31	294	Leeds to Wakefield	2	9	I
32	63	Liverpool to Prescot	1	27	I
33	42	Marylebone	1	4	L
34	35	Maidenhead to Sonning	1	11	R
35	34	New Cross	1	8	L

	Trust no.	Trust	A	B	C
36	270	New Road	2	3	L
37	483	Northampton to Old Stratford	2	11	R
38	13	Old Stratford to Dunchurch	1	28	R
39	176	Ripon to Boroughbridge	2	6	R
40	366	Sparrows Herne to Aylesbury	2	28	R
41	247	Skipton to Colne	2	12	I
42	23	Stamford Hill	1	14	L
43	301	Stockbridge to Winchester	2	10	R
44	173	Taunton	2	64	R
45	27	Trentham	1	10	I
46	413	Wadhurst to West Farleigh	2	16	R
47	706	Wellingborough to Northampton	3	11	R
48	301	Winchester to Southampton	2	11	R
49	311	Windsor Forest	2	16	R
50	422	Wrotham Heath	2	19	R

Key: as for Sample 2.

Appendix 3

A Contract Agreement for the Repair of the Keighley to Kendal Road, 1753

'The Trustees present entered into an Agreement with Joshua Parsons of Newton in Bolland Mason for Repair of a certain part of the said Road leading from a certain Gate at the Back Lane and going upon Brayshaw Scars to an Under Bridge at the bottom of Rawlinshaw Brow to Mrs Lupton in manner following, that is to say,

The said part of the said Road is to be cast seven Yards wide between the Ditches and Well and Equally formed in a Turnpike like manner and sufficiently raised where the Ground's low or soft—

The low places in the low parts of the Road to be raised as much as possible and the high places taken down in order to make the Road as near as can be level and no Bank to ascend more than five inches in the Yard—

Conduits and drains to be made where necessary and sufficiently strong and large not exceeding two feet square—

The Road to be so formed to the satisfaction of the Surveyor and then stoned five Yards broad and two Yards in the Middle to be twelve inches thick after sufficiently broke and to decrease in thickness gradually to each side to four inches—

The stones to be well broke half way thro' to the Satisfaction of the Surveyor and then covered with such Gravel or earth as can be had at the sides of the Road and where the sides of the Road do not afford good Gravel to the Surveyors Satisfaction the said Joshua Parsons must provide the same elsewhere—The Gravel to be four Yards broad along the Middle and five inches thick—

When the said part of the sd. Road is well repaired and amended as aforesd. the said Joshua Parsons is to preserve & maintain & keep the same in like Order and Condition for the whole Year from the Day of the

Date of the Certificate hereinafter mentioned And also shall and will make reasonable Satisfaction to the owners of enclosed Lands or Grounds for the Diging forgeting Stones or Gravel in order to perfect the said part of the said Road as aforesaid And indemnify the said Trustees and other Trustees appointed or to be appointed to be put the said Act in Execution for the Damage to be done thereby—

And for the Considerations aforesd. the said Trustees or their Treasurer for the time being shall and will pay unto the said Joshua Parsons for the amending and repairing the sd. part of the said Road after the rate of One hundred and five pounds for one measured Mile in manner following—that is to say, the sum of six shillings per Rood immediately after the perfecting of each ten Roods as producing a Certificate in writing under the hand of the Surveyor for that purpose and the remainder of the Consideration money when and soon as the whole of that part of the Road contracted to be repaired is amended and repaired to the good liking of five of the said Trustees and the Surveyors in writing under their hands & on giving satisfactory Security to keep the said Road in sufficient repair for one whole year And also shall direct permit and suffer the said Joshua Parsons to have the use and benefit of the Statute Work by the said Act directed to be performed in proportion to the length of the said part of the said Road in each Township in which the same lies. NB The said work is by the said Agreement to be perfected on or before the 25th Day of March next As by the same Agreement in the Hands of the Clerk more fully appears.'

Source: Keighley to Kendal Minutes, 9 Aug. 1753 (WR).

Appendix 4

Cost of the Collingham Trust's Renewal Act, 1791

The Trustees of the Turnpike Road from Collingham to York.

To J. Hebden Do—

1791
Sept.

	£	s	d
Attending a Meeting of the Commiss[rs.] at Wetherby when it was resolved to Apply to Parliament for a fresh Act		13	4
Journey to Chesterfield in Derbyshire to wait upon Mr Maynard Steward to the Duke of Devonshire upon this Business	3	3	0
Coach Hire and Expenses	2	0	0
Drawing Advertizement that Application wo[d] be made the next Session of Parliam[t] for an Amendment of the Act		3	6
Making Copy for the York Printer 1[s]/8[d] Writing therewith 3[s]/4[d]		5	0
Making some Alterations in the Advertizement on Acco[t] of the proposed Deviation		2	0
Copy thereof for the Printer and Writing therewith		3	6
Making four Copies to put at Knaresborough and York Sessions		6	8
Oct. 4.			
Journey to Knaresbro' Sessions to put up the Notice there	1	1	0
Horse hire and Expenses		15	0
Journey to York to put up like Notice at the Sessions held for the Ainstie	2	2	0
Coach hire and Expenses	1	5	0
Paid for Advertizing in the York Courant	1		10

		£	s	d
Drawing Petition to Parliament for leave to bring in a Bill for renewing the Act 'c			5	0
Ingrossing thereof and Parchment			5	0
Journey to Wetherby to Attend a Meeting of the Trustees in order to get the Petition Signed & on other Business		1	1	0
Horse hire and Expenses			10	
	carr'd over	£15	1	10

Account of Expences in passing the Collingham Road Bill
G & J White, H? of Commons

1792	£	s	d
Making Copies of Committee on Petition		10	0
Settling Report and drawing order of Leave		10	0
Perusing Settling & altering the Bill & drawing New Clauses	1	1	0
Making Copy for the House		7	0
Briefs and Copy for the Speaker		13	4
D? Lord Cathcart & Attending him	1	1	0
Copies Committee on Bill		10	0
Prefacing Amendment for the Committee with references to folios and Liners of House Bill		10	0
Filling up Bills for the Committee		10	0
Making Copies Trustees Names		2	0
Paid House Fees on Petition and Bill	29	18	8
Committees Clerks D?	9	1	0
Housekeepers & Messengers d.°	2	5	0
Doorkeepers for delivering Bills	1	1	0
Ingrossing Fees and Gratuity to Waiters	5	4	6
Making 2 Bills complete for Ingrossers & press		4	0
Assistance to examine Ingrossm.! & proof		6	0
Paid Gratuities to Housekeeper & Mess.rs & others as usual	2	7	0

	£	s	d
for Printing Bill & Act	4	10	0
House Fees at Lords	54	0	0
for Order for Committee & List	1	1	0
Committee Clerks ffee and Gratuity	4	4	0
Yeoman Usher & Doorkeepers d?	5	5	0
for Swearing Witness		2	0
Porters Postage & other Small Expences	2	2	0
Solicitation ffee	21	0	0
	£148	6	4

	£	s	d
1792 Bro.ᵗ over	15	1	10
Drawing Draft of the proposed Act and Copy	1	11	6
Journey to Wetherby & other places to collect the Books & papers belonging to the Road together & obtain Names of New Commissioners & out 2 Days	2	2	0
Horse hire and Expences		15	0
Journey to, and from, London and Attending their folliciting this Bill from 29.ffebry to the 5th April inclusive being 37 days at 1 gᵃ per day	38	17	0
Coach hire and Expences to London	4	17	0
Expences in London 33 Days at 10/6 per days	17	6	6
Coach hire & Expences from London	4	17	0
April 28th The House breaking up for Easter Hollidays Expences going again to London (I only charge one half having other Business)	2	10	0
To my Journey to & from London & Attendance there from the 20ᵗʰ April to the 14 May inclusive 24 days	25	4	0
To one Moiety of Expences in London 20 days for the before mentioned reason	5	5	0
To D? Expences returning from London	2	10	0
paid Messʳˢ White's of the House of Commons their Bill for ffees &ᶜ amounting to	148	6	4
Solicitors ffee on Obtaining this Act	21	0	0
Carriage of Parcels postage of Letters &ᶜ in London	2	2	0
	£292	5	2

Bibliography

Primary Sources

Bedford County Record Office

Accounts of the Stage Coaches from Bedford and
    Kettering to London 1803–12   X37/1–27

Occupations Index
Index of Wills proved in the Archdeaconry of
    Bedford

Berkshire County Record Office

Hungerford to Sousley Water Trust, Account
    Book 1772–1813   D/ELm 019

Maidenhead Bridge to Sonning Lane Trust,
    Statement of Income, 1728–34   D/EHy 09/3

Windsor Forest Trust, Account Book 1759–67   D EGh 01

Birmingham Reference Library

Hagley Trust, Minute Book 1753–72   ZZ 33

Bristol Archives Office

Register of Halliers, Brewers and Glassmakers,
    1718–56   No ref.

Ordinances for City Companies   No ref.

Cambridge:

Cambridge Record Office

Biggleswade to Alconbury Hill Trust, Account
  Book 1780–9   DDX 40/2

Cambridge to Ely Trust, Account Book
  1791–1837   No ref.

Kneesworth to Caxton Trust, Account Book
  1780–1818   T/K/FA 1

Account Book of a Lynn Carrier, 1792   No ref.

Cambridge University Library

University Carriers' Papers:	Bonds 1663–1711	T1V 1
	Licences 1699–1791	T1V 2
	Miscellaneous	T1V 3
	Licences 1665–1781	T1V 4

Vice-Chancellors' Court Records:
Acta Curiae (Neat Book)	1718–28	Vc Ct I 16
	1728–35	Vc Ct I 17
(Loose Papers)	1713–35	Vc Ct I 90–100
	1735–1800	Vc Ct I 101–9

Cumbria Record Office

Military Road, Minute Book 1751–91   CA/Road Books

Account Book of Robert Dawson, Carrier,
  1750–60   No ref.

Sir John Lowther's Memorandum Book, c. 1699. D/Law/L

Letter from John Hopper to Sir James Lowther,
  6 Nov. 1766   D/Lons/L/Survey
                      List 2

Cusworth Hall, Doncaster

Doncaster to Saltersbrook Trust,
  Account Book 1764–71
  Toll Book, Harper Stables Gate 1765–6
  Toll Book, Ardsley Gate 1769–70

Typescript notes concerning MSS of Richard Milne, Carrier.
The documents at Cusworth Hall are not numbered

Derbyshire Record Office

Duffield to Wirksworth Trust,
   Toll Accounts 1783–90   D5 unlisted
           1790–97   ,,

East Sussex Record Office

Flinwell Vent to Hastings Trust,
   Ticehurst Gate Returns 1769–70
   List of Gatekeepers 1756–1800   Dunn MS 52/19

Gloucestershire Record Office

Burford to Preston Trust,
   Minute and Account Book 1753–1801   D 1070

Chapel-on-the-Heath to Bourton-on-the-Hill
   Trust, Account Book 1731–67   D 621/X4

Gloucester to Birdlip Hill Trust, Minute and
   Account Book 1761–73   D 204/3/1

Gloucester to Hereford Trust,
   Minute Book 1726–68   D 204/2/2
   Account Book 1788–1812   D 204/2/8

Guildford Muniment Room

The Proposal for Removing the Godalming
   Turnpike considered (printed document,
   1767)   Loseley MSS

Hampshire Record Office

Gosport to Chawton Trust,
   Account Book 1775–97   36 M/72

Ringwood to Wimborne District,
   Minute Book 1759–89   8 M 47/3

Stockbridge to Winchester District,
   Minute Book 1758–81   4 M 30/1
   Account Book 1773–1801   4 M 30/5

Winchester to Romsey District,
Minute Book 1759–84   CC

Winchester to Southampton District,
Account Book 1773–1801   4M 30/14

Hertford County Record Office

Cheshunt Turnpike, Minute Book 1725–59   TP 1/1
                    Minute Book 1759–79   TP 1/2

Hockerill Turnpike, Minute Book 1744–85   TP 3/1

St Alban's Turnpike, Account Book 1759–76   TP 5/14

Stevenage to Biggleswade Turnpike,
    Register of Promissory Notes   TP 6/37
    Promissory Notes   TP 6/38
    Miscellaneous Papers   TP 6

Watton Turnpike, Minute Book 1757/78   TP 8/1
                 Minute Book 1778/1819   TP 8/2

Welwyn Turnpike, Minute Book 1726–55   TP 9/1

Kent Archives Office

Canterbury to Barham Trust,
    Account Book 1797–1802   T 6/1

Chalk Trust, Minute Book 1761–1809   T 7/A1

Dover to Sandwich Trust,
    Account Book 1797–1833   T 11/F1

Kippings Cross to Cranbrook Trust,
    Minute Book 1765–1827   T 1/1

New Cross Trust,
    Minute and Account Book 1718–23   T 9/A1/14
    Minute Book 1746–65   T 9/A1/1

Rochester to Maidstone Trust,
    Minute Book 1728–41   T 12/1

Tonbridge to Maidstone Trust,
    Minute Book 1765–1804   T 2/1

Wadhurst to West Farleigh Trust,
Minute and Account Book 1765–88   T 15/1

Wrotham Heath Trust, Account Book 1768–74   U442–058

Lancashire Record Office

Blackburn to Burscough Bridge Trust,
Minute Book 1755–93   TTE 1
Account Book 1755–93   TTE 2

Liverpool to Prescot Trust,
Minute and Account Book 1726   TTG 1

Preston to Garstang Trust,
Minute Book 1751–82   TTD 1

Skipton to Colne Trust,
Account Book 1787–1875   TTI 2

London:

Chiswick Library

Brentford Trust, Minute Book 1717–29
Minute Book 1738–57

Finsbury Library

Old Street Trust, Minute Book 1753–78

Hounslow Library

Isleworth District, Minute Book 1767–83
Minute Book 1783–1813

The documents in these Libraries are not numbered.

Islington Library

Islington Trust, Minute Book 1717–23   Y B208, Cr 98299
Minute and Account Book 1758–67   Y B208, Cr 98302

Minutes of Committees 1766–74   Y B208, Cr 98305
Cancelled Bills   Y B208, Cr 98339

Kensington Library

Fulham Trust, Minute Book 1730–50	MS 58/7039
Minute Book 1750–65	MS 58/7040
Minute Book 1765–70	MS 58/7041

Kensington, Chelsea and Fulham Trust,

Minute Book 1726–34	MS 58/7001
Minute Book 1734–40	MS 58/7002
Minute Book 1758–71	MS 58/7006
Account Book 1772–1806	MS 58/7042

Hyde Park Gate, Weighing Machine Receipt Book 1795–7	MS 58/7029
Weekly Account of Cash paid to Labourers 1771–8	MS 58/9374

Marylebone Library

Marylebone Trust, Minute Book	1740–52	MTT/1/2
Account Book	1721–36	MTT/3/1
	1736–53	MTT/3/2
	1753–64	MTT/3/3
	1764–73	MTT/3/4

Middlesex County Record Office

Edgware Trust, Minute Book	1775–97	LA/HW/709
	1797–1810	LA/HW/710
Account Book	1730–1810	LA/HW/712
Surveyor's Accounts	1743–72	LA/HW/713
Ledger Accounts	1772–85	LA/HW/714

Hounslow Heath to Bagshot Trust, Minute Book 1728–57	Tp BED 1
Maidenhead Bridge to Cranford Bridge Trust, Minute Book 1728–84	Tp COL 1

Northamptonshire Record Office

Banbury to Lutterworth Trust, Account Book 1765–1800	Box 1118

Northampton to Hanborough Trust Plan, 1740   Fisher Sanders 61/68

Northampton to Old Stratford Trust,
Minute and Account Book 1778–1800   Box 775

Old Stratford to Dunchurch Trust,
Account Book 1765–9   D 3390

Peterborough to Northampton Trust Plan, 1753   No ref.

Wellingborough to Northampton Trust,
Account Book 1797–1819   Box 1023

Oxford:

Bodleian Library

Oxford Carriers' List, c. 1670.   Rawlinson D. 317B fo. 177.

University Carriers' Papers   Archives Univ. Oxon Hyp. fo. 2.
Twyne–Langbein MSS, Vol. 4
MSS Wood 276A/318

Ryton Bridge to Banbury Trust,
Account Book 1755–86   Ms Top Oxon 8.373

Christ Church Library

Leatherhead to Guildford Trust,
Account Book 1758–94   Evelyn MS 102

Leatherhead to Horsham Trust,
Account Book 1772–8   Evelyn MS 103

Oxfordshire County Record Office

Oxford Mileways,
Account Book 1771–5   I/I

Stokenchurch to Woodstock Trust,
Minute Book 1740–93   CH/S/II/i/1

Sheffield City Library

Rotherham to Wentworth Trust,
Surveyor's Account Book 1767–73   WWM A1286

Sheffield to Wakefield Trust,
Account Book 1765–75 — TC 364
Surveyor's Account Book 1774 — TC 304/57
Old Mill Bar Toll Book 1760–2 — TC 363/43–5

Miscellaneous Turnpike Papers — TC 363, 4

Fitzwilliam correspondence re the affairs of John
Hick — WWM F106/99–107

Articles of Agreement between Thomas Lidgard
and Richard Gardiner — PC 1088

Somerset Record Office

Ilminster Trust, Minute Book 1759–1803 — D/T/ilm 1

Taunton Trust,
Minute and Account Book 1752–77 — D/T/ta 5

Wells Trust, Minute Book 1753–67 — D/T/WEL 2
1767–99 — 3

Yeovil Trust, Minute Book 1753–1810 — D/T/Yeo 13

Stafford:

Staffordshire Record Office

Oakmore District, Account Book 1762–84 — D239M Box 4

Tean to Wetley Rocks District Account Book
1762–1830 — D239M Box 5

William Salt Library

Ipstones District, Account Book 1770–1804 — 52/31

Trentham Trust, Account Book 1772–1802 — 272/32

West Riding Registry of Deeds

Collingham to York Trust,
Minute Book 1775–1825 — Box 44

Doncaster to Tadcaster Trust,
Minute Book 1741–1835   Box 54

Doncaster to Wakefield Trust,
Minute Book 1741–1830   Box 54a
Account Book 1741–1812   Box 54a

Grassington to Wetherby Trust,
Minute Book 1775–1870   Box 30b

Harrogate to Boroughbridge Trust,
Minute Book 1752–1870   Box 27

Harrogate to Hutton Moor Trust,
Minute Book 1752–1814   Box 30b
Account Book 1752–1814   Box 28c

Keighley to Kendal Trust,
Minute Book 1753–63   Box 22
                1787–1815   Box 22

Knaresborough to Green Hammerton Trust,
Minute Book 1752–1878   Box 27

Knaresborough to Pateley Bridge Trust,
Minute Book 1759–1851   Box 27
Account Book 1759–1880   Box 27

Leeds to Wakefield Trust,
Account Book 1768–91   Box 45c

Ripon to Boroughbridge Trust,
Minute and Account Book 1752–1814   Box 28c

Tadcaster to Otley Trust, Plan 1753   Box 45c

Tadcaster to York Trust,
Minute Book 1745–99   Box 17

Toller Lane End to Colne Trust,
Minute Book 1755–1823   Box 50

Wakefield to Halifax Trust,
Minute Book 1741–62   Box 32b

Wakefield to Weeland Trust,
Minute Book 1741–1826   Box 54

Wiltshire County Record Office

Devizes Trust, Accounts 1707–8 Account Book 1745–83	Quarter Sessions Records, A3/7/4
Salisbury to Eling Trust, Minute Book 1753–95	No. 339
Seend to Box Trust, Minute Book 1753–91	No. 519
Studley Bridge to Toghill Trust, Minute Book 1727–68	No. 119

Worcestershire Record Office

Droitwich Trust, Minute Book 1754–93	BA704; b705; 584.
Stourbridge to Colley Gate Trust, Minute Book 1762–79	899:31 BA3762/4 (iv)

Parliamentary Material

Acts of Parliament, 1696–1800.

Journals of the House of Commons, Vols 1–55.

Statutes at Large, Vols 1–16.

Parliamentary Papers (BPP):

Report of the Committee appointed to take into Consideration the Acts now in force, regarding the Highways and Turnpike Roads in England and Wales. . . .
1810–11 (240) III: 855

Report from the Select Committee on the Highways of the Kingdom. . . .
1819 (509) V: 339

Report from the Select Committee appointed to consider the Acts now in force regarding Turnpike Roads and Highways in England and Wales.
1821 (747) IV: 343

Report from the Select Committee appointed to inquire into the Receipts, Expenditure and Management of the several Turnpike Trusts within ten miles of London. . . .
1825 (355) V: 167

First Report of the Commissioners of the Metropolis Turnpike Roads north of the Thames. . . .
1826–27 (339) VII: 23

Second Report from the Lords on Fees on Turnpike Road Bills.
1833 (703) XV: 409

Report from the Select Committee appointed for the purpose of ascertaining how far the formation of Railroads may affect the interests of Turnpike Trusts, and the Creditors of such Trusts.
1839 (295) IX: 369

Report of the Commissioners for inquiring into the State of the Roads in England and Wales.
1840 (256) XXVII: 1

Appendix to the Report of the Commissioners for inquiring into the State of the Roads in England and Wales.
1840 (280) XXVII: 15

Abstract of the General Statements of the Income and Expenditure of the Several Turnpike Trusts in England and Wales, 1838.
1840 (289) XLV. 391

1st Report of the Commissioners of Inland Revenue, on the Inland Revenue.
1857 (2199) IV. 65: Appx. 24.

Primary Published and Printed Sources

Aikin, J., *A Description of the Country from Thirty to Forty Miles round Manchester*, London (1795).
Andrews, C. B. (ed.), *The Torrington Diaries*, London (1934).
Burn, R., *The Justice of the Peace*, London (1755).

Cary, J., *Cary's Survey of the High Roads from London*, London (1790).

Clark, A., *Register of the University of Oxford*, Vol. II (1571–1622) Part I, Oxford (1887).

Cole, G. D. H. and M. (eds), *Cobbett's Rural Rides*, 3 vols (1930).

D'Archenholz,M., *Picture of England*. Dublin (1791).

Defoe, D., *A Tour through the Whole Island of Great Britain*, Everyman's Library, 2 Vols, London (1962).

Defoe, D., *An Essay on Projects.*, London (1697).

Delaune, T., *The Present State of London*, London (1681).

A Description of the City of Chester, Chester (1781).

Elsas, M. (ed.), *Iron in the Making: Dowlais Iron Company Letters 1782–1860*, Glamorgan County Council (1960).

Fielding, H., *The History of Tom Jones, a Foundling*, London: reprinted (1962).

Fowle, J. P. M. (ed.), *Wiltshire Quarter Sessions and Archives, 1736*, Wilts. Arch. and Nat. Hist. Society, Records Branch, XI., Devizes (1955).

Hardy, W. le (ed.), *Calendar to the Sessions Books, Sessions Minute Books and Other Sessions Records*: Vol. VI: 1658–1700, Vol. VII: 1700–52 (1930, 31).

Hinde, A., *Merchants and Traders Necessary Companion*, London (1715).

Homer, H., *An Enquiry into the Means of Preserving and Improving the Public Roads of this Kingdom*, London (1767).

Hutton, W. H., *A History of Derby*, London (1791).

Hutton, W. H., *A History of Birmingham*, Birmingham (1795).

Hutton, W. H., *Remarks upon North Wales*, Birmingham (1803).

Kalm, Pehr, *Kalm's Account of his visit to England*, translated by Joseph Lucas, London (1892).

Mann, J. de L., *Documents Illustrating the Wiltshire Textile Trades in the Eighteenth Century*, Wilts. Arch. and Nat. Hist. Society, Records Branch, Vol. XIX, Devizes (1964).

Marshall, W., *The Rural Economy of the West of England*, Vol. I, London (1796).

Marshall, W., *The Rural Economy of the Southern Counties*, Vol. 2, London (1798).

Marshall, W., *On the Landed Properties in England*, London (1804).

Mather, E., *Of Repairing and Mending the Highways*, London (1696).

Moritz, C., *Travels of Carl Philipp Moritz in England in 1782*, translated, London (1924).

Morris, C. (ed.), *The Journeys of Celia Fiennes*, London (1947).

Nicholson, J. and Burn, R., *The History and Antiquities of the Counties of*

Westmoreland and Cumberland, Vol. 1, London (1777).

Parnell, Sir Henry, *Treatise on Roads*, London (1834).

Paterson, D., *Paterson's Roads*, 15th Ed., London (1811).

Phillips, R., *A Dissertation concerning the Present State of the High Roads of England*, London (1737).

Phillips, J., *The General History of Inland Navigation*, 4th Ed., London (1803).

Priestley, J., *Historical account of the navigable rivers, canals, and railways of Great Britain*, London (1831).

de Saussure, C., *A Foreign View of England in the Reigns of George I and II*, translated by Madame van Muyden, London (1902).

Scott, J., *Digests of the General Highway and Turnpike Laws*, London (1778).

Shapleigh, J., *Highways: a Treatise showing the Hardships and Inconveniences of Presenting and Indicting Parishes, Townships, etc., for not repairing the Highways*, London (1749).

Taylor, J., *The Carriers Cosmographie*, London (1637).

Travellers' & Chapmans' Instructor, (1705).

The Universal British Directory of Trade, Commerce and Manufacture, (1790).

Vaisey, D. G. (ed.), 'Probate Inventories of Lichfield and District 1568–1680', *Collections for a History of Staffordshire*, 4th Series, Vol. 5, Staffs. Record Society (1969).

Wrightson, R., *The New Triennial Directory of Birmingham*, Birmingham (1818).

Young, A., *A Six Week Tour through the Southern Counties of England and Wales*, London (1769).

Young, A., *A Six Months Tour through the North of England*, Vols 2–4, London (1771).

Board of Agriculture Reports

Entitled 'A General View of the Agriculture of the County of . . .'

Bailey, J. and Culley, G.	1797	Northumberland, Cumberland and Westmoreland
Bailey, John	1810	Durham
Batchelor, Thomas	1808	Bedford
Billingsley, John	1798	Somerset

Boys, John	1796	Kent
Brown, Robert	1799	West Riding of Yorks
Clark, John	1794	Brecon*
Davis, Thomas	1813	Wiltshire
Dickson, R. W.	1815	Lancashire*
Duncomb, John	1805	Hereford
Gooch, Rev. W.	1813	Cambridgeshire
Holland, Henry	1808	Cheshire
Holt, John	1795	Lancashire
Kent, Nathaniel	1796	Norfolk
Lowe, Robert	1798	Nottingham
Mavor, William	1809	Berkshire
Middleton, John	1798	Middlesex
Middleton, John	1809	Middlesex
Parkinson, R.	1811	Huntingdon
Pitt, William	1808	Stafford
Pitt, William	1813	Worcester
Pitt, William and Parkinson, Richard	1813	Leicester and Rutland*
Plymley, Joseph	1803	Shropshire
Priest, Rev. St John	1810	Buckinghamshire
Rudge, Thomas	1807	Gloucester
Stevenson, William	1812	Dorset
Stevenson, William	1809	Surrey*
Strickland, H. E.	1812	East Riding of Yorkshire*
Tuke, John	1800	North Riding of Yorkshire
Vancouver, Charles	1808	Devon
Vancouver, Charles	1813	Hampshire
Worgan, G. B.	1815	Cornwall*
Young, Arthur	1799	Lincoln
Young, Arthur	1804	Hertford
Young, Arthur	1804	Suffolk
Young, Arthur	1807	Essex
Young, Arthur	1808	Sussex
Young, Arthur	1809	Oxford

*These Reports were not used in the analysis in Chapter 10.

Newspapers

Farley's Bristol Newspaper (1725–41).

The Oracle, Bristol Weekly Advertiser (1742–5).

Felix Farley's Bristol Journal, (1744–84) Bristol Reference Library.

Derby Mercury, (1722–1800) Derby Borough Library.

Gloucester Journal, (1721–1800) Gloucester Reference Library.

Jackson's Oxford Journal, (1753–1800) Bodleian Library.

London—*Flying Post, Daily Courant, London Post* (1704), Burney Collection, British Museum.

Maps

Bryant, A., A map of the county of Oxford from actual survey, (1823). 1:42,240.

Cary, John, Cary's New and Correct English Atlas, (1787). 1:520,000.

Cruchley, G. F., Cruchley's environs of London extending thirty miles from the metropolis, (1828). c1:55,000.

Davis, Richard, A new map of the county of Oxford, (1797). c1:32,000.

Donn, B., Map of the country 11 miles round the city of Bristol, (1769). c1:44,000.

Gream Thomas, A map of Sussex, (1799). c1:63,360.

Greenwood, C. and J., A Map of the county of Berks from an actual survey, (1824). c1:63,360.

Greenwood, C. and J., A Map of the county of Sussex from an actual survey, (1825). 1:63,360.

Neele, S. J., A new plan of London, XXIX miles in circumference, (1797). c1:9,900.

Paterson, Daniel, Paterson's twenty-four miles round London, (1802). c1:115,000.

Rocque, John, A Map of the County of Berks, (1761). 1:32,800.

Unpublished Theses

Andrews, J. H., 'Geographical Aspects of the Maritime Trade of Kent and Sussex, 1650–1750' Ph.D., University of London (1954).

Clarke, C. A. A., 'The Turnpike Trusts of Marylebone and Islington from 1700 to 1825' M.A., University of London (1955).

Dicks, T. R. B., 'The South-Western peninsular of England and Wales: studies in agricultural geography, 1550–1900' Ph.D., Aberystwyth (1964).

Dyos, H. J., 'The Suburban Development of Greater London, South of the Thames: 1836–1914' Ph.D., University of London (1952).

Fuller, G. J., 'A Geographical Study of the Development of Roads through the Surrey–Sussex Weald to the South Coast during the period 1700–1900' Ph.D., University of London (1950).

Ginarlis, J. E., 'Road and Waterway Investment in Britain, 1750–1850' Ph.D., University of Sheffield (1970).

Goodwin, A. K., 'Road Development in Ayrshire' M.Litt., University of Strathclyde (1970).

Isaac, D. G. D., 'A Study of Popular Disturbances in Britain, 1715–1754' Ph.D., Edinburgh University (1953).

Lambert, A. M., 'Oxfordshire about 1800: a study in human geography' Ph.D., University of London (1953).

Lewis, A. H. T., 'The Development and Administration of Roads in Carmarthen, 1763–1800' M.A., University of Wales, Swansea (1968).

McGrath, P. V., 'The Marketing of Food, Fodder and Livestock in the London Market area in the Seventeenth Century' M.A., University of London (1948).

Neale, D., 'The History of Navigation on the Thames above Oxford' B.A., University of Leicester (1972).

Patten, J. H. C., 'The Urban Structure of East Anglia during the sixteenth and seventeenth centuries' Ph.D., University of Cambridge (1972).

White, A. W. A., 'Economic Growth in Eighteenth Century Warwickshire' Ph.D., University of Birmingham (1972).

Secondary Sources

Albert, W. I., *The Turnpike Road System in England 1663–1840*, Cambridge (1972).

Ashton, T. S., *The Industrial Revolution: 1760–1830*, London (1948).

Ashton, T. S., *An Economic History of England: The 18th Century*, London (1955).

Ashton, T. S., *Economic Fluctuations in England, 1700–1800*, Oxford (1959).

Bagwell, Philip S., *The Transport Revolution from 1770*, London (1974).

Baines, Thomas, *History of the Commerce and Town of Liverpool*, London (1852).

Baker, Dennis, 'The Marketing of Corn in the First Half of the Eighteenth Century: North-East Kent', *Agricultural History Review*, Vol. 18 (1970), 126–50.

Barber, William J., *A History of Economic Thought*, London (1967).

Barker, T. C. and Harris, J. R., *A Merseyside Town in the Industrial Revolution: St. Helens, 1750–1900*, Liverpool (1954).

Barker, T. C. and Savage, C. I., *An Economic History of Transport*, London (1975).

Beavington, F., 'Early Market Gardening in Bedfordshire', *Transactions of the Institute of British Geographers*, Vol. 37 (1965), 91–100.

Beresford, M. W., 'Commissions of Enclosure', *Ec.H.R.*, 1st Series, Vol. XVI (1946), 130–40.

Brandon, P. F., *The Sussex Landscape*, London (1974).

Brown, A. F. J., *Essex at Work, 1700–1815*, Chelmsford (1969).

Butlin, R. A., 'Rural Change in Northumberland, 1600–1880', in *Environment, Man and Economic Change*, ed. A. D. M. Phillips and B. J. Turton, London (1975).

Campbell, R. H., *Scotland since 1707: The Rise of an Industrial Society*, Oxford (1965).

Chalklin, C. W., *The Provincial Towns of Georgian England*, London (1974).

Chalklin, C. W. and Havinden, M. A. (eds), *Rural Change and Urban Growth 1500–1800*, London (1974).

Chambers, J. D. and Mingay, G. E., *The Agricultural Revolution, 1750–1880*, London (1966).

Clarkson, L. A., *The pre-industrial economy in England, 1500–1750*, London (1971).

Cleveland-Stevens, E., *English Railways: Their Development and Relation to the State*, London (1915).

Clifford, F., *A History of Private Bill Legislation*, Vol. 2, London (1887).

Cootner, Paul H., 'The Role of Railroads in United States Economic Growth', *Journal of Economic History*, Vol. XXIII (1963), 477–521.

Cordeaux, E. H. and Merry, D. H., *A Bibliography of Printed Works relating to the University of Oxford*, Oxford (1968).

Court, W. H. B., *The rise of the Midland industries, 1600–1838*, London (1938).

Davis, Dorothy, *A History of Shopping*, London (1966).

Deane, Phyllis and Cole, W. A., *British Economic Growth: 1688–1959*, Cambridge (1962).

Demsetz, H., 'Toward a Theory of Property Rights', *American Economic Review*, Vol. LVII (1967), 347–59.

Dowdell, E. G., *A hundred years of Quarter Sessions, the government of Middlesex from 1660 to 1760*, Cambridge.

Dyos, H. J., *Review. Journal of Transport History*, Vol. II (1956), 185–6.

Dyos, H. J. and Aldcroft, D. H., *British Transport*, Leicester (1969).

East, W. G., 'Land Utilization in England at the end of the Eighteenth Century', *Geographical Journal*, Vol. LXXXIX (1937), 156–72.

Emmison, F. G., 'The Earliest Turnpike Bill—1622', *Bulletin of the Institute of Historical Research*, Vol. XII (1934), 108–12.

Everitt, Alan, 'Urban Growth, 1570–1770', *Local Historian*, Vol. VIII (1968), 118–25.

Everitt, Alan, *Ways and Means in Local History*, London (1971).

Everitt, Alan, 'Town and Country in Victorian Leicestershire: The Role of the Village Carrier', in *Perspectives in English Urban History*, ed. A. Everitt, London (1973).

Fisher, F. J., 'The Development of the London Food Market, 1540–1640', *Ec.H.R.*, 1st Series, Vol. V (1935), 46–64.

Fishlow, Albert, *American Railroads and the Transformation of the Ante–Bellum Economy*, Cambridge, Mass. (1965).

Flinn, M. W., *Men of Iron*, Edinburgh (1962).

Flinn, M. W., *Origins of the Industrial Revolution*, London (1966).

Fogel, R. W., *Railroads and American Economic Growth*, Baltimore (1964).

Freeman, M. J., 'The Stage-coach system of South Hampshire, 1775–1851', *Journal of Historical Geography*, Vol. 1 (1975), 259–81.

Fussell, G. E. and Goodman, C., 'Eighteenth Century Traffic in Livestock', *Economic History*, Vol. III (1936), 214–36.

Fussell, G. E. and Goodman, C., 'The Eighteenth Century Traffic in Milk Products', *Economic History*, Vol. III (1936), 380–87.

Gayer, A. D., Rostow, W. W. and Schwarz, A. J, *The Growth and Fluctuation of the British Economy, 1790–1850*, Oxford (1953).

Grigg, David, *The Agricultural Revolution in South Lincolnshire*, Cambridge (1966).

Gunderson, Gerald, 'The Nature of Social Saving', *Ec.H.R.*, 2nd Series, Vol. XXIII (1970), 207–19.

Haggett, Peter, *Locational Analysis in Human Geography*, London (1965).

Hamilton, Henry, *The Industrial Revolution in Scotland*, Oxford (1932).

Hamilton, Henry, *An Economic History of Scotland in the Eighteenth Century*, Oxford (1963).

Hart, Cyril, *The Industrial History of Dean*, Newton Abbot (1971).

Hart, H. W., 'Some Notes on Coach Travel, 1750–1848', *Journal of Transport History*, Vol. IV (1960), 146–60.

Hartwell, R. M., *The Industrial Revolution and Economic Growth*, London (1971).

Harvey, David, *Explanation in Geography*, London (1969).

Havinden, M. A., Lime as a means of Agricultural improvement: the Devon example, Chapter 5 of Chalklin and Havinden (1974).

Hawke, G. R., *Railways and Economic Growth in England and Wales, 1840–1870*, Oxford (1970).

Hawke, G. R., *Review*, *Ec.H.R.*, 2nd Series, Vol. XXVI (1973), 156–7.

Hicks, John, *A Theory of Economic History*, Oxford (1969).

Hirschman, Albert O., *The Strategy of Economic Development*, New Haven (1958).

Holderness, B. A., 'Capital Formation in agriculture', in *Aspects of capital investment in Great Britain 1750–1850*, ed. J. P. P. Higgins and S. Pollard, London (1971).

Holdsworth, Sir William, *A History of English Law*: Vol. X, London (1938).

Horsfield, T. W., *The History, Antiquities and Topography of the County of Sussex*, Vol. 1, Lewes (1824).

Hunter, Holland, 'Transport in Soviet and Chinese Development', *Economic Development and Cultural Change*, Vol. XIV (1965), 71–84.

Jackman, W. T., *The Development of Transportation in Modern England*, Cambridge (1916).

John, A. H., 'Aspects of English Economic Growth in the First Half of the Eighteenth Century', *Economica*, Vol. XXVIII (1961), 176–90.

Johnson, B. L. C., 'The Charcoal iron industry in the early eighteenth century', *Geographical Journal*, Vol. CXVII (1951), 167–77.

Johnson, B. L. C., 'The Foley Partnerships: The Iron Industry at the End of the Charcoal Era', *Ec.H.R.*, 2nd Series, Vol. IV (1952), 322–40.

Jones, E. L., 'Agricultural Conditions and Changes in Herefordshire, 1660–1815', *Woolhope Transactions*, Vol. XXXVII (1961), 32–55.

Jones, E. L. (ed.), *Agriculture and Economic Growth*, London (1967).

Joyce, H., *The History of the Post Office from its Establishment down to 1836*, London (1893).

Kahn-Freund, Otto, *The Law of Carriage by Inland Transport*, London (1939).

Kellett, J. R., *The Impact of Railways on Victorian Cities*, London (1969).

Kennett, D. H., 'The Geography of Coaching in Early Nineteenth Century Northamptonshire', *Northamptonshire Past and Present*, Vol. V, no. 2, (1974), 317–20.

Kindleberger, C. P., *Economic Development*, 2nd Ed., New York (1965).

Kuznets, Simon, *Economic Growth and Structure*, London (1966).

Langton, John, 'Coal Output in South-West Lancashire, 1590–1799', *Ec.H.R.* 2nd Series, Vol. 25 (1972), 28–54.

Latimer, John, *Annals of Bristol in the Eighteenth Century*, Frome (1893).

Law, C. M., 'Some Notes on the Urban Population of England and Wales in the Eighteenth Century', *The Local Historian*, Vol. 10 (1972), 13–26.

Leader, R. E., *Sheffield in the eighteenth century*, Sheffield (1901).

Lobel, M. D. (ed.), *Historic Towns*, London (1969).

Mantoux, Paul, *The Industrial Revolution in the Eighteenth Century*, London (1961).

Marshall, J. D. (ed.), *The Autobiography of William Stout of Lancaster, 1655–1752*, Manchester (1967).

Mathias, Peter, *The First Industrial Nation*, London (1969).

McKendrick, N., 'Josiah Wedgwood: An Eighteenth Century Entrepreneur in Salesmanship and Marketing Techniques', *Ec.H.R.*, 2nd Series, Vol. XII (1960), 408–33.

Millward, Roy, 'The Cumbrian town between 1600 and 1800', Chapter 8 of Chalklin and Havinden (1974).

Minchinton, W. E., 'Bristol—Metropolis of the West in the eighteenth century', *Transactions of the Royal Historical Society*, 5th Series, no. 4, (1954), 69–89.

Minchinton, W. E. (ed.), *Industrial South Wales, 1750–1914*, London (1969).

Mitchell, B. R., *Abstract of British Historical Statistics*, Cambridge (1962).

Mitchell, B. R., 'The Coming of the Railway and U.K. Economic Growth', *Journal of Economic History*, Vol. XXIV (1964), 315–36.

Moir, Esther, 'Local Government in Gloucestershire, 1775–1800', *Publications of British and Glos. Arch. Soc.* (Record Section), Vol. VIII (1969).

Nef, J. U., *The rise of the British coal industry*, 2 vols, London School of Economics, *Studies in Economics*, 6, London (1932).

Parris, H. W., *Government and Railways in Nineteenth Century Britain*, London (1965).

Perkin, Harold, *The Age of the Railway*, Newton Abbot (1970).

Pratt, E. A., *A History of Inland Transport and Communication in England*, London (1912).

Pratt and Mackenzie, *Pratt and Mackenzie's Law of Highways*, 21st Ed., ed. H. Parrish and Lord de Manley, 21st Ed. (1967).

Presnell, L. S., *Country Banking in the Industrial Revolution*, Oxford (1956).

Raistrick, A., *The West Riding Landscape*, London (1970).

Reed, M. C., *Investment in Railways in Britain, 1820–44—a study in the development of the capital market*, Oxford (1975).

Robinson, E., 'Eighteenth Century Commerce and Fashion: Matthew Boulton's Marketing Techniques', *Ec.H.R.*, 2nd Series, Vol. XVI (1963), 39–60.

Robinson, H., *Britain's Post Office*, London (1953).

Robson, Brian T., *Urban Growth: an Approach*, London (1973).

Rogers, E. M. and Shoemaker, F. F., *Communication of Innovations—A Cross-Cultural Approach*, New York (1971).

Rostow, W. W., *The Stages of Economic Growth—A Non-Communist Manifesto*, 2nd Ed., Cambridge (1971).

Savage, C. I., *An Economic History of Transport*, London (1959).

Schumpeter, Joseph A., *The Theory of Economic Development*, Cambridge, Mass. (1934).

Schumpeter, Joseph A., *Business Cycles: a theoretical, historical and statistical analysis of the capitalist process*, New York (1939).

Sherrington, C. E. R., *A Hundred Years of Inland Transport, 1830–1933*, London (1934).

Smith, Adam, *The Wealth of Nations*, ed. Edwin Cannan, London (1904).

Smith, Wilfred, *An Historical Introduction to the Economic Geography of Great Britain*, 2nd Ed. London (1968).

Summerson, John, *Georgian London*, London (1962).

Sylvester, D., *The Rural Landscape of the Welsh Borderland*, London (1969).

Tawney, A. J. and R. H., 'An Occupational Census of the Seventeenth Century' *Ec.H.R.*, First Series, Vol. V (1934), 25–64.

Taylor, Christopher, *The Cambridgeshire Landscape*, London (1973).

Thirsk, J. and Cooper, J. P., *Seventeenth Century Economic Documents*, Oxford (1972).

Thompson, Allan, *The Dynamics of the Industrial Revolution*, London (1973).

Trinder, B., *The Industrial Revolution in Shropshire*, Chichester (1973).

Turnbull, G. L., 'Pickfords and the canal carrying-trade, 1750–1850', *Transport History, 6* (1973), 5–29.

Unwin, George, *Samuel Oldknow and the Arkwrights*, Manchester (1924).

Vamplew, Wray, 'Railways and the Transformation of the Scottish Economy' *Ec.H.R.*, 2nd Series, Vol. XXIV (1971), 37–54.

Vigier, Francois, *Change and Apathy: Liverpool and Manchester during the Industrial Revolution*, Cambridge, Mass. (1970).

de Villiers, E., *Swinford Toll Bridge*, Eynsham Local History Society (1969).

Wadsworth, A. P. and Mann, Julia de L., *The Cotton Trade and Industrial Lancashire 1600–1780*, Manchester (1931).

Ward, J. R., *The Finance of Canal Building in Eighteenth Century England*, Oxford (1974).

Webb, S. and B., *English Local Government: The Parish and the County*, London (1906).

Webb, Sidney and Beatrice, *English Local Government—the Story of the King's Highway*, London (1920).

Webb, Sidney and Beatrice, *English Local Government: Statutory Authorities for Special Purposes*, London (1922).

Webb, W. A., *The early years of Stage coaching on the Bath road*, Ealing (1922).

Wiles, R. M., *Freshest Advices: early Provincial Newspapers in England*, Columbus (1965).

Willan, T. S., *River Navigation in England*, Oxford (1936).

Willan, T. S., 'The River Navigation and Trade of the Severn Valley 1600–1750' *Ec.H.R.*, First Series, Vol. VIII (1937), 68–79.

Willan, T. S., *The English Coasting Trade 1600–1750*, Manchester (1938).

Willan, T. S., *An Eighteenth Century Shopkeeper: Abraham Dent of Kirkby Stephen*, Manchester (1970).

Williams, D., *The Rebecca Riots, A Study in Agrarian Discontent*, Cardiff (1955).

Wilson, C. H., 'The Entrepreneur in the Industrial Revolution in Britain', *History,* Vol. XLII (1957), 101–17.

Wilson, R. G., 'Transport dues as indices of economic growth, 1775–1820' *Ec.H.R.,* 2nd Series, Vol. XIX (1966), 110–23.

Wilson, R. G., *Gentlemen Merchants: The merchant community in Leeds, 1700–1830,* Manchester (1971).

Wrigley, E. A., 'A Simple Model of London's Importance in Changing English Society and Economy, 1650–1750', *Past and Present,* no. 37 (1967), 44–70.

Young, Allyn A., 'Increasing Returns and Economic Progress' *Economic Journal,* Vol. XXXVIII (1928), 527–42.

Youngson, A. J., *Overhead Capital: A Study in Development Economics,* Edinburgh (1967).

Local Turnpike Studies

These are the most useful local studies. Those marked * have not been referred to in the text, but they have been used to check the accuracy of the maps in Chapter 5:

*Cossons, A., 'The Turnpike Roads of Nottinghamshire', *Historical Association Leaflet,* no. 97, London (1934).

*Cossons, A., 'The Turnpike Roads of Warwickshire', *Transactions of Birmingham Arch. Soc.,* Vol. LXIV (1946).

*Cossons, A., 'The Turnpike Roads of Northamptonshire with the Soke of Peterborough', *Northamptonshire Past and Present,* Vol. 1 (1950).

*Cossons, A., 'The Turnpike Roads of Norfolk', *Norfolk Archaeology,* Vol. XXX (1952), 189–212.

*Cossons, A., 'Roads', *The Victoria History of the Counties of England: Wiltshire,* Vol. IV (1959), 256–71.

Dodd, A. H., 'The Roads of North Wales, 1750–1850', *Archaeology Cambriensis,* Vol. LXXX (1925), 121–48.

Elliston-Erwood, F. C., 'Miscellaneous Notes on some Kent Roads', *Archaeologia Cantiana,* Vol. LXX (1956), 201–20.

*Emmison, F. G., 'Turnpike Roads and Tollgates of Bedfordshire', *Beds.*

Historical Record Society (Survey of Ancient Buildings), Vol. 33 (1936), 1–26.

Ffooks, E. J., 'The Kensington Turnpike Trust', Typescript, Kensington Borough Library (1955).

Hall, Peter, 'The development of communications' in *Greater London*, eds J. T. Coppock and Hugh C. Prince, London (1964).

Iredale, D., 'Industry, Trade and People' in *History of Congleton*, ed. W. B. Stephens, Manchester (1970).

Lewis, Anthony, H.T., 'The Early Effects of Carmarthenshire Turnpike Trusts, 1760–1800', *Carmarthenshire Historian* Vol. IV (1967), 41–54.

MacMahon, K. A., 'Roads and Turnpike Trusts in Yorkshire', East Yorkshire Local History Series, no. 18 (1964).

Payne, P. L., 'The Bermondsey, Rotherhithe and Deptford Turnpike Trust, 1776–1810', *Journal of Transport History*, Vol. II (1956), 132–43.

*Russell, P., 'Roads', *The Victoria History of the Counties of England: Leicestershire*, Vol. 3 (1955), 79–91.

Scott, J. 'The Turnpike Roads of Derbyshire', *Derbyshire Miscellany*, (1973), 198–208.

Sharpe-France, R., 'The Highway from Preston into the Fylde', *Trans. Hist. Soc. of Lancs. and Cheshire*, Vol. XCVII (1945), 27–58.

Sheppard, F. H. W., *Local Government in St. Marylebone 1688–1835*, London (1958).

Spry, N., 'The Northgate Turnpike', *Gloucestershire Society for Industrial Archaeology, Journal* (1971), 1–55.

Thomas, Annie Longton, 'Geographical Aspects of the Development and Communications in North Staffordshire during the Eighteenth Century', *Collections for a History of Staffordshire*, William Salt Archaeological Society (1934).

*Tupling, G. H., 'The Turnpike Trusts of Lancashire', *Memoirs and Procs. of the Manchester Literary and Philosophical Society*, Vol. XCIV (1953).

*Williams, David, *The Rebecca Riots*, Cardiff (1955).

Williams, L. A., *Road Transport in Cumbria in the Nineteenth Century*, London (1975).

Subject Index

Index of Places